Communications
in Computer and Information Science   1802

Rationale

The CCIS series is devoted to the publication of proceedings of computer science conferences. Its aim is to efficiently disseminate original research results in informatics in printed and electronic form. While the focus is on publication of peer-reviewed full papers presenting mature work, inclusion of reviewed short papers reporting on work in progress is welcome, too. Besides globally relevant meetings with internationally representative program committees guaranteeing a strict peer-reviewing and paper selection process, conferences run by societies or of high regional or national relevance are also considered for publication.

Topics

The topical scope of CCIS spans the entire spectrum of informatics ranging from foundational topics in the theory of computing to information and communications science and technology and a broad variety of interdisciplinary application fields.

Information for Volume Editors and Authors

Publication in CCIS is free of charge. No royalties are paid, however, we offer registered conference participants temporary free access to the online version of the conference proceedings on SpringerLink (http://link.springer.com) by means of an http referrer from the conference website and/or a number of complimentary printed copies, as specified in the official acceptance email of the event.

CCIS proceedings can be published in time for distribution at conferences or as post-proceedings, and delivered in the form of printed books and/or electronically as USBs and/or e-content licenses for accessing proceedings at SpringerLink. Furthermore, CCIS proceedings are included in the CCIS electronic book series hosted in the SpringerLink digital library at http://link.springer.com/bookseries/7899. Conferences publishing in CCIS are allowed to use Online Conference Service (OCS) for managing the whole proceedings lifecycle (from submission and reviewing to preparing for publication) free of charge.

Publication process

The language of publication is exclusively English. Authors publishing in CCIS have to sign the Springer CCIS copyright transfer form, however, they are free to use their material published in CCIS for substantially changed, more elaborate subsequent publications elsewhere. For the preparation of the camera-ready papers/files, authors have to strictly adhere to the Springer CCIS Authors' Instructions and are strongly encouraged to use the CCIS LaTeX style files or templates.

Abstracting/Indexing

CCIS is abstracted/indexed in DBLP, Google Scholar, EI-Compendex, Mathematical Reviews, SCImago, Scopus. CCIS volumes are also submitted for the inclusion in ISI Proceedings.

How to start

To start the evaluation of your proposal for inclusion in the CCIS series, please send an e-mail to ccis@springer.com.

Anand Kumar M · Bharathi Raja Chakravarthi ·
Bharathi B · Colm O'Riordan · Hema Murthy ·
Thenmozhi Durairaj · Thomas Mandl
Editors

Speech and Language Technologies for Low-Resource Languages

First International Conference, SPELLL 2022
Kalavakkam, India, November 23–25, 2022
Proceedings

Editors
Anand Kumar M ⓘ
National Institute of Technology Karnataka
Mangalore, India

Bharathi B ⓘ
Sri Sivasubramaniya Nadar College
of Engineering
Kalavakkam, India

Hema Murthy ⓘ
Indian Institute of Technology Madras
Chennai, India

Thomas Mandl ⓘ
University of Hildesheim
Hildesheim, Germany

Bharathi Raja Chakravarthi ⓘ
National University of Ireland
Galway, Ireland

Colm O'Riordan
National University of Ireland
Galway, Ireland

Thenmozhi Durairaj ⓘ
Sri Sivasubramaniya Nadar College
of Engineering
Kalavakkam, India

ISSN 1865-0929   ISSN 1865-0937 (electronic)
Communications in Computer and Information Science
ISBN 978-3-031-33230-2   ISBN 978-3-031-33231-9 (eBook)
https://doi.org/10.1007/978-3-031-33231-9

This Springer imprint is published by the registered company Springer Nature Switzerland AG
The registered company address is: Gewerbestrasse 11, 6330 Cham, Switzerland

Preface

We are excited to present the proceedings of the First International Conference on SPEech and Language Technologies for Low-Resource Languages (SPELLL 2022) which was held at Sri Sivasubramaniya Nadar College of Engineering (SSN), Chennai, India, during 23 to 25 November, 2022. The conference was organized by a research group consisting of people from various academic institutions and industries across the globe. In particular, general chairs of SPELLL 2022 Anand Kumar M., Bharathi Raja Chakravarthi, Durairaj Thenmozhi, B. Bharathi, Subalalitha C. N. and Malliga Subramanian meticulously worked on all the finer details towards the successful organization of this conference. The aim of this series of conferences is to provide an international platform to discuss, exchange, disseminate and cross-fertilize innovative ideas that solicit experimental, theoretical work and methods in solving problems and applications of current issues of speech and language technologies for low-resourced languages.

The enthusiastic response received for this first edition of the conference was overwhelming. The papers presented at the conference were across a spectrum of areas such as language resources, language technologies, speech technologies and multi-modal analysis. We reached out to more than 100 experts in the fields of natural language processing to review the papers received. Each submitted paper went through comprehensive reviews by at least 3 reviewers and their review comments were communicated to the authors before the conference. Out of 70 papers received through the EquinOCS submission management system, only 27 papers were accepted, from which 25 papers were registered and presented by authors from India and abroad. Our volume editors Anand Kumar M. of National Institute of Technology Karnataka, India, Bharathi Raja Chakravarthi and Colm O'Riordan of University of Galway, Durairaj Thenmozhi and B. Bharathi of Sri Sivasubramaniya Nadar College of Engineering, India, Hema Murthy of Indian Institute of Technology Madras, India and Thomas Mandl of Universität Hildesheim, Germany played a significant role in selecting these papers. The final submissions were checked by the program committee to ensure that all the comments had been addressed.

Two workshops were collocated with SPELLL 2022 on the topics "Fake News Detection in Low-Resource Languages (RegionalFake)" and "Low Resource Cross-Domain, Cross-Lingual and Cross-Modal Offensive Content Analysis (LC4)". A pre-conference tutorial was conducted on 23rd November 2022 in emerging topics of natural language processing with hands-on sessions. This tutorial had 30 participants and the sessions were handled by Praveen S. V. of NIT Trichy and Subalalitha C. N. of SRMIST.

The conference proceedings were inaugurated on November 24, 2022. Five keynote talks were delivered in the conference. Fairness and Ethics in ML was delivered by Deepak Padmanabhan of Queen's University Belfast, UK. The Creation of Datasets for Training Language Models for Low-Resource Languages was delivered by Dias P.G.V. of University of Moratuwa, Sri Lanka. Kalika Bali of Microsoft Research India gave a talk on Building Technology for Low Resource Languages: Lessons Learnt. Kevin Scannell of Saint Louis University, USA delivered a note on 20 Years a' Growing: The

Past, Present, and Future of Irish NLP. Miguel Ángel García Cumbreras and Salud María Jiménez-Zafra of University of Jaén, Spain gave a talk on Corpus compilation for NLP shared tasks: the Spanish case.

Martin Klinkigt, Research Scientist of Kyocera Future Design Labs delivered a talk on Human Augmentation Technology: Using Multimodal NLP and Vision Technology to Improve Quality of Life, Dhivya Chinnappa of Thomson Reuters gave a talk on Multimodal Machine Learning and Anushiya Rachel of Vellore Institute of Technology, Chennai delivered a keynote address on Text-to-Speech System in the LC4 workshop. Jamal Abdul Nasir of University of Galway delivered a keynote address on How to Leverage a High-resource Language to Contribute to Fake News Detection in Low-resource Languages? in the RegionalFake workshop. Presentations of the accepted papers were organized as 5 tracks, which included 3 tracks for SPELLL and 1 for each workshop: RegionalFake and LC4.

This volume contains revised versions of all the twenty-five papers presented at the conference. We sincerely hope that these papers provide significant research contributions and advancements in the fields of speech and language technologies for low-resourced languages. We thank the Sri Sivasubramaniya Nadar College of Engineering for their support and encouragement to host the first edition of SPELLL 2022, and Springer for publishing these proceedings. We thank all the program committee members, reviewers, session chairs, organizing committee members and the participants for their contributions towards the success of the conference.

November 2022   Anand Kumar M.
                                                        Bharathi Raja Chakravarthi
                                                                   Bharathi B.
                                                               Colm O'Riordan
                                                                   Hema Murthy
                                                             Thenmozhi Durairaj
                                                                  Thomas Mandl

Organization

General Chairs

Durairaj Thenmozhi — Sri Sivasubramaniya Nadar College of Engineering, India
Anand Kumar M. — National Institute of Technology Karnataka, India
Bharathi Raja Chakravarthi — University of Galway, Ireland
Subalalitha C. N. — SRM Institute of Science and Technology, India
Malliga Subramanian — Kongu Engineering College, India

Program Committee Chairs

B. Bharathi — Sri Sivasubramaniya Nadar College of Engineering, India
Colm O'Riordan — University of Galway, Ireland
Hema A. Murthy — Indian Institute of Technology Madras, India
Thomas Mandl — Universität Hildesheim, Germany
Dhanalakshimi V. — Subramania Bharathi School of Tamil Language & Literature, India
Ratnavel Rajalakshmi — Vellore Institute of Technology, India
Zia Ush Shamszaman — Teesside University, UK
Paul Stynes — National College of Ireland, Ireland

Program Committee

Alexander Gelbukh — National Polytechnic Institute, Mexico
Aline Villavicencio — University of Sheffield, UK
Alla Rozovskaya — Queens College (CUNY), USA
Aytuğ Onan — İzmir Katip Çelebi Üniversitesi, Bilgisayar Mühendisliği Bölümü, Turkey
Bharathi Ganesh — Resilience Business Grids LLP, India
Bianca Pereira — University of Galway, Ireland
Brian Davis — Dublin City University, Ireland
Christiane D. Fellbaum — Princeton University, USA
Deepak Padmanabhan — Queen's University, Belfast, UK
Dhanalakshimi V. — Pondicherry University, India
Dhivya Chinnappa — Thomson Reuters, USA

Dinesh Kumar Vishwakarma	Delhi Technological University, India
Emily Prudhommeaux	Boston College, USA
Eswari Rajagopal	National Institute of Technology Tiruchirappalli, India
Eva Schaeffer-Lacroix	Sorbonne University and INSPE Paris, France
Fausto Giunchiglia	Universita di Trento, Italy
Grigori Sidorov	Centro de Investigación en Computacion, Mexico
Hamdy Mubarak	Qatar Computing Research Institute (QCRI), Qatar
Hanmin Jung	Korea Institute of Science and Technology Information (KISTI), Korea
Hung-Yu Kao	National Cheng Kung University, Taiwan
Jamin Shin	Hong Kong University of Science and Technology, China
José Antonio García-Díaz	University of Murcia, Spain
Kalika Bali	Microsoft Research, India
Kathleen McKeown	Columbia University, USA
Kevin Patrick Scannell	Saint Louis University, USA
Krisana Chinnasarn	Burapha University, Thailand
Malvina Nissim	University of Groningen, The Netherlands
Marcos Zampieri	Rochester Institute of Technology, USA
Marissa Griesel	University of South Africa, South Africa
Mathieu d'Aquin	University of Galway, Ireland
Manikandan Ravikiran	Hitachi Research and Development, India
Marta R. Costajussa	Universitat Politècnica de Catalunya, Spain
Md. Rezaul Karim	Fraunhofer FIT and RWTH Aachen University, Germany
Md. Shajalal	Fraunhofer FIT and University of Siegen, Germany
Melvin Johnson	Google, USA
Menno Van Zaanen	North-West University, South Africa
Miguel Ángel García	Universidad de Jaén, Spain
Monojit Choudhury	Microsoft Research, India
Pascale Fung	Hong Kong University of Science and Technology, China
Paul Buitelaar	University of Galway, Ireland
Prasanna Kumar Kumaresan	Indian Institute of Information Technology and Management Kerala, India
Priya Rani	Insight SFI Research Centre for Data Analytics, Galway
Rahul Ponnusamy	Indian Institute of Information Technology and Management-Kerala, India
Rafael Valencia-Garcia	Universidad de Murcia, Spain

Ruba Priyadharshini	Gandhigram Rural Institute-Deemed to be University, India
Sajeetha Thavareesan	Eastern University, Sri Lanka
Salud María Jiménez-Zafra	Universidad de Jaén, Spain
Sinnathamby Mahesan	University of Jaffna, Sri Lanka
H. L. Shashirekha	Mangalore University, India
Subalalitha C. N.	SRM Institute of Science and Technology, India
Taraka Rama	University of Texas, USA
Thomas Mandl	Universität Hildesheim, Germany
Valerio Basile	University of Turin, Italy
Viktor Hangya	Ludwig Maximilian University of Munich, Germany
Viviana Patti	Università di Torino, Italy
Yuta Koreeda	Hitachi, Ltd., USA

Workshop Chairs

Sangeetha Sivanesan	National Institute of Technology, Trichy, India
Eswari Rajagopal	National Institute of Technology, Trichy, India
Zia Ush Shamszaman	Teesside University, UK
Elizabeth Sherly	Kerala University of Digital Sciences, India
Dhivya Chinnappa	Thomson Reuters, USA
S. Angel Deborah	Sri Sivasubramaniya Nadar College of Engineering, India

Additional Reviewers

Shubhanker Banerjee
Malliga S.
Kogilavani Shanmugavadivel
Kavi Priya S.
Angel Deborah S.
Nandhini Kumaresh
Ratnavel Rajalakshmi
Soubrayalu Sivakumar
Kingsy Grace R.
Arjun Paramarthalingam
Abirami Murugappan
Ramesh Kannan
Betina Antony
C. Jerin Mahibha
Rajalakshmi Sivanaiah
Josephine Griffith

Kayalvizhi Sampath
Rajeswari Natarajan
Kingston Thamburaj
Miguel Ángel García Cumbreras
Sangeetha Sivanesan
Richard Saldanha
Hariharan R. L.
György Kovács
Sripriya N.
Lakshmi Kanthan Narayanan
Deepak P.
Briskilal J.
Hosahalli Shashirekha
Anushiya Rachel Gladston
Manikandan Ravikiran

Contents

Speech Technologies

Multimodal Data Analysis

Workshop 1: Fake News Detection in Low-Resource Languages (Regional-Fake)

Workshop 2: Low Resource Cross-Domain, Cross-Lingual and Cross-Modal Offensive Content Analysis (LC4)

Language Resources

KanSan: Kannada-Sanskrit Parallel Corpus Construction for Machine Translation

Asha Hegde$^{(\boxtimes)}$ and Hosahalli Lakshmaiah Shashirekha

Department of Computer Science, Mangalore University, Mangalore, India
hegdekasha@gmail.com

Abstract. Machine Translation (MT) is the process of automatic conversion of text from the source language into a target language preserving the meaning in the source text. Large parallel corpora are the essential resources to build any MT model. However, most of the languages are under-resourced due to lack of computational tools and digital resources with respect to parallel corpora for MT. Further, translation of under-resourced languages with complex morphological structures are more challenging. In view of these factors, this paper describes the practical approaches to develop MT systems for Kannada-Sanskrit language pair from scratch. This work comprises of the construction of *KanSan* - a parallel corpus for Kannada-Sanskrit language pair and implementation of MT baselines for translating Kannada text to Sanskrit text and vice versa. The models, namely: Recurrent Neural Network (RNN), Bidirectional Recurrent Neural Network (BiRNN), transformer-based Neural Machine Translation (NMT) with and without subword tokenization, and Statistical Machine Translation (SMT) are implemented for MT of Kannada text to Sanskrit text and vice versa. The performance of MT models is measured in terms of Bilingual Evaluation Understudy (BLEU) score. Among all the models, the transformer-based model with subword tokenization performed best with BLEU scores of 9.84 and 12.63 for Kannada to Sanskrit and Sanskrit to Kannada MT respectively.

Keywords: Parallel Corpus Construction · Kannada · Sanskrit · Machine Translation

1 Introduction

In recent years, MT techniques have seen rapid growth, especially for high-resource language pairs; for instance, English-French, English-German, and English-Spanish. With many practical applications including technical translations, translation of proposals and tender documentation, legal translations like translation of contracts, policies, and confidential agreements, translations in fraud investigations, etc., most of the MT models are built for high-resource languages. While the translation quality of many MT systems is comparable to that of human translations, a relatively large parallel corpus is required to train such MT systems [1]. However, most of the languages around the globe are under-resourced languages mainly due to the common issue pertaining to lack of resources. This huge gap between high-resource languages and under-resourced languages creates a language barrier and MT is the only solution to bridge this gap mainly due to its speed, consistency, and low cost compared to that of human translators.

Anand Kumar M et al. (Eds.): SPELL 2022, CCIS 1802, pp. 3–18, 2023.
https://doi.org/10.1007/978-3-031-33231-9_1

MT has considerable potential in a multilingual country like India where majority of the languages, such as Kannada, Sanskrit, Tamil, Telugu, Malayalam, etc., are under-resourced languages, in spite of having the history of thousands of years, a rich collection of articles, and a rich morphological structure.

Sanskrit, one of the oldest languages in the world, has a credible influence on Indo-European languages [2]. With a history dating back to hundreds of years, Sanskrit is one of the scheduled languages of India and is written in Devanagari script. The literature of Sanskrit holds the privilege of being used in ancient poetry, drama, and sciences, as well as in philosophical texts [3]. Sanskrit language consists of 16 vowels and 36 consonants and is rich in vocabulary, phonology, grammar, morphological features, and agglutinativeness. It is a highly inflected language in nature and was portrayed in the form of eight chapters written by *Panini* to make it more structured and easy to grasp *(Panini Asthadhyayi)* [4]. From the literature, it is evident that this ancient language has a well-structured grammar and can be used to analyze modern languages [5, 6].

Kannada, one of the major Dravidian languages, is also one of the scheduled languages of India and the official and administrative language of the state of Karnataka. It is a language spoken predominantly by the people of Karnataka. There are more than 40 million Kannada speakers throughout the world and it is also spoken as a second and third language by over 12.6 million non-Kannada speakers in Karnataka. Similar to Sanskrit, Kannada has rich inflections, agglutinativeness, and morphologies [7]. The compound words in Kannada are formed by combining one or more root words and suffixes and the sequence of words forms the phrase or sentence. By convention, it is a free word order language and usually sentences have verbs at the end.

According to the Indian census of 1991, there were 49,736 Sanskrit speakers in India and this number is reduced to 24,821 in 2011[1]. This number is likely to decline in the future resulting in the number of Sanskrit speakers becoming scarce. Despite the fact that a few parallel corpora are constructed using the epics *Ramayana* and *Mahabharata* available in *shloka* form (which is composed in a specific metre or *chandas* with a specific number of lines and a specific number of words in each line) [8,9] no parallel corpora are available for the conventional Sanskrit text paired with any other language. In addition to implementing MT models, the parallel corpus is beneficial in developing bilingual embeddings, dictionaries, and lexicons.

In view of the lack of parallel corpora for Kannada-Sanskrit MT, this paper contributes *KanSan* - a Kannada-Sanskrit parallel corpus for MT and presents the comprehensive results of popular MT models using this dataset. In most of the cases, parallel corpora involve monolingual text in each language of the language pair. Contrary to this, the proposed parallel corpus also has English words in Latin script which makes it unique. Further, the motivation behind choosing Sanskrit and Kannada for MT is the under-resourceness and the rich morphological features of these languages.

The remainder of the paper is organized as follows: Sect. 2 presents the recent research works on parallel corpus construction for MT. Details about parallel corpus construction are given in Sect. 3 followed by the experimental setup of the baseline MT systems in Sect. 4. Experiments and results are described in Sect. 5 and Sect. 6 concludes the paper along with the future scope.

---

[1] https://censusindia.gov.in/2011Census/C-16_25062018_NEW.pdf.

2   Related Work

In recent decades, MT which requires a large sentence-aligned parallel corpus has got immense attention from researchers to build effective MT systems. However, few under-resourced Indian languages like Sanskrit [11] and Kannada [12] are rarely explored in this direction. Some efforts made for such languages to construct parallel corpora for MT are described below:

Ramesh et al. [12] developed *Samanantar* - a massive collection of parallel corpora for 11 Indian languages (Assamese, Bengali, Gujarati, Hindi, Kannada, Malayalam, Tamil, Telugu, Marathi, Oriya, and Punjabi) with 49.7 million sentence pairs between English and Indian languages. They collected 12.4 million parallel sentences from publicly available resources and extracted 37.4 million parallel sentences by combining many existing corpora, tools, and methods (web crawling, document OCR, multilingual representation models for aligning sentences, and nearest neighbor approach for searching parallel sentences). Further, they also extracted 83.4 million parallel sentences between 55 Indian language pairs using English as the pivot language. They trained transformer-based multilingual NMT models with the newly constructed dataset and found that their models outperformed Google NMT (GNMT) [13], Multilingual Bidirectional and Auto-Regressive Transformer (mBART) model [14], and Multilingual Text to Text Transformer (mT5) model [15] - the state-of-the-art models for translation.

A large-scale Sanskrit-English parallel corpus is built by Aralikatte et al. [16] considering 93,000 Sanskrit *shlokas* from two Indian epics *Ramayana* and *Mahabharata* and their English translations written by Manmathnaath Dutta [17] and Bibek Debroy [18] respectively. They have extracted the text from these two books available in public domain using Google's Optical Character Recognition (OCR) Application Program Interface (API)[2] and verified the output manually. Using this dataset, the authors implemented SMT system using Moses tool kit[3] and transformer-based NMT model to translate Sanskrit text into English text and vice versa. Among the two models, the transformer-based models outperformed the other models with BLEU scores of 7.49 and 7.59 for Sanskrit to English and English to Sanskrit translations respectively.

Parida et al. [19] extracted 29,346 sentence pairs from the publicly available Bible written in Odiya and Latin script to develop Odiya-English parallel corpus for MT. During preprocessing, removal of duplicate sentences and normalization of text, sentence segmentation, sentence alignment, and manual verification of Odiya-English parallel sentences are carried out. Both Phrase Based SMT (PBSMT) and transformer-based NMT systems were implemented to translate Odiya text to English text and PBSMT model outperformed the transformer-based model with BLEU score of 12.72. Parida et al. [20] developed an extended version of the English-Odiya parallel corpus of 98,308 sentence pairs for MT. The authors extracted text data using web-scraping and OCR-based data acquisition methods from the available sources, namely English-Odiya Parallel Bible, Odisha Government Portal, Odisha Government Home Department Portal, and Odia Digital Library. During preprocessing, they adopted standard text data preparation procedures, namely: extracting plain text, sentence segmentation, sentence

---

[2] https://cloud.google.com/vision/docs/pdf.
[3] https://github.com/moses-smt/mosesdecoder.

alignment, and manual verification of the parallel text. The authors used OpenNMT-py[4] [21] to implement NMT baseline with Vanilla RNN and obtained 5.2 and 8.6 BLEU scores for English to Odiya and Odiya to English translations respectively.

Using web-crawling, an English-Punjabi parallel corpus with 20,000 sentence pairs was built by Jolly et al. [22]. They trained GNMT system to translate English sentences into Punjabi sentences. To evaluate the model, they used the string matching algorithms: Hamming matching, Levenshtein matching, Jaccard matching, and regular expression and the matching scores were calculated based on string overlappings. Among all the string matching algorithms, Jaccard matching behaved better with a similarity score of 0.69. Jindal et al. [23] developed an English-Punjabi parallel corpus with 2,50,000 sentence pairs to develop an MT system. They collected parallel text data from various data sources, namely: EMILLE Corpus, Gyan Nidhi corpus, Health Text corpus, Bible, Sri Guru Granth Sahib corpus, E-books of Punjab School Education Board, Bilingual newspaper, and named entity corpus. During data preparation, the authors applied common preprocessing techniques like noise removal, textual attribute tagging for identifying the source of the data, text alignment, and manual verification followed by text indexing. Haddow et al. [24] collected parallel corpora of English pairing with 13 major Indian languages[5] consisting of 56,000 parallel sentences for each language pair. They implemented a web-crawler[6] and used Moses splitter[7] for sentence segmentation [25] followed by Hunalign [26] and Vecalign [27] pretrained models for sentence alignment. Further, they implemented an NMT baseline with encoder-decoder based RNN model for each language pair and their model obtained a maximum BLEU score of 23.4 for Hindi to English text translation.

From the literature, it is clear that the parallel corpus is the fundamental need to build efficient MT models and under-resourced languages are rarely explored in this direction. To the best of our knowledge, this is the first work that describes the construction of a Kannada-Sanskrit parallel corpus that contains general Sanskrit text for MT.

3   Kannada-Sanskrit Parallel Corpus Construction

One of the objectives of this work is to construct *KanSan* - a Kannada-Sanskrit parallel corpus for MT and the framework for the construction is shown in Fig. 1. The textual content of *Mann Ki Baat*[8] - a radio program hosted by Mr. Naredra Modi, Prime Minister of India, is available as temporally aligned parallel corpus in many Indian languages including Kannada and Sanskrit. However, as this corpus contains only 23,758 parallel sentences, it is not sufficient to build an efficient MT system and hence text data from other resources are also used in the parallel corpus construction.

---

[4] https://github.com/OpenNMT/OpenNMT-py.

[5] http://data.statmt.org/pmindia.

[6] https://github.com/bhaddow/pmindia-crawler.

[7] https://github.com/moses-smt/mosesdecoder/blob/master/scripts/ems/support/split-sentences. perl.

[8] https://www.pmindia.gov.in/en/mann-ki-baat/.

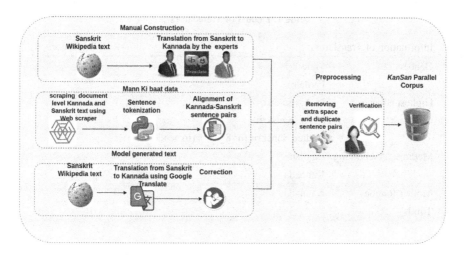

Fig. 1. Framework of the *KanSan* parallel corpus construction

The first step in the construction of *KanSan* corpus is extracting monolingual Sanskrit text from Wikipedia[9] by web-crawling[10]. The text collected from Wikipedia dumps have lot of noise, such as empty lines, lines consisting of only digits, symbols, English letters, and urls. This noise is removed from the text using handcrafted code[11] subjected to sentence tokenization using indicNLP library[12] which resulted in 9,38,184 Sanskrit sentences. Part of this data is used in the manual construction and Model Generated Text (MGT) approaches to create *KanSan* corpus. The approaches used to create *KanSan* corpus are described below:

i) Manual Construction - 25,000 Sanskrit sentences are randomly selected from cleaned Sanskrit Wikipedia text which are then manually translated into Kannada with the help of three native Kannada speakers who have expertise in Sanskrit and the details about the translators is given in Table 1. Each sentence is translated by a minimum of two translators according to the following guidelines provided to them:

– The context of the source sentence must be clearly conveyed in the target sentence
– During translation, the adequacy and fluency of the target language must be considered
– Words in the source sentence that do not belong to the source language must be entered in the target sentence in the same form as they appeared in the source sentence
– Digits must be written either using the target language phonetics or in the number format

---

[9] https://sa.wikipedia.org/wiki/.

[10] https://github.com/hegdekasha/wikiextractor.

[11] https://github.com/hegdekasha/wikiextractor/wikipreprocessing.

[12] https://github.com/anoopkunchukuttan/indic_nlp_library.

Table 1. Details of Translators

Information of Translators		# of Translators
Gender	Male	1
	Female	2
Highest education	M.A. (Sanskrit)	1
	M.A. (Sanskrit)	1
	studied Sanskrit for 8 years (in academics)	1
Medium of schooling	English	0
	Kannada	3
Mother tongue	Kannada	3
Total		3

Using these guidelines, each sentence is translated in two phases: i) all the sentences are translated by one or the other translator ii) the translator who is not involved in the first phase verifies and corrects the sentences in the second phase.

ii) Model Generated Text - uses pretrained models or open sourced services/API to generate text [28]. Motivated by this, MGT is considered as one of the sources of data in the construction of *KanSan* corpus using Google Translate[13] (GT) - an open sourced translation API. Recently GT added Sanskrit to its system which provides decent translations from Sanskrit text to Kannada text [11]. 25,000 non-overlapping Sanskrit sentences randomly selected from the cleaned Sanskrit Wikipedia text obtained earlier are translated to Kannada text by the GT API. The output of GT is manually verified by the experts to check the fluency and adequacy of the target language and corrections are made wherever required.

iii) Mann Ki Baath Data - *Mann Ki Baath* online repository[14] contains multilingual parallel data of 13 Indian languages including Kannada and English. A web-scraper[15] is used to extract Kannada text from this repository at the document level. Further, Sanskrit text of *Mann Ki Baath* data which is also at the document level is obtained from the online Sanskrit documents website[16]. Both Kannada and Sanskrit documents are temporally aligned and are then tokenized using the indicNLP library followed by the manual verification of sentence alignment. This process yields 23,758 Kannada-Sanskrit sentence pairs. It may be noted that the verification of sentence alignment has consumed a significant amount of time as the parallel text is temporally aligned. The sentence alignment has the significant role in building a comprehensive parallel corpus and hence on the quality of MT.

---

[13] https://translate.google.co.in/.

[14] https://www.pmindia.gov.in/en/mann-ki-baat/.

[15] https://github.com/MSKantulu/Mann-Ki-Baat.

[16] https://sanskritdocuments.

The above three approaches together yielded 73,758 Kannada-Sanskrit sentence pairs and the sample sentences along with their English translations are given in Table 2. In addition to these approaches, Back-Translation (BT) (discussed in Sect. 4.5) is also used to add more Kannada-Sanskrit sentence pairs to *KanSan* corpus.

Table 2. Sample Sanskrit sentences and their Kannada and English translations from the *KanSan*

Sanskrit (as source)	Kannada (as target)	English translation
अद्य अशेष-देश: रक्षाबंधन-पर्व आयोजयति (adya aśeṣa-deśaḥ rakṣābaṃdhana-parva āyōjayati)	ಇಂದು ಸಂಪೂರ್ಣ ದೇಶ ರಕ್ಷಾಬಂಧನದ ಹಬ್ಬವನ್ನು ಆಚರಿಸುತಿದೆ (imdu sampūrNa deśa rakṣābaṃdhanada habbavannu ācharisutide)	Today the entire country is celebrating the festival of Rakshabandhan
अस्य यानस्य अग्रम् अरि उपहतम् (asya yānasya agram ari upahatam)	ಈ ಗಾಡಿಯ ಮುಂದಿನ ಚಕ್ರ ಮುರಿದಿದೆ. (I gaadiya mumndina chakravu muridide)	The front wheel of this cart is broken.
ओक्टोबर-मासे द्वितीये दिनाङ्क, तत: परम् ऐषम: वर्षत्रयं पूर्ण भविता (oktobara-māse dvitīye dināṅka, tataḥ param eeṣamaḥ varṣatrayam pūrṇa bhavitā)	ಈ ಅಕ್ಟೋಬರ್ 2 ಕ್ಕೆ ಅದಕ್ಕೆ 3 ವರ್ಷ ತುಂಬುತ್ತವೆ (I actōbar 2 kke adakke 3 varṣa tumbuttave)	It will be 3 years this October 2
पुस्तकमिदं NarendraModi इत्यत्र e-book रूपेणापि समुपलभ्यते (pustakamidam NarendraModi ityatra e-book rūpeṇāpi samupalabhyate)	ಈ ಪುಸ್ತಕವು NarendraModi-website ನಲ್ಲಿ e-book ರೂಪದಲ್ಲಿ ಲಭ್ಯವಿದೆ. (I pustakavu NarendraModi-website nalli e-book rūpadalli labhyavide)	This book is available in e-book form on NarendraModi-website.

4   Baseline Machine Translation Models

The primary objective of this work is to build *KanSan* - a parallel corpus with decent amount of Kannada-Sanskrit sentence pairs to train the MT models to translate Kannada text to Sanskrit text and vice versa. Techniques which are used in implementing MT models are described below:

4.1   Preprocessing

The impact of preprocessing in improving the quality of MT output has been reported in several research works [29, 30]. Apart from removing the noise that reduce the quality of the corpus, preprocessing will also evaluate the corpus semantically, stimulating a tendency for the creation of sentence alignments. Hence, during preprocessing, extra space such as initial space, end space, empty lines, double white space, and duplicate sentence pairs are removed resulting in 72,671 Kannada-Sanskrit sentence pairs out of 73,758 sentences pairs.

4.2   Subword Tokenization

Subword tokenization is a popular tokenization method in which rare words are split into the most frequently occurring words and are represented as a pair of bytes in a sequence with an unused byte [31]. Usage of subword tokenization is intended to avoid

Out-Of-Vocabulary (OOV) issues that occur when a word is present in the Test set but not in the Train set. Further, OOV issue occurs specifically in morphologically rich languages due to lengthy morphemes. Byte Pair Encoding (BPE)[17] - a popular subword tokenization technique developed based on data compression algorithm is used in this work to obtain subword units. In BPE, the frequent words are represented by a single token along with a special symbol (_) and the rare words are broken down into two or more subword tokens. OOV words will be broken down into more frequently occurring subwords. It may be noted that, in this work, BPE with a vocabulary size of 50,000 for both Kannada and Sanskrit is used in building vocabulary for both source and target text which are then transformed into vectors to train the transformer-based models. Table 3 shows the sample Sanskrit sentences and Kannada inferences and their English translations followed by the BPE subword tokenization of the words in these sentences.

4.3 Statistical Machine Translation

SMT is a statistical model proposed by Brown et al. [32], where in translations are carried out based on the probability distribution of the parallel sentences. This model considers every sentence 'b' to be a potential translation of sentence 'a', where 'b' represents the target sentence and 'a' represents the source sentence. For every sentence pair (a, b), translation probability can be defined as $p(b|a)$ where b is the translation of 'a'. This can be achieved through Language Model (LM) and Translation Model (TM). LM gives the probability distribution of each target sentence i.e., p(b) and TM gives the product of the probability of the source sentence given the target sentence $(p(a|b))$ and the LM (p(b)). Then the best translation is calculated by searching the maximum probability value considering the Bayes theorem. The mathematical expression of this theorem to get the probability of target words is given below:

$$\arg \max_b p(b|a) = \arg \max_b p(a|b)p(b) \tag{1}$$

4.4 Neural Machine Translation

Essentially an NMT system predicts a sequence of words B = $(b_1,\ldots, b_k)$ in the target language for a given source language sentence A = $(a_1,\ldots, a_k)$ [33]. This conditional probability distribution is modeled using encoder-decoder architectures and the basic encoder-decoder architecture is shown in Fig. 2. The encoder converts the variable length source language sentence into a fixed length vector. As this fixed length vector (sentence embedding) contains the context of the input sentence, it is also called as a context vector. Taking this context vector as an input, the decoder predicts the output words based on the context of each word. Mathematically, it can be represented as follows:

$$log\ p(b|a) = \sum_{t}^{k=1} log\ p(b_k|b_{k-1}, \ldots b_1, a, c) \tag{2}$$

---

[17] https://bpemb.h-its.org/.

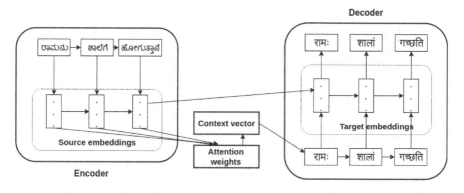

Fig. 2. Encoder-decoder based Neural Machine Translation model

Encoder - Basically, encoders transform sentences into vector values, which represent their context. It is necessary to obtain word representations, often known as word embeddings, of source language words before feeding them into the encoder network. Encoder network transforms these word embeddings into sentence embeddings thereby generating the context vector consisting of the context of the source sentence [33]. By convention, the encoder network can be constructed using RNN and can also be constructed either using BiRNN [34], or transformers [35]. Unlike RNN, BiRNN has two RNNs to compute forward and backward hidden state sequences [36]. Further, the transformer-based encoder network extracts the features of all words in the source sentence using self-attention mechanism.

Table 3. Sample BPE subword tokenization of Sanskrit and Kannada sentences and their English translations

Language	Original sentence	English Translation	Tokenized sentence using BPE
Sanskrit	अद्य अशेष-देश: रक्षाबंधन-पर्व आयोजयति (adya aśeṣa-deśaḥ rakṣābaṃdhana-parva āyōjayati)	Today the entire country is celebrating the festival of Rakshabandhan	['_ಇದು', '_ಸಂಪೂರ್ಣ', '_ದೇಶ', '_ರಕ್ಷಾ', 'ಬಂಧ', 'ನದ', '_ಹಬ್ಬವನ್ನು', '_ಆಚರಿಸ', 'ುತ', 'ಿ°ದ']
Kannada	ಇದು ಸಂಪೂರ್ಣ ದೇಶ ರಕ್ಷಾಬಂಧನದ ಹಬ್ಬವನ್ನು ಆಚರಿಸುತಿದೆ (imdu sampūrNa deśa rakṣābaṃdhanada habbavannu ācharisutide)	Today the entire country is celebrating the festival of Rakshabandhan	['_अद्य', '_अ', 'शेष', '-', 'देश:', '_रक्षा', 'बंधन', '-', 'पर्व', '_आयोजयति']

Decoder - The decoder network is initialized by the final layer of the encoder network i.e. context vector and the decoder network can be either RNN, BiRNN, or transformer based on the type of the encoder network. The target language words (tgt) are predicted based on the sentence embeddings obtained at the encoder, previously predicted target words and the contextual information of each source word. From Eq. 2, $p(b_k|b_{k-1}, ..b_1, a, c) = tgt$ can be obtained as,

$$tgt = g(b_{k-1}, f(h_{k-1}, k-1, c_k), c_k) \tag{3}$$

where, g is a nonlinear function, b_{k-1} is the previously predicted target word, c_k contextual information of each word, and h_{k-1} is the hidden state in the decoder at (k-1) step.

Longer source sentences with rich morphological features make it more challenging for the machine to remember the context and this will increase the probability of incorrect target word predictions. This problem is alleviated by assigning weights randomly focusing on certain parts of the input sentence while predicting the kth target word and this mechanism is known as Attention Mechanism [37]. The Attention Mechanism generates attention weights by comparing target hidden states with source hidden states and the context vector is computed based on the attention vector. These vector values are then used as input to the decoder to predict the target words.

4.5   Back-Translation

Data Augmentation (DA) is one of the popular approaches to increase the size of any corpus. Back-translation (BT) is one of the simplest and more effective DA techniques [38] which exploits the monolingual data for translation and it can be used to increase the size of the parallel corpus [31] by translating the target language text into the source language text creating synthetic data. In this work, 72,671 preprocessed Kannada-Sanskrit sentence pairs (T_c) obtained as mentioned in Sect. 4.1 are used for BT. Out of these 72,671 sentence pairs in T_c, 10,000 sentence pairs are chosen randomly and the Kannada sentences from these pairs are used to test and the remaining sentence pairs are used to train the Transformer+BPE model.

The steps that are used to carry out BT are given below:

1. 10,000 Kannada (source) sentences in the Test set are translated into Sanskrit (target) sentences
2. The reverse translation is carried out by training the Transformer+BPE model using the interchanged Kannada (source) and Sanskrit (target) language text (obtained in step 1)
3. The Sanskrit (target) sentences that were obtained in step 2 are considered as the Test sentences for reverse translation to generate Kannada sentences (source)
4. To overcome the biasing, Steps 1, 2, and 3 are repeated four times with non-overlapping Test sets to get the Kannada (source) sentences in parallel to the Sanskrit (target) sentences

The Kannada-Sanskrit sentence pairs obtained by BT are manually verified and added to T_c. Further, duplicate sentence pairs in the new T_c are removed to get the final corpus. Thus, BT contributed 27,500 Kannada-Sanskrit parallel sentences in the construction of *KanSan* corpus resulting in 1,01,171 parallel sentences. The number of parallel sentences obtained from each data source including BT and the statistics of *KanSan* corpus are given in Table 4 and 5 respectively.

Table 4. Statistics of the *KanSan* parallel sentences collected from different data sources

Data source	# of Kannada-Sanskrit sentences extracted
Manual Translation	25,000
Mann Ki Baat	23,758
Model Generated Text	25,000
Total (before preprocessing)	73,758
Total (after preprocessing)	72,671
Back-translation	27,500
Total	1,00,171

Table 5. Statistics of the *KanSan* parallel corpus and details about Train and Test set

Languages	# of Tokens	# of Unique words	Average words in a sentence
Sanskrit	3,89,556	51,259	9
Kannada	3,57,117	50,953	11
Total # of Sentences	1,01,171		
Language pair	**Train set**	**Test set**	
san-kan	1,00,171	1,000	

Table 6. Hyper-parameters and their values used in NMT model

Hyper-parameters	Values
word vector size	512
encoding layers	2
decoding layers	2
heads	8
learning rate	1.0
dropout	0.3
batch size	64
train steps	1,00,000
encoder type	transformer
rnn type	lstm
position encoding	True
optimization	sgd
check-point	10,000
maximum-sequence-length-src	default
maximum-sequence-length-tgt	default

5   Experimental Setup and Results

After extensive preprocessing, both SMT system and NMT baselines, namely: RNN, BiRNN and transformer-based models are implemented to set the benchmark on newly constructed *KanSan* corpus. The SMT system is implemented using Moses toolkit[18] and NMT models are implemented using Open source Neural Machine Translation (OpenNMT-py)[19] to translate Kannada sentences to Sanskrit sentences and vice versa. Basically, OpenNMT-py provides a well structured encoder-decoder architecture with attention mechanism to perform sequence-to-sequence prediction tasks [21].

Several experiments are carried out by fine-tuning hyper-parameters to obtain the best results. Different encoder-types, namely: RNN baseline, BiRNN, and transformer, and other hyper-parameters are fine-tuned to obtain the best results. In addition to different encoder types, different RNN architectures, namely: Long Short Term Memory (LSTM) and Gated Recurrent Unit (GRU) are also experimented to get the best hyper-parameter set. The hyper-parameters and their values used to build NMT models that gave the best results are shown in Table 6.

Table 7. Performance measure of the MT models in terms of BLEU score

Models	Kannada-Sanskrit	Sanskrit-Kannada
SMT	4.53	5.42
RNN baseline	6.48	8.32
BiRNN	7.32	9.93
Transformer	8.53	11.56
Transformer+BPE	**9.84**	**12.63**
Google translator	7.13	12.28

To measure the performance of MT models, BLEU scores are chosen as evaluation metrics. This approach counts the n-grams in the candidate translation that match the n-grams in the reference text and comparison is made without considering word order. In general, more the matches between the candidate and reference translation, better is the translation [39]. By this, it is possible to automatically evaluate the MT models similar to human evaluation. Performance measure of MT models in terms of BLEU scores given in Table 7 indicates that all the NMT models performed better than SMT model in terms of BLEU scores indicating that the NMT models are always winners over SMT models in sequence prediction task [40]. BiRNN model has shown slight improvement in the BLEU scores for both Kannada-Sanskrit and Sanskrit-Kannada translations over RNN baseline. Transformer-based models due to its self-attention mechanism, outperformed BiRNN with BLEU scores of 1.21 and 1.63 for Kannada-Sanskrit and Sanskrit-Kannada translations respectively. However, when the transformer-based models are

[18] https://github.com/moses-smt.
[19] https://github.com/OpenNMT/OpenNMT-py.

compared to Transformer+BPE, this extended model performed better than all the previous models with improved BLEU scores. Further, the performance of GT trained on zero-shot translation technique is compared with the proposed models to measure the performance of the SMT and NMT models. The BLEU scores of GT are slightly less for Sanskrit-Kannada translations compared to that of Transformer+BPE. However, the BLEU scores of Kannada-Sanskrit translations are little surprising because of Kannada sentences getting translated into Hindi. This may be due to the reason that both Hindi and Sanskrit text are written in the same script.

The sample Sanskrit to Kannada translations obtained from RNN baseline and Transformer+BPE models along with the actual translations are given in Table 8. Comparison of the model predictions is conducted only for RNN baseline and Transformer+BPE models, since, a slight improvement in the BLEU score does not influence the model predictions. In Table 8, translations obtained from RNN baseline and Transformer+BPE models for the sample sentences 1 and 2 are almost similar to the actual translations and both models convey the context of the source sentences. The reason for these accurate translations is the simple structure of the source sentences with more frequent verbal inflections. However, for the sample source sentences 3 and 4, outputs of RNN baseline fail to capture the context of the input sentences and predicts only the first word. Transformer+BPE model successfully predicts more number of words compared to that of RNN baseline model with the correct word order because of its self-attention and subword tokenization features. Further, the sample Kannada to Sanskrit translations obtained from the RNN baseline and Transformer+BPE models along with the ground truths are given in Table 9. Similar to Sanskrit to Kannada translations, outputs obtained from the Transformer+BPE model captured more accurate context compared to that of the RNN baseline for Kannada to Sanskrit translations. Consequently, simple source sentences (sample sentences 1 and 2) are translated successfully using both RNN baseline and Transformer+BPE models.

Table 8. Sanskrit to Kannada translation samples

Sanskrit to Kannada Translation				
SL. No	Source sentences	Output 1 (RNN baseline)	Output 2 (Transformer+BPE)	Actual Translation
1.	महेशः फलम् आदत् (maheśaḥ phalam ādat)	ಮಹೇಶ ಹಣ್ಣು ತೆಗೆದುಕೊಳ್ಳುತ್ತಾರೆ (mahēśa haṇṇannu tegedukoḷḷuttāne)	ಮಹೇಶ ಹಣ್ಣನ್ನು ತೆಗೆದುಕೊಳ್ಳುತ್ತಾನೆ (mahēśa haṇṇu tegedukoḷḷuttāne)	ಮಹೇಶನು ಹಣ್ಣನ್ನು ತೆಗೆದುಕೊಳ್ಳುತ್ತಾನೆ (mahēśanu haṇṇannu tegedukoḷḷuttāne)
2.	रामः ऋणं स्वीकरोति (rāmaḥ ṛṇam svīkarōti)	ರಾಮ ಸಾಲ ಪಡೆಯುತ್ತಾನೆ (rāma sāla padeyuttāne)	ರಾಮ ಸಾಲವನ್ನು ಪಡೆಯುತ್ತಾನೆ (rāma sālavannu padeyuttāne)	ರಾಮನು ಸಾಲವನ್ನು ಸ್ವೀಕರಿಸುತ್ತಾನೆ (rāmanu sālavannu svīkarisuttāne)
3.	भारतस्य संविधानं निर्मातुं संविधानसमितेः रचना अभूत् (bhāratasya samvidhānam nirmitum samvidhānasamiteḥ rachanā abhūt)	ಭಾರತದ ಸುಪ್ರೀಂ ಬದಲಾವಣೆಯಾಗಿದೆ (bhāratada suprīm badalāvaṇeyāgide)	ಭಾರತದ ಸಂವಿಧಾನವನ್ನು ರಚಿಸಲಾಯಿತು (bhāratada samvidhānavannu rachisalāyitu)	ಭಾರತದ ಸಂವಿಧಾನವನ್ನು ನಿರ್ಮಿಸಲು ಸಂವಿಧಾನ ಸಮಿತಿಯ ರಚನೆ ಆಯಿತು (bhāratada samvidhānavannu nirmisalusalu samvidhāna sabheya rachane āyitu)
4.	अयं दुर्गः एकस्मिन् उपशैले स्थितः अस्ति (ayam durgaḥ ekasmin upaśaile sthitaḥ asti)	ಈ ಕೋಟೆಯು ಬೆಟ್ಟದ ಕೇಂದ್ರವಾಗಿದೆ (ī kōṭeyu beṭṭada kēmdravāgide)	ಈ ಕೋಟೆಯು ಉಪ ಬೆಟ್ಟದ ಮೇಲೆ ಇದೆ (ī kōṭeyu upa beṭṭada mēle ide)	ಈ ಕೋಟೆಯು ಒಂದು ಹತ್ತಿರದ ಬೆಟ್ಟದ ಮೇಲೆ ಇರುತ್ತದೆ (ī kōṭeyu omdu hattirada beṭṭada mēle iruttade)

Table 9. Kannada to Sanskrit translation samples

	Kannada to Sanskrit Translation			
SL No	Source sentences	Output 1 (RNN baseline)	Output 2 (Transformer+BPE)	Actual Translation
1.	ಮಹೇಶನು ಹಣ್ಣನ್ನು ತೆಗೆದುಕೊಳ್ಳುತ್ತಾನೆ (maheśānu haṇṇannu tegedukoḷḷuttāne)	महेश फलं आदत्ते (maheśa phalaṃ ādatte)	महेशः फलम् आदत्ते (maheśaḥ phalam ādatte)	महेशः फलम् आदत् (maheśaḥ phalam ādat)
2.	ರಾಮನು ಸಾಲವನ್ನು ಸ್ವೀಕರಿಸುತ್ತಾನೆ (rāmanu sālavannu svīkarisuttāne)	रामः ऋणं स्वीकरोति (rāmaḥ ṛṇam svīkarōti)	रामः ऋणं स्वीकरोति (rāmaḥ ṛṇam svīkarōti)	रामः ऋणं स्वीकरोति (rāmaḥ ṛṇam svīkarōti)
3.	ಭಾರತದ ಸಂವಿಧಾನವನ್ನು ನಿರ್ಮಿಸಲು ಸಂವಿಧಾನ ಸಮಿತಿಯ ರಚನೆ ಆಯಿತು (bhāratada samvidhānavannu nirmisalusalu samvidhāna sabheya rachane āyitu)	भारतस्य बहुविधेषु वाणिजेषु प्रमुखेषु च प्रदर्शयति (bhāratasya bahuvidheṣu vāṇikeṣu pramukheṣu ca pradarśayati)	भारतस्य संविधानस्य निर्माणार्थं संविधानसमिति: निर्मितवती (bhāratasya samvidhānasya nirmāṇārtham samvidhānasamitiḥ nirmitavatī)	भारतस्य संविधानं निर्मातुं संविधानसमिते: रचना अभूत् (bhāratasya samvidhānam nirmitum samvidhānasamiteḥ rachanā abhūt)
4.	ಈ ಕೋಟೆಯು ಒಂದು ಹತ್ತಿರದ ಬೆಟ್ಟದ ಮೇಲೆ ಇರುತ್ತದೆ (ī kōṭeyu omdu hattirada beṭṭada mēle iruttade)	अयं दुर्ग: पर्यटकानां आकर्षणकेन्द्रम् अस्ति (ayam durgah paryaṭkānām ākarṣaṇakendram astī)	अयं दुर्ग: समीपस्थे पर्वते अस्ति (ayam durgah samīsthe parvate asti)	अयं दुर्ग: एकस्मिन् उपशैले स्थित: अस्ति (ayam durgah ekasmin upaśaile sthitaḥ asti)

6 Conclusion and Future Work

This paper describes the construction of *KanSan* - a parallel corpus, for MT and the MT baselines to translate Kannada text to Sanskrit text and vice versa. *KanSan* corpus is constructed both manually and also using MGT and BT approaches. This is the first work which describes the construction of Kannada-Sanskrit parallel corpus for MT. Using this newly constructed parallel corpus, the models: SMT, RNN baseline, BiRNN, Transformer, and Transformer+BPE are implemented to translate Kannada text to Sanskrit text and vice versa. Among all the models, Transformer+BPE model outperformed the other models with BLEU scores of 9.84 and 12.63 for Kannada-Sanskrit and Sanskrit-Kannada MT respectively. As future work, hybrid MT models utilizing linguistic features of Sanskrit and Kannada with suitable preprocessing techniques will be explored.

References

1. Wu, Y., et al.: Google's neural machine translation system: bridging the gap between human and machine translation. arXiv preprint arXiv:1609.08144 (2016)
2. Beekes, R.S.P.: Comparative Indo-European Linguistics: An Introduction. John Benjamins Publishing, Amsterdam (2011)
3. Keith, A.B.: A History of Sanskrit Literature. Motilal Banarsidass Publisher, New Delhi (1993)
4. Kak, S.C.: The Paninian approach to natural language processing. Int. J. Approx. Reasoning 1(1), 117–130 (1987)
5. Huet, G.: Shallow syntax analysis in Sanskrit guided by semantic nets constraints. In: Proceedings of the 2006 International Workshop on Research Issues in Digital Libraries, pp. 1–10 (2006)

6. Antony, P.J., Soman, K.P.: Computational morphology and natural language parsing for Indian languages: a literature survey. Int. J. Sci. Eng. Res. (2012)
7. Prathibba, R.J., Padma, M.C.: Shallow parser for Kannada sentences using machine learning approach. Int. J. Comput. Linguist. Res. 158–170 (2017)
8. Singh, M., Kumar, R., Chana, I.: Corpus based machine translation system with deep neural network for Sanskrit to Hindi translation. Procedia Comput. Sci. 2534–2544 (2020)
9. Bawa, S., Kumar, M.: A comprehensive survey on machine translation for English, Hindi and Sanskrit languages. J. Ambient Intell. Humanized Comput. 1–34 (2021)
10. Kashyap, D., Bharati, S., Dhubri, A.: Spoken Sanskrit movement in India: a study. Global Res. Methodol. J. 1–5 (2013)
11. Bapna, A., et al.: Building machine translation systems for the next thousand languages. arXiv preprint arXiv:2205.03983 (2022)
12. Ramesh, G., et al.: Samanantar: the largest publicly available parallel corpora collection for 11 Indic languages. Trans. Assoc. Comput. Linguist. 145–162 (2022)
13. Johnson, M., et al.: Google's multilingual neural machine translation system: enabling zero-shot translation. Trans. Assoc. Comput. Linguist. 339–351 (2017)
14. Chipman, H.A., George, E.I., McCulloch, R.E., Shively, T.S.: mBART: multidimensional monotone BART. Bayesian Anal. 515–544 (2022)
15. Xue, L., et al.: mT5: a massively multilingual pre-trained text-to-text transformer. arXiv preprint arXiv:2010.11934 (2020)
16. de Lhoneux, M., Kunchukuttan, A., Aralikatte, R., Søgaard, A.: Itihasa: a large-scale Corpus for Sanskrit to English translation. In: WAT, pp. 145–162 (2021)
17. Dutt, M.N. (ed.): A Prose English Translation of the Mahabharata: (tr. Literally from the Original Sanskrit Text. HC Dass, Elysium Press, Kolkata (1897)
18. Debroy, B.: The Valmiki Ramayana. Penguin Random House India Private Limited (2017)
19. Parida, S., Bojar, O., Dash, S.R.: Building English-Punjabi parallel corpus for machine translation. In: Smart Intelligent Computing and Applications, pp. 495–504. Springer, Cham (2020)
20. Parida, S., Dash, S.R., Bojar, O., Motlicek, P., Pattnaik, P., Mallick, D.K.: OdiEnCorp 2.0: Odia-English parallel corpus for machine translation. In: Proceedings of the WILDRE5-5th Workshop on Indian Language Data: Resources and Evaluation, pp. 14–19 (2020)
21. Klein, G., Kim, Y., Deng, Y., Senellart, J., Rush, A.M.: OpenNMT: open-source toolkit for neural machine translation. arXiv preprint arXiv:1701.02810 (2017)
22. Jolly, S., Agrawal, R.: Building English–Punjabi parallel corpus for machine translation. In: Gupta, D., Khanna, A., Bhattacharyya, S., Hassanien, A.E., Anand, S., Jaiswal, A. (eds.) International Conference on Innovative Computing and Communications. AISC, vol. 1165, pp. 377–385. Springer, Singapore (2021). https://doi.org/10.1007/978-981-15-5113-0_28
23. Jindal, S., Goyal, V., Bhullar, J.S.: Building English-Punjabi parallel corpus for machine translation. Int. J. Eng. Sci. Math. 223–229 (2018)
24. Haddow, B., Kirefu, F.: PMIndia-a collection of parallel corpora of languages of India. arXiv preprint arXiv:2001.09907 (2020)
25. Koehn, P., et al.: Moses: open source toolkit for statistical machine translation. In: Proceedings of the 45th Annual Meeting of the Association for Computational Linguistics Companion Volume Proceedings of the Demo and Poster Sessions, pp. 177–180 (2007)
26. Varga, D., Halácsy, P., Kornai, A., Nagy, V., Németh, L., Trón, V.: Parallel corpora for medium density languages. Amsterdam Stud. Theory History Linguist. Sci. Ser. 247 (2007)
27. Thompson, B., Koehn, P.: Vecalign: improved sentence alignment in linear time and space. In: Proceedings of the 2019 Conference on Empirical Methods in Natural Language Processing and the 9th International Joint Conference on Natural Language Processing (EMNLP-IJCNLP), pp. 1342–1348 (2019)

28. Lowphansirikul, L., Polpanumas, C., Rutherford, A.T., Nutanong, S.: A large English-Thai parallel corpus from the web and machine-generated text. Lang. Resour. Eval. 477–499 (2022)
29. Oudah, M., Almahairi, A., Habash, N.: The impact of preprocessing on Arabic-English statistical and neural machine translation. arXiv preprint arXiv:1906.11751 (2019)
30. Narasimha Raju, B.N.V., Bhadri Raju, M.S.V.S., Satyanarayana, K.V.V.: Effective preprocessing based neural machine translation for English to Telugu cross-language information retrieval. IAES Int. J. Artif. Intell. 306–314 (2021)
31. Sennrich, R., Haddow, B., Birch, A.: Improving neural machine translation models with monolingual data. arXiv preprint arXiv:1511.06709 (2015)
32. Pietra, D., Vincent, J.: The mathematics of statistical machine translation: parameter estimation. Using Large Corpora 223–311 (1994)
33. Sutskever, I., Vinyals, O., Le, Q.V.: Sequence to sequence learning with neural networks. In: Advances in Neural Information Processing Systems, pp. 3104–3112 (2014)
34. Premjith, B., Anand Kumar, M., Soman, K.P.: Neural machine translation system for English to Indian language translation using MTIL parallel corpus. J. Intell. Syst. 387–398 (2019)
35. Vaswani, A.: Attention Is All You Need. In: Advances in Neural Information Processing Systems (2017)
36. Schuster, M., Paliwal, K.K.: Bidirectional recurrent neural networks. IEEE Trans. Signal Process. 2673–2681 (1997)
37. Bahdanau, D., Cho, K., Bengio, Y.: Neural machine translation by jointly learning to align and translate. arXiv preprint arXiv:1409.0473 (2014)
38. Hegde, A., Banerjee, S., Chakravarthi, B.R., Priyadharshini, R., Shashirekha, H., McCrae, J.P.: Overview of the shared task on machine translation in Dravidian languages. In: Proceedings of the Second Workshop on Speech and Language Technologies for Dravidian Languages, pp. 271–278 (2022)
39. Papineni, K., Roukos, S., Ward, T., Zhu, W.J.: BLEU: a method for automatic evaluation of machine translation. In: Proceedings of the 40th annual meeting of the Association for Computational Linguistics, pp. 311–318 (2002)
40. Mahata, S.K., Mandal, S., Das, D., Bandyopadhyay, S.: SMT vs NMT: a comparison over Hindi & Bengali simple sentences arXiv preprint arXiv:1812.04898 (2018)

A Parsing Tool for Short Linguistic Constructions

A Case Study for Indian Languages

Priyanka Jain[1]([⊠]) [ID], N. K. Jain[1], Hemant Darbari[1], and Virendrakumar C. Bhavsar[2]

[1] Centre for Development of Advanced Computing, Delhi, India
priyankaj@cdac.in
[2] Faculty of Computer Science, University of New Brunswick, Fredericton, Canada

Abstract. In the current trend of unstructured language usage in simpler and shorter conversations, we identified a need of language analysis tool (a language parser) to find semantic relations within the sentence constituents. Earley's algorithm is used in this paper to propose a parsing approach based on the Tree Adjoining Grammar (TAG) formalism. It is able to extract dependency relations in the derivation tree form. A generalized TAG tree-grammar pertaining to Subject-Object-Verb (SOV) syntactic pattern is also presented corresponding to the proposed algorithm. This grammar is targeted to be suitable for short dialogues in low resource languages which have scarcity of enough data for ML/DL based approaches. The process flow is presented using the combinatory tree-set formation and parsing. Two implementations are carried out using XML and LISP notation data structure. Examples from an Indian language are presented in a step-by-step manner that illustrates parsing in a controlled grammar environment for linguistically not-very complex syntactic constructions. Results along with findings are presented for execution time and memory consumption.

Keywords: Tree adjoining grammar · Natural Language Processing · Syntactic Parser · Rule-based approaches · Ealey's algorithm

1 Introduction

A simple parsing tool is proposed with minimal complexity and response time to handle the unstructured shorter linguistic constructions. The proposed simplified parser is designed to use the customized controlled grammar pertaining to Subject-Object-Verb (SOV) oriented Indian language (IL) structure. The motivation of the parser algorithm and corresponding grammar is to fulfill the requirement of often-used simpler sentences where the complexity of linguistic constructions is smaller. These constructions especially belong to dialogue communication, not to grammatically correct form (as found in literature). The proposed parsing tool can be applied in the linguistic applications like Chatbot, Machine Translation, Summarizer, Expert system, Knowledge Engineering and as a heuristic rule-base input for many Machine-Learning oriented systems.

© The Author(s), under exclusive license to Springer Nature Switzerland AG 2023
Anand Kumar M et al. (Eds.): SPELLL 2022, CCIS 1802, pp. 19–34, 2023.
https://doi.org/10.1007/978-3-031-33231-9_2

We consider parsing of a MoR-FWO (Morphological rich and free word order) [3] Indian languages as a case-study. These languages have complexities like free-word-order nature, linguistic divergence, automation complexity, resource deficiency and semantic ambiguity [7]. The proposed work maintains the state-chart while parsing that helps in obtaining close dependency-relations of the constituents. These semantic relations are required for identifying long-distance dependencies from parsing of free-word-order Indian languages.

This paper is organized in Sections. Here, Sect. 2 provides the review on the TAG related works and the Earley's Algorithm. Section 3 presents our IL TAG Parser. Section 4 focuses on specific simpler TAG Grammar targeted to identify semantic relation in-between the sentence constitutes. Section 5 gives a parsing example. Experiment and result analysis are provided in Sect. 6. Section 7 presents the conclusion of the paper.

2   Related Work

The research work in this paper considers adapting the Earle's algorithm [4, 5] as a base, so that it has the capability of handling Tree Adjoining Grammar (TAG) formalism and ease of processing like Context Free Grammar (CFG). Works in [2, 3, 19] show various parsing strategies for Free-Word Order Languages. A constraint-based approach that incorporates grammatical notions from Computational Paninian Grammar (CPG) to build a generalized parser is proposed by [6]. TAG produces derivation trees, which are significant semantically and syntactically [17]. TAG formalism works well for modeling sentential structures of languages having long distance relations [11]. The significant work on TAG is presented in [14–16]. TAG for German language [1] shows that the dependencies involved in scrambling are beyond the generative capacity of the CFG. Some reported work [8, 9] to apply TAG [10–13] parsing for Hindi. Research work in [6, 20] offers innovative work to translate the syntax of language grammars using TAG formalism in linguistic significance. Lexicalized Tree Adjoining Grammar formalism (LTAG) [10] has attractive properties towards Natural Language Processing attaching Lexicons with the trees. An approach in [19] proposes to take out LTAG spinal tree-bank [21] from dependency structures of HyDT [2] for the Hindi language parsing. As a restricted TAG, Tree Insertion Grammar (TIG) [21] wraps auxiliary trees leaving only left and right auxiliary trees. An Earley's algorithm for the TAG formalism given by [20] uses the concepts of dotted rule on four dots in a tree-node and modified states. TAG [11] using Tree forms has two direction movements left to right and top to bottom. This makes TAG stronger to use adjunction operations.

3   Proposed IL TAG Parser

The workflow diagram for proposed parsing tool is presented in Fig. 1. Here, modifications at five parts of the operations are highlighted in yellow color. The details are discussed later in corresponding sections. On contrary to TAG, CFG has unidirectional possibility of traversing only left to right. Taking that into account, instead of four-dots, we propose to use two dots on every node for left to right traversal in a TAG tree. The depth of tree nodes is handled by balanced parentheses. Figure 2 presents an example with comparison of tree traversal in four-dot and two-dot notations on a sample tree. An equivalent LISP-notation is also illustrated. Similar to CFG, the substitution process is context free insertion of child tree into parent tree. The adjunction process in TAG is a context sensitive insertion before and after the foot node. Figure 3(a) shows the substitution where the constituents of the substitution tree are inserted into main tree's constituents.

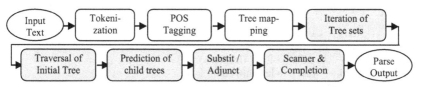

Fig. 1. Workflow Diagram with highlighted proposed parser tool

In Fig. 3(b), the root node of adjunction tree is inserted into the main tree node and the children of main tree node are adjuncted into foot node of adjunct tree. To perform the operations, we had implementations using a data structure in LISP and XML notation. In the line of TIG [21], it allows only left and right operations. There is no issue of handling nullable production in the proposed approach as it is a lexicalized grammar based on LTAG [10]. Influenced by simpler parsing in CFG and TIG like restricted TAG, a modified Earley's algorithm with controlled grammar is proposed.

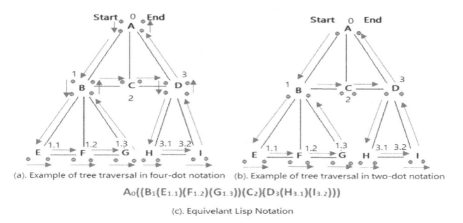

(a). Example of tree traversal in four-dot notation   (b). Example of tree traversal in two-dot notation

$$A_0((B_1(E_{1.1})(F_{1.2})(G_{1.3}))(C_2)(D_3(H_{3.1})(I_{3.2})))$$

(c). Equivalent Lisp Notation

Fig. 2. Comparison of tree traversals

The Substitution and Adjunction operations are performed by nodes embedding in parent tree. In the line of the Earley's algorithm, the Substitution Predictor operation predicts the appropriate initial trees. Dissimilar to [20], our process is modified at the four points; the algorithm is shown in Fig. 4 for proposed process.

Point 1: To parse a given string w, we use a collection of trees as TAG Tree set Ts(G). Trees in Ts(G) are arranged as per the grammatical categories of the input tokens. Trees

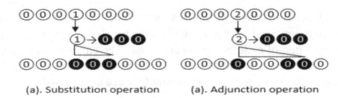

(a). Substitution operation   (a). Adjunction operation

Fig. 3. Difference of tree traversals

```
Declare ARAY S;
Function INIT(w)
        S ← CREARE-ARRAY (length(w) + 1)
        For k ← from 0 to length(w) do
        S[k] ← EMPTY-ORDERED-SET
function Proposed-PARSE(Iₛ, w, Tₛ(G) )
        ENQUEUE(currentTree, currentNode, parentTree, oCount) in S
        for each node in Iₛ do
                maintain oCount
                if next-of('•') is a non-terminal X then
                        PREDICTOR(Iₛ, X, S, Tₛ(G)) // for case 'α•Xβ' in Iₛ'
                else if next-of('•') is close-bracket then
                        COMPLETER(S) // for case 'α•)β' in Iᵢ'
MOVE-NEXT
        SCANNER(Iₛ, w, oCount, Tₛ(G))
        return chart
end
procedure PREDICTOR(Iₛ, X, S, Tₛ(G)) // for (X → I_q)
        if Lexical-Index(I_q) in-between Lexical-Indexes(Iₛ)
        insert I_q into Iₛ
        add-to-S(I_q, X, Iₛ, oCount)
                remove (X → I_q) from Tₛ(G)
end
procedure COMPLETER (S) // for case 'α•)β' in Iᵢ'
        find Sⱼ and X such that X is the last predicted node in S
        add-to-S(Sⱼ) // e.g. null for parent tree of Iₛ'
end
procedure SCANNER(Iₛ, w, oCount, T_w(G))
        if oCount?(0) and Tₛ(G)?(0) then
                for j ← from 0 to length(w) do
                        if order-of lex-of(Iₛ) matches wⱼ
                                return successful
                else return fail
end
```

Fig. 4. Algorithm of parsing module

are lexicalized at head node with its lexical index and category. If the token of the input string is at index '5' with category 'VM', it is represented as an anchor node '5VM◇' as shown in Eq. (1). The root of TAG tree is considered as a left side non-terminal of a production. The states are maintained while parsing to generate the derivation tree post-parsing. A LISP notation of Is with dot '•' is shown in Eq. (2):

$$I_s = \bullet \, ((S)((NP\downarrow))((VP)((V)(5VM\lozenge)))) \; // \; \text{TAG Tree in LISP form} \qquad (1)$$

$$S \to NP \; VP \; V \; 5VM\lozenge \; // \; \text{Equivalent CFG} \; (S \to XYZai) \qquad (2)$$

Point 2: The prediction in Early's algorithm adds state (Y → γk) to S(k). It is done with Y on the left-hand side (Y → γ) for every production in the grammar. Instead of adding all productions for a single node, we pre-compute the ambiguities in trees selection process. The brute-force analysis gets appropriate combination of trees in a Tree set Ts(G) by enumerating all possible solutions successively. Unlike the scanner operation in Early's algorithm after every prediction, we perform the scanner only once on completion of parsing process. This resolves conflicts in multiple adjunctions based on combinatory Tree sets. Extension to look-ahead prediction in Earley's algorithm, we predict the trees with suitable lexicon index. These should be in accordance with the already performed indexes in Is. Use of this combinatory Tree sets and contextual index help in controlling multiple recursions as each index has assigned a specific tree to operate. On completion of the operations, the trees are removed from the Tree set.

$$I_s = ((S)((NP.r)((NP)((N)(1NN\lozenge)))((P)(2PSP\lozenge)))((VP.r)((NP)(\bullet \, (N)(4NN\lozenge)))((VP.f)((V)(5VM\lozenge)))))$$
$$(3)$$

In the given example in Eq. (3), the prediction at position •(N) seeks for a tree which has anchor node index between 2PSP$\lozenge$ and 4NN$\lozenge$.

Point 3: We reduced the state tuples according to reduction in dots on nodes, as in Eq. (4). Here, α is the current-tree and 'node' is the current node in being processed. The tree α' is the parent tree of current tree α. The 'content' is the count of open braces/nodes at an instance while traversing Is. At the end, content c(x) = 0 indicates the generation of a balanced and completed derived tree.

$$s = [\alpha, \text{node}, \alpha', \text{content}] \qquad (4)$$

Point 4: Parsing process traverses a LISP notation of I_s from left to right. It is like a pre-order parsing in a tree structure. While parsing tree, it performs prediction and completion operations. On completing the parsing process, the scanner operation matches the lexical sequence in I_s with input string w. It uses four tasks:

- Task1: Operation 'Move-Next' moves the dot '•' in I_s from left to right while maintaining content.
- Task2: 'Prediction' performs three operations for every node Y of the form α •Y β in Is, where (Y → • γ):

  – If Y has substitution symbol, then check for (Y → •γ) where γ should be an Initial tree in T_s(G) else seek as auxiliary tree.
  – Insert LISP of tree (Y → •γ) into Is as non-terminal Y is the root node of tree.

– Add to state S (γ, Y, γ', content). The dot moves next.

• Task3: Operation 'Completion' closes the current node for further processing. Since the next position of '•' is a closing bracket, it performs the two operations:

– Find last item with predicted node X in S so Completion is not performed on X.
– Add to state S (γ, X, γ', content). The dot moves next.

• Task4: Operation 'Scanner' recognizes the input string on completing the parsing process. A parser is successful on the satisfaction of the following three conditions:

– iff content $= 0$, i.e. the count of all processed open brackets is equal to count of all processed closed brackets. It means Isis a balanced and complete tree.
– iff $|T_s(G)| = 0$, all the trees from Tree set $T_s(G)$ are utilized.
– The order of lexicons in Isis same as the tokens in input string w.

If the predicted substitutable tree is totally recognized, the 'Substitution Completer' recognizes the rest of the tree in the parent tree. For 'Adjunction Predictor', the sub-tree pushed under the recognized foot then 'Predictor' recognizes the other half of the auxiliary tree. On total recognition of the auxiliary tree, the 'Completer' recognizes the rest of the tree in parent tree. The dot moves next for further processing in predicted tree. In case of no prediction also, the dot moves to next node in parent tree. The length of Ts(G) is reduced by removing the current operated tree. On a successful parse, the parser generates the derivation tree by the states with 'completer' operations. Sample instances of Points 1 to 4 are explained in Table 4 with an example.

4 Customized TAG Grammar

Free-word-order nature of language tends to generate a vague linguistic structure, which leads to the ambiguity in language processing. To handle the issue, a grammar is crafted by identifying inter-constituent dependency for extremely finest controlled parsed structured of Indian language. Minimum ambiguity remains using this grammar and it generates appropriate precise structures emphasizing the postposition relations and its grouping to head noun. This grammar is able to handle simple, compound, and complex sentences and it is expandable to larger scope in linguistic. Here, we discuss a few possible constructions corresponding to selected categories pertaining to the research scope due to space limitations; the details of other categories are given in the doctoral thesis of one of the authors. Final 10 trees are given in Table 1.

Finite Verb: These sentential trees of verb are the surface representation of sentence's syntax pertaining to grammar. Here, the root node of sentential tree is 'S', denoting a sentence. The anchor node 'V' is lexical node and carries the IL token corresponding to verb category. The intermediate 'NP' and 'VP' nodes are free for further adjunction and extension of parsing process.

- **T1 (nx0-V)** is a most suitable sentential initial TAG tree of verb. A basic TAG tree of noun category 'nxn' is appropriate for substitution at 'NP' substitutable node. This can handle transitive or di-transitive verb constructions by left adjunction of noun tree at 'VP' node. There is an auxiliary TAG tree named T4 ('nxvx') for noun category, which allows left adjunction of noun at VP node.
- **T2 (nx0e-V)** is for imperative sentence construction where 'esp' at subject node indicated a null string. These often appear to be with missing subjects and use a verb to begin the sentence. The construction "किताब पढ़ो"[Read a book] is handled by left adjunction of noun tree T4 ('nxvx') at 'VP' node.

NOUN: The anchor node 'N' is the lexical node with the IL token in noun tree. The recursive 'noun' to 'noun' attachment is handled in pre-processing and POS chunking using morphological analyser.

- **T3 (nxn)** is most suitable initial tree of noun. As discussed for trees T1 and T2, this noun tree T3 substitutes root node 'NP' in NP substitutable node of parent verb tree. The Nodes 'NP' and 'N' further can be adjuncted with relevant trees.
- **T4 (nxvx)** is an auxiliary tree and used for left adjunction at 'VP' node. Root node of this tree is 'VP' and anchor node 'N' is lexical node. Intermediate nodes 'VP', 'NP', and 'N' are used for further adjunction with relevant trees. Consider an example - "लड़के ने पेन किताब पर रखा"[The boy kept the pen on book]. Using this tree, the incorrect noun-to-noun adjunction is prevented where two nouns are not dependent. Notice that 'पेन' and 'किताब'are two different consecutive nouns so instead of multiple adjunction nouns on noun, this tree helps in correct attachment on 'VP' node of sentential initial tree of verb.

Postposition: As name implies, postpositions in Indian languages are modifiers that follow the nouns. The suitable postposition phase for example is 'NP1 PP' like "चौकोर-टेबल पर"[on square table] which is a noun phrase and postposition followed.

- **T5(nPx)** is an auxiliary tree with 'NP' as a root node and it gets adjunct at 'NP' node of noun tree. The node 'P' is postposition node to carry lexical information.

Adjective: Adjectives are mostly preceded the heading noun. An example of this tree is - "लाल किताब"[Red book]. The recursive 'Adj' to 'Adj' attachment is handled in pre-processing like morphological analyser and POS chunking.

- **T6(An)** is auxiliary tree with anchor node 'Adj' for the lexical information. It has root node 'N', with a left adjunctable to 'N' node for noun tree.

Adverb: The adverbs modify verbs, adjectives, or other adverbs. The placement of adverb varies widely in a language. It is relocated in pre-processing for easy parsing.

- **T7(ARBv)** is auxiliary tree with anchor node 'Adv' for the lexical information. To simplify the broader coverage of adverbs, these are collected, chunked, and placed before the verb. Therefore, only one tree is considered to be in final for adverb.

Table 1. Final 10 TAG Tree set for TAG Grammar

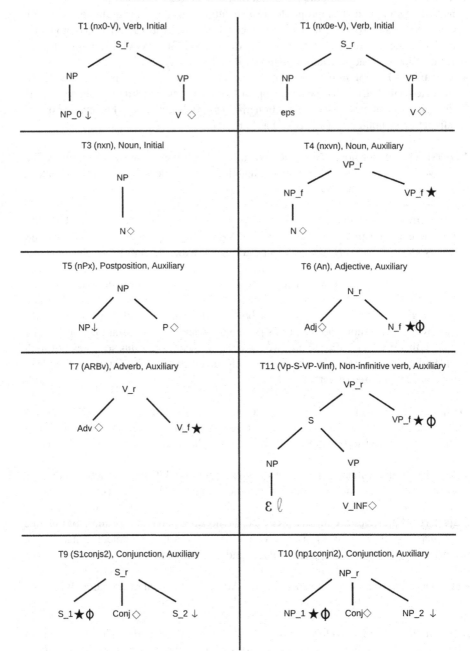

Non-finite Verb: A verb form that cannot serve as the root of an independent clause is called nonfinite verb form. It has no subject, tense or number. It functions as a noun or an adjective or an adverb or infinitives, participles or gerunds.

- **T8(Vp-S-VP-Vinf)** is an auxiliary tree with anchor node of nonfinite verb based on their syntactic construction. The intermediate nodes are used for further operation of adjunctions and substitution.

Conjunction: The common Indian Language conjunctions join nouns, adjective, adverbs, verbs, sub-clauses and sentences. Both the conjunction trees are auxiliary trees with anchor node 'conj' having lexical token.

- **T9(S1conjs2)** has root node 'S' as it is sentential conjunction to adjunct two sentence initial trees at 'S' node for compound sentence.
- **T10(np1conjnp2)** is a noun conjunction tree to join two nouns with a conjunction.

5 Parsing Example for Short Linguistic Notation

The basic constructions of SOV ordered languages are in a pattern: $((N + (P*))?)*V$. This implies that zero or multiple occurrences of Noun-Preposition phrases are possible before Verb. The Postposition (modifier) is also optional in NP Phrase. The possibility of multiple NP heads before the final verb aids further ambiguity in SOV construction. Some of the sample equivalent language phrases are shown here for input string: 'जंगल में काला हाथी है'(There is a black elephant in the Jungle).

Sanskrit: तत्र वने कृष्णा गज: अस्ति	Gujrathi: જંગલમાં કાળો હાથી છે
Aasammes: হাবতি এটা ক' লা হাতী আছে	Urdu: جنگل میں ایک کالا ہاتھی ہے
Manipuri: ঢ়াল্বহ্ন ঔহ্ধ্বু অহ্হৄঠ ঢ়হ্হ টঁ	Marathi: जंगलात एक काळा हत्ती आहे
Mizo: Ramhnuai a sai dum awm	Odia: ଜଙ୍ଗଲରେ ଏକ କଳା ହାତୀ ଅଛି
Maithili: जंगल मे एकटा कारी हाथी अछि	Punjabi: ਜੰਗਲ ਵਿਚ ਇਕ ਕਾਲਾ ਹਾਥੀ ਹੈ
Sindhi: ٻيلي ۾ هڪ ڪارو هاٿي آهي	Kannada: ಕಾಡಿನಲ್ಲಿ ಕಪ್ಪು ಆನೆ ಇದೆ
Bangla: বনের মধ্যে একটি কালো হাতি রয়েছে	Telugu: అడవిలో ఒక నల్ల ఏనుగు ఉంది

In case of agglutination as composition of a sequence of morphemes, a pre-processing stage is applied, that takes care of sandhi split as stemmer using Morphological Analyzer. Basically, the input of the Parser would be a POS tagger which would take care of initial steps and provide a grammatical category of each token in the language. The tree annotations are constant with the XTAG [22, 23] conventions except that our TAG grammar has trees with single anchor mapped with string as headp T. The node substp T and footp T demotes the substitution and foot node. The node labels are presented by node name and the subscript denotes the actual node subscript string. A tree-map Tm(G) is shown in Table 2 for input string - 'जंगल में काला हाथी है'. The isomorphism between elementary tree schema to show the equivalence of trees in LISP, XML and graphical form is presented in Fig. 5.

Table 2. Tree-map $T_m(G)$ output

Token	Category	POS	Tree 1	Tree 2	Tree 3
जंगल / Jungle	NOUN	NN	nxvx	nxn	-
में / in	Postposition	PSP	nPx	-	-
काला / black	Adjective	JJ	An	-	-
हाथी / elephant	NOUN	NN	nxvx	nxn	-
है / is	VERB	VM	nx0-v	-	-

Our parsing process is done on the pre-processed input string w = (a1, a2,.....,an). A tree-map Tm(G) is formed of all the relevant trees from TAG Grammar T(G) based on grammatical category of tokens ai and syntactic nature of neighboring tokens in w. A single token may carry multiple trees based on its grammatical context. Whereas, a parser instance needs a single tree per input token at a time.

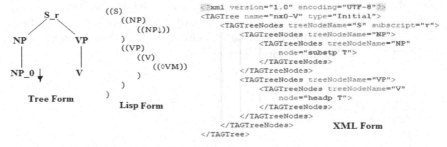

Fig. 5. Isomorphism between elementary tree schemas

We use (most) straightforward brute-force approach to enumerate all possible solutions. It prepares the collection of Tree sets $T_s(G)$ as each elementary tree with each possible pos-tag token. For the $T_m(G)$ in Table 1, total four combinations of $T_s(G)$ are prepared as shown in Table 3. These combinations are processed one-by-one in a loop. In our approach, the parser proceeds greedily trying to compute a single successful sequence of actions. Verb category trees are sentence initial trees that initiate the parsing process. Parsing starts with a dot traversal in the main sentence initial tree (T1 from Table 1 in our case). It keeps executing the operations by maintaining a chart of all possible matches, both partial and complete. These are organized into the States as mentioned in design of the parser. Initially, current node is S_0, parent-tree is null and content is 0. Table 4 shows some of the steps of a complete successful parse from Tree set 2. For the sake of brevity, we are providing only few initial and some last execution steps instead of all steps. The example shows both left and right adjunctions by corresponding auxiliary trees. On complete traversing of the tree T1, we check for its success by verifying conditions.

Table 3. Examples of four Tree-sets

Tree set	1/NN/ जंगल	2/PSP/ में	3/JJ/ काला	4/NN/ हाथी	5/VM/ है
Tree set 1	nxn	nPx	An	nxn	nx0-v
Tree set 2	nxn	nPx	An	nxvx	nx0-v
Successful PARSER OUTPUT and loop break					
Tree set 3	nxvx	nPx	An	nxn	nx0-v
Tree set 4	nxvx	nPx	An	nxvx	nx0-v

The parse is successful as the content $= 0$, Ts(G) is empty and the lexical token's sequence is same as the input string 'जंगल में काला हाथी है'in final production i.e. Eq. (5).

$$((S)((NP.r)((NP)((N)(1/जंगल)))((P)(2/में)))((VP.r)((NP)(((N.r)((Adj)(3/काला))((N)(4/ हाथी)))))((VP.f)((V)(5/ है))))))$$

(5)

Table 4 presents the State Set in TAG Parsing. Here, the Blue color indicates the operation performed in that step. Figure 6 presents a graphical representation of the trees in Tree set 2 that are responsible for a successful parse of input string w. On a successful parse, a derived tree Fig. 7(a) and a derivation tree Fig. 7(b) is constructed from state set S. It represents the syntactic and semantic relations between the sentence constituents.

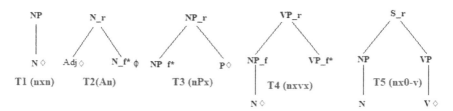

Fig. 6. Trees in Trees set 2 for successful parse

Table 4. State Set in TAG Parsing

S.	Sentence Initial Tree I_s	State S	Operation
1	•((S)((NP↓))((VP)((V)(5^VM◊))))	(T5, S_0, null, 0)	Predict Adjunction: at "S" Node
2	((S)•((NP↓))((VP)((V)(5^VM◊))))	(T5, S_0, null, +1)	Predict Substitution: at "NP" Node of T5
3	((S)•((NP)((N)(1^NN◊)))((VP)((V)(5^VM◊))))	(T1, NP, T5, +1)	Predict Adjunction: at "NP" Node of T1
4	((S)•((NP.r)((NP)((N)(1^NN◊)))((P)(2^PSP◊)))((VP)((V)(5^VM◊))))	(T2, NP, T1, +1)	Move Next:
5	((S)((NP.r)•((NP)((N)(1^NN◊)))((P)(2^PSP◊)))((VP)((V)(5^VM◊))))	(T2, NP, T1, +2)	Predict Adjunction: at "NP" node from T2 Move Next:
6	((S)((NP.r)((NP)•((N)(1^NN◊)))((P)(2^PSP◊)))((VP)((V)(5^VM◊))))	(T2, N, T1, +3)	Predict Adjunction: at "N" node from T2
7	((S)((NP.r)((NP)((N)•(1^NN◊)))((P)(2^PSP◊)))((VP)((V)(5^VM◊))))	(T2, ◊, T1, +4)	Move Next:
8	((S)((NP.r)((NP)((N)(1^NN◊)•))((P)(2^PSP◊)))((VP)((V)(5^VM◊))))	(T2, ◊, T1, +4)	Move Next:
9	((S)((NP.r)((NP)((N)(1^NN◊))•)((P)(2^PSP◊)))((VP)((V)(5^VM◊))))	(T2, N, T1, +3)	Completion: "N" from (6)
…	……..	……..	……..
..	……..	……..	……..
34	((S)((NP.r)((NP)((N)(1^NN◊)))((P)(2^PSP◊)))((VP.r)((NP)(((N.r)((Adj)(3^JJ◊))((N)(4^NN◊)))))((VP.f)((V)(5^VM◊)))•))	(T3, V, T5, +2)	Completion: "V"
35	((S)((NP.r)((NP)((N)(1^NN◊)))((P)(2^PSP◊)))((VP.r)((NP)(((N.r)((Adj)(3^JJ◊))((N)(4^NN◊)))))((VP.f)((V)(5^VM◊)))•)	(T3, V, T5, +1)	Completion: "VP"
36	((S)((NP.r)((NP)((N)(1^NN◊)))((P)(2^PSP◊)))((VP.r)((NP)(((N.r)((Adj)(3^JJ◊))((N)(4^NN◊)))))((VP.f)((V)(5^VM◊))))•	(T3, V, T5, 0)	Completion: "S"

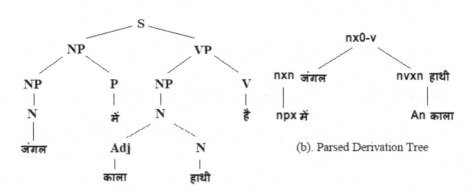

(a). Parsed Derived Tree

(b). Parsed Derivation Tree

Fig. 7. (a). Derived tree and (b). Derivation tree

6 Performance Analysis

We did not find any baseline algorithm for TAG grammar and parsing algorithm pertaining to Hindi language. Therefore, we are not able to provide a comparative study of performance of the proposed algorithm. However, we are presenting the time taken for the proposed process. The linguistic and semantic complexity for a language parsing cannot be measured by the length of the input string and the number of operations performed for parsing. We have prepared a test-bed of 27 sentences with increasing number of tokens along with increasing numbers of TAG operations. The test-bed consists of simple and compound grammatical constructions having repetitive noun-postposition phrases.

The performance in terms of execution time and memory usage is presented in Fig. 8 and Fig. 9 respectively. It is observed that the increased no. of tokens along with no. of substitution/adjunction operations demands the resources exponentially. The modified algorithm with reduced tuples in State increases the memory consumption drastically. At the same time, the operations performed in data structures like XML ad LISP make the execution faster. Table 5 shows the time and memory consumption during the execution of test sentences. The time and memory consumption increase with increase in the complexity of sentences. The maximum time taken is 209.60 ms by XML Parser, whereas the LISP Parser takes 197.37 ms for the longest sentence of length 32 tokens. In this case, total 29 operations are performed with 4 substitutions and 25 adjunctions. For the same sentence, the maximum memory is 582.60 MB for XML Parser and 2329.20 MB for LISP Parser. The system configuration used for testing the algorithm is Intel(R) Core(TM) i7-3770, CPU @ 3.40 GHz, 4 GB RAM on Windows 7 Professional (64 bit) OS, Net Beans IDE 8.0.2 for Java:1.8.0.77 (64-Bit).

Table 5. Test sentences, execution time (ms) and memory consumption (mb)

S. No	Test Sentences	No. of Tokens	No. of operations		Memory (MB)		Time (MS)	
			Subst	Adjnct	XML	LISP	XML	LISP
1	Sen 1	4	2	1	0.10	2.60	1.80	0.10
2	Sen 2	5	2	2	0.10	3.40	2.60	0.10
3	Sen 3	6	2	2	0.10	7.20	2.60	0.10
4	Sen 4	7	2	3	0.10	8.20	2.40	0.10
5	Sen 5	7	2	4	0.10	18.00	5.80	5.13
6	Sen 6	8	2	5	0.10	17.60	6.20	5.12
7	Sen 7	9	3	5	0.10	19.60	7.00	5.12
8	Sen 8	10	3	6	5.00	19.20	7.20	5.12

(continued)

Table 5. (*continued*)

S. No	Test Sentences	No. of Tokens	No. of operations		Memory (MB)		Time (MS)	
			Subst	Adjnct	XML	LISP	XML	LISP
9	Sen 9	11	3	7	5.00	22.40	7.20	5.12
10	Sen 10	12	3	8	5.00	34.40	9.00	5.12
11	Sen 11	13	3	9	5.00	31.40	10.80	5.12
12	Sen 12	15	3	11	5.00	60.80	21.20	5.12
13	Sen 13	16	3	12	5.00	74.60	20.20	5.14
14	Sen 14	17	3	13	5.00	115.80	35.80	15.44
15	Sen 15	18	3	14	5.00	116.20	39.00	15.36
16	Sen 16	19	3	15	10.00	119.60	40.00	15.46
17	Sen 17	20	3	16	35.00	317.00	93.40	56.43
18	Sen 18	21	3	17	35.00	308.40	105.40	56.43
19	Sen 19	22	3	18	40.00	316.00	111.80	61.62
20	Sen 20	24	4	18	40.00	328.00	107.40	58.51
21	Sen 21	25	4	19	40.00	330.60	110.00	61.70
22	Sen 22	26	4	20	40.00	320.80	111.20	61.54
23	Sen 23	28	4	21	117.00	729.00	260.60	174.55
24	Sen 24	28	4	22	126.80	730.40	268.40	174.55
25	Sen 25	29	4	23	128.00	708.80	279.20	179.67
26	Sen 26	31	4	24	188.40	2217.20	554.60	198.09
27	Sen 27	32	4	25	209.60	2329.20	582.60	197.37

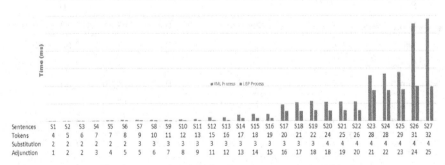

Fig. 8. Execution time for the test sentences in Table 4

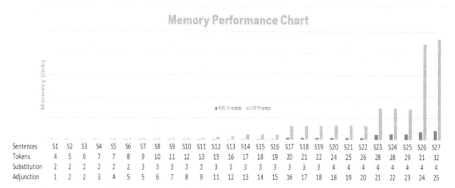

Fig. 9. Memory consumption for the test sentences in Table 4.

7 Conclusion

We have proposed a modified Earley's algorithm for a TAG Parser in this paper. We needed a simpler and faster implementation of a TAG Parser for short linguistic constructions; therefore we proposed modification in the tree traversal from 4 dots to 2 dots. This also takes into account references to the CFG and TIG Approach. It simplifies the parsing process using lexicalized LTAG grammar based for shorter linguistic structures. Our proposed parsing tool can be used for handling such constructions in many Indian languages. We discussed the modifications in the Earley's algorithm at the processing steps and reduced state tuple for small memory consumption. Combinatory tree sets with customized TAG Grammar are used for executing Parser.

We demonstrated the design, process flow and an example of Hindi text using a step-by-step parsing process. We used two data structures for TAG trees in the LISP and XML form. The results of implementation are presented. The proposed implementation is efficient in terms of time and space consumption. The proposed system can be extended for handling complex sentences and more complex grammar.

References

1. Becker, T., Joshi, A. K. and Rambow, O.: Longdistance scrambling and tree ad-joining grammars. In: Proceedings of the Fifth Conference of the European Association for Computational Linguistics. Berlin (1991)
2. Begum, R., Husain, S., Dhwaj, A., Sharma, D., Bai, L., Sangal, R.: Dependency annotation scheme for indian languages. In: Proceedings of The Third International Joint Conference on Natural Language Processing (IJCNLP), India (2008)
3. Bharati, A., Sangal R.: Parsing free word order languages in the paninian framework. In: Proceedings of ACL, vol. 93 (1993)
4. Earley, J.: An Efficient Context-Free Parsing Algorithm, PhD Thesis, Carnegie-Mellon University (1968)
5. Earley, J.: An efficient context-free parsing algorithm. Commun. ACM **13**(2), 94–102 (1970)
6. Eisner, J., Satta, G.: A faster parsing algorithm for lexicalized tree adjoining grammars, In: Proceedings of the Fifth International Workshop on Tree Adjoining Grammar and Related Frameworks, (TAG5), Université Paris 7 (2000)

7. Husain, S.: A Generalized Parsing Framework Based on Computational Paninian Grammar. Ph. D. Thesis, IIIT Hyderabad, India (2011)

8. Jain, P., Bhavsar, R., Kumar, A., Pawar, B.V., Darbari, H., Bhavsar, V.C.: Tree Adjoining Grammar based Parser for a Hindi text-to-scene conversion system in 4th International Conference (I2CT). IEEE Xplore (2018)

9. Jain, P., Darbari, H., Bhavsar, V.C.: Vishit: A Visualizer for Hindi Text. In: Fourth International Conference (CSNT), IEEE Xplore, pp. 886–890 (2014)

10. Joshi, A.K.: An introduction to tree adjoining grammars. In: Manaster-Ramer, A. (ed.) Mathematics of Language. John Benjamins, Amsterdam (1987)

11. Joshi, A.K., Schabes, Y.: Tree-adjoining grammars and lexicalized grammars. In: Nivat, M., Podelski, A. (eds.) Tree Automata and Languages. Elsevier (1992)

12. Joshi, A.K., Schabes, Y.: (1997): Tree-adjoining grammars. In: Rozenberg, G., Salomaa, A. (eds.) Handbook of Formal Languages, vol. 3, p. 69123. Springer, Berlin. https://doi.org/10.1007/978-3-642-59126-6_2

13. Joshi, A.K., Levy, L.S., Takahashi, M.: Tree adjunct grammars. J. Comput. Syst. Sci. **10**(1) (1975)

14. Vijay-Shanker, K., Joshi, A.K.: Feature structure based TAG. In: Proceedings of the 12th International Conference on Computational Linguistic, pp. 714–719 (1988)

15. Khandelwal, D.: Tree adjoining grammar. In: Automating Data-Driven Modelling of Dynamical Systems. Springer Theses. Springer, Cham (2022). https://doi.org/10.1007/978-3-030-903 43-5_4

16. Khandelwal, D., Schoukens, M., Tóth, R.: A Tree Adjoining Grammar Representation for Models of Stochastic Dynamical Systems. Automatica, vol. 119, 109099 (2020). ISSN 0005-1098. https://doi.org/10.1016/j.automatica.2020.109099

17. Knuth, D.E.: A Characterization of parenthesis languages. Inform. Control **11**, 269–289 (1967)

18. Ma, M.: Automatic conversion of natural language to 3D animation. Ph.D. thesis, University of Ulster, Derry, Ireland, pp. 1–250 (2006)

19. Mannem, P., Abhilash, A., Bharati, A.: LTAGspinal treebank and parser for hindi. In: ICON-2009: International Conference on Natural Language Processing (2009)

20. Rambow, O., Joshi, A.K.: A processing model for free word order languages. In: Clifton, C., Frazier, L., Rayner, K. (eds.) Perspectives on Sentence Processing, p. 267301. Lawrence Erlbaum Associates, Hillsdale, NJ (1994)

21. Schabes, Y., Joshi, A.K.: An Earley-type parsing algorithm for tree adjoining grammars. In: Proceedings of the 26th Association for Computational Linguistics, pp. 258–269 (1988)

22. XTAG Group: A lexicalized tree adjoining grammar for English. In: Technical Report, IRCS-01-03, University of Pennsylvania (2001)

23. Yumnam, N., Sharma, U.: An initial study of tree-adjoining grammar formalism for parsing manipuri language. Int. J. Comput. Appl. Technol. Res. **10**, 142–148 (2021). https://doi.org/10.7753/IJCATR1006.1003

TamilEmo: Fine-grained Emotion Detection Dataset for Tamil

Charangan Vasantharajan[1], Ruba Priyadharshini[2],
Prasanna Kumar Kumaresan[3], Rahul Ponnusamy[3],
Sathiyaraj Thangasamy[4], Sean Benhur[5], Thenmozhi Durairaj[6(✉)],
Kanchana Sivanraju[5], Anbukkarasi Sampath[7],
and Bharathi Raja Chakravarthi[8]

[1] University of Moratuwa, Moratuwa, Sri Lanka
charangan.18@cse.mrt.ac.lk
[2] ULTRA Arts and Science College, Madurai, India
[3] Indian Institute of Information Technology and Management-Kerala,
Kazhakkoottam, India
{prasanna.mi20,rahul.mi20}@iiitmk.ac.in
[4] Sri Krishna Adithya College of Arts and Science Coimbatore, Kovaipudur, India
sathiyarajt@skacas.ac.in
[5] PSG College of Arts and Science, Peelamedu, India
kanchana@psgcas.ac.in
[6] Sri Sivasubramaniya Nadar College of Engineering Chennai, Kalavakkam, India
theni_d@ssn.edu.in
[7] Kongu Engineering College Erode, Perundurai, India
[8] University of Galway, Galway, Ireland
bharathiraja.asokachakravarthi@universityofgalway.ie

Abstract. Emotional Analysis from textual input has been considered both a challenging and interesting task in Natural Language Processing. However, due to the lack of datasets in low-resource languages (e.g. Tamil), it is difficult to conduct research of high standards in this area. Therefore we introduce a large manually annotated dataset of more than 42k Tamil YouTube comments, labeled for 31 emotions for emotion recognition. The goal of this dataset is to improve emotion detection in multiple downstream tasks in Tamil. We have also created three different groupings of our emotions namely 3-class, 7-class, and 31-class, and evaluated the models' performance in each category of the grouping. We ran several baselines of different models and our MuRIL model has achieved the highest macro F1 score of 0.67 across our 3-class group dataset. In 7-class and 31-class groups, the MuRIL and Random Forest models performed well with a macro F1 score of 0.52 and 0.29 respectively.

Keywords: Emotion Detection · Fine-grained Dataset · Low Resource · Tamil

Anand Kumar M et al. (Eds.): SPELLL 2022, CCIS 1802, pp. 35–50, 2023.
https://doi.org/10.1007/978-3-031-33231-9_3

1   Introduction

The emotional analysis is the classification task of mining emotions in texts, which finds use in various natural language applications such as reviews analysis in e-commerce, public opinion analysis, extensive search, personalized recommendation, healthcare, and online teaching [13]. Emotions are the psychological states that are often expressed through behavior or language. Emotional analysis helps to analyze the text and extract the emotions which are expressed in the text. This is why emotional analysis plays a significant role in Natural Language Processing (NLP) and its applications.

In this paper, we describe the creation of a monolingual corpus for Tamil (a Dravidian language). Tamil is the official language in Sri Lanka and Singapore. Moreover, Tamil is widely spoken by millions of people around the world. But the tools and resources available for developing robust NLP applications are under-developed for Tamil [20]. In Tamil, the most complex words are formed by stringing together morphemes without changing them in spelling or phonetics [15]. Also, the writing system is a phonemic abugida written from left to right, and at one point in history, it used Tamili, Vattezhuthu, Chola, Pallava, and Chola-Pallava scripts. Today's modern Tamil script was retrieved from the Chola-Pallava script that was conceived around the 4th century CE [16].

With regards to Dravidian languages, many recent works have aimed to create more resources in Tamil, Kannada, and Malayalam [1] which focuses on Offensive Language Detection, Hate Speech Detection, and Sentiment Analysis. In this work, we created a dataset for fine-grained emotion detection.

The contributions of this paper are:

1. We present a dataset in Tamil for the emotional analysis fine-grained task.
2. This monolingual dataset contains 31 types of fine-grained emotions as labels with 42,686 comments.
3. This dataset was evaluated on traditional machine learning models and benchmark results of the pre-trained transformer models are also provided.

2   Related Work

2.1   Datasets for Emotion Detection

In the past decade, several researchers have released emotion recognition datasets in several languages for a variety of domains, but they contained only a very small number of emotions, about 4 to 7, and also contained a smaller number of samples. Recently [14] released an Empathetic dialogues dataset which consisted of text conversations labeled with 32 emotions and [4] released GoEmotions which consists of Reddit comments labeled with 27 emotion categories for around 52k samples. To the best of our knowledge, there are no previous emotion recognition and fine-grained classification datasets available for Tamil. This is the first work to create a large dataset of fine-grained emotions in the Tamil language.

Fig. 1. Overview of the data collection process.

2.2 Emotion Classification

Emotion classification is a type of text classification task that is used to detect emotions. Both traditional machine learning and deep learning models can be employed to classify emotions. Machine Learning methods such as SVM, random forest, and logistic regression are often employed for these types of tasks. In addition to this lexicons such as Valence Arousal Dominance Lexicon [11] can be also used as a feature extraction with these models. Deep Learning Models such as RNN, LSTMs, and Transformer models can also be employed for this task. Transfer learning methods such as BERT [5], and Roberta [10] have achieved a state of the art results in major NLP tasks. [3] fine-tuned different pre-trained models such as BERT, DistilBert, Roberta, XLNet, and Electra and Roberta provided better results. [7,18] used a method to incorporate knowledge from emotion lexicons into an attention mechanism to improve emotion classification. In our work, we have used traditional machine learning models and multilingual transformer models (since it is also pre-trained on Tamil corpus [5]) to provide a strong baseline for this dataset.

3 Tamil Emotion Dataset

3.1 Scraping Raw Data

Data in social media platforms such as Twitter, Facebook, and YouTube, changes rapidly and can alter the perception or reputation of an individual or community drastically [19]. This highlights the importance of automation in emotional analysis. YouTube is a popular social media platform in the Indian subcontinent due to its wide range of content available, such as movies, trailers, songs, tutorials, product reviews, etc. YouTube allows users to create content as well as allows other users to engage and interact with this content through actions such as liking or commenting. Because of this, there is more user-generated content in under-resourced languages.

Hence, we chose YouTube to extract comments to create our dataset. We collected data from movie trailers and teasers to create our dataset because movies are quite popular among the Tamil-speaking populace in most countries. This significantly increases the chance of getting various views on one topic from different people. Figure 1 shows the steps that we followed to create our dataset.

We used a YouTube Comment Scraper tool[1] for crawling comments from the YouTube videos and processing the collected comments to make the datasets for

---

[1] https://youtubecommentsdownloader.com/.

emotional analysis with manual annotations. We intended to collect comments that contain purely monolingual texts in the native Tamil script, with enough representation for each emotion class, so we also removed the codemixed Tamil text. As a part of the preprocessing steps to clean the data, we utilized langdetect library[2] to capture different languages and to eliminate the unintended languages and codemixed scripts. Also, to maintain data privacy, we made sure that all the user-related information was removed from the corpora by dropping the features associated with it. As a part of the text-preprocessing, we removed redundant information such as URL and comments that are nearly the same as other comments according to the Levenshtein Distance using a python library[3]. Moreover, we retained all the emojis, emoticons, punctuation, etc that are presented in the text to faithfully preserve real-world usage.

Methodology of Annotation. We contacted the Indian Institute of Information Technology and Management to find volunteers for the annotation process. We created Google Forms that contain 25 comments on one page to collect annotations from annotators and send them through email. The student volunteer annotators received the link to Google Forms and did the annotations on their personal computers or mobile phones. During the annotation process, we checked the medium of schooling and the native language of the annotator to check whether the person has sufficient knowledge to annotate. The annotators were asked to identify emotions expressed by the writer of the text from the predefined emotions (see Appendix A) provided to them. The annotators were cautioned that the user suggestions may have aggressive language. They were given a provision to discontinue the annotation process in case the content is too upsetting to deal with.

They were requested not to be partial to a specific individual, circumstance, or occasion during the annotation process. The annotators were also instructed to agree on the annotation guidelines before they were allowed to proceed further. We finished the annotation process in three stages.

To ensure the high quality of the dataset, we set up a "dry run" phase, where two annotators annotated each comment, for which the inter-annotator agreement value is provided in Sect. 3.3. After the dry run phase, each comment was annotated by a single annotator to check for an annotation if both annotators' choices are different for a comment.

3.2   Annotator Statistics

Since we called the volunteers from various Universities and Colleges, the types of annotators in the task are different. From Table 1, we can see that 9 male and 7 female annotators volunteered to contribute to the task. The distribution of male annotators is slightly higher than female annotators in the task. The majority of the annotators have received undergraduate levels of education.

---

[2] https://pypi.org/project/langdetect/.

[3] https://pypi.org/project/pylev/.

Table 1. Annotators Statistics for emotional analysis task.

Language		Tamil
Gender	Male	09
	Female	07
	Transgender	00
Higher Education	Undergraduate	12
	Postgraduate	04
Medium of Schooling	English	09
	Native language	07

We were also unable to find volunteers from the transgender community to annotate our dataset. From Table 1, we can observe that the majority of the annotators' medium of schooling is English even though their mother tongue is Tamil.
Since most of the participants' medium of education was the English language,
we were careful that it would not affect the annotation process by ensuring that
all of them are fully proficient in using the Tamil language.

Once the forms were created, a sample form (first assignment) was annotated
by experts, and a gold standard was created. Then, we manually compared the
volunteer's submission form with gold standard annotations. Then, we eliminated the annotators for the following reasons during the first assignment to
control the quality of annotation. They are:

– Annotators delayed unreasonably by not responding.
– labeled all sentences with the same label.
– More than 10 annotations in a form were wrong, which was compared with
  gold standard annotations.

After the elimination of 5 volunteers due to the lack of Tamil proficiency, a
total of 16 volunteers were involved in the annotation task. Once they completed
the given Google Forms, 10 Google Forms (250 comments) were sent to them. If
an annotator offered to volunteer more, the next set of Google Forms was sent
to them with another set of 250 comments and in this way, each volunteer chose
to annotate as many comments from the corpus as they wished.

3.3   Inter-Annotator Agreement

The inter-annotator agreement is the measure of how well two or more annotators
can make the same annotation decision for a certain category. This is important
to verify that the annotation process is consistent and that different annotators
can label the same emotion label to a given comment. Generally, two questions
arise about the inter-annotator agreement. They are:

- How do the raters agree or disagree in their annotation?
- How much of the observed agreement or disagreement among the annotators might be due to chance?

To answer these questions and to ensure the annotation reliability, we used both Krippendorff's alpha(α) [9] and Cohen's Kappa as a inter-annotator agreement measure.We used **agreement** module from nltk[4] for calculating α. The result of an inter-annotator agreement between our annotators in the dry run phase is 0.7452 Krippendorff's alpha(α) and 0.72 Cohen's Kappa.

3.4 Selecting and Curating YouTube Comments

We choose YouTube videos with at least 500 comments and remove non-English comments. Generally, YouTube comments contain biased data about a particular video. So to reduce biased training data, we process the dataset through a series of data-curating methods as below. Therefore, we can develop fully representative emotion models using our dataset and can ensure our data does not comment that is emotion-specific or language biases.

Manual Review. We read the comments manually to detect and remove harmful comments towards a particular religion, ethnicity, gender, sexual orientation, or disability, to create the best dataset for our judgment.

Length Filtering. The comments that contain less than three tokens and more than 512 tokens were eliminated using NLTK's word tokenizer library[5].

Code-Mixed Filtering. A code-mixed comment is a comment with a mixing of two or more languages. The comments that contain non-Tamil words were eliminated using NLTK's words dictionary.

Levenshtein Distance. Levenshtein distance is a measure to calculate the distance between two strings as the minimum number of characters needed to insert, delete or replace in a given string to transform it into another string. Using **pylev**[6], we remove the comments which has more than 80% similarity among the dataset.

4 Data Analysis

Table 2 contains the summary statistics of this dataset. Figure 2 shows the distribution of emotion labels, we can notice that emotion Admiration holds up the highest number of examples and desire is the lowest count.

---

[4] https://www.nltk.org/.
[5] https://nltk.org/api/nltk.tokenize.html.
[6] https://pypi.org/project/pylev/.

Table 2. Dataset Statistics.

Description	Count
No of examples	42686
No of emotions	31
Max.no of tokens in text	2988
Min.no of tokens in text	2
Max.no of data in class	6682-admiration
Min.no of data in class	208-desire

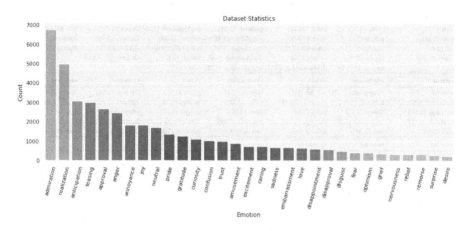

Fig. 2. Dataset Statistics

4.1 Keywords

We extract the top words associated with the emotion category by calculating the log odds ratio, informative Dirichlet prior [12] for each token. The log odds ratio quantifies the association between a word in one emotion category to another emotion category by building on word frequency counts and an estimate of prior word probability, this helps us to extract the important keywords of each emotion. The log odds are z-scored, all values greater than 1 indicate an association with the corresponding emotion. We list the top 5 tokens of each emotion in Table 3. We can note that the keywords are highly correlated with the emotion (e.g. amusement with tokens such as ஹேத்துனா, மாங்கல்யம், pride with "நிமிர்ந்த."

Table 3. Top 5 words associated with each emotion. The log odds ratios are shown in parentheses.

admiration	amusement	anger	annoyance	anticipation	approval	caring
வாழ்த்துக்கள் (30.37)	ஹேத்துனா (3.63)	நாயே (5.04)	ஏண்டா (2.58)	வேண்டும் (8.96)	அல்ல (2.86)	கவலை (1.6)
சார்பாக (22.16)	தந்துனானே (3.59)	டெய் (4.54)	வன்னிய (2.53)	போடுங்க (6.11)	இல்லை (2.58)	பனை (1.38)
பெற்றி (21.05)	மாங்கல்யம் (3.53)	நாய்களை (4.01)	போங்குடா (2.5)	ஆதரவு (5.4)	அண்ணா (2.44)	முடிந்த (1.29)
பெற (19.23)	ஜீவன (3.09)	நாய்கள் (4)	ஏன்டா (2.45)	தூருங்கள் (4.35)	தான் (2.34)	கவளமாக (1.23)
வாழ்க (16.08)	போட்றா (2.78)	திருட்டு (3.76)	அவன் (2.35)	விடியோ (4.1)	என்பது (2.11)	வேண்டாம் (1.2)

confusion	curiosity	desire	disappointment	disapproval	disgust	embarrassment
நல்லைமாக (2.22)	ஆர்வமாக (2.44)	ஆவலாய் (1.59)	விடியல் (2.41)	மெய்த்து (2.23)	அநாகரீகம் (1.73)	சாம் (1.3)
சந்தேகம் (1.9)	சொல்லுங்க (2.37)	மனஸ்ராக (1.36)	ரூபாய் (1.94)	ஆரியர்களான (2.05)	உடலுறவு (1.56)	வேதனை (1.1)
ஆகளம் (1.9)	பாகம் (2.22)	பருத்ததிவளார் (1.19)	கிளோ (1.86)	கூறுகிறான் (1.89)	டித்து (1.56)	
தெறி (1.84)	எய்ப (2.17)	ஆசை (1.18)	பள்ளர்கள் (1.75)	பிராமணர்கள் (1.81)	பபலே (1.43)	
கல்வெட்டு (1.77)	அடுத்த (2.13)	தடைவைக்கு (1.07)	தேர்தலுக்கு (1.54)	இல்லை (1.65)	போடா (1.4)	

excitement	fear	gratitude	grief	joy	love	nervousness
சூப்பர் (2.65)	பயமா (3.47)	நன்றி (21.42)	ஓடினேன் (1.94)	வாழ்த்துக்கள் (7.55)	அக்கா (3.7)	டாப்ளிட்டர் (2.34)
அட்ரா (2.58)	தமிழ்நாடு (2.85)	மிக்க (8.42)	நம்முதிரிகளும் (1.94)	சார்பாக (5.96)	பிடிக்கும் (2.74)	அவர்கள் (1.74)
மாஸ் (2.09)	தொண்டை (2.11)	நன்றிகள் (7.01)	நாயர்களும் (1.94)	மகிழ்ச்சி (5.93)	அம்மா (2.53)	ஆயம் (1.12)
சுபர்ஸ்ட் (1.89)	இருமல் (1.96)	சகோ (3.79)	பிடிப்புகளுக்கு (1.9)	வெற்றி (5.61)	செல்லக்குட்டி (2.19)	என் (2)
அடொடா (1.76)	வாத்திகள் (1.94)	தகவல்களுக்கு (3.3)	கையொளானகாது (1.57)	படம் (4.81)		

neutral	optimism	pride	realization	relief	remorse	sadness
மலைபாளி (3.58)	சம்மந்தியாக (1.94)	தமிழன் (6.1)	உண்மை (3.29)	ஐங்க (1.67)	அவளது (2.06)	ஆழிரத்தில் (3.81)
ஆலங்காலங்குருடி (3.12)	உள்நாட்டு (1.44)	பெருமை (5.94)	என்று (3.12)	ஓய்க்கு (1.59)	வாக்கை (1.96)	ஹஹார் (2.89)
ஆகாசத்து (3.12)	போனை (1.41)	தமிழ் (5.65)	தான் (3.09)	தமிழ்ா (1.59)	சரியானதுக (1.94)	ஒருவன் (2.26)
செயலளார் (2.85)	வெல்வோம் (1.36)	நிமிர்ந்து (4.81)	அவர்கள் (2.99)	அனுப்புவோம் (1.45)	வேலைவாய்ப்பு (1.44)	நட்டேன் (2.23)
தழுவி (2.68)	நாம் (1.34)	நில்லடா (4.6)	என்பது (2.85)	குரானை (1.35)	தேவைக்கு (1.44)	கண்ணீர் (1.59)

surprise	teasing	trust
தயாரிச்சது (1.59)	திருப்பி (3.86)	கிரு (3.17)
வாங்கினா (1.59)	மாமா (3.38)	கடவுள் (3.06)
ஆச்சரியமாக (1.45)	குருமா (3.33)	நம்புகிறேன் (2.01)
ஆச்சரியம் (1.38)	கொடுக்காத (3.25)	நல்லது (1.99)
செய்தியா (1.19)	விருதை (3.14)	இறைவனை (1.73)

5   Modeling

5.1   Data Preparation

After the annotation process, each comment was labeled by at least three annotators. So we filter out emotion labels selected by only a single annotator to reduce the noise in our data. After the cleaning process 97% of the data was retained as the original. Finally, we randomly split the dataset into the train (80%), dev (10%), and test (10%) sets. Once our model was finalized, dev and test sets were used to validate and evaluate our model respectively.

Grouping Emotions. We create three different groups of our taxonomy and evaluated the model's performance in each category of the grouping. A sentiment level(Group 01) divides the labels into 3 categories positive (நேர்மறை), negative (எதிர்மறை) and ambiguous (தெளிவற்ற). A further grouping inspired from [6] divides the labels into 7 categories. They are love-அன்பு (maps to caring, love, anticipation, excitement, joy, desire, and curiosity), Pathos-அழுகை (maps to disgust, embarrassment, sadness, grief, relief, and remorse), Disgrace-இளிவரல் (maps to annoyance, disappointment, anger, nervousness, fear, confusion, and disapproval), Laughter-நகை (maps to teasing, and amusement),

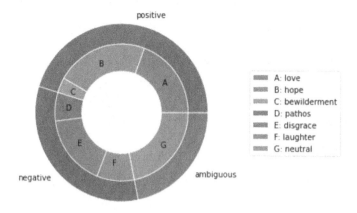

Fig. 3. 3-Class Group Mapping

neutral-நடுவுநிலை (maps to realization, approval, and neutral), hope-நம்பிக்கை (maps to trust, pride, admiration, and optimism), and Bewilderment-மருட்கை (maps to surprise and gratitude). Figure 3 and 4 show the mapping between the emotion classes.

5.2 Baseline Experiments

In this section, we will describe our methodology for building a baseline system for developing an Emotion detection system for the created dataset. We experiment with both traditional Machine Learning models and pre-trained multilingual models such as mBERT and MuRIL.

Machine Learning Models. We train traditional Machine learning models as a baseline for this dataset. We experimented with Logistic Regression, K-Nearest Neighbors classifier, Linear Support Vector Machines (SVM) [2], Decision Trees, and Random Forest. For all the models we encode the text into TF-IDF vectors of uni-grams and pass it to the respective models.

mBERT: This model was pre-trained using the same pretraining strategy that was employed to BERT [5], which is Masked Language Modelling (MLM) and Next Sentence Prediction (Next Sentence Prediction). It was pre-trained on the Wikipedia dump of 104 languages. For having a balanced set of all languages exponentially smoothed weighting of data was performed during data creation and vocabulary creation. This results in high-resource languages being undersampled while low-resourced languages are being over-sampled.

MuRIL: MuRIL [8] is a pre-trained model, trained in 16 different Indian Languages and English languages, it was trained on both the MLM and Translated

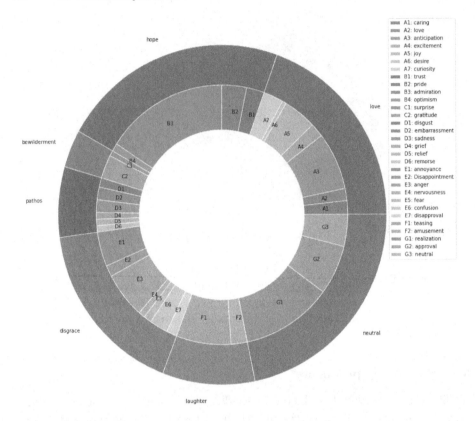

A1: caring
A2: love
A3: anticipation
A4: excitement
A5: joy
A6: desire
A7: curiosity
B1: trust
B2: pride
B3: admiration
B4: optimism
C1: surprise
C2: gratitude
D1: disgust
D2: embarrassment
D3: sadness
D4: grief
D5: relief
D6: remorse
E1: annoyance
E2: Disappointment
E3: anger
E4: nervousness
E5: fear
E6: confusion
E7: disapproval
F1: teasing
F2: amusement
G1: realization
G2: approval
G3: neutral

Fig. 4. 7-Class Group Mapping

Language Modelling (TLM) objectives. The model was trained with Common crawl OSCAR corpus and Wikipedia corpus.

5.3   Experiment Settings

We removed the unwanted noises in the text such as URLs, punctuation, digits, unwanted symbols, and emojis during the preprocessing step.

Machine Learning Models. We trained all the models with uni-grams extracted from the TF-IDF technique. All the parameters are summarized in Table 4. In Logistic Regression the *lbfgs* optimizer was used with the l2 regularizer, a maximum of 2000 iterations is taken for a solver to converge. For SVM we have used *rbf* kernel for a maximum of 2000 iterations with a tolerance of 1e-3. In the Random Forest model, we used 100 trees with *gini* criterion, which is used to measure the quality of the split in the tree. The additive feature of Naive Bayes is set to 1 and *classprior* and *fitprior* is set to None. For the Decision Tree, a *gini* criterion was used to split the tree with the best split based on node. The hyper-parameters used during the training are shown in Table 4.

Table 4. Hyperparameters for Machine Learning Models

Model	Parameters
Logistic Regression	optimizer='lbfgs', penalty='l2'
Support Vector Machine	max_iter=2000, kernel='rbf', tol=0.0001
Multinomial Naive Bayes	alpha=1.0, class_prior=None, fit_prior=None
Random Forest	criterion='gini', n_estimators=100
K Nearest Neighbors	n_neighbors=5, algorithm='brute'

Pre-Trained Models. We fine-tuned mBERT and MuRIL pre-trained models for 10 epochs with a batch size of 64 and a maximum sequence length of 128. A linear scheduler with 2e-5 as an initial learning rate is used along with *AdamW* optimizer and a Cross-Entropy loss function. We found that training for more epochs causes over-fitting of the model.

5.4 Results and Discussion

Overall, MuRIL achieved the best macro F1 score in 3-class and 7-class taxonomy while Random Forest holds the same place in 31-class taxonomy. Table 5 summarizes the results of all the models on the different groupings of the data while table 6, 7 and 8 summarize the results of the best performing models on 3-class, 7-class, and 31-class taxonomy respectively.

In 3-class taxonomy, all models performed well compared to the other taxonomy classes. Particularly, MuRIL achieved the highest macro F1 of 0.67 while the decision tree was the lowest with a macro F1 score of 0.41. Among all the models, transformer-based models are holding higher F1 scores than machine-learning models. In terms of individual F1 scores, the positive class reached the highest with a macro F1 score of 0.77 followed by the "negative" (0.69) and "ambiguous" (0.56) classes.

The transformer-based models performed well on 7-class taxonomy compared to the machine learning models with the higher F1 score difference. Here also, MuRIL beat the other models with a macro F1 score of 0.52 while mBERT holds the second highest with a macro F1 score of 0.51. Machine learning models performed poorly in this taxonomy, particularly the decision tree reached 0.23 F1 score which is the lowest. Among the 7 classes, MuRIL classified "Hope" well with a macro F1 score of 0.66 while showing poor performance in classifying "Pathos" (F1 score of 0.30).

In contrast to the 3-class and 7-class taxonomy, all models performed poorly on the 31-class taxonomy. The highest F1 score is 0.29 achieved by random forest (nearly equal to the lowest F1 score of 7-class taxonomy) followed by mBERT with a macro F1 score of 0.23. It is due to the lower number of class samples

Table 5. Macro Average Precision, Recall, and F1 Score on test set for all the Models. The highest scores in each taxonomy are in bold.

Model	3-class Group			7-classs Group			31-class Group		
	P	R	F1	P	R	F1	P	R	F1
Logistic Regression	0.54	0.53	0.52	0.35	0.36	0.32	0.17	0.18	0.16
Support Vector Machine	0.54	0.53	0.52	0.39	0.35	0.33	0.24	0.14	0.14
K-Nearest Neighbors	0.51	0.50	0.50	0.37	0.35	0.35	0.30	0.21	0.23
Multinomial Naive Bayes	0.54	0.49	0.48	0.49	0.28	0.28	0.11	0.07	0.05
Decision Tree	0.42	0.41	0.41	0.23	0.24	0.23	0.11	0.08	0.08
Random Forest	0.61	0.55	0.56	0.49	0.41	0.42	0.47	0.25	**0.29**
mBERT	0.67	0.65	0.66	0.54	0.50	0.51	0.30	0.23	0.23
MuRIL-Base	0.69	**0.67**	0.67	0.52	0.52	**0.52**	0.16	0.18	0.16

Table 6. Results of MuRIL on 3-class taxonomy

Sentiment	Precision	Recall	F1
positive	0.75	0.79	0.77
negative	0.67	0.71	0.69
ambiguous	0.64	0.50	0.56
macro avg	**0.69**	**0.67**	**0.67**

Table 7. Results of Muril on 7-class taxonomy

Emotion	Precision	Recall	F1
Hope	0.64	0.69	0.66
Neutral	0.61	0.55	0.58
Love	0.53	0.59	0.56
Bewilderment	0.54	0.59	0.56
Disgrace	0.53	0.52	0.53
Pathos	0.41	0.24	0.30
Laughter	0.41	0.44	0.42
macro avg	**0.52**	**0.52**	**0.52**

in the dataset. The "admiration" which contains the most number of samples in the dataset and "grief" are holding the highest and lowest macro F1 scores (0.45, 0.16) respectively in 31-class taxonomy (Table 8).

In addition to the results, confusion matrices for 3-class, and 7-class are visualized for the best-performed models (MuRIL) in Fig. 5. Finally, the results show that it is significantly hard for ML models to compare emotions in fine-grained settings.

Table 8. Results of Random Forest on 31-class Taxonomy

Emotion	Precision	Recall	F1	Emotion	Precision	Recall	F1
admiration	0.32	0.76	0.45	gratitude	0.55	0.56	0.55
amusement	0.61	0.18	0.18	grief	0.50	0.10	0.16
anger	0.41	0.28	0.34	joy	0.38	0.23	0.29
annoyance	0.39	0.23	0.29	love	0.18	0.18	0.18
anticipation	0.36	0.29	0.32	nervousness	0.50	0.12	0.20
approval	0.41	0.26	0.31	neutral	0.39	0.20	0.26
caring	0.57	0.21	0.31	optimism	0.44	0.16	0.23
confusion	0.39	0.19	0.25	pride	0.30	0.32	0.31
curiosity	0.35	0.18	0.24	realization	0.38	0.42	0.40
desire	0.45	0.22	0.29	relief	0.60	0.19	0.29
disappointment	0.73	0.23	0.35	remorse	0.33	0.12	0.18
disapproval	0.41	0.14	0.21	sadness	0.64	0.24	0.35
disgust	0.50	0.18	0.26	surprise	0.43	0.22	0.29
embarrassment	0.73	0.15	0.25	teasing	0.25	0.43	0.32
excitement	0.50	0.15	0.23	trust	0.61	0.18	0.27
fear	0.82	0.33	0.47	**macro avg**	**0.47**	**0.25**	**0.29**

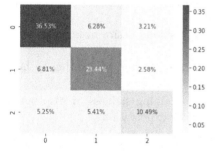
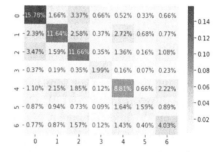

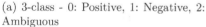

(a) 3-class - 0: Positive, 1: Negative, 2: Ambiguous

(b) 7-class - 0: Trust, 1: Neutral, 2: Love, 3: Bewilderment, 4: Disgrace, 5: Pathos, 6: Laughter

Fig. 5. Confusion Matrix of MuRIL Model: 3-class vs 7-class

6   Conclusion

We propose TamilEmo, a large dataset for fine-grained emotion detection that has been extensively annotated manually. We present a detailed data analysis that demonstrates the accuracy of the annotations over the whole taxonomy with a high inter-annotator agreement in terms of Krippendorff's alpha and Cohen's Kappa. Also, for each class group, we give the results of all models in terms of precision, recall, and F1 score. We anticipate that this resource will enable researchers to tackle new and fascinating Tamil research on the topics of emotion detection.

We also released the dataset through a shared task [17] and made the source code used for model training, publicly available in GitHub[7].

A   Emotion Definitions

- **Admiration** (போற்றுதல்): Comments containing respect and warm approval.
- **Amusement** (கேளிக்கை): Comments containing the state or experience of finding something funny.
- **Anger** (கோபம்): Comments containing a strong feeling of being upset or annoyed because of something wrong or bad.
- **Annoyance** (எரிச்சல்): Comments containing the feeling or state of being annoyed; irritation.
- **Anticipation** (எதிர்பார்ப்பு): Comments containing the act of looking forward especially, to expect something to happen / excitement about the future.
- **Approval** (ஒப்புதல்): Comments containing the action of approving something.
- **Caring** (அக்கறை): Comments containing kindness and concern for others.
- **Confusion** (குழப்பம்): Comments that are uncertain about what is happening, intended, or required.
- **Curiosity** (ஆர்வம்): Comments containing a strong desire to know or learn something.
- **Desire** (ஆசை): Comments containing a strong feeling of wanting to have something or wishing for something to happen.
- **Disappointment** (ஏமாற்றம்): Comments containing sadness or displeasure caused by the non-fulfillment of one's hopes or expectations.
- **Disapproval** (மறுப்பு): Comments containing possession or expression of an unfavourable opinion.
- **Disgust** (அருவருப்பு): Comments containing a strong feeling of dislike for something that has a very unpleasant appearance, taste, smell, etc.
- **Embarrassment** (சங்கடம்): Comments containing a feeling of self-consciousness, shame, or awkwardness.
- **Excitement** (உற்சாகம்): Comments containing a feeling of great enthusiasm and eagerness.
- **Fear** (பயம்): Comments containing a feeling of anxiety and agitation caused by the presence or nearness of danger, evil, pain, etc.
- **Gratitude** (நன்றியறிதல்): Comments containing the quality of being thankful; readiness to show appreciation for and to return kindness.
- **Grief** (துக்கம்): Comments containing intense sorrow, especially caused by someone's death.

---

[7] https://github.com/Chaarangan/TamilEmo.

– **Joy** (மகிழ்ச்சி): Comments containing a feeling of great pleasure and happiness.
– **Love** (அன்பு): Comments containing a feeling of strong or constant affection for a person.
– **Nervousness** (பதட்டம்): Comments containing the quality or state of being nervous.
– **Neutral** (நடுவுநிலை): Comments that are not supportive or helpful to either side in a conflict, disagreement, etc.
– **Optimism** (எதிர்காலத்தைப் பற்றிய நம்பிக்கை): Comments containing hopefulness and confidence about the future or the success of something.
– **Pride** (பெருமை): Comments containing a feeling of deep pleasure or satisfaction derived from one's achievements, the achievements of those with whom one is closely associated, or from qualities or possessions that are widely admired.
– **Realization** (உண்மையை உணர்தல்): Comments containing an act of becoming fully aware of something as a fact.
– **Relief** (துயர்நீக்கம்): Comments containing a feeling of reassurance and relaxation following release from anxiety or distress.
– **Remorse** (குற்றமுணர்ந்ததால் ஏற்படும் வருத்தம்): Comments containing deep regret or guilt for a wrong committed.
– **Sadness** (சோகம்): Comments associated with, or characterized by, feelings of disadvantage, loss, despair, grief, helplessness, disappointment, and sorrow.
– **Surprise** (ஆச்சரியம்): Comments containing a completely unexpected occurrence, appearance, or statement.
– **Teasing** (கிண்டல்): Comments intended to provoke or make fun of someone in a playful way.
– **Trust** (நம்பிக்கை): Comments containing assured reliance on the character, ability, strength, or truth of someone or something.

References

1. Chakravarthi, B.R., Jose, N., Suryawanshi, S., Sherly, E., McCrae, J.P.: A Sentiment Analysis Dataset for Code-Mixed Malayalam-English. In: SLTU (2020)
2. Cortes, C., Vapnik, V.: Support-vector networks. Machine learning **20**(3), 273–297 (1995)
3. Cortiz, D.: Exploring Transformers in Emotion Recognition: A Comparison of BERT. DistillBERT, RoBERTa, XLNet and ELECTRA (2021)
4. Demszky, D., Movshovitz-Attias, D., Ko, J., Cowen, A., Nemade, G., Ravi, S.: GoEmotions: A Dataset of Fine-Grained Emotions. In: Proceedings of the 58th Annual Meeting of the Association for Computational Linguistics, pp. 4040–4054. Association for Computational Linguistics, Online (Jul 2020). https://doi.org/10. 18653/v1/2020.acl-main.372
5. Devlin, J., Chang, M.W., Lee, K., Toutanova, K.: BERT: Pre-training of Deep Bidirectional Transformers for Language Understanding. In: Proceedings of the 2019 Conference of the North American Chapter of the Association for Computational Linguistics: Human Language Technologies, Volume 1 (Long and Short

Papers), pp. 4171–4186. Association for Computational Linguistics, Minneapolis, Minnesota (Jun 2019). 10.18653/v1/N19-1423
6. Ekman, P.: Psychological Review. Psychol. Rev. **99**(3), 550–553 (1992)
7. Khanpour, H., Caragea, C.: Fine-Grained Emotion Detection in Health-Related Online Posts. In: Proceedings of the 2018 Conference on Empirical Methods in Natural Language Processing, pp. 1160–1166. Association for Computational Linguistics, Brussels, Belgium (Oct-Nov 2018). https://doi.org/10.18653/v1/D18-1147
8. Khanuja, S., et al.: MuRIL: Multilingual Representations for Indian Languages (2021)
9. Krippendorff, K.: Estimating the Reliability, Systematic Error and Random Error of Interval Data. Educ. Psychol. Measure. **30**(1), 61–70 (1970). https://doi.org/ 10.1177/001316447003000105
10. Liu, Y., et al.: RoBERTa: A Robustly Optimized BERT Pretraining Approach (2019)
11. Mohammad, S.M.: Obtaining Reliable Human Ratings of Valence, Arousal, and Dominance for 20,000 English Words. In: Proceedings of The Annual Conference of the Association for Computational Linguistics (ACL). Melbourne, Australia (2018)
12. Monroe, B.L., Colaresi, M.P., Quinn, K.M.: Fightin' words: lexical feature selection and evaluation for identifying the content of political conflict. Polit. Anal. **16**(4), 372–403 (2017). https://doi.org/10.1093/pan/mpn018
13. Peng, S., et al.: A survey on deep learning for textual emotion analysis in social networks. Digital Commun. Netw. (2021). https://doi.org/10.1016/j.dcan.2021.10. 003
14. Rashkin, H., Smith, E.M., Li, M., Boureau, Y.L.: Towards Empathetic Open-domain Conversation Models: A New Benchmark and Dataset. In: Proceedings of the 57th Annual Meeting of the Association for Computational Linguistics, pp. 5370–5381. Association for Computational Linguistics, Florence, Italy (Jul 2019). https://doi.org/10.18653/v1/P19-1534
15. Sakuntharaj, R., Mahesan, S.: A novel hybrid approach to detect and correct spelling in Tamil text. In: 2016 IEEE International Conference on Information and Automation for Sustainability (ICIAfS), pp. 1–6 (2016)
16. Sakuntharaj, R., Mahesan, S.: Detecting and correcting real-word errors in Tamil sentences. Ruhuna J. Sci. **9**(2), 150 (2018)
17. Sampath, A., et al.: Findings of the Shared Task on Emotion Analysis in Tamil. In: Proceedings of the Second Workshop on Speech and Language Technologies for Dravidian Languages, pp. 279–285. Association for Computational Linguistics, Dublin, Ireland (May 2022). https://doi.org/10.18653/v1/2022.dravidianlangtech-1.42
18. Suresh, V., Ong, D.C.: Using Knowledge-Embedded Attention to Augment Pre-trained Language Models for Fine-Grained Emotion Recognition. In: 2021 9th International Conference on Affective Computing and Intelligent Interaction (ACII), pp. 1–8 (2021). https://doi.org/10.1109/ACII52823.2021.9597390
19. Vasantharajan, C., Thayasivam, U.: Hypers@DravidianLangTech-EACL2021: Offensive Language Identification in Dravidian Code-Mixed YouTube Comments and Posts. In: Proceedings of the First Workshop on Speech and Language Technologies for Dravidian Languages, pp. 195–202. Association for Computational Linguistics, Kyiv (Apr 2021)
20. Vasantharajan, C., Thayasivam, U.: Towards offensive language identification for tamil code-mixed youtube comments and posts. SN Comput. Sci. **3**(1), 1–13 (2021). https://doi.org/10.1007/s42979-021-00977-y

Context Sensitive Tamil Language Spellchecker Using RoBERTa

Ratnavel Rajalakshmi[1]([✉]), Varsha Sharma[1], and Anand Kumar M[2]

[1] Vellore Institute of Technology, Chennai, Tamil Nadu, India
rajalakshmi.r@vit.ac.in
[2] National Institute of Technology, Mangaluru, Karnataka, India

Abstract. A spellchecker is a tool that helps to identify spelling errors in a piece of text and lists out the possible suggestions for that word. There are many spell-checkers available for languages such as English but a limited number of spell-checking tools are found for low-resource languages like Tamil. In this paper, we present an approach to develop a Tamil spell checker using the RoBERTa (xlm-roberta-base) model. We have also proposed an algorithm to generate the test dataset by introducing errors in a piece of text. The spellchecker finds out the mistake in a given text using a corpus of unique Tamil words collected from different sources such as Wikipedia and Tamil conversations, and lists out the suggestions that could be the potential contextual replacement of the misspelled word using the proposed model. On introducing a few errors in a piece of text collected from a Wikipedia article and testing it on our model, an accuracy of 91.14% was achieved for error detection. Contextually correct words were then suggested for these erroneous words detected. Our spellchecker performed better than some of the existing Tamil spellcheckers in terms of both higher accuracy and lower false positives.

Keywords: Tamil · Spellchecker · Error Detection · Error Correction · XLM-RoBERTa

1 Introduction

Spelling mistakes are the errors made while writing a piece of text or a word in a specific language. These errors are unacceptable hence there arises a need to develop a system that identifies these mistakes and gives suggestions for correcting the same. These spellchecker tools can become handy in a lot of workspaces such as educational institutions or offices. While many spellchecking tools are available for English language, only a few number of such works are found for Indic languages such as Tamil. In many of the existing works [14,41], it was found that there is no proper benchmark dataset available for testing the spellchecker. Some spellcheckers have used the BERT and Levenshtein distance technique [17] for correcting a misspelled word.

To enhance the existing work and overcome the issues faced by existing spellcheckers, we propose a spellchecker model that finds out the misspellings

Anand Kumar M et al. (Eds.): SPELLL 2022, CCIS 1802, pp. 51–61, 2023.
https://doi.org/10.1007/978-3-031-33231-9_4

in a given input text and lists out the suggestions for the misspelled word. To perform this task, we have designed a suitable deep learning approach applying a multi-lingual XLM-RoBERTa model with an end-to-end pipeline for detecting and correcting the spelling mistakes in Tamil language texts. We studied the performance of the proposed spellchecker on the corpus created by us and showed that an accuracy of 91.14% could be acheived with a detailed experimental analysis. Also, we have evaluated its performance by comparing with the existing Tamil spell checkers viz., Vaani [3] and Thamizha Solthiruthi [2] and observed that, our proposed Tamil spellchecker outperforms the existing works, with a better accuracy and reduced the false positive rate to zero. The highlights of our spellchecker are summarized below:

- Creation of corpus/dictionary of unique Tamil words.
- Designing an algorithm to introduce errors in a given text which can then be used to test a spellchecker
- Using a pretrained XLM-RoBERTa model which is a multilingual version of RoBERTa and thus faster than BERT to find out contextually similar words for the misspelled word.
- Comparison of our spellchecker with the existing spellcheckers to show the efficiency of our model.

The organization of the paper is as follows: Sect. 2 describes the related works in this field of research. The proposed methodology is presented in Sect. 3 followed by the detailed error analysis in Sect. 4. The experimental results are discussed in Sect. 5 with a comparative study in Sect. 6. The concluding remarks are given in the last section.

2   Related Works

There are a variety of works and approaches found for the development of spell-checkers. [17] have used the lookup dictionary and named entity recognition for error detection and, Levenshtein distance and BERT for error correction. They have not explored models like ALBERT and RoBERTa for the spellcheckers and other non-English languages such as Tamil, Telugu, etc. [8] have developed a spellchecker using the phonetic spellchecking approach. They have used the phonetic encoding to gather candidates and then these suggestions are sorted based on their general frequency in the English language. [12] have developed a spellchecking toolkit that offers ten different spelling correction models. Out of those ten models, six of them are GNU Aspell, JamSpell, SC-LSTM, CHAR-LSTM-LSTM, CHAR-CNN-LSTM, and BERT.

[7] has trained a transformer-based masked language model using more than two terabytes of CommonCrawl data that contains around one hundred languages. The model was then tested on cross-lingual benchmarks and it was found that their proposed model performs better than the multilingual BERT (mBERT). [16] used edit distance to find the candidate suggestions. The most suitable suggestion is then selected based on the word that has the maximum value for the weighted sum of cosine similarity, edit-distance-based similarity, Double Metaphone-based

similarity, and a binary value indicating whether or not the candidate appears in the target text. [11] have used the dictionary lookup and character bi-grams to find the similarity coefficient in order to find the most correct similar word. [6] have used a self-created benchmark dataset and followed the Damerau-Levenshtein distance and n-grams approach to develop their spellchecker.

[14] has developed a spellchecker for the Tamil language using the minimum edit distance to find the possible words and a Matrix Formation Algorithm to generate a matrix of cost of operations required to get the target word. They mention that they faced an issue in finding a benchmark dataset for Tamil, unlike other languages. [35] have used a hybrid approach using a tree-based algorithm with n-gram and stemming techniques to construct their spell-checker model. Confidence classifiers for checking and correcting words and the n-grams language model were used by [42] for their spellchecker. For short text classification feature weighting method [21,22], Machine learning [23,25], Deep learning [19,20] and transfer learning approach [29] have been proposed.

Many existing works [10,13,31,32,34] have been found in low-resource languages such as Hindi, Marathi, Tamil [26,28], etc. Ensemble based approach [18, 27,30] has been carried in various text classification tasks. [30] has implemented machine learning methods to carry out a sentiment analysis on the code-mixed Hinglish datasets, including decision trees, SVC, logistic regression, multinomial nave Bayes, and SGD classifier. This was followed by the implementation of the XGBoost ensemble algorithm, which produced an F1 score of 83.10%. In order to improve the contextual classification of a word in a text, [37] utilized the attention-extracted deep contextual characteristics from BERT and fed them into the BGRU using transfer learning. An F1 score of 95.57, 86.66, and 80.29% for IMDB, Polarity, and OLID dataset (weighted) was obtained with the suggested attention-extracted BERT-bidirectional gated recurrent unit (i.e., AeBERT-BGRU).

[24] has suggested a relevance-based measure that uses statistics to separate code borrowing from code mixing in order to process multilingual queries quickly. The efficiency of the suggested relevance metric was investigated by doing several tests on the social media data corpus including more than 2.5 lakh tweets. In another work, IndicBERT, XLM Roberta, and Masked LM models have been used by [33] to embed tweet data. After that, classification techniques like Logistic Regression, Support Vector Machine, Ensembling, and Neural Network-based approaches were used to carry out classification of Hinglish tweets as hate speech or not. Ensembling was determined to be the best approach after experiments were conducted using the code-mixed data and IndicBERT, yielding a macro F1-score of 62.53%. As part of the FIRE2021 shared task, Hate Speech and Offensive Content Identification in English and Indo-Aryan Languages, [27] has carried a task of identifying hate speech and offensive content for the languages of English, Hindi, and Marathi (HASOC-2021). For the subtask of categorizing the tweets as offensive or non-offensive, the Random Forest Classifier received macro F1 scores of 75.19% and 73.12% on the Marathi and Hindi tweet datasets, respectively. The XGBoost, on the other hand, scored 46.5% macro F1 on the subtask of further identifying Hindi tweets as hate speech, offensive or profane. Sentiment analysis on social media [9,36,39] contents have been studied with self attention [38] based approach.

In our approach, we have used masked language modeling as used by some other existing spellchecker models as well. Many existing works have used the BERT transformer models as well. However, we have used the XLM-RoBERTa pretrained model to develop the Tamil spellchecker which is faster than the BERT transformers.

3 Model

In our spellchecker model, we have used xlm-roberta-base model which is a pre-trained model on 2.5 TB of filtered CommonCrawl data containing 100 languages. Our spellchecker takes an input text, finds out the misspelled word and lists out the possible suggestions for the misspelled word.

3.1 Dictionary Creation

A dictionary or corpus of 1441654 unique Tamil words was made after collecting texts from various sources. Around 100+ articles were collected from Wikipedia Tamil articles [5]. A set of Tamil words was gathered from the Wikipedia dumps [40]. Words from the HASOC training dataset and their stem words (found using the IndicNLP MA [15]) were added. After gathering all the words from different sources, they were added to a text file which was then processed to remove all the special symbols, English letters and numbers, if any. Only the unique words were kept in the final file and all the duplicates were removed.

3.2 Test Dataset Creation

From many of the existing works, it was noticed that they faced any issue of finding a proper benchmark dataset for testing their spellchecking algorithms or models. Hence, we propose a method of introducing the errors in a given text and thus generating a dataset for testing any spellchecker.

An algorithm is developed that takes a word at random from the input text. From this chosen word, a letter is selected at random. Either of the two types of errors i.e., del or swap is introduced in the data. The error del is introduced after deleting the selected letter from the selected word while the error swap is generated after swapping the chosen letter and its adjacent letter. Hence, a dataset with a specific number of erroneous words is obtained as an output.

The test data contains a total of 255 words out of which 79 words have been introduced with a del or swap error. Following is the example of the generated error sentence

Example of generated errors மையச் செயற்பகுதி அல்லது மையச் செயலகம் என்பது கணன நிரல்களின் கட்ளைடகளை , அந்தக் கட்டளைகள் சுட்டும் எண்ணியல் , எளவை-யிய்ல (தருக்வகியல்) , கட்டுபாட்டியல் , உள்ளீட்டு , வெளயீட்டு வினைகளை , செய்றபடுத்தும் ஒரு மின்னனியல் சுற்றமைப்பு ஆகும் .

Original Sentence மையச் செயற்பகுதி அல்லது மையச் செயலகம் என்பது கணினி நி-
ரல்களின் கட்டளைகளை, அந்தக் கட்டளைகள் சுட்டும் எண்ணியல் , எளவையியல் (தருக்-
கவியல்) , கட்டுபாட்டியல் , உள்ளீடு , வெளியீட்டு விளைகளை , செயற்படுத்தும் ஒரு மின்-
னனியல் சுற்றமைப்பு ஆகும்.
(A central processing unit or central office is an electronic circuit that executes
the commands of computer programs, the arithmetic, mathematical (logical),
control, input, and output functions that those commands execute) (Table 1).

Table 1. Types of Error Generated

S. No	Error Category	Errors Generated
1	Del and Swap	79
2	Space	0
3	Correct words labelled as mis-spelt	0
4	Incorrect words	79

3.3   XLM-RoBERTa-base Model

The corpus of the unique Tamil words was loaded. The words for the dictionary
have been stored as a single text in a text file. This corpus of words and the test
dataset were opened. Both these texts were tokenized using the NLTK library
to obtain a list of the words.

Error Detection. A word is categorized as misspelt if it is not found in the dic-
tionary/corpus in a similar manner as followed in the n-grams and edit distance
approach.

Error Correction. A pre-trained xlm-roberta-base model is used from the
Hugging Face library [4]. The misspelled word in a verse is masked by replacing
it with the ⟨mask⟩ token. This sentence is then passed into the transformer
model which then lists out the possible words that could be replaced with the
mask token.

Thus, the possible suggestions for a misspelled word are obtained. These
suggestions are contextually correct for a given sentence.

The hyper parameters used in the experimentation are the number of words
in the dictionary and the number of words in the test file. Increasing the number
of words in the dictionary can improve the overall error detection accuracy of
the spellchecker.

The basic idea of masking the misspelled word and then feeding it to the
transformer was taken from [17]. However, they have used the BERT model
whereas, we propose the spellchecker using the RoBERTa model since the
RoBERTa model outperforms BERT in many aspects. Also, we propose word
suggestions for the misspelled word that are contextually correct.

4   Error Analysis

The error categories that can be found in any test dataset are as follows:

Error Categories

- Deletion of a character from a word (del)
  A character is selected at random from a specific chosen word and the chosen character is then deleted. Hence, a misspelled or the erroneous word is obtained.
- Swapping two characters in a word (swap)
  A character is selected at random from a specific chosen word. The selected character and its next adjacent letter are then swapped to obtain a misspelled word.
- Space error (space)
  These are the errors in a text that is due to the missing space between two or more words.
- Correct words labelled as misspelled (corr)
  These are correct words but are labelled as misspelled by the spellchecker. This is because these words are absent in the corpus that is used as dictionary.
- Incorrect word (incorr)
  These are the words that are actually incorrect. Thus, they are not present in the dictionary, Hence, these erroneous words are detected by the spellchecker (Fig. 1).

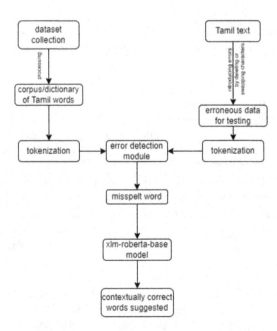

Fig. 1. Overall Architecture of the Spellchecker

5   Experiments

In this section, we list out the experiments carried out for the spellchecker on a part of text collected from a Tamil Wikipedia article. 79 errors were introduced in the Wikipedia test set. These involved the errors that were introduced by our algorithm. This algorithm introduced errors by selecting a word at random from a piece of text and randomly selecting a letter from that word. This letter was then either deleted or swapped with its adjacent letter.

5.1   Experiment: Xlm-roberta-base Model on Wikipedia Article [1]

The text in which errors were introduced by our algorithm was tested with the xlm-roberta-base spellchecker and the corresponding spelling suggestions were listed out. A 'score' is calculated by the pre-trained model, xlm-roberta-base and generated for each word replacement for the masked token. For example,

Correct sentence மரபாக இச்சொல் முதன்மை நினைவகம், உள்ளீட்டகம், வெளியீட்டகம் ஆகிய கணினியின் புறநிலை அணிகளைத் தவிர்த்து உள்ளகட்டுப் பகுதிகளாகிய செயற்-பகுதியையும் கட்டுபாட்டுப் பகுதியையும் மட்டுமே குறித்தது.

(Traditionally, this term refers only to the functional and control areas of the computer, excluding the main memory, input, and output components of the computer) (Table 2).

Sentence after introducing the error மரபகா இச்சொல் முதன்மை நினைவகம், உள்-ளீட்டகம், வெளியீட்டகம ஆகயி கணினியனி புறநிலை அணிளைத் தவிர்த்து உள்ளகட்டுப் பகுதிகளாகிய செயற்பகுதியையும் ட்டுபாட்டுப் பகுதியையும் டம்டுமே குறித்தது.

Misspelled word: அணிளைத்
Suggestions generated

Table 2. Suggestions generated and their corresponding scores

S. No.	Suggestion	Score
1.	பையத்	0.5445
2.	களைத்	0.13048
3.	பைய	0.12446
4.	களை	0.040219
5.	கள்	0.0332665

The spellchecker successfully identified 72 errors out of 79 errors that were introduced in a total of 255 words.

The errors identified are as below (Table 3):

Table 3. Categories of the errors identified

S. No	Error Category	Errors Detected
1	Del and Swap	72
2	Space	0
3	Correct words labelled as misspelled	0
4	Incorrect words	72

The error detection accuracy of the algorithm is thus

$$\frac{No.of\ errors\ detected}{No.of\ errors\ introduced} = \frac{72}{79} = 91.14\% \tag{1}$$

The words suggested for the replacement of the incorrect spellings are the words that are contextually correct for a given sentence.

6   Comparison with Tamil Spellcheckers

We have compared the performance of our spellchecker with other spellcheckers as well by testing those spellcheckers on our Wikipedia test dataset. The total misspelt words in the test dataset are 79.
The performance metrics used are:

$$Error\ detection\ accuracy = \frac{Total\ errors\ detected\ correctly}{Total\ errorss\ in\ the\ text} \tag{2}$$

$$Incorrect\ error\ detection\ percentage = \frac{False\ Positives}{Total\ errors\ highlighted} \tag{3}$$

The results obtained are tabulated in the following table (Table 4).

Table 4. Comparison of proposed spellchecker with existing spellcheckers

Spell Checker	Total Errors Highlighted	Total Errors Detected Correctly	Error Detection Accuracy	Incorrect Error Detection Percentage
Vaani [3]	96	44	55.69%	54.17%
ThamiZha! Solthiruthi (Tamil spellchecker) [2]	157	78	98.73%	50.32%
Proposed Method	**72**	**72**	**91.13%**	**0%**

7   Conclusion

We have developed a spellchecker using xlm-roberta-base model. The benchmark dataset was created using our own designed algorithm and tested on our proposed spellchecker. The performance of the spellchecker was compared with two other Tamil spellcheckers as well. It was found that our spellchecker does not misclassify any word as misspelt unlike the other Tamil spellcheckers such as Vaani and ThamiZha! Solthiruthi. We can work on improving our dictionary by adding more Tamil words to it which can then lead to increased efficiency. Other techniques such as n-grams and edit distance can also be explored for the development of the spellchecker model.

References

1. https://ta.wikipedia.org/s/azh
2. Thamizha! solthiruthi (tamil spellchecker). https://addons.mozilla.org/en-US/firefox/addon/thamizha-solthiruthi/
3. Vaani. http://vaani.neechalkaran.com
4. xlm-roberta-base. https://huggingface.co/xlm-roberta-base
5. Annaswamy, R.: Tamil wikipedia articles. https://www.kaggle.com/datasets/disisbig/tamil-wikipedia-articles
6. Chaabi, Y., Allah, F.A.: Amazigh spell checker using damerau-levenshtein algorithm and n-gram. J. King Saud Univ.-Comput. Inf. Sci. **34**, 6116–6124 (2021)
7. Conneau, A., et al.: Unsupervised cross-lingual representation learning at scale. arXiv preprint arXiv:1911.02116 (2019)
8. Downs, B., et al.: Kidspell: A child-oriented, rule-based, phonetic spellchecker. In: Proceedings of the 12th Language Resources and Evaluation Conference, pp. 6937–6946 (2020)
9. Ganganwar, V., Rajalakshmi, R.: Implicit aspect extraction for sentiment analysis: a survey of recent approaches. Procedia Comput. Sci. **165**, 485–491 (2019)
10. Ganganwar, V., Rajalakshmi, R.: Mtdot: a multilingual translation-based data augmentation technique for offensive content identification in tamil text data. Electronics **11**(21) (2022). https://doi.org/10.3390/electronics11213574. https://www.mdpi.com/2079-9292/11/21/3574
11. Jain, A., Jain, M.: Detection and correction of non word spelling errors in Hindi language. In: 2014 International Conference on Data Mining and Intelligent Computing (ICDMIC), pp. 1–5. IEEE (2014)
12. Jayanthi, S.M., Pruthi, D., Neubig, G.: Neuspell: a neural spelling correction toolkit. arXiv preprint arXiv:2010.11085 (2020)
13. Kannan, R.R., Rajalakshmi, R., Kumar, L.: Indicbert based approach for sentiment analysis on code-mixed tamil tweets, vol. 3159, p. 8 (2021)
14. Kumar, P., Kannan, A., Goel, N.: Design and implementation of nlp-based spell checker for the tamil language. In: Presented at 1st International Electronic Conference on Applied Sciences, vol. 10, p. 30 (2020)
15. Kunchukuttan, A.: Indic nlp library. https://github.com/anoopkunchukuttan/indic_nlp_library

16. Nagata, R., Takamura, H., Neubig, G.: Adaptive spelling error correction models for learner English. Procedia Comput. Sci. **112**, 474–483 (2017)
17. Pal, A., Mustafi, A.: Vartani spellcheck - automatic context-sensitive spelling correction of ocr-generated hindi text using BERT and levenshtein distance. CoRR abs/2012.07652 (2020). https://arxiv.org/abs/2012.07652
18. Rajalakshmi, R., Reddy, B.Y.: DLRG@hasoc 2019: an enhanced ensemble classifier for hate and offensive content identification. In: Mehta, P., Rosso, P., Majumder, P., Mitra, M. (eds.) Working Notes of FIRE 2019 - Forum for Information Retrieval Evaluation, Kolkata, India, 12–15 December 2019, CEUR Workshop Proceedings, vol. 2517, pp. 370–379. CEUR-WS.org (2019). http://ceur-ws.org/Vol-2517/T3-26.pdf
19. Rajalakshmi, R., Tiwari, H., Patel, J., Kumar, A., Karthik, R.: Design of kids-specific URL classifier using recurrent convolutional neural network. Procedia Comput. Sci. **167**, 2124–2131 (2020)
20. Rajalakshmi, R., Tiwari, H., Patel, J., Kumar, A., Karthik., R.: Design of kids-specific url classifier using recurrent convolutional neural network. Proceedia Comput. Sci. **167**, 2124–2131 (2020). https://doi.org/10.1016/j.procs.2020.03.260, https://www.sciencedirect.com/science/article/pii/S1877050920307262
21. Rajalakshmi, R., Xaviar, S.: Experimental study of feature weighting techniques for URL based webpage classification. Procedia Comput. Sci. **115**, 218–225 (2017)
22. Rajalakshmi, R.: Supervised term weighting methods for URL classification. J. Comput. Sci. **10**(10), 1969–1976 (2014)
23. Rajalakshmi, R.: Identifying health domain URLs using SVM. In: Proceedings of the Third International Symposium on Women in Computing and Informatics, pp. 203–208 (2015)
24. Rajalakshmi, R., Agrawal, R.: Borrowing likeliness ranking based on relevance factor. In: Proceedings of the Fourth ACM IKDD Conferences on Data Sciences, pp. 1–2 (2017)
25. Rajalakshmi, R., Aravindan, C.: An effective and discriminative feature learning for URL based web page classification. In: 2018 IEEE International Conference on Systems, Man, and Cybernetics (SMC), pp. 1374–1379. IEEE (2018)
26. Rajalakshmi, R., Duraphe, A., Shibani, A.: DLRG@ DravidianLangTech-ACL2022: abusive comment detection in Tamil using multilingual transformer models. In: Proceedings of the Second Workshop on Speech and Language Technologies for Dravidian Languages, pp. 207–213 (2022)
27. Rajalakshmi, R., Mattins, F., Srivarshan, S., Reddy, L.P.: Hate speech and offensive content identification in Hindi and Marathi language tweets using ensemble techniques (2021)
28. Rajalakshmi, R., More, M., Shrikriti, B., Saharan, G., Samyuktha, H., Nandy, S.: DLRG@ tamilnlp-acl2022: offensive span identification in Tamil using BiLSTM-CRF approach. In: Proceedings of the Second Workshop on Speech and Language Technologies for Dravidian Languages, pp. 248–253 (2022)
29. Rajalakshmi, R., Ramraj, S., Ramesh Kannan, R.: Transfer learning approach for identification of malicious domain names. In: Thampi, S.M., Madria, S., Wang, G., Rawat, D.B., Alcaraz Calero, J.M. (eds.) SSCC 2018. CCIS, vol. 969, pp. 656–666. Springer, Singapore (2019). https://doi.org/10.1007/978-981-13-5826-5_51
30. Rajalakshmi, R., Reddy, P., Khare, S., Ganganwar, V.: Sentimental analysis of code-mixed Hindi language. In: Congress on Intelligent Systems, pp. 739–751. Springer, Heidelberg (2022). https://doi.org/10.1007/978-981-16-9113-3_54

31. Rajalakshmi, R., Reddy, Y., Kumar, L.: DLRG@DravidianLangTech-EACL2021: Transformer based approach for offensive language identification on code-mixed Tamil. In: Proceedings of the First Workshop on Speech and Language Technologies for Dravidian Languages, pp. 357–362. Association for Computational Linguistics, Kyiv (2021). https://aclanthology.org/2021.dravidianlangtech-1.53
32. Rajalakshmi, R., Selvaraj, S., R., F.M., Vasudevan, P., M., A.K.: Hottest: hate and offensive content identification in Tamil using transformers and enhanced stemming. Comput. Speech Lang. **78**, 101464 (2023). https://doi.org/ 10.1016/j.csl.2022.101464. https://www.sciencedirect.com/science/article/pii/ S0885230822000870
33. Rajalakshmi, R., Srivarshan, S., Mattins, F., Kaarthik, E., Seshadri, P.: Conversational hate-offensive detection in code-mixed hindi-english tweets 3159, 11. https:// ceur-ws.org/Vol-3159/T1-47.pdf
34. Ravikiran, M., et al.: Findings of the shared task on offensive span identification fromCode-mixed Tamil-English comments. In: Proceedings of the Second Workshop on Speech and Language Technologies for Dravidian Languages, pp. 261–270. Association for Computational Linguistics, Dublin (2022). https:// doi.org/10.18653/v1/2022.dravidianlangtech-1.40, https://aclanthology.org/2022. dravidianlangtech-1.40
35. Sakuntharaj, R., Mahesan, S.: A novel hybrid approach to detect and correct spelling in Tamil text. In: 2016 IEEE International Conference on Information and Automation for Sustainability (ICIAfS), pp. 1–6. IEEE (2016)
36. Sharen, H., Rajalakshmi, R.: DLRG@ LT-EDI-ACL2022: detecting signs of depression from social media using XGBoost method. In: Proceedings of the Second Workshop on Language Technology for Equality, Diversity and Inclusion, pp. 346– 349 (2022)
37. Sivakumar, S., Rajalakshmi, R.: Context-aware sentiment analysis with attention-enhanced features from bidirectional transformers. Social Netw. Anal. Min. **12**(1), 1–23 (2022)
38. Soubraylu, S., Rajalakshmi, R.: Analysis of sentiment on movie reviews using word embedding self-attentive LSTM. Int. J. Ambient Comput. Intell. **12**, 33–52 (2021). https://doi.org/10.4018/IJACI.2021040103
39. Soubraylu, S., Rajalakshmi, R.: Hybrid convolutional bidirectional recurrent neural network based sentiment analysis on movie reviews. Comput. Intell. **37**(2), 735–757 (2021)
40. Shrinivasan, T.: Tamil wikipedia word list. https://github.com/tshrinivasan/tamil-wikipedia-word-list
41. Uthayamoorthy, K., Kanthasamy, K., Senthaalan, T., Sarveswaran, K., Dias, G.: Ddspell - a data driven spell checker and suggestion generator for the tamil language. In: 2019 19th International Conference on Advances in ICT for Emerging Regions (ICTer), vol. 250, pp. 1–6 (2019). https://doi.org/10.1109/ICTer48817. 2019.9023698
42. Whitelaw, C., Hutchinson, B., Chung, G.Y., Ellis, G.: Using the web for language independent spellchecking and autocorrection (2009)

Correlating Copula Constructions in Tamil and English for Machine Translation

Vadivelu Dhanalakshmi[1]([✉]) and S. Rajendran[2]

[1] School of Tamil, Pondicherry University, Pondicherry, India
dhanagiri@pondiuni.ac.in
[2] CEN, Amrita Vishwa Vidyapeetham, Coimbatore, India

Abstract. Translation between language pairs of linguistic divergence is complex. Human mind can establish correlations that exist between the linguistically divergent languages. But making a machine to understand this correlation is quite difficult. The complexity arises while finding the equivalent replacement from source language to target language. Copula construction in which the subject is linked to its complement in the predicate position by a link verb known as copula verb is found in many languages with different realizations. Tamil makes use of mainly two types of copula construction: one is zero copula construction and another is verbal copula construction. English does not make use of zero copula construction; it makes use of only verbal copula construction. When we try to correlate Tamil copula constructions with English copula constructions or vice versa we come across a lot of mismatches and complexities. In this paper we discuss about the realization of these mismatches which are crucial for Machine Translation between Tamil and English and vice versa.

Keywords: Tamil Language · Tamil Grammar · Copula · Machine Translation

1 Introduction

A copula construction is a construction carrying a copula verb. In linguistics, a copula is a word or phrase that links the subject of a sentence to a subject complement. The word copula derives from the Latin noun for a "link" or "tie" that connects two different things. For example in English sentence "The girl is beautiful", 'the girl' is subject and the subject complement is 'beautiful'; the verb linking verb is copula verb. Copulative or copular verbs are other names for copula verbs. A copula is most commonly used to connect a clause's subject to its subject complement. Frequently, a copular verb is seen as a part of the predicate, with the other words being referred to as predicative expressions. The example below shows a simple clause with a copula. The book is on the table.

Anand Kumar M et al. (Eds.): SPELLL 2022, CCIS 1802, pp. 62–70, 2023.
https://doi.org/10.1007/978-3-031-33231-9_5

In that sentence, the noun phrase 'the book' is the subject, the verb 'is' serves as the copula, and the prepositional phrase 'on the table' is the predicative expression. The whole expression 'is on the table' may (in some theories of grammar) be called a predicate or a verb phrase[1]. Copulas are conventionally defined functionally as a means of relating elements of clause structure, especially subject and complement, and considered to be semantically empty or meaningless [7].

Curnow [2] in his study of Cross-linguistic Typology of Copula Constructions found four strategies to encode identity and group membership relations of copula constructions. (1) Verbal copula construction - This is a common strategy in which copular verb exists as similar to English "be". (2) Particle copula construction - consist of Copula subject + Copula complement + non-verb (3) 'Inflectional' copula construction - the Copula complement is treated as though it were a verb. (4) Zero' copula constructions - the Copula subject and Copula complement are simply juxtaposed.

Tamil makes use of mainly two types of copula construction: one is zero copula construction and another is verbal copula construction. Dorr [3] states that "Translation divergence occurs when the common translation of one language into another results in a very different form than that of the original". So, translation between languages of linguistic divergence pair are complex. This paper discuss about the divergence in Copula construction translation and brings forth the machine readable rules which are crucial for Machine Translation between Tamil and English language pair.

2   Zero Copula Construction

The term "zero copula" refers to a linguistic phenomenon in which the subject and predicate are connected without any explicit indication of relationship like the copula "to be" in English. One can distinguish languages that simply do not have a copula and languages that have a copula that is optional in some contexts[2]. Sentences with nominal predicates are equative sentences, which lack the copula or the verb 'to be' in most of the languages [4]. Overt expletives and copulas are not present in the existential sentences of all languages [6]. The zero copula construction in which the subject and the subject complement are juxtaposed without any linking verb appears to be the major format of copula construction in Tamil. A non-lexical copula verb like 'be' in English is not generated in Modern Tamil to express such a proposition [5].

Tamil has sentences which can be expanded as NP+NP in which the first is a subject and the second is a complement to the subject NP which is in the predicate position. This can be equated with English as NP+ Copula verb BE+ NP. The copula BE can be realized as present tense form 'is', past tense form 'was' and future tense form 'will be'. The zero copula construction in Tamil can

---

[1] https://en.wikipedia.org/wiki/Copula(linguistics).
[2] https://en.wikipedia.org/wiki/Zerocopula.

denote only the present tense. The different tenses can be taken care of by iru-
copula constructions discussed latter. The transfer from zero copula construction
in Tamil to English can be stated by the following rule.

Rule 1: NPs + NPcom = NPs + BE +NPcom

- avar oru aaciriyar / (NPs + NPcom)
  He one teacher
- He is a teacher / (NPs +BE +NPcom)

- avaL oru ndaTikai /(NPs + NPcom)
  she one actress
- She is an actress / (NPs +BE +NPcom)

In Tamil the subject and the subject complements are nominal. There is
another type sentences in Tamil which can be expanded as NP+NP in which the
second NP is a pronominzlized adjective which can be expanded as N+ADJV-
PN. (ADJV stands denote adjectivalizer and PN stands to denote pronominalizer.) The pronominalizer will be in agreement with the subject NP by person,
number and gender.

- avaL azhk-aana-vaL
  she beauty-ADJV-PN
- 'She is beautiful'

The pronominalized adjectival noun in Tamil can be equated with adjective
itself in English which is linked with the subject noun by a copula verb as given
the below.

- She is beautiful
- *avaL oru azhak-aana
  she one beautiful

'she one beautiful' is not a complete sentence. The adjectival form needs the
support of the pronominalizer which agrees with the subject noun. The equation
between Tamil and English copula constructions can be stated as a transfer rule
as given below:

Rule 2: NPs + N-ADJV-PN = NPs + BE + ADJ

- avaL azhak-aana-vaL (NPs + N-ADJV-PN)
  she beauty-become-ADJP-she
- She is beautiful (NPs + BE + ADJ)

Similarly the adjectives like 'nalla' cannot occupy the predicative position
alone. It need to be inflected for pronominal suffix in agreement with the subject.

- avaL nalla-vaL (NPs + ADJ-PN)
  she is good-she
- She is good (NPs + BE + ADJ)

The adjectival participle form of aaku is anna which is grammticalized into an adjective forming suffix: inimaiy-aana 'sweet', cuttam-aana 'pure'. In the above sentences with aa-na can be considered as a copula construction in which the copula aaku is inflected for past adjectival participle (aa-na) to which the pronominal suffix in agreement with the subject is added.

3   Copula Construction with 'aaku' as the Copula Verb

The Tamil construction without a copula verb can optionally take a copula verb aaku inflected for future tense and pronominal agreement. aaku is originally a verb denoting the sense 'to become'. But the future tense form the verb aaku is grammaticalized to denote the copula sense 'is' [8]. The future tense marker stand to denote present tense only. The equation between Tamil and English copula construction can be given as a transfer rule as given below.

Rule 3: NPs + NPcom+ aa-FUT-PN = NPs + BE+ NPcom

- avar oru aaciriyar aa-v-aan (NPs + NPcom+ aa-FUT-PN)
  he one teacher become-FUT-he
- He is a teacher (NPs + BE+ NPcom)

- avaL our ndaTikai aa-v-aaL (NPs + NPcom+ aa-FUT-PN)
  she one actor become-fut-she
- She is an actress (NPs + BE+ NPcom)

In the above sentence aaku can occur as a neuter-cum-emphatic form aakkum too (at least in colloquial speech).

- avan oru aaciriyar aakkum
  he one teacher is
- He is a teacher

- avaL oru ndaTikai aakkum
  She one teacher is
- She is a teacher

The inflected forms with future tense suffix -v- is ambiguous as it denotes the future tense sense too when required.

- avar oru aaciriyar aa-v-aan
  He one teacher become-FUT-he
- He will become a teacher

- avaL our ndaTikai aa-v-aaL
  She one actor become-fut-she
- She will become an actress

The copula verb in the above constructions cannot be used to denote the past tense 'was' as a be-verb. Of course it can be inflected to denote past, present and future in the 'become' sense.

- avar aaciriyar aa-n-aar
  he teacher become-PAS-he
- He became a teacher
  *He was a teacher

The sentence cannot be glossed as 'He was a teacher', but as 'He became a teacher'. Similar is the case the following sentence.

- avar aaciriyar aa-kiR-aar
  he teacher become-PRE-he
- He becomes a teacher
- *He is a teacher'

This sentence cannot be glossed as 'He is a teacher', but as 'He becomes a teacher'.

The negative counter part of 'aaku' is 'illai'. The negative verb does not inflect for tense and PNG in agreement with the subject. In formal Tamil 'alla' is used to negate nominal predications and 'illai' for the rest [1]. This diction is lost in the contemporary Tamil and only 'illai' is used in both cases. The rule of transfer can be given as follows:

Rule 4: NPs + NPcom+ illai = NPs + BE+ not+ NPcom

- avar oru aaciriyar illai (NPs + NPcom+ illai)
  he one teacher not
  He is not a teacher NPs + BE+ not+ NPcom
- avaL our ndaTikai illai (NPs + NPcom+ illai)
  she one actor not
  She is not an actress (NPs + BE+ not+ NPcom)

The negative verbs il- 'be not' (to negate existential, locative, copula usages) and al- (to negate copula usage) are not inflected for tense but marked only for third neuter plural as ill-ai, all-a, but agree with both singular and/or plural subjects [4]. In contemporary Tamil 'illa' and 'alla' become unanalyzable single units without marking the diction between singular and pluaral. The example is given below.

- avarkaL aaciriyar-kaL illai
  They teacher-s not
- 'They are not teachers'

The comparative constructions of the following types take the copula 'aaku' optionally.

- avaL avan-ai viTa muuttavaL (aavaaL)
  she he-ACC than elder-she

– She is elder than him

There are many long sentences in which 'aakum' appears by default even though the omission does not make them wrong. A number of such sentences are found in Tamil corpus. For the sake of brevity the lengthy sentences are given in reduced format.

– atu nTandtatu enpatu mikavum varuttam aLikkum vishayam aakum
  that happened that very sorrowful matter is
– 'It is a sorrowful matter that it happened'
– rayilvee sTeeshan avaikkaveeNTum enpatu aaraNi makkaLin ndiiNTa naaL
  koorikkai aakum
  railway station should-be-established that AraNi people long day demand is
– 'Establishing a railway station is the demand of Arani people'

There are instances in which 'aaku' is obligatory when it is used with the non-copula sense such as 'become, necessary, take etc'.

– aRuvai cikiccaikku pattaayiram ruupaay celavu (aakum)
  operation treatment ten thousand rupees expenditure necessary
– 'The operation treatment will take rupees ten thousand as expenditure'
– inta tiTTattiRu 100 kooTi (aakum)
  this plan hundred crore need
– 'This plan needed hundred crores'

4 Copula Construction with 'iru' as the Copula Verb

The copula construction with locative noun phrase takes iru 'be' as the copula verb. The verb iru inflect for all the three tenses (Tens) and person, number gender (PNG) as usual. The copula verb aaku cannot occur there. English makes use of the same copula verb (i.e. be verb) to link the locative prepositional phrase (LocPP) with the subject noun phrase. The transfer rule can be given as follows.

Rule 5: NPs + NPLoc + iru-Tens-PNG = NPs + BE+ LocPP

– avan viiTT-il iru-kkiR-aan (NPs + NPLoc + iru-Tens-PNG)
  he house-Loc be -PRE-he
– 'He is in the house' (NPs + BE+ LocPP)
– avaL cennaiy-il iru-kkiR-aaL(NPs + NPLoc + iru-Tens-PNG)
  she Chennai-Loc be-PRE-she
– 'She is in Chennai'(NPs + BE+ LocPP)

The negative counter part of iru too is illai. The negative verb does not inflect for tense and does not inflect to agree with the subject. English makes use of the negative copula complex 'be not' in this context.

Rule 6: NPs + NPLoc + illai = NPs + BE+ not+ LocPP

- avan viiTT-il illai (NPs + NPLoc + illai)
  he house-Loc not
- 'He is not in the house' (NPs + BE+ not+ LocPP)
- avaL cennaiy-il illai (NPs + NPLoc + illai)
  she Chennai-Loc
- 'She is not in Chennai' (NPs + BE+ not+ LocPP)

5 Copula Construction with 'aaka-Iru' as the Copula Verb

The zero copula construction can optionally take aaka-iru as the copula verb. English makes use of the same 'be-verb' in this context.

Rule 7: NPs + NP-aaka + iru-Tens-PNG = NPs + BE+ NP

- avar oru aaciriyar-aaka iru-kkiR-aar (NPs + NPLoc + iru-Tens-PNG)
  he one teacher-become-INF be-PRE-he
- 'He is a teacher' (NPs + BE+ LocPP)
- avaL oru ndaTikai aaka iru-kkiR-aaL(NPs + NPLoc + iru-Tens-PNG)
  she one actress-become-INF be-PRE-she
- 'She is an actress' (NPs + BE+ LocPP)

The construction NP-aaka iru can be re-analyzed as NP-aaka-iru. The lexical gap left by 'aaka' not to function as full-fledged be verb denoting 'is' and 'was' is compensated by 'aaka-iru'.

- avar oru aaciriyar-aaka iru-nt-aar
  he one teacher-become-INF be-PAS-he
- 'He was a teacher'
  avaL oru ndaTikai aaka iru-nd-aaL
  she one actress-become-INF be-PRE-she
- 'She was an actress'

The lexical gap left by 'aaku' not to complement an adjective is compensated by 'aaka-iru'

- avaL azhak-aaka iru-kkiR-aaL
  she beauty-become-INF be-PRE-she
- 'She is beautiful'

The suffix '-aaka' is generally considered as an adverb forming suffix. But functionally it is not always the case.

- avaL oru ndaTikaiy-aaka iru-kkiR-aaL
  she one actor-become-INF be-PRE-she
- 'She is an actress'

Here too the negative counter part of 'iru' is 'illai' which does not inflect for tense and PNG in agreement with the subject.

Rule 8: NPs + NP-aaka + illai = NPs + BE+ not+ NP

- avar oru aaciriyar-aaka illai
  he one teacher-become-INF not
- 'He is not a teacher'

Note that English copula complex BE+not allows the manifestation of the three tenses where as Tamil allows the realization of only the present tense.

6   Copula Construction as Embedded Sentences

Copula construction can occur as an embedded sentence complemented by enRu 'that'

- avan oru aaciriyar enRu eNN-in-een
  he one teacher that think-PAS-I
- 'I thought that he is a teacher'

But the following sentence with copula verb appears to be odd.

- avan oru aaciriyar aa-v-aan enRu eNN-in-een
  he one teacher be-FUT-he think-PAS-I
- *'I thought that he is a teacher'

This sentence can be glossed as 'I thought that he would become a teacher'.

7   Problematic Cases

The definition and scope of the concept of a copula is not necessarily precise in any language. As noted above, though the concept of the copula in English is most strongly associated with the verb 'to be', there are many other verbs that can be used in a copular sense as well. The following example will illustrate the point.

- The boy became a man.
- The girl grew more excited by seeing him.
- The dog felt tired from the activity.
- The milk turned sour.
- The food smells good.
- You seem upset.

In that case the verb 'aaku' with the sense 'become' a part of copula construction. In Tamil, the verbs of feeling verb such as ini 'be/feel sweet', kaca 'be/feel bitter', paci 'feel hungry', kuLir 'feel cold' etc. and the verbs of perception such as teri 'be visible, maNa 'smell', keeL 'be heard', etc., need to considered as a part of copula construction.

- paal ini-kkiR-atu
  milk be sweet-PRE-it
- 'The milk is sweet'
- maruntu kaca-kkiR-atu
  medicine be-bitter-PRE-it
- 'The medicine is bitter'
- enakkup paci-kkiR-atu
  I-DAT feel hungry-PRE-it
- 'I feel hungry'
- enakku kuLir-kiR-atu
  I-DAT feel cold-PRE-it
- 'I feel cold'

8   Conclusion

The copula construction in which the subject is linked to its complement in the predicate position by a link verb known as copula verb is found in many languages with different realizations. We have seen that Tamil uses two main types of copula construction: zero copula construction and verbal copula construction. English only uses verbal copula construction and does not use zero copula construction. There are numerous mismatches and complexities present when attempting to match Tamil copula constructions with English copula constructions. For machine translation between Tamil and English and vice versa, the realisation of these discrepancies is essential. This research identified all of those mismatches and produced computer-readable rules to aid in machine translation between the Tamil and English language pairs.

References

1. Asher, R.E.: Tamil: Descriptive Grammar (Croom Helm Descriptive Grammar). Routledge, Abingdon (1990)
2. Curnow, T.: Towards a cross-linguistic typology of copula constructions. In: Conference of the Australian Linguistic Society (2000)
3. Dorr, B.J.: Machine Translation: A View from the Lexicon, p. 182. MIT Press, Cambridge (1993)
4. Krishnamurti, B.: The Dravidian Languages (Cambridge Language Surveys). Cambridge University Press, Cambridge (2003)
5. Lehmann, T.: A Grammar of Modern Tamil, p. 172. Pondicherry Institute of Linguistics and Culture, Pondicherry (1993)
6. Myler, N.: Complex copula systems as suppletive allomorphy. Glossa J. Gen. Linguist. **51**, 1–43 (2018)
7. Pustet, R.: Copulas: Universals in the Categorization of the Lexicon. Oxford University Press, Oxford (2003)
8. Rajendran, S.: Grammaticalization of verbs in Tamil. Int. J. Dravid. Linguist. **49**, 85–115 (2020)

Language Technologies

Tamil NLP Technologies: Challenges, State of the Art, Trends and Future Scope

S. Rajendran[1], M. Anand Kumar[2](✉), Ratnavel Rajalakshmi[3],
V. Dhanalakshmi[4], P. Balasubramanian[5], and K P Soman[1]

[1] CEN, Amrita Vishwa Vidyapeetham, Coimbatore, India
[2] National Institute of Technology Karnataka, Surathkal, India
m_anandkumar@nitk.edu.in
[3] Vellore Institute of Technology,Chennai, India
rajalakshmi.r@vit.ac.in
[4] Pondicherry University,Pondicherry, India
dhanagiri@pondiuni.ac.in
[5] National Institute of Technology, Tiruchirappalli, India

Abstract. This paper aims to summarize the NLP-based technological development of the Tamil language. Tamil is one of the Dravidian languages that are serious about technological development. This phenomenon is reflected in its activities in developing language technology tools and the resources made for technological development. Tamil has successfully developed tools or systems for speech synthesis and recognition, grammatical analysis of grammar, semantics and social media text, along with machine translation. There are many types of research undertaken to orient towards this achievement. Similarly, many activities are developing resources to facilitate technological development. The activities include preparing text corpora for text including monolingual, parallel and lexical along with speech with lexical resources and grammar. What is needed now is to stock-take the achievement made so far and found out where Tamil is in the arena of technological development and looks forward further to its fast technological development. Computational linguistics in Tamil NLP is gaining more attraction, and various data sets available for research is highlighted in this work for further exploration.

Keywords: Tamil Dravidian Language · Natural Language Processing · Deep Learning

1 Introduction

Technological development for Tamil has had a head start with respect to languages belonging to the Indian subcontinent. Using the opportunities given, the Tamil language, through various projects, has made itself suitable for digitization and accessible through multiple information systems. The liberal funding

© The Author(s), under exclusive license to Springer Nature Switzerland AG 2023
Anand Kumar M et al. (Eds.): SPELLL 2022, CCIS 1802, pp. 73–98, 2023.
https://doi.org/10.1007/978-3-031-33231-9_6

provided by the government agencies both at the state/ provincial level[1] and at the central[2] level, have played a significant role in the technological development of Tamil. The support provided by government organizations has helped in the development of systems and utilities such as the Indo WordNets, Machine translation and other NLP systems. A significant contribution has been made by private entities too in the development of resources for Tamil. Several noteworthy individuals from India and abroad have worked for the advancement of Tamil computing[3]. In terms of technological developments in Tamil a key role has been played by organizations such as Tamil Virtual Academy, Central Institute of Indian Languages (CIIL), Tamil University, AUKBCRC, Amrita Vishwa Vidyapeetham, and Madras University.

Among the government agencies, the Department of Electronics and Information Technology (popularly known as DeitY, has been the principal funding agency for projects involving Tamil resources. The CIIL has contributed significantly to the creation of digital resources in Tamil. The "Resource Centre for Indian Language Technology Solutions (RCILTS) - projects" established at Anna University with the financial support from the Govt. of India's Ministry of Information Technology has also made significant contributions in the same area. "Tamil Virtual Academy" in Tamil Nadu, has sponsored several technological projects for the development of Tamil. The Tamil Internet Conference, conducted annually by the International Forum for Information Technology in Tamil (INFITT) provides a platform to encourage and showcase the technological developments made in the Tamil language.

2   Risks and Challenges in the Technological Development of Tamil

Some of the risks and challenges faced in the technological development of Tamil include,

- Adopting Unicode fonts from among the various other fonts being used,
- Using font converters to converting available digitized material into the Unicode format,
- Creating linguistic resources to be used in digitization and computational systems for Tamil, and
- Digitization.

Distortions such as slang, ungrammatical and corrupt expressions, and code-mixed text exist in the digital media for Tamil at the risk or loss levels. These practices may cause the loss of cultural inflections, linguistic and some features that are unique to a language.

---

[1] http://www.tamilvu.org/en/research-development.
[2] https://tdil.meity.gov.in/Research_Effort.aspx.
[3] https://github.com/nlpc-uom.

The process of converting textual information into the digital form is called digitalization. In the digitalized form the information is represented by units of data called bits, these bits are separately addressed in groups of bytes. The digital form of representing data is required for as computing system understand and operate on binary data. The Digital India initiative has launched some incredible projects such as simultaneous digitization of text and images. Digitization of images and text can happen simultaneously: text images can be captured by scanners and stored as bitmaps. An optical character recognition (OCR) program is used where analysis of bitmaps for areas with respect to dark and bright regions is performed to identify and convert the characters into ASCII form.

Digitizing data helps make it easier to store and share information. An example for this can be a scenario where an original physically accessible manuscript is digitized, then it can be accessed from any device. This obvious advantage has led to a trend of digitalizing culturally and historically significant documents. Sanga Tamil literary pieces and other essential works in Tamil have been digitalized by the Tamil Virtual Academy (TVA), Project Madurai and other organisations.

Several forms of input methods exist for the Tamil language developed specifically to type Tamil language characters. Programs like NHM writer and Azhagi provide fixed and phonetic type layouts. We have listed below the challenges [56] of the present Unicode for the Tamil language.

- The presently available code space for Tamil does not represent about 90% of the characters used in general Tamil text exchanges.
- Combinations of vowel-consonant form the majority of the code space that get excluded. Just like characters in the English Alphabet, vowel-consonant combinations are essential to Tamil, some examples for this are *ka, kA, ki, kI*, etc., but unlike the assumptions made for unicode these are not conjunct characters, ligatures, or glyphs and hence get excluded.
- On an average vowel-consonants constitute 64 to 70% of a plain Tamil text with about 25 to 30% of consonant characters while vowels makeup about 5 to 6% of the text, hence dividing frequently occurring letters such as vowel-consonants and representing them as glyphs is not an efficient approach.
- This form of encoding is based on ISCII (1988). The natural order of sequence is not followed to represent the characters. In order to arrange them in the natural order of a sequence, a complex collation algorithm is needed.
- In this approach multiple code points are used to render single characters. The use of multiple code points cause more harm and can lead to security vulnerabilities and ambiguous combinations being created that require the use of normalization.

3   Language Resources: Data, Knowledge Base, and Resources

The corpus is a significant collection of text in the context of NLP. A corpus can be of various types, such as corpora for text, image, speech corpus and so on.

3.1 Text Corpora

As part of the Technology Development Scheme for Indian Languages (TDIL), a
45 million-word corpus[4] in Scheduled Languages has been developed under the
coordination of the CIIL. The information on the Tamil Text and Speech Corpus
in CIIL is detailed in Table.1. The same has been converted into UNICODE
format by CIIL in association with Lancaster University. Users have access to
this format of corpora as well as the Lancaster University corpora[5].

Tamil Virtual Academy, Chennai seeks to develop a Tamil corpus bank of
international standards. A corpus of 200 million words is now being extracted
from Sangam, Medieval, and Modern Tamil. Tamil POS-tagged monolingual
corpus was developed by Jawaharlal Nehru University, New Delhi as part of the
Indian Languages, Corpora Initiative phase-II (ILCI phase-II) project, which
was sponsored by the MeitY, Government of India.

NLP team at Amrita developed Tamil POS tagged corpus[6] of size 227k words
are available on request [79]. AUKBC provides access to a sizable (515K tokens),
manually annotated POS-tagged corpus[7] for Tamil.

3.2 Corpora for Speech

According to the report of ILTPDC,Tamil Speech Data - ASR is available for
download. More than 62000 audio files from 1000 Tamil speakers are included in
this corpus. The Tamil Speech data file contains words, phonetic representations,
and text transcripts for audio. The size of this corpus, which was created for the
Agricultural Product domain, is 5.7 GB.

In this database of Tamil speech recognition, 450 native Tamil speakers were
chosen from Tamil Nadu based on their age (16–20, 21–50, and 51+), gender,
dialectal region, and surroundings (such as public spaces, offices and home environments). Each speaker used an in-built microphone recorder to capture text in
a noisy environment. The stereo recordings, along with the extracted channels
are included in the relevant files. This data contains a text file, an audio file, and
ZIP-encoded NIST files.

3.3 Parallel Corpora

As a part of EILMT project [35], the parallel corpora for English-Tamil has been
developed and available at TDIL[8] website. Bilingual English-Tamil data for NLP
research has been gathered from publicly accessible sources under the project
"EnTam: An English-Tamil Parallel Corpus" [121]. These parallel corpora include
texts from domains like news, movie and Bible. In the shared task on Machine

---

[4] http://corpora.ciil.org/wordcorpora.htm.
[5] http://www.emille.lancs.ac.uk/home.htm.
[6] POS tagged corpus is available on request http://www.nlp.amrita.edu/nlpcorpus.html.
[7] http://www.au-kbc.org/nlp/corpusrelease.html.
[8] http://tdil-dc.in.

Translation in Indian languages (MTIL) [71], English-Tamil parallel corpora[9] of size 139k (including 92k from TDIL) was released by CEN, Amrita in 2017.

Table 1. Corpus Statistics.

Text Corpus	
Corpus Name	**Word Count**
Tamil CIIL Corpus	8068759
Tamil Magazine Corpus	1805164
Tamil News paper (Web Crawled)	1059561
Total Raw Text	10933484
Annotated Corpus	
POS tagged	
Tagset Name	**Word Count**
BIS Tagset	1881646
LDC-IL Tagset	58557
Chunking	
Statistics Type	**Count**
Sentence Count	20972
Chunk Count	160386
Speech Corpus	
Statistics Type	**Count**
Total Speakers	453
Total Hours	213:37:27

3.4 Lexical Resources

WordNets can be used as online lexical databases designed to discover information across languages for machine translation, information extraction, and other NLP applications. Under the Dravidian WordNet project supported by DietY, Tamil WordNet was developed based on Hindi WordNet. The four main Dravidian languages have been connected to about 30,000 synsets [103]. The Dravidian WordNet is a part of the IndoWordNet project.

Amrita Vishwa Vidyapeetham, Coimbatore has constructed Tamil visual Onto-thesaurus constituting of 50000 words. Tamil Virtual Academy, Chennai funded it. Tamil vocabulary is taxonomically organized and characterised by many types of lexical or semantic relationships. [133] propose building Ontological structure for Tamil vocabulary and how this is converted into a knowledge representation and user-friendly retrieval system. English-Tamil glossary and the parallel corpora prepared by the NLPC, University of Moratuwa are available online [50].

---

[9] Parallel Corpus is available on request http://www.nlp.amrita.edu/nlpcorpus.html.

3.5 Grammars

Tamil holds all types of grammar, from classical to contemporary, including Chomskiian transformational generative grammar principles. For computing Tamil, formalizations based on Paniniyan grammar, Dependency Grammar, Tag Grammar, LFG (Lexical Functional Grammar), Context-Free Grammar (CFG), Context-Sensitive Grammar (CSG), and Phrase Structure Grammar (PSG) have been used. The ILMT project developed Paniyan formalism, while the ELMT project supported by CDAC, Pune, utilized Tag formalism. To create its own MT system between English and Tamil Amrita Vishwa Vidyapeetham adopted Dependency Grammar.

4   Language Technology: Tools, Grammatical Technologies and Applications

Notable grammatical analysis of natural language consists of three phases: phonological analysis, morphological analysis and syntactic analysis. The word order, verb tense, and inflection of Tamil are all comparatively open. The words in Tamil are created by combining many morphemes because the language is agglutinative. Tamil words are constructed from a root and further grammatical accretions. The roots of Tamil words can be found at the monosyllabic level regardless of their length, complexity, or word type by carefully removing consecutive accretions. Traditionally, a Tamil word is divided into a maximum of six parts : a) *pakuthy* (prime-stem), b) *sandhi*—(junction), c) *vihaaram* (variation), d)*iTainilai* (middle part), e) *saariyai* (enunciator) and f) *vikuti* (terminator) in that order. For example, a word, *ndaTantanan* meaning '(He) walked', is made up of the morphemes: *naTa* + *t(n)* + *t* + *an* + *an*. The prime-stem has two grammatical additions: the middle section and the terminator. The terminator designates the gender, while the middle part designates the tense. Typically, the primary component of a word that determines its meaning is the prime-stem.

4.1 Word Segmentation or Tokenization

The method of tokenizing involves dividing the provided text into token-sized pieces. The tokens could be letters, numbers, or punctuation. Word boundaries are located through tokenization to accomplish this task. Word boundaries are the location where one word ends and the following word begins. Word segmentation is another name for tokenization. The agglutinative languages, like Tamil, do not, and text segmentation in those languages is a big undertaking that necessitates understanding of the vocabulary and morphology of the language's terms. All Tamil-focused machine translation systems must begin with tokenization or word segmentation.

4.2 Stemming and Lemmatization

Stemming reduces inflected words to their word stem, base, or root form-typically a written word form-in linguistic morphology and information retrieval.

Related words are often sufficient to map to the same stem, even if it is not a valid root, rather than requiring the stem to match the word's morphological root exactly. Since the 1960 s,s, computer science has investigated stemming algorithms. Many search engines use query expansion, or conflation, as a method of treating terms with the same stem as synonyms. A stemming programme, stemming algorithm, or stemmer is a computer programme or subroutine that stems words. For Tamil, numerous stemmers have been created. [148]. They operate with a corpus of texts that have been divided up into words or tokenized. The author demonstrated speech synthesis using a Hidden Markov Model (HMM) in Tamil. [132]. In order to maintain the underlying word, Vallikannu R et el. developed a simpler stemming method. He also used Tamil SentiWordNet to classify the sentiment of Tamil movies (TSWN) [119].

A word's inflected forms are removed during the lemmatization process in linguistics so that the word's lemma, or dictionary form, can be used to represent it as a single entity. Lemmatizer is the term for a computer system that lemmatizes text. Lemmatizers have been created by Anna University, Amrita Vishwa Vidyapeetham and AUKBC [69],. An method created by Rethanya et al. stems and generates the lemma utilising two distinct modules. [129]. Mercy Evangeline and colleagues created a frequency-based feature extraction technique for Tamil text document classification. The traditional preprocessing of documents has been implemented, and word tagging is carried out using Tamil-specific morphophonemic criteria. [48]. A model for categorising Tamil documents based on LSTM was proposed by Rajkumar et al. Tamil documents are classified using the model, which also includes the customary preprocessing procedures of feature extraction, feature selection, and classification. [109]. A method for identifying missing words in Tamil texts using n-grams was given by Sakuntharaj et al. [131].

To improve Tamil text summarization for online Tamil news items, Dhivyaa et al. presented the Generative Pre-trained Transformer 2 (GPT-2) model. [47]. Vasantharajan et al. created an ensemble method that blends deep learning and transfer learning models to find offensive YouTube video. [150]. Sakthivel used computational linguistics and python libraries to discuss the preprocessing methods, applications, and problems of text mining. [151]. After completing text prepossessing from Dravidian code-mixed data in order to categorise objectionable language, Agalya proposed SVM and Logistic classifier model for training. [2].

4.3   Morphological Analysis

The process of dissecting words into their individual morphemes and determining the morpheme's class is known as morphological analysis. Such a strategy is impossible in languages like Tamil, a heavily agglutinated Indian language, where each dictionary entry has thousands of potential word variants. For many NLP applications, including machine translation, developing morphological analyzer is essential (MT). Based on the module's foundation in the Anusaraka Project, Rajendran created the first morphological analyzer for Tamil. AUKBCRC later made improvements to it. CIIL made the largest contribution in creating a morphological analyzer for Tamil. [51,53], AUKBCRC [83,116,155,156], Anna University [10], Amrita Vishwa Vidyapeetham, Coimbatore [6,7,44,73,82,86], Tamil University [102,104,108], Central University, Hyderabad [17,34,123], Madras University [37] and Annamalai University [52]. There are also some efforts made by individuals, such as the morphological analyzer created by Ganesan and the Tamil Word Processor by Deyvasundram. Akilan et al. have developed a morphological analyzer for classical text using a rule-based methodology. Different morphological analyzers have been created for Tamil that employ various methodologies, including rule-based methodology, sequence labelling methodology, and machine learning methodology. Other nations have made a few important contributions as well. [78,87,120,124,125,138].

Suriyah et al. developed Piripori, a morphological analyser for Tamil. It follows word-level morphological rules [145]. Krishnan et al. presented the foremost word analogy dataset for Tamil language and rules-based segmenter was used for capturing morphology as well as meta-embedding techniques [67]. Rajasekar and Angelina Geetha proposed three approaches for morphological analysis, and they are based on rules, paradigms and n-grams for Gynecological Tamil documents [101]. Premjith and Soman are implemented a morphological synthesis at the character level using Deep learning models, namely, RNN, LSTM and GRU [94].

4.4 Morphological Generation

Morphological production, which changes a word's internal representation into its surface form, is the opposite of morphological analysis. Morphological generators are computers that do morphological generation. The morphological generator or word generator was created by Tamil-targeting machine translation systems. The morphological generator for Tamil was developed with help from the ILILMT and EILMT consortium projects To meet the needs of their NLP projects, Central University in Hyderabad, CIIL ([34,122]), AUKBCRC ([85]), Amrita Vishwa Vidyapeetham ([6,86]), and Anna University ([10]) have created a morphological generator for Tamil. ThamizhiMorph parser designed using Finite-State-Transducer (FST) by Sarveswaran et al. which serves as extendable Morphological Analyser cum Generator (MAG) for Tamil [139].

4.5 Part-of-speech Tagging

Identify the parts of speech for each word in the following phrase. Numerous parts of speech can be used with many common words. Such ambiguity is present in some languages but not in others. Such ambiguity is especially common in languages with little inflectional morphology, like English. For the purpose of POS tagging Indian languages, including Tamil, numerous tagsets have been created. According to Baskaran (2008):1, Microsoft, India tried to create "A standard part of speech tagset architecture for Indian Languages." The tagset is hierarchical. Flat tagset is the alternative tagset for Tamil. For all Deity-funded projects, including the Indian Language Corpora Initiative (ILCI) project, TDIL created the BIS tagset for Indian languages. The POS tagger is the name of the programme that determines the parts of speech in each word. Many organisations and individuals use BIS tagsets to create POS taggers for Tami.lPOS tagger for Tamil has been created by CIIL, AUKBCRC ([16,91]), Amrita Vishwa Vidyapeetham ([7,31,43]), Anna University ([54,90]), and a few other people. There are some noteworthy contributions from other countries as well; see Ranganathan 2001:1 and Thayaparan 2018. There are initiatives to enhance the current POS tagging systems, according to Selvam (2009:1). Rule-based techniques and machine learning approaches are the two primary categories of POS tagging approaches. [7,43]. [105] discusses the complexity of POS tagging in Tamil. [68] proposes an LSTM based POS tagger for the Tamil language which used the character to word model instead of a traditional word lookup table.

Sarveswaran and Dias developed ThamizhiPOSt to provide an efficient contextual neural POS tagger [137]. Ezhilarasi and Uma Maheswari proposed a neural model like Bi-LSTM model for POS Tag classification ans prediction of words from the Palaeographic stone inscription script [49]. Visuwalingam et al. presented a deep learning-based POS tagger for Tamil language using Bi-LSTM [154]. Sivasankar et al. proposed an ESD-DA model that used enhanced tamil dictionary with multi-domain datasets for Tamil reviews sentimental analysis [141]. Authors utilized Ripple down rules-based POS tagger (RDRPOS) for the translated source and target domain reviews. The authors proposed sequential deep learning models to address the problem of POS tagging for the Tamil language [13]. Selvi et al. proposed hybrid POS tagger algorithm for Tamil language using cross-lingual transformation learning techniques [140]. The performance of the proposed model, which combines methods like the Mining-based methodology (MT), the Keyword-based tagging algorithm (KT), the Verb pattern-based tagging algorithm (VT), and the Unique pair occurrence-tagging algorithm (UT), has significantly improved.

4.6 Chunking

Instead of using the time-consuming and expensive complete syntactic parsing, Chunking Task has been chosen. Sentence chunking is sufficient for NLP tasks like machine translation. Chunker separates a sentence into its main, non-overlapping phrases and gives each chunk a label. Many go beyond just straightforward chunking, while others look for NPs. Between tagging and complete parsing, chunking lies. Tamil has a complex morphological and syntactical structure because it is an agglutinate language. It is a reasonably free word order language, yet in phrasal and clausal construction, it behaves like a fixed word order language. Consequently, chunking in Tamil is a less difficult process than POS tagging. AUKBC-RC developed a Noun Phrase chunker for Tamil [115]. An elaborate work on chunking in Tamil was undertaken by [42,43].

4.7 Named Entity Recognition (NER)

Information extraction (IEsub-task)'s of named entity recognition (NER) looks for and classifies specific entities in a body or bodies of texts. Entity identification, entity chunking, and entity extraction are all common names for NER.The NER System extracts from a given stream of text the elements that correspond to proper names, such as names of people or places, and the type of each such name (e.g. person, location, organisation). A few attempts have been made to create general NER systems for Tamil. There have been a few tries to develop general NER approaches for Tamil. These are machine learning techniques, including SVMs, CRFs, Hidden Markov Models, and Maximum Entropy Markov Models (CRF) [80,81,153] [1]. [57] propose an LSTM-based model for NER for the Tamil language using distributed representation. [38] [128] summarises the disaster management dataset's named entity extraction from online social media content in Tamil using n-gram embedding.

4.8 Shallow Parsing

Following are the four modules that make up the shallow parser: I a part-of-speech tagger that assigns POS tags to tokenized texts, I Chunker, which divides a sentence into its key, distinct phrases (noun phrase, verb phrase, etc.) (ii) Morphological Analyzer, which analyses the words into morphemes and provides English glosses (iii) Chunker, which determines which relations the chunks in a sentence have with the main verb given the POS tag and chunks in the sentence (subject, object, location, etc.). Dhanalakshmi started the field of shallow parsing study in Tamil. [42,43]. The primary objective of the study was to create a Tamil shallow parser. In an effort to extract meaningful syntactic information from Sri Lankan Tamil sentences, ariaratnam (2014) aimed to construct a shallow parser that assigns a partial structure to natural language sentences.

4.9 Syntactic Parsing

Parsing allows for the grammatical analysis (parse tree) of a given sentence. The two primary types of parsing are Constituency parsing and Dependency parsing. Dependency parsing focuses on the relationships between words in a phrase (identifying things like Primary Objects and predicates)(PCFG), while constituency parsing concentrates on creating the Parse Tree using a probabilistic context-free grammar (PCFG). Tamil "cite" shanmugam2004 has a parse representation created by AUKBC. For Tamil, various syntactic parser types have been tried They consist of lexical parsing, dependency parsing, statistical parsing, and TAG formalism-based parsing. Semantic parsing, Penn Treebank-Based Syntactic Parsing, Shallow Parsing, Structural Parsing Using Phrase Structure Hybrid Language, Structural Parsing Using Phrase Structure Hybrid Language Model, Dependency Parsing Using Rule-Based and Corpus-Based Approaches, and Dependency Parsing Using Rule-Based and Corpus-Based Approaches were all developed. Dependency Parser for Tamil Classical Literature: kuruntokai [45], is used to find the dependency structure and the relations of the words with the main verb or the root word in kuruthokai, Tamil classical literature.

ThamizhiUdp, created by Sarveswaran et al., is a neural network-based dependency parser that offers a full pipeline for the dependency parsing of Tamil language text using the Universal Dependency formalism. [136]. Kumar et al. presented an innovative method that uses word-to-word dependency tagging with BERT models to enhance the Tamil malt parser's performance. Parameswari et al. built morphosyntactically annotated treebank for modern written Tamil language [66]. In this work, Universal Dependencies (UD) approach employed that support the implementation and evaluation of Tamil dependency parsers. Anbukkarasi and Varadhaganapathy proposed a combination of neural network and rule-based approach to develop a Tamil grammar checker. It has been used for spell-checking, consonant error handling, subject-verb agreement errors and long component letter error [14].

4.10   Identification of the Clause Boundary

The smallest grammatical articulate that can express a proposition is a clause. A verb or verb group (a verb plus its auxiliary) and any explicit or implicit arguments for the verb are contained in this group of words, which are ordered in a specific order. [110]. A number of NLP systems, such as machine translation, parallel corpus alignment, information extraction, syntactic parsing, automatic summarization, and speech applications, are enhanced by the inclusion of clause boundaries in a phrase. On clause boundary identification in Tamil, AUKBC-RC has made significant progress. [110,114]. [46] used dependency parsing to attempt to identify Tamil clause boundaries.

4.11   Speech Recognition

Text to voice, sometimes known as STT(Speech To Text), is a challenging NLP problem. Yegnanarayana, Hema A. Murthy, A.G. Ramakrishnan, and T. Nagarajan citekhan2001development provided the foundation for converting voice into text.Utilizing neural networks and finite-state transducers, A.G. Ramakrishnan created an automatic speech recognition system for Tamil that can identify utterances using a wide range of vocabulary. Tamil speech to text converter is available on Google Play. Azhagi for Android Voice input is a STT in more than 100 languages (Voice input or Speech recognition). Users of the Azhagi Android app can type, speak, and write messages in a number of languages, including Tamil.With Solvan, a sophisticated Tamil text-to-speech system, Sellinam is the most widely used input method app for mobile devices on both Android and Mac. [146,147] Authors made a contribution to Tamil STT system development. [59] proposes an efficient Continuous Tamil Speech Recognition technique. [77] proposes a bidirectional RNN with a self-organizing map for Tamil speech recognition. Zhang et al. examined three languages such as Tamil, Malay and English and extracted robust features using music processing and vector representation learning [157]. Extended byte pair encoding (BPE) and the Morfessor tool were developed by

Bharathi et al. to segment words into smaller units for automatic speech recognition. [93]. The model used a weighted finite state transducers (WFST) architecture and maximum likelihood (ML) and Viterbi estimation approaches to learn the subword dictionary from a sizable text corpus.

4.12 Speech Synthesis

There have been numerous attempts to render written text as speech. IIT Chennai, IISc Bangalore, and the International School of Dravidian Linguistics (ISDL), Trivandrum, are the pioneering institutes participating in the development of TTS synthesis. ISDL created a very effective Tamil TTS synthesis system [144]. Yegnanarayana, an IIT Chennai student at the time, started the TTS synthesis of Tamil research. Following him, his student Hema A. Murthy made significant contributions to this field of study. Tamil text to speech software was created by A.G. Ramachandran from IISc, Bangalore. [117]. T. Nagarajan created a Tamil Speech-Enabled Interactive Enquiry System with funding from Chennai's Tamil Virtual Academy (https://www.tamilvu.org/en/content/tamil-computing-tools). The SSN team has put out a technique to enhance signal quality and maintain understandability in the presence of stationary and non-stationary noise.

4.13 Optical Character Recognition

OCR identifies the text that corresponds to an image of printed text. Tamil has seen the development of numerous OCR systems. OCR for Tamil was created by Krishnamoorthy, who is well recognised for it. [33]. The Indian Language Technology Proliferation and Deployment Center (ILTPDC) offers a free OCR programme called e-Aksharayan-Tamil OCR. An extensive OCR for Tamil was created by IISc Bangalore. The font and size of the input are irrelevant to how the Tamil OCR technology operates [15]. Other systems are attempted by some researchers [36] [97] [96].

5   Semantic Analysis

Finding synonyms, disambiguating word sense, building question answering systems, translating across natural languages, and populating a knowledge base are only a few of the complicated tasks that can be categorized under the subject of semantics. Before attempting to fix a semantic issue, one must do a full morphological and syntactical study.

5.1   Word Sense Disambiguation

In this context, various definitions may be used. With the use of a WSD system, the right meaning can be selected from among several possibilities. A number of people have made serious efforts to create WSD systems in Tamil. As far as

I can tell, only [21] has made any serious effort to do WSD in Tamil. WSD in Tamil has been attempted previously by [106] and [149], but with little success. In [8] , the author presents a WSD solution in Tamil by employing feature-rich support vector machines. Cross-lingual preposition disambiguation for machine translation is promoted as a compelling use case for a WSD system, and both [8,74] support this approach. [134] proposed combining WSD and Semantic Web for statistical machine translation from Tamil to English.

5.2   Question Answering

Find the solution to a problem posed in natural language. Unlike the usual questions, which have one right answer (such as "What is the capital of Tamilnadu?"), more philosophical inquiries (such as "What is the meaning of life?") are also taken into account. Complex issues have been explored in recent works. Some question-and-answer systems have been written in Tamil. [152] created software to generate questions in Tamil automatically.

5.3   Relationship Extraction

Given a portion of text, relationship extraction determines the connections between identified entities (e.g. who is married to whom). In [84] cause-effect relations in Tamil using CRFs have been explored.

5.4   Paraphrase Identification

Identifying a paraphrase is the task of figuring out if two sentences mean the same thing or not. The first open-source corpora for detecting paraphrases in Indian languages like Tamil are being released by the DPIL 2016 shared task [75]. This particular dataset is now available[10] for research activities [9].

5.5   Automatic Text Summarization

A text summarization algorithm turns a piece of text into an easy-to-read synopsis. It is often used to understand well-known types of text, like newspaper articles in the business section. A few different systems were made to instantly simplify different kinds of Tamil texts [20,130]. Sarika et al. altered the Text Rank algorithm to sum up both Tamil and English newsgroup datasets [135].

5.6   Co-reference Resolution

The coreference resolution algorithm figures out which words ("makes mention of") in a given sentence or larger piece of text refer to the same topics ("entities"). Anaphora resolution is a kind of task that has to do with making sure that pronouns are used with the right nouns or names. The AUKBCRC lab has done a number of related research projects [3–5,111–113] [40,41,142] [92].

---

[10] DPIL corpus is available on request http://www.nlp.amrita.edu/nlpcorpus.html.

5.7   Text Generation

Text creation is the process of turning information stored in computer databases or semantic meanings into a form that people can read. A system or programme that can make text can be called a "text generator." The generation of Tamil lyrics from melodies was something that [11,12] tried out. In [64] researchers have come up with a way for the automatic generation of Tamil content. The idea in [143] is to make a language relationship to synthesize Tamil stories using hints provided.

5.8   Machine Translation

Machine translation is software that automatically converts text from one human language to another. It's a tough one, and it belongs to a class of issues known as "AI-complete," meaning that they can only be solved using all the many kinds of information that humans have (grammar, facts, etc.).

Anusaraka for Tamil. Rajendran started making the first MT system (Anusaraka) for Hindi to Tamil translation at IIT in Kanpur using the Anusaraka framework, which was later completed by AUKBCRC.

ANUVADAKSH. The consortium institutes behind ANUVADAKSH have integrated TAG (tree-adjoining grammar), MTs based on statistics (SMT), rules (AnalGen), and examples (EBMT) into a single system. CDAC-Pune serves as the consortium's leader with help from TDIL.

Indian Language to Indian Language Machine Translation. Machine translation (MT) systems for Indian languages were created as part of a collaboration project called "Indian Language to Indian Language Machine Translation," which was supported by TDIL. Several MT systems with a focus on Tamil have been created for this initiative. There are several such systems, including one that converts Hindi, Telugu, and Malayalam to Tamil.

Other Systems. For his dissertation, Anand Kumar M (2013) [79] used computational linguistics to create a statistical machine translation system that can translate between English and Tamil. A derived statistical machine translation technique from English to Tamil was proposed in [70]. There is a group working on an automated method to translate between Tamil and English called Machine Translation in Indian Languages [71]. Machine translation from English to Tamil has been proposed using a rule-based MT system [107] [63,72].

The AUKBCRC has created a rule-based MT framework for English-to-Tamil translation [39]. The Russian-to-Tamil translation project at Tamil University began quite some time ago [32]. Rajendran attempted to create a linguistic machine translation aid [60].

With the use of pre-trained word representations and fine-tuning the hyperparameters, the Encoder-Decoder based approach for translation is enhanced in [58]. In order to increase the accuracy of translations, the authors of [65] offer a work based on the divergence index (DI) and how it is constructed. Researchers in [24,25,30] looked into how using orthographic data could enhance translation software for Dravidian languages. The impact of phrase-induced mixed computer translation of English to Tamil is proposed and investigated in [88].

6   Social Media Text Analysis

In recent days, the usage of Tamil language in social media contents has increased, as many people prefer to post their comments in their native language.

6.1   Sentiment Analysis

In order to evaluate "polarity" towards particular products, sentiment analysis frequently uses online reviews to extract subjective information from documents. It is useful for assessing public sentiment in marketing and social media. Many attempts of various types have undertaken for developing sentiment analysis in Tamil [18], [62,89], [118] A corpus containing code-mixed Tamil language was developed by Bharathiraj et al., [27] for sentiment analysis. This dataset contains 15,744 Youtube comments which is a gold-standard annotated corpus for sentiment analysis in Tamil-English. To encourage the NLP research community, shared task has been organized for sentiment analysis of Dravidian languages [29], in which 44,020 Code-mixed Tamil comments with 5 different categories are released. Many machine learning and deep learning architectures were employed by the researchers to perform the sentiment analysis [22,61].

6.2   Offensive Content Identification

Advancements in technology has helped the people in various ways to disseminate the information quickly. But, it has also a downside, as people use social media to express their opinion or offensive comments publicly. To identify such offensive posts in social media, an exclusive Tamil dataset has been created by Bharathiraja et al., in addition to code-mixed Tamil-English dataset. The first one contains Tamil YouTube comments in native script and has a total of 6531 comments, with 1271 offensive comments and 5260 non-offensive comments. [26]. Many approaches were tried to categorize these offensive comments in Tamil. As Tamil is a rich morphological language, the effect of stop words with enhanced Stemming algorithm has been applied with transformer based models to identify the offensive text by [100]. As the dataset is a highly imbalanced one with less offensive comment, different techniques were used to address this issue with multi-linugal translation based approaches [55]. The code-mixed Tamil-English dataset for offensive content identification is also made available for the researchers, in which six categories of tweets, viz., Offensive Targeted Insult Group (2557), Offensive Targeted Insult Individual (2343), Offensive Targeted Insult Other (454), Offensive Untargeted (2906), Not Offensive (25425), and not-Tamil (1454). This code-mixed dataset also has an imbalanced distribution. [28]. Many teams participated in this task and various approaches were tried to identify the offensive content in code-mixed Tamil [19, 99].

In addition to the above offensive content classification tasks, the datasets are available for toxic span identification also, in Tamil language, that was developed by Ravikiran et.al. [126]. This dataset consists of 4786 Tamil-English comments with 6202 annotated spans. Different teams attempted to find the solution for this problem of offensive span identification [127]. Transformer based models [76]and sequence based models [98] were tried by the teams and there is a scope for further improvement.

The abusive comments analysis is also explored on Tamil YouTube comments by [95]. This dataset contains 12,785 Tamil abusive comments that are categorized to Homophobia, Misandry, Counter-speech, Misogyny, Xenophobia, Transpho-bic. Many attempts made by various researchers show that, [23, 98] the deep learning methods with suitable embedding techniques can improve the performance of classifiers in detecting abusive comments.

7   Conclusion and Future Scope

The use of software for language processing in the Tamil language began much before any other Indian language. The use of machine translation for bidirectional translation between Russian and Tamil started in the early 1980 s.s. Work on using computing for the Tamil language by universities, industries and other institutions started even earlier than this period. There is no doubt that Tamil has overcome many of the difficulties and challenges thrown at it during its technological development. It has solved the problem of having a standard code representation during the digitization phase by adapting to the Unicode format. Today, there is a standard way for computing systems to accept Tamil as input due to adopting a standard format. Now, one can read, write and transmit text without any technical problems with respect to format and representation. This has resulted in the resolution of issues in text analysis and text generation, along with the development of quite a few of the text-to-speech and speech recognition systems in use today. Tangible results have been realized in the form of the various forms of digital corpora available in Tamil, along with readily available lexical resources in the form of machine-readable dictionaries and the WordNet built for it. Today, Google offers an excellent English-to-Tamil translator along with OCR and speech recognition systems. The digitization program promoted by the government of India has been successfully implemented for Tamil. Computer Scientists and Linguistic experts (including language experts) have worked for hand in hand to meet the scheduled targets within the stipulated time. Government agencies and departments, both at the state and the centre, have made significant contributions to funding the technological development of Tamil.

Due to the early adoption of digitization in the Tamil language, many natural language processing tools have been developed that include machine translation systems. Several monolingual, bilingual, and multilingual parallel corpora have been developed. These corpora can be used for compiling monolingual, bilingual and multilingual machine-readable dictionaries. Several lexical resources for Tamil have been developed, which can be used for many NLP-oriented tasks in research. The development of computing systems for Tamil has touched all the aspects of NLP, including speech processing and developing text-to-speech and speech-to-text systems. Tamil is at the forefront among Indian languages when considering statistical-based and neural network-based machine translation systems. Many chat-oriented interactive systems are also being developed for the Tamil language. These achievements made in the computing systems for Tamil point to the bright prospects of NLP in Tamil. The widely available benchmark Tamil data sets that are created from Social Media Posts, also gain attraction from various international researchers towards this Tamil language. In the future, one will find many robots talking in Tamil and taking commands.

Acknowledgments. This paper is based on the White paper designed on the META-NET. We express our gratitude to Dr. George Rehm (Head of the META-NET), Prof. Joseph Mariani and Prof.Girish Nath Jha from School of Sanskrit and Indic Studies for the white paper development through close interactions. The complete resource links are available in the Tamil data portal, https://sites.google.com/view/tamilnlp.

References

1. Abinaya, N., John, N., Ganesh, B.H., Kumar, A.M., Soman, K.: Amrita_cen@ fire-2014: Named entity recognition for indian languages using rich features. In: Proceedings of the Forum for Information Retrieval Evaluation, pp. 103–111 (2014)
2. Agalya, T.: Comparative analysis for offensive language identification of Tamil text using SVM and logistic classifier (2021)
3. Akilandeswari, A., Devi, S.L.: Conditional random fields based pronominal resolution in Tamil. Int. J. Comput. Sci. Eng. **5**(6), 567 (2013)
4. Akilandeswari, A., Lalitha Devi, S.: Anaphora Resolution in Tamil Novels. In: Prasath, R., O'Reilly, P., Kathirvalavakumar, T. (eds.) MIKE 2014. LNCS (LNAI), vol. 8891, pp. 268–277. Springer, Cham (2014). https://doi.org/10.1007/978-3-319-13817-6_26
5. Akilandeswari, A., Devi, S.L.: Tamil pronominal resolution boosted by sentence transformation. Aust. J. Basic Appl. Sci. **9**(23), 566–572 (2015)
6. Anand Kumar, M., Dhanalakshmi, V., Rekha, R., Soman, K., Rajendran, S.: A novel data driven algorithm for Tamil morphological generator. Int. J. Comput. Appl. **975**, 8887 (2010)
7. Anand Kumar, M., Dhanalakshmi, V., Soman, K., Rajendran, S.: A sequence labeling approach to morphological analyzer for Tamil language. (IJCSE) Int. J. Comput. Sci. Eng. **2**(6), 1944–195 (2010)
8. Anand Kumar, M., Rajendran, S., Soman, K.: Tamil word sense disambiguation using support vector machines with rich features. Int. J. Appl. Eng. Res. **9**(20), 7609–20 (2014)

9. Anand Kumar, M., Singh, S., Ramanan, P., Sinthiya, V., Soman, K., et al.: Creating paraphrase identification corpus for Indian languages: Opensource data set for paraphrase creation. In: Handbook of Research on Emerging Trends and Applications of Machine Learning, pp. 157–170. IGI Global (2020)
10. Anandan, P., Saravanan, K., Parthasarathi, R., Geetha, T.: Morphological analyzer for Tamil. In: International Conference on Natural language Processing. **3**, 12–22 (2002)
11. Ananth Ramakrishnan, A., Devi, S.L.: An alternate approach towards meaningful lyric generation in Tamil. In: Proceedings of the NAACL HLT 2010 Second Workshop on Computational Approaches to Linguistic Creativity, pp. 31–39 (2010)
12. Ananth Ramakrishnan, A., Kuppan, S., Devi, S.L.: Automatic generation of Tamil lyrics for melodies. In: Proceedings of the workshop on computational approaches to linguistic creativity, pp. 40–46 (2009)
13. Anbukkarasi, S., Varadhaganapathy, S.: Deep learning based Tamil parts of speech (POS) tagger. Technical Sciences, Bulletin of the Polish Academy of Sciences (2021)
14. Anbukkarasi, S., Varadhaganapathy, S.: Neural network-based error handler in natural language processing. Neural Comput. Appl., pp. 1–10 (2022)
15. Aparna, K.G., Ramakrishnan, A.G.: A Complete Tamil Optical Character Recognition System. In: Lopresti, D., Hu, J., Kashi, R. (eds.) DAS 2002. LNCS, vol. 2423, pp. 53–57. Springer, Heidelberg (2002). https://doi.org/10.1007/3-540-45869-7_6
16. Arulmozhi, P., Sobha, L., Kumara Shanmugam, B.: Parts of speech tagger for Tamil. In: Symposium on Indian Morphology, Phonology Language Engineering, pp. 19–21 (2004)
17. Arulmozhi, S.: Aspects of inflectional morphophonology - a computational approach. Unpublished Ph.D. Thesis (1998)
18. Arunselvan, S., Anand Kumar, M., Soman, K.: Sentiment analysis of Tamil movie reviews via feature frequency count. Int. J. Appl. Eng. Res. **10**(20), 17934–17939 (2015)
19. Bharathi, B., Agnusimmaculate, A.S.: SSNCSE_NLP@DravidianLangTech-EACL2021: Offensive language identification on multilingual code mixing text. In: Proceedings of the First Workshop on Speech and Language Technologies for Dravidian Languages, pp. 313–318. Assoc. Comput. Linguist., Kyiv (2021), https://aclanthology.org/2021.dravidianlangtech-1.45
20. Banu, M., Karthika, C., Sudarmani, P., Geetha, T.: Tamil document summarization using semantic graph method. In: International Conference on Computational Intelligence and Multimedia Applications (ICCIMA 2007) 2, pp. 128–134 IEEE (2007)
21. Baskaran, S.: Semantic analyser for word sense disambiguation. Unpublished MS Thesis (2002)
22. Bharathi, B., Samyuktha, G.: Machine learning based approach for sentiment analysis on multilingual code mixing text. In: Working Notes of FIRE 2021-Forum for Information Retrieval Evaluation. CEUR (2021)
23. Bharathi, B., Varsha, J.: Ssncse nlp@ tamilnlp-acl2022: Transformer based approach for detection of abusive comment for Tamil language. In: Proceedings of the Second Workshop on Speech and Language Technologies for Dravidian Languages, pp. 158–164 (2022)
24. Chakravarthi, B.R.: Leveraging orthographic information to improve machine translation of under-resourced languages. Ph.D. thesis, NUI Galway (2020)

25. Chakravarthi, B.R., Arcan, M., McCrae, J.P.: Comparison of Different Orthographies for Machine Translation of Under-Resourced Dravidian Languages. In: 2nd Conference on Language, Data and Knowledge (LDK 2019). Open Access Series in Informatics (OASIcs) 70, pp. 61–614. Schloss Dagstuhl-Leibniz-Zentrum fuer Informatik, Dagstuhl, Germany (2019). https://doi.org/10.4230/OASIcs.LDK. 2019.6,http://drops.dagstuhl.de/opus/volltexte/2019/10370
26. Chakravarthi, B.R., et al.: Overview of the HASOC-DravidianCodeMix Shared Task on Offensive Language Detection in Tamil and Malayalam. In: Working Notes of FIRE 2021 - Forum for Information Retrieval Evaluation. CEUR (2021)
27. Chakravarthi, B.R., Muralidaran, V., Priyadharshini, R., McCrae, J.P.: Corpus creation for sentiment analysis in code-mixed Tamil-English text. CoRR abs/2006.00206 (2020). https://arxiv.org/abs/2006.00206
28. Chakravarthi, B.R., Priyadharshini, R., Kumar M, A., Krishnamurthy, P., Sherly, E.: Proceedings of the First Workshop on Speech and Language Technologies for Dravidian Languages. Assoc. Comput. Linguist., Kyiv (2021). https:// aclanthology.org/2021.dravidianlangtech-1.0
29. Chakravarthi, B.R., etal.: Findings of the sentiment analysis of dravidian languages in code-mixed text. CoRR abs/2111.09811 (2021), https://arxiv.org/abs/ 2111.09811
30. Chakravarthi, B.R., Rani, P., Arcan, M., McCrae, J.P.: A survey of orthographic information in machine translation. arXiv e-prints pp. arXiv-2008 (2020)
31. Chandrakanth, D., Anand Kumar, M., Gunasekaran, S.: Part-of-speech tagging for Tamil language. Proc. Int. J. Commun. Eng. 6(6), 1 (2012)
32. Chellamuthu, K.: Russian to Tamil machine translation system at Tamil university. In: Proceedings of Tamil Internet 2002 Conference. http://infitt.org/ti2002/ papers/16CHELLA. pdf) (2002)
33. Chinnuswamy, P., Krishnamoorthy, S.G.: Recognition of handprinted Tamil characters. Pattern Recogn. 12(3), 141–152 (1980)
34. Cruz, W.: Parsing and generation of Tamil verbs in GSMORPH. Unpublished M.Phil. Dissertation (2002)
35. Darbari, H., et al.: Enabling linguistic idiosyncrasy in anuvadaksh. Vishwabharat, July-Dec (2013)
36. Deepa, R.A., Rao, R.R.: A novel nearest interest point classifier for offline Tamil handwritten character recognition. Pattern Anal. Appl. 23(1), 199–212 (2020)
37. Deivasundaram, N., Gopal, A.: Computational morphology of Tamil. Word Structure in Dravidian, Kuppam: Dravidian University, pp. 406–410 (2003)
38. Devi, G.R., Kumar, M.A., Soman, K.: Extraction of named entities from social media text in Tamil language using n-gram embedding for disaster management. In: Studies in Computational Intelligence, pp. 207–223 (2020)
39. Devi, S.L., Pralayankar, P., Menaka, S., Bakiyavathi, T., Ram, R.V.S., Kavitha, V.: Verb transfer in a Tamil to Hindi machine translation system. In: 2010 International Conference on Asian Language Processing, pp. 261–264. IEEE (2010)
40. Devi, S.L., Ram, V.S., Rao, P.R.: Anaphora resolution system for Indian languages. In: Proceedings of 2nd Workshop on Indian Language Data: Resources and Evaluation (WILDRE). LREC2014, Reykjavik, Iceland (2014)
41. Devi, S.L., Ram, V.S., Rao, P.R.: A generic anaphora resolution engine for Indian languages. In: Proceedings of COLING 2014, the 25th International Conference on Computational Linguistics: Technical Papers, pp. 1824–1833 (2014)
42. Dhanalakshmi, V., Kumar, A.M., Rajendran, S., Soman, K.: POS tagger and chunker for Tamil language. In: Proceedings of the 8th Tamil Internet Conference. Cologne, Germany (2009)

43. Dhanalakshmi, V., Kumar, A.M., Soman, K., Rajendran, S.: Chunker for Tamil using machine learning. In: 7th International Conference on Natural Language Processing 2009 (ICON 2009), IIIT Hyderabad, India (2009)
44. Dhanalakshmi, V., Padmavathy, P., Soman, K., Rajendran, S.: Chunker for Tamil. In: 2009 International Conference on Advances in Recent Technologies in Communication and Computing, pp. 436–438. IEEE (2009)
45. Dhanalakshmi V, Anand Kumar M, Murugesan, C.: Dependency parser for Tamil classical literature: kurunthokai. In: Proceedings of Tamil Internet Conference, pp. 147–152 (2012)
46. Dhivya, R., Dhanalakshmi, V., Anand Kumar, M., Soman, K.P.: Clause Boundary Identification for Tamil Language Using Dependency Parsing. In: Das, V.V., Ariwa, E., Rahayu, S.B. (eds.) SPIT 2011. LNICST, vol. 62, pp. 195–197. Springer, Heidelberg (2012). https://doi.org/10.1007/978-3-642-32573-1_32
47. Dhivyaa, C., Nithya, K., Janani, T., Kumar, K.S., Prashanth, N.: Transliteration based generative pre-trained transformer 2 model for Tamil text summarization. In: 2022 International Conference on Computer Communication and Informatics (ICCCI), p. 1–6. IEEE (2022)
48. Evangeline, M.M., Shyamala, K., Barathi, L., Sandhya, R.: Frequency Based Feature Extraction Technique for Text Documents in Tamil Language. In: Singh, M., Tyagi, V., Gupta, P.K., Flusser, J., Ören, T., Sonawane, V.R. (eds.) ICACDS 2021. CCIS, vol. 1441, pp. 76–84. Springer, Cham (2021). https://doi.org/10. 1007/978-3-030-88244-0_8
49. Ezhilarasi, S., Maheswari, P.U.: Depicting a neural model for lemmatization and POS tagging of words from PALAEO graphic stone inscriptions. In: 2021 5th International Conference on Intelligent Computing and Control Systems (ICI-CCS), pp. 1879–1884. IEEE (2021)
50. Fernando, A., Ranathunga, S., Dias, G.: Data augmentation and terminology integration for domain-specific Sinhala-English-Tamil statistical machine translation. (2020) arXiv preprint arXiv:2011.02821
51. Ganesan, M.: Functions of the morphological analyser developed at CIIL, Mysore. In: Automatic Automatic Translation (seminar proceedings), Thiruvananthapuram: ISDL (1994)
52. Ganesan, M.: Computational morphology of Tamil. Word Structure in Dravidian, Kuppam: Dravidian University, pp. 399–405 (2003)
53. Ganesan, M., Ekka, F.: Morphological analyzer for Indian languages. Information Technology Applications in Language, Script and Speech, New Delhi: BPB Publication (1994)
54. Ganesh, J., Parthasarathi, R., Geetha, T.V., Balaji, J.: Pattern Based Bootstrapping Technique for Tamil POS Tagging. In: Prasath, R., O'Reilly, P., Kathirvalavakumar, T. (eds.) MIKE 2014. LNCS (LNAI), vol. 8891, pp. 256–267. Springer, Cham (2014). https://doi.org/10.1007/978-3-319-13817-6_25
55. Ganganwar, V., Rajalakshmi, R.: MTDOT: A multilingual translation-based data augmentation technique for offensive content identification in Tamil text data. Electronics 11(21), 3574 (2022)
56. HandWiki: Tamil_all_character_encoding (2020)
57. Hariharan, V., Kumar, M.A., Soman, K.: Named entity recognition in Tamil language using recurrent based sequence model. In: Lecture Notes in Networks and Systems, 74 (2019)
58. Jain, M., Punia, R., Hooda, I.: Neural machine translation for Tamil to English. J. Stat. Manage. Syst. 23(7), 1251–1264 (2020)

59. Kalamani, M., Krishnamoorthi, M., Valarmathi, R.: Continuous Tamil speech recognition technique under non stationary noisy environments. Int. J. Speech Technol. **22**(1), 47–58 (2019)
60. Kamakshi, S., Rajendren, S.: Preliminaries to the preparation of a machine aid to translate linguistics texts written in English into Tamil. Language in India **3** (2004)
61. Kannan, R.R., Rajalakshmi, R., Kumar, L.: Indic-BERT based approach for sentiment analysis on code-mixed Tamil tweets (2021)
62. Kausikaa, N., Uma, V.: Sentiment analysis of English and Tamil tweets using path length similarity based word sense disambiguation. Int. Organ. Sci. Res. J. **1**, 82–89 (2016)
63. Kavirajan, B., Kumar, M.A., Soman, K., Rajendran, S., Vaithehi, S.: Improving the rule based machine translation system using sentence simplification (English to Tamil). In: 2017 International Conference on Advances in Computing, Communications and Informatics (ICACCI), pp. 957–963. IEEE (2017)
64. Kohilavani, S., Mala, T., Geetha, T.: Automatic Tamil content generation. In: 2009 International Conference on Intelligent Agent Multi-Agent Systems, p. 1–6. IEEE (2009)
65. Krishnamurthy, P.: Development of Telugu-Tamil transfer-based machine translation system: an improvisation using divergence index. J. Intell. Syst. **28**(3), 493–504 (2019)
66. Krishnamurthy, P., Sarveswaran, K.: Towards building a modern written tamil treebank. In: Proceedings of the 20th International Workshop on Treebanks and Linguistic Theories (TLT, SyntaxFest 2021), pp. 61–68 (2021)
67. Krishnan, A.S., Ragavan, S.: Morphology-aware meta-embeddings for Tamil. In: Proceedings of the 2021 Conference of the North American Chapter of the Association for Computational Linguistics: Student Research Workshop, pp. 94–111 (2021)
68. Krishnan, K.G., Pooja, A., Kumar, M.A., Soman, K.: Character based bidirectional LSTM for disambiguating Tamil part-of-speech categories. Int. J. Control Theory Appl **10**, 229–235 (2017)
69. kumar, A.M., Soman, K.: Amrita_cen@ fire-2014: morpheme extraction and lemmatization for Tamil using machine learning. In: Proceedings of the Forum for Information Retrieval Evaluation, pp. 112–120 (2014)
70. Kumar, M.A., Dhanalakshmi, V., Soman, K., Rajendran, S.: Factored statistical machine translation system for English to Tamil language. Pertanika J. Soc. Sci. Humanit. **22**(4) (2014)
71. Kumar, M.A., Premjith, B., Singh, S., Rajendran, S., Soman, K.P.: An overview of the shared task on machine translation in Indian languages (MTIL)–2017. Journal of Intelligent Systems **28**(3), 455–464 (2019). https://doi.org/10.1515/jisys-2018-0024https://doi.org/10.1515/jisys-2018-0024
72. Kumar, M.A., Premjith, B., Singh, S., Rajendran, S., Soman, K.: An overview of the shared task on machine translation in Indian languages (MTIL)-2017. J. Intell. Syst. **28**(3), 455–464 (2019)
73. Kumar, M.A., Rajendran, S., Soman, K.: Cross-lingual preposition disambiguation for machine translation. Procedia Comput. Sci. **54**, 291–300 (2015)
74. Kumar, M.A., Rajendran, S., Soman, K.: Cross-lingual preposition disambiguation for machine translation. Procedia Comput. Sci. **54**, 291–300 (2015)
75. Anand Kumar, M., Singh, S., Kavirajan, B., Soman, K.P.: Shared Task on Detecting Paraphrases in Indian Languages (DPIL): An Overview. In: Majumder, P.,

Mitra, M., Mehta, P., Sankhavara, J. (eds.) FIRE 2016. LNCS, vol. 10478, pp. 128–140. Springer, Cham (2018). https://doi.org/10.1007/978-3-319-73606-8_10

76. LekshmiAmmal, H., Ravikiran, M., et al.: Nitk-it_nlp@ tamilnlp-acl2022: Transformer based model for toxic span identification in Tamil. In: Proceedings of the Second Workshop on Speech and Language Technologies for Dravidian Languages, pp. 75–78 (2022)

77. Lokesh, S., Kumar, P.M., Devi, M.R., Parthasarathy, P., Gokulnath, C.: An automatic Tamil speech recognition system by using bidirectional recurrent neural network with self-organizing map. Neural Comput. Appl. **31**(5), 1521–1531 (2019)

78. Lushanthan, S., Weerasinghe, A., Herath, D.: Morphological analyzer and generator for tamil language. In: 2014 14th International Conference on Advances in ICT for Emerging Regions (ICTER), pp. 190–196. IEEE (2014)

79. Anandkumar, M.: Morphology based prototype statistical machine translation system for English to Tamil language. Unpublished PhD Thesis (2013)

80. Malarkodi, C., Lex, E., Devi, S.L.: Named entity recognition for the agricultural domain. Res. Comput. Sci. **117**, 121–132 (2016)

81. Malarkodi, C., Sobha, L.: Twitter named entity recognition for Indian languages. In: Proceedings of 18th International Conference on Computational Linguistics and Intelligent Text Processing (2018)

82. Manone, V., Soman, K., Rajendran, S.: A synchronous syntax for English-Tamil language pair for machine translation. In: 4th International Symposium on Natural Language Processing (NLP'15), Kochi, Kerala, Co-affiliated with 4th International Conference in Computing, Communications and Informatics (ICACCI-2015) (2015)

83. Marimuthu, K., Amudha, K., Bakiyavathi, T., Devi, S.L.: Word boundary identifier as a catalyzer and performance booster for Tamil morphological analyzer. In: Proceedings of 6th Language and Technology Conference, Human Language Technologies as a challenge for Computer Science and Linguistics, Poznan, Poland. (2013)

84. Menaka, S., Malarkodi, C., Devi, S.L.: A deep study on causal relations and its automatic identification in tamil. In: Proceedings of 2nd Workshop on Indian Language Data: Resources and Evaluation. LREC2014, Reykjavik, Iceland (2014)

85. Menaka, S., Ram, V.S., Devi, S.L.: Morphological generator for Tamil. Proceedings of the Knowledge Sharing event on Morphological Analysers and Generators, LDC-IL, Mysore, India, pp. 82–96 (2010)

86. Menon, D.A., Saravanan, S., Loganathan, R., Soman, D.K.: Amrita morph analyzer and generator for Tamil: a rule based approach. In: Proceedings of Tamil Internet Conference, pp. 239–243 (2009)

87. Mokanarangan, T., et al.: Tamil Morphological Analyzer Using Support Vector Machines. In: Métais, E., Meziane, F., Saraee, M., Sugumaran, V., Vadera, S. (eds.) NLDB 2016. LNCS, vol. 9612, pp. 15–23. Springer, Cham (2016). https://doi.org/10.1007/978-3-319-41754-7_2

88. Mrinalini, K., Nagarajan, T., Vijayalakshmi, P.: Pause-based phrase extraction and effective OOV handling for low-resource machine translation systems. ACM Transactions on Asian and Low-Resource Language Information Processing (TALLIP) **18**(2), 1–22 (2018)

89. Padmamala, R., Prema, V.: Sentiment analysis of online Tamil contents using recursive neural network models approach for Tamil language. In: 2017 IEEE International Conference on Smart Technologies and Management for Computing, Communication, Controls, Energy and Materials (ICSTM), pp. 28–31. IEEE (2017)

90. Pandian, S.L., Geetha, T. V.: CRF Models for Tamil Part of Speech Tagging and Chunking. In: Li, W., Mollá-Aliod, D. (eds.) ICCPOL 2009. LNCS (LNAI), vol. 5459, pp. 11–22. Springer, Heidelberg (2009). https://doi.org/10.1007/978-3-642-00831-3_2

91. Pattabhi, R., Rao, T., Ram, R.V.S., Vijayakrishna, R., Sobha, L.: A text chunker and hybrid pos tagger for indian languages. In: Proceedings of International Joint Conference on Artificial Intelligence Workshop on Shallow Parsing for South Asian Languages, IIIT Hyderabad, Hyderabad, India (2007)

92. Pattabhi, R., Sobha, L.: Identifying similar and co-referring documents across languages. In: Proceedings of the 2nd workshop on Cross Lingual Information Access (CLIA) Addressing the Information Need of Multilingual Societies, pp. 10–17 (2008)

93. Pilar, B., et al.: Subword dictionary learning and segmentation techniques for automatic speech recognition in Tamil and Kannada. (2022) arXiv preprint arXiv:2207.13331

94. Premjith, B., Soman, K.: Deep learning approach for the morphological synthesis in Malayalam and Tamil at the character level. Trans. Asian Low-Resource Lang. Inf. Proc. **20**(6), 1–17 (2021)

95. Priyadharshini, R., et al.: Overview of abusive comment detection in Tamil-ACL 2022. In: Proceedings of the Second Workshop on Speech and Language Technologies for Dravidian Languages, pp. 292–298 (2022)

96. Raj, M.A.R., Abirami, S.: Junction point elimination based Tamil handwritten character recognition: An experimental analysis. J. Syst. Sci. Syst. Eng. **29**(1), 100–123 (2020)

97. Raj, M.A.R., Abirami, S.: Structural representation-based off-line Tamil handwritten character recognition. Soft. Comput. **24**(2), 1447–1472 (2020)

98. Rajalakshmi, R., Duraphe, A., Shibani, A.: Dlrg@ dravidianlangtech-acl2022: Abusive comment detection in Tamil using multilingual transformer models. In: Proceedings of the Second Workshop on Speech and Language Technologies for Dravidian Languages, pp. 207–213 (2022)

99. Rajalakshmi, R., Reddy, Y., Kumar, L.: Dlrg@ dravidianlangtech-eacl2021: Transformer based approachfor offensive language identification on code-mixed Tamil. In: Proceedings of the First Workshop on Speech and Language Technologies for Dravidian Languages, pp. 357–362 (2021)

100. Rajalakshmi, R., Selvaraj, S., Vasudevan, P., et al.: Hottest: Hate and offensive content identification in Tamil using transformers and enhanced stemming. Computer Speech Language, p. 101464 (2022)

101. Rajasekar, M., Geetha, A.: Comparison of Machine Learning Methods for Tamil Morphological Analyzer. In: Raj, J.S., Palanisamy, R., Perikos, I., Shi, Y. (eds.) Intelligent Sustainable Systems. LNNS, vol. 213, pp. 385–399. Springer, Singapore (2022). https://doi.org/10.1007/978-981-16-2422-3_31

102. Rajendran, S.: Spell and grammar checker for tamil. In: Paper read in 27th All India Conference of Dravidian Linguists held in ISDL, Thiruvananthapuram. **17** (1999)

103. Rajendran, S.: Preliminaries to the preparation of a word net for Tamil. Lang. India **2**(1), 467–497 (2002)

104. Rajendran, S.: Parsing in Tamil: Present state of art. Lang. India **6**, 8 (2006)

105. Rajendran, S.: Complexity of Tamil in POS tagging. Lang. India 7(1) (2007)

106. Rajendran, S.: Resolution of lexical ambiguity in Tamil. Lang. India 14(1) (2014)

107. Rajendran, S., Kumar, M.A.: Computing tools for Tamil language teaching and learning. In: 17th Tamil Internet Conference. Tamil Agricultural University, Coimbatore (2018)
108. Rajendran, S., Viswanathan, S., Kumar, R.: Computational morphology of Tamil verbal complex. Lang. India 3(4) (2003)
109. Rajkumar, N., Subashini, T., Rajan, K., Ramalingam, V.: An efficient feature extraction with bidirectional long short term memory based deep learning model for Tamil document classification. J. Comput. Theor. Nanosci. **18**(3), 568–585 (2021)
110. Ram, R.V.S., Lalitha Devi, S.: Clause Boundary Identification Using Conditional Random Fields. In: Gelbukh, A. (ed.) CICLing 2008. LNCS, vol. 4919, pp. 140–150. Springer, Heidelberg (2008). https://doi.org/10.1007/978-3-540-78135-6_13
111. Ram, R.V.S., Devi, S.L.: Coreference resolution using tree-CRF. A. Gelbukh (ed), Comput. Linguist. Intell. Text Proc. 7181, 285–296 (2012)
112. Ram, R.V.S., Devi, S.L.: Pronominal resolution in Tamil using tree CRFS. In: 2013 International Conference on Asian Language Processing, pp. 197–200. IEEE (2013)
113. Ram, R.V.S., Devi, S.L.: Two layer machine learning approach for mining referential entities for a morphologically rich language. Asian J. Inf. Technol. **15**, 2831–2838 (2016)
114. Ram, R.V.S., Sobha, L.D.: Tamil clause boundary identification: Annotation and evaluation. In: Workshop on Indian Language and Data: Resources and Evaluation. p. 122. LREC, Istanbul (2012)
115. Ram, R., Devi, S.L.: Noun phrase chunker using finite state automata for an agglutinative language. In: Proceedings of the Tamil Internet-2010 at Coimbatore, India, pp. 23–27 (2010)
116. Ram, V.S., Menaka, S., Devi, S.L.: Tamil morphological analyser. In: Proceedings of the Knowledge Sharing event on Morphological Analysers and Generators, Mona Parakh, LDC-IL, Mysore, India, pp. 1–18 (2010)
117. Ramakrishnan, A., Kaushik, L.N., Narayana, L.: Natural language processing for Tamil TTS. In: Proc. 3rd Language and Technology Conference, Poznan, Poland, pp. 192–196 (2007)
118. Ramanathan, V., Meyyappan, T., Thamarai, S.: Predicting Tamil movies sentimental reviews using Tamil tweets. J. Comput. Sci. **15**(11), 1638–1647 (2019)
119. Ramanathan, V., Meyyappan, T., Thamarai, S.: Sentiment analysis: an approach for analysing tamil movie reviews using Tamil tweets. Recent Adv. Mathe. Res. Comput. Sci. **3**, 28–39 (2021)
120. Ramasamy, L., Bojar, O., Žabokrtský, Z.: Morphological processing for English-Tamil statistical machine translation. In: Proceedings of the Workshop on Machine Translation and Parsing in Indian Languages, pp. 113–122 (2012)
121. Ramasamy, L., Bojar, O., Žabokrtský, Z.: ENTAM: An English-Tamil parallel corpus (ENTAM v2. 0) (2014)
122. Ramaswamy, V.: A morphological generator for Tamil. Unpublished Ph.D. Dissertation (2000)
123. Ramaswamy, V.: A morphological analyzer for Tamil. Unpublished Ph.D. Dissertation (2003)
124. Ranganathan, V.: A lexical phonological approach to Tamil word by computer. Int. J. Dravidian Linguist. **26**(1), 57–70 (1997)
125. Ranganathan, V.: Computational Approaches To Tamil Linguistics, chap. 3. CRE-A Publications (2016)

126. Ravikiran, M., Annamalai, S.: DOSA: dravidian code-mixed offensive span identification dataset. In: Proceedings of the 1st Workshop on Speech and Language Technologies for Dravidian Languages, pp. 10–17. Assoc. Comput. Linguist., Kyiv (2021). https://aclanthology.org/2021.dravidianlangtech-1.2

127. Ravikiran, M., et al.: Findings of the shared task on toxic span identification in Tamil. In: Proceedings of the 2nd Workshop on Speech and Language Technologies for Dravidian Languages. Assoc. Comput. Linguist. (2022)

128. Remmiya Devi, G., Anand Kumar, M., Soman, K.: Co-occurrence based word representation for extracting named entities in Tamil tweets. J. Intell. Fuzzy Syst. **34**(3), 1435–1442 (2018)

129. Rethanya. V, Dhanalakshmi, V., Soman, M., Rajendran, S.: Morphological stemmer and LEMMATIZER for Tamil. In: Proceedings of 18th Tamil Internet Conference. International Forum for Information Technology in Tamil (INFITT) (2019)

130. RK Rao, P., Devi, S.L.: Patent document summarization using conceptual graphs. Int. J. Nat. Lang. Comput. (IJNLC) 6 (2017)

131. Sakuntharaj, R., Mahesan, S.: Missing word detection and correction based on context of tamil sentences using n-grams. In: 2021 10th International Conference on Information and Automation for Sustainability (ICIAfS), pp. 42–47. IEEE (2021)

132. Samuel Manoharan, J.: A novel text-to-speech synthesis system using syllable-based hmm for Tamil language. In: Shakya, S., Du, K.L., Haoxiang, W. (eds.) Proceedings of Second International Conference on Sustainable Expert Systems, pp. 305–314. Springer, Singapore (2022). https://doi.org/10.1007/978-981-16-7657-4_26

133. Sankaralingam, C., Rajendran, S., Kavirajan, B., Kumar, M.A., Soman, K.: Ontothesaurus for Tamil language: Ontology based intelligent system for information retrieval. In: 2017 International Conference on Advances in Computing, Communications and Informatics (ICACCI), pp. 2396–2396. IEEE (2017)

134. Santosh Kumar, T.: Word sense disambiguation using semantic web for Tamil to English statistical machine translation. IRA-Int. J. Technol. Eng. **5**(2), 22–31 (2016)

135. Sarika, M., et al.: Comparative analysis of Tamil and English news text summarization using text rank algorithm. Turkish J. Comput. Mathe. Educ. (TURCOMAT) **12**(9), 2385–2391 (2021)

136. Sarveswaran, K., Dias, G.: THAMIZHIUDP: A dependency parser for Tamil. (2020) arXiv preprint arXiv:2012.13436

137. Sarveswaran, K., Dias, G.: Building a part of speech tagger for the Tamil language. In: 2021 International Conference on Asian Language Processing (IALP), pp. 286–291 IEEE (2021)

138. Sarveswaran, K., Dias, G., Butt, M.: Thamizhifst: A morphological analyser and generator for Tamil verbs. In: 2018 3rd International Conference on Information Technology Research (ICITR). pp. 1–6. IEEE (2018)

139. Sarveswaran, K., Dias, G., Butt, M.: THAMIZHIMORPH: a morphological parser for the Tamil language. Mach. Transl. **35**(1), 37–70 (2021)

140. Selvi, S.S., Anitha, R.: J. Intell. Fuzzy Syst. (Bilingual corpus-based hybrid POS tagger for low resource Tamil language: A statistical approach), 1–20 (2022)

141. Sivasankar, E., Krishnakumari, K., Balasubramanian, P.: An enhanced sentiment dictionary for domain adaptation with multi-domain dataset in Tamil language (ESD-da). Soft. Comput. **25**(5), 3697–3711 (2021)

142. Sobha, L.: Pronominal resolution in south dravidian languages. 23rd South Asian Language Analysis, University of Texas, Austin 446 (2003)

143. Sridhar, R., Janani, V., Gowrisankar, R., Monica, G.: Language relationship model for automatic generation of Tamil stories from hints. Int. J. Intell. Inf. Technol. (IJIIT) **13**(2), 21–40 (2017)
144. Subramoniam, V., Bhattacharya, M., Lohy, A., Tarai, S.: Speech synthesis (Tamil oriya): an application for the blind. Department of Science and Technology, Govt. of India III.5(35) 2001-ET (2001)
145. Suriyah, M., Anandan, A., Narasimhan, A., Karky, M.: Piripori: morphological analyser for tamil. In: International Conference On Artificial Intelligence, Smart Grid And Smart City Applications. pp. 801–809. Springer (2019) https://doi.org/10.1007/978-3-030-24051-6_75
146. Thangarajan, R., Natarajan, A.: Syllable based continuous speech recognition for Tamil. South Asian lang. rev. **18**(1), 72–85 (2008)
147. Thangarajan, R., Natarajan, A., Selvam, M.: Word and triphone based approaches in continuous speech recognition for Tamil language. WSEAS Trans. Signal Proc. **4**(3), 76–86 (2008)
148. Thangarasu, M., Manavalan, R.: Stemmers for Tamil language: performance analysis. (2013) arXiv preprint arXiv:1310.0754
149. Thenmozhi, D., Aravindan, C.: Ontology-based Tamil-English cross-lingual information retrieval system. Sadhana - Academy Proc. Eng. Sci. **43**(10), 1–14 (2018)
150. Vasantharajan, C., Thayasivam, U.: Towards offensive language identification for Tamil code-mixed YouTube comments and posts. SN Computer Science **3**(1), 1–13 (2022)
151. Vel, S.S.: Pre-processing techniques of text mining using computational linguistics and python libraries. In: 2021 International Conference on Artificial Intelligence and Smart Systems (ICAIS). pp. 879–884. IEEE (2021)
152. Vignesh, N., Sowmya, S.: Automatic question generator in Tamil. International J. Eng. Res. Technol. (IJERT) 2 (2013)
153. Vijayakrishna, R., Sobha, L.: Domain focused named entity recognizer for tamil using conditional random fields. In: Proceedings of the IJCNLP-08 workshop on named entity recognition for South and South East Asian Languages (2008)
154. Visuwalingam, H., Sakuntharaj, R., Ragel, R.G.: Part of speech tagging for Tamil language using deep learning. In: 2021 IEEE 16th International Conference on Industrial and Information Systems (ICIIS), pp. 157–161 IEEE (2021)
155. Viswanathan, S.: Tamil morphological analyser. Unpublished MS Thesis (2000)
156. Viswanathan, S., Ramesh Kumar, S., Kumara Shanmugam, B., Arulmozi, S., Vijay Shanker, K.: A tamil morphological analyser. In: Proceedings of the International Conference on Natural Language Processing (ICON), CIIL, Mysore, India (2003)
157. Zhang, H., Shi, K., Chen, N.F.: Multilingual speech evaluation: Case studies on English, Malay and Tamil. (2021) arXiv preprint arXiv:2107.03675

Contextualized Embeddings from Transformers for Sentiment Analysis on Code-Mixed Hinglish Data: An Expanded Approach with Explainable Artificial Intelligence

Sargam Yadav[1]([✉])(iD) and Abhishek Kaushik[2](iD)

[1] Dublin Business School, Dublin D02 WC04, Ireland
sargam.yadav@edhec.com
[2] Dundalk Institute of Technology, Dundalk A91 K584, Ireland
Abhishek.Kaushik@dkit.ie

Abstract. Transformer-based models have gained traction for giving breakthrough performance on various Natural Language Processing (NLP) tasks in recent years. A number of studies have been conducted to understand the type of information learned by the model and its performance on different tasks. YouTube comments can serve as a rich source for multilingual data, which can be used to train state-of-the-art models. In this study, two transformer-based models, multilingual Bidirectional Encoder Representations from Transformers (mBERT) and RoBERTa, are fine-tuned and evaluated on code-mixed 'Hinglish' data. The representations learned by the intermediate layers of the models are also studied by using them as features for machine learning classifiers. The results show a significant improvement compared to the baseline for both datasets using the feature-based method, with the highest accuracy of 92.73% for Kabita Kitchen's channel and 87.42% for Nisha Madhulika's channel. Explanations of the model predictions using the Local Interpretable Model-Agnostic Explanations (LIME) technique show that the model is using significant features for classification and can be trusted.

Keywords: Bidirectional encoder representations from transformers · Natural Language Processing · Sentiment Analysis · Cookery Channels · Bertology · Transformers · Hinglish · Explainable Artificial Intelligence · Local Interpretable Model-Agnostic Explanations

1 Introduction

YouTube is a major media-sharing platform that is host to a variety of content. India is the largest user base of YouTube, with approximately 467 million monthly visitors [1]. User engagement on YouTube channels can be measured through user comments, likes, and channel subscriptions. It is crucial for creators

Anand Kumar M et al. (Eds.): SPELLL 2022, CCIS 1802, pp. 99–119, 2023.
https://doi.org/10.1007/978-3-031-33231-9_7

to understand how the users are perceiving their content to enable subsequent improvements. In order to determine overall user opinion on the variety of comments posted online, NLP tools can be trained to provide automatic predictions. Sentiment analysis is a powerful NLP tool to analyse user opinion on the content posted by creators, as it can work with large amounts of text data and eliminates the need for manual analysis. The content posted on social media platforms in India is in the form of a mix-code of Hindi and English, sometimes abbreviated as 'Hinglish'. Code-mixed Hinglish consists of romanized Hindi and English words. Figure 1 displays an example image of a code-mixed sentence in Hinglish from Nisha Madhulika's dataset.

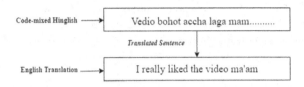

Fig. 1. Example of code-mixed Hinglish statement

However, there have been a limited number of studies performed on 'Hinglish' in NLP [2,3]. Previous studies have implemented Term Frequency - Inverse Document Frequency (TF-IDF) vectorizer and machine learning models [4], Multilayer Perceptron (MLP) [5], and other transformers-based approaches [6] for sentiment classification. Introduction of the transformer architecture [7] was a turning point in NLP. BERT [8] is a transformer-based language model and has improved upon several benchmarks with task-specific fine-tuning on the specific datasets. There are several language specific and multilingual variations of BERT available such as AlBERTo for Italian [9], BERTje for Dutch [10], and more [11,12].

Since machine learning models are being implemented to solve several crucial real-world tasks, it is imperative that a level of trust can be placed in the model's decisions. Black-box models such as neural networks provide excellent results on many tasks, but the decision making process is opaque and not interpretable by humans. Empirical metrics should not be considered as a definite measure of model performance, and Explainable Artificial Intelligence (XAI) provides a complementary tool to understand model behavior. To increase trust in the decisions made by a model, XAI provides tools and frameworks that can allow for the responsible deployment of Artificial Intelligence models in the real world [13]. LIME [14] is a model agnostic XAI technique that provides human-interpretable explanations of the predictions made by black-box models by creating local approximations of prediction instances.

In this study, two transformer-based models, mBERT [8] and RoBERTa [15], are used to perform sentiment analysis on the comments in code-mixed Hindi and English collected from two YouTube cookery channels: Kabita Kitchen's [16] and Nisha Madhulika's channel [17,18].

This study also explores a hybrid approach where features of the intermediate layers of the two models are fed to machine learning classifiers such as Logistic Regression (LR), Support Vector Machines (SVM), K-Nearest Neighbours (KNN), and Naive Bayes (NB). Features from individual layers are combined using the following strategies:

1. Features from the last layer
2. Features from the second last layer
3. Sum (Addition) of features from the last 4 layers
4. Concatenation of features from the last 4 layers

The performance of the machine learning classifiers is evaluated for both datasets. In order to determine if the results given by the model are trustworthy, the LIME framework has also been used to explain predictions of the hybrid approach.

The remaining sections of the paper are as follows: Section 3 covers the relevant literature on transformer-based models, previous work on the 'Hinglish' language, and XAI. Section 4 explains the datasets and the methodology used in our study. Section 5 explores the results obtained by the experiment, analysis, statistical testing and explanations of the results using LIME. Section 6 discusses the findings of the study with respect to our research questions. Section 7 outlines the conclusions derived from the study and the future work that needs to conducted in the field.

2 Motivation

This study aims to analyse the performance of two transformer-based models, mBERT and RoBERTa, on the task of sentiment analysis of code-mixed Hindi and English data. Two approaches are considered for the study: In the first approach, the model is fine-tuned with a fully-connected linear layer for classification. In the second approach, features are extracted from the intermediate layers of the model and fed into downstream machine learning classifiers. 'Hinglish' is an under-resourced language with a limited amount of toolkits [2], and there is a scarcity of BERT-based pre-trained language models available for sentiment analysis on YouTube comments in Indian languages [3]. A large portion of online content posted in India is code-mixed, and a deeper look at the performance of current state-of-the-art models on 'Hinglish' is essential.

As many high-impact decisions are increasingly relying on machine learning models, it is important to understand the decision-making process of a black-box model to avoid enforcing biased and incorrect decisions. The LIME framework [14,19] provides a faithful and human-readable explanation of model decisions. To our knowledge, there has been no previous study on using a feature-based approach for downstream classification on the code-mixed 'Hinglish' language and generating explanations through LIME.

The hypothesis to be explored in the experiment is as follows:

Hypothesis: *The hybrid approach of training machine learning classifiers on features generated through BERT-based models can outperform standard state-of-the-art language models in performing sentiment analysis on code-mixed 'Hinglish' data.*

The research questions designed to explore the hypothesis are listed as follows:

1. Which transformer-based model, multilingual BERT or monolingual RoBERTa, provides better results for sentiment analysis on code-mixed Hinglish data?
2. Do the final layers of the models provide accurate sentence-level representations for classification?
3. Are the results obtained by the study statistically significant?
4. Are the explanations for classifications provided by the models trustworthy?

3   Related Work

In this section, the relevant literature for our study is reviewed and supporting conclusions are derived.

3.1   Pre-trained Language Models

The transformer architecture was introduced by Vaswani et al. [7], and relies on multi-headed self-attention to obtain representations of the input text. BERT [8] is a breakthrough language model based on the transformer architecture that can be applied to many NLP tasks with minimum fine-tuning and achieves great results. BERT has outperformed traditional machine learning and deep learning algorithms in several Natural Language Understanding (NLU) tasks. BERT is implemented in 2 steps: pre-training and fine-tuning. The model is pre-trained on a large corpus of data using the Masked Language Modeling (MLM) objective and Next Sentence Prediction (NSP) objective, and captures long-range dependencies in the text through the self-attention mechanism. The multilingual version of BERT, mBERT, is trained on a corpus of 102 languages. The RoBERTa model [15] implements a robust training approach to the BERT architecture by removing the next sentence prediction objective, increasing training time and learning rates, training on longer sequences, etc. As opposed to BERT which uses static masking while training, RoBERTa was trained using dynamic masking. It outperforms BERT and achieved state-of-the-art results on General Language Understanding Evaluation (GLUE), Reading Comprehension dataset from Examinations (RACE), and Stanford Question Answering Dataset (SQuAD).

The reason for the outstanding performance of BERT-based models is not very well understood. A field of study named 'BERTology' has recently emerged and tries to explore the inner workings of BERT [20]. Devlin et al. [8] studied the output of specific BERT layers for the CoNLL-2003 Named Entity Recognition task [21] without fine-tuning the model. The highest F1 score of 96.1 was achieved when the token representations from the top four hidden layers were concatenated and BiLSTM was used as a classifier, suggesting that BERT-based models are effective in generating contextual features. Yang et al. [22] capture complementary representations from the hidden states of RoBERTa layers and the approach gives results comparable to state-of-the-art models. Su et al. [23] propose SesameBERT, a fine-tuning method that extracts information from all layers through Squeeze and Excitation and outperforms BERT on the HANS dataset [24].

3.2 Sentiment Analysis on Hinglish

Kaur et al. [4] used supervised and unsupervised machine learning algorithms to perform classification on Kabita Kitchen's and Nisha Madhulika's datasets using the count vectorizer, TF-IDF vectorizer and term frequency vectorizer. The best accuracy was of 74.01% achieved by LR with the term frequency vectorizer in Nisha Madulika's dataset and 75.37% in Kabita's Kitchen channel. Yadav et al. [6] conducted a similar study on the same datasets, where word embeddings were calculated by taking mean of all the token representations from the last layer of a fine-tuned BERT model, and machine learning algorithms were applied on the resulting vectors. The highest accuracy for Nisha Madhulika's dataset was 72% and for Kabita kitchen's channel was 76%. Donthula et al. [5] trained deep learning models on the same datasets using different feature engineering techniques. The highest accuracy of 98.53% on Kabita's dataset and 98.48% on Nisha Madhulika's dataset using an MLP with a count vectorizer.

Kazhuparambil and Kaushik [25] performed sentiment analysis on Malayalam-English mix-code data using BERT-based models and compared their results with conventional deep learning classifiers. The XLM model performed the best, with an accuracy of 67.31%. MLP with term frequency vectorizer produced the best results out of all the deep learning models with an accuracy of 65.98%. BERT-based models have also been implemented in various shared tasks for sentiment analysis in mix-code languages. The SemEval-2020 Task on Overview of Sentiment Analysis of Code-Mixed Tweets achieved the highest F1 score of 75.0% for Hinglish and 80.6% F1 for 'Spanglish' using BERT-based models [26]. In the study done by Bhange and Kasliwal [27], classical machine learning models are shown to have a performance competitive with transformer models on Hinglish sentiment detection.

3.3 LIME

LIME [14] is an XAI technique that provides explanations of the predictions of black-box models in an interpretable and human-readable manner. LIME works by forming a local approximation of any black-box model around a given instance. Providing interpretable explanations can help increase trust in the model, and can also be an indicator of model performance along with empirical evaluation metrics. LIME explanations for BERT-based models have been previously studied for the task of fake news detection [28], hate speech classification [19], etc.

The equation for an explanation ξ given by LIME for a sample x by a model $g \in G$ is given as:

$$\xi(x) = \underset{(g \, \epsilon \, G)}{argmin} \, \mathcal{L}(f, g, \pi_x) + \Omega(g) \tag{1}$$

where G is a class of potentially interpretable models, $g \, \epsilon \, G$ is a model presented to the user as an explanation, π_x is the measure of complexity, and $\mathcal{L}(f, g, \pi_x)$ is a measure of how unfaithful g is in approximating f in the locality defined by π_x. An optimal trade-off must be achieved between $\mathcal{L}(f, g, \pi_x)$ (local fidelity) and π_x (interpretability).

The review of related literature supports further exploration of transformer-based models for performing sentiment analysis on 'Hinglish' YouTube comments. The break-through performance of transformer-based language models for classification and generation of contextualized features suggests that the models must be further studied on unseen data. Baseline studies on the dataset suggest that using state-of-the-art models could improve upon the results. The LIME framework has allowed for the generation of explanations for decisions made by black-box models, which can be analysed to understand the rationale used by the model for making predictions.

4   Methodology

In this section, we discuss the dataset used in the study and the experimental methodology that is followed for performing sentiment analysis.

4.1   Dataset

The dataset is composed of comments collected from the YouTube channels of Nisha Madhulika [17] and Kabita Kitchen [16]. The comments are labelled as one of the following categories: 'Praising', 'Undefined', 'Hybrid', 'Gratitude', 'About recipe', 'About video', and 'Suggestion and queries'. Each label has 700 comments each, making the total number of comments for each dataset equal to 4900. Each dataset is perfectly balanced. The dataset consists of comments both in English and code-mixed Hindi and English.

In the baseline study done by Kaur et al. [4], parametric and non-parametric machine learning classifiers were trained and evaluated, and LR with the term frequency vectorizer gives the highest accuracy of 74.01% accuracy in Nisha Madulika's dataset and 75.37% accuracy in Kabita's Kitchen dataset.

4.2   Experiment

For this study, two approaches for performing sentiment analysis on the Hinglish datasets are explored. In the first approach, standard fine-tuning of two transformer-based pre-trained language models, mBERT and RoBERTa, is performed on the respective datasets.

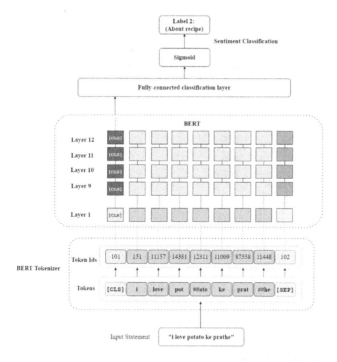

Fig. 2. Experimental Flowchart of the 1st Approach for a sample sentence using mBERT

The BERT-base-multilingual-uncased[1] model is case insensitive and consists of 12 layers of transformer blocks. The RoBERTa-base model[2] was pre-trained on English and is case sensitive. It also consists of 12 layers of transformers block with a hidden size of 768.

In this study, the following hyper-paramaters are used to fine-tune mBERT for both datasets: learning rate = 4e−5, training and evaluation batch size = 8, Adam's optimizer with epsilon value = 1e−08, and 2 training epochs. The hyper-parameters used for fine-tuning RoBERTa for both datasets are as follows: learning rate = 3e−5, training and evaluation batch size = 8, Adam's optimizer with epsilon value = 1e−08, and 2 training epochs. The sequence length for both models was set to 256 tokens.

Figure 2 displays the experimental flowchart of the first approach for a sample sentence using the mBERT model. The sequence is first split up into sub-words according to the WordPiece model. Two special tokens, [CLS] and [SEP], are added to the beginning and end of the sequence respectively. The [CLS] token is used by BERT-based models to encode a sentence level vector that can be used for classification purposes. The tokens are then assigned token ids and passed

---

[1] https://huggingface.co/bert-base-multilingual-uncased.
[2] https://huggingface.co/roberta-base.

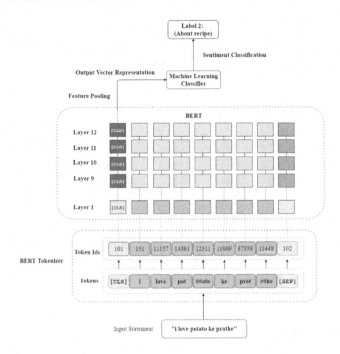

Fig. 3. Experimental Flowchart of the 2nd Approach for a sample sentence using mBERT

as input to the BERT model. The BERT-base model consists of 12 layers. The [CLS] embedding obtained from the last transformers layer is passed through a fully-connected layer for sentiment analysis.

Figure 3 displays the experimental flowchart for the second approach. In the second approach, the feature vectors of the [CLS] token are extracted from the final layers of both fine-tuned models, pooled through four combination strategies, and fed to downstream machine learning classifiers. The vector representations are selected from the last four layers, as they contain more task-specific embeddings [20]. The sequence length was set to 64 tokens while performing feature extraction.

The four pooling strategies considered are as follows [29,30]:

1. Selecting features from the last layer
2. Selecting features from the second last layer
3. Taking sum of features from the last four layers
4. Concatenating the features of the last four layers

Both parametric and non-parametric machine learning algorithms are used for downstream classification. Parametric algorithms, such as LR, NB (Gaussian and Bernouilli), and SVM-Linear kernel (SVM-L), require a fixed number of parameters for training. In non-parametric algorithms, such as KNN and SVM-Radial Basis Function kernel (SVM-RBF), the number of features are infinite and increase with the training data.

The pre-trained language models are implemented using the HuggingFace Transformers library [31] and PyTorch [32]. Machine learning algorithms are implemented with the Scikit-learn library [33]. For both approaches, the data is split into 75% training samples and 25% testing samples. In order to perform parameter tuning of the machine learning algorithms, grid search for optimal parameters is conducted. A range of 10^{-3} to 10^{+3} is used for the following parameters: α (alpha) for Bernoulli Naive Bayes (NB-B); C for LR and SVM-L; and C and γ (gamma) for SVM-RBF. For Gaussian Naive Bayes (NB-G), Laplace smoothing has been performed. For KNN, the number of neighbours are considered in the range of 15 to 20. K-fold cross-validation with k = 10 is conducted on the training data.

Table 1. Results of Approach-1 (fine-tuning) for Kabita Kitchen's Dataset

Model	Accuracy	MCC	Macro-F1
RoBERTa	**85.06**	**0.8261**	**0.8496**
mBERT	84.57	0.8204	0.8439

Table 2. Results of Approach-1 (fine-tuning) for Nisha Madhulika's Dataset

Model	Accuracy	MCC	Macro-F1
RoBERTa	**81.79**	**0.7877**	**0.8176**
mBERT	80.97	0.7787	0.8082

4.3 Evaluation Metrics

Model performance is evaluated on the following evaluation criteria: accuracy, macro-F1 score, Mathews correlation coefficient (MCC), Log loss, and Area Under the Receiver Operating Characteristic Curve (ROC-AUC) score. These are some of the most widely used evaluation metrics for sentiment analysis [34]. Model accuracy is calculated as the total number of correct predictions over the total number of validation samples. The F1 score is the harmonic mean of precision and recall, and the macro-weighted average of F1-score is considered for this study. Log loss, or cross-entropy loss measures how close the prediction probability is to the predicted value [35]. The value of log loss ranges from 0 to ∞, and a model with a lower value is preferred. The ROC-AUC score measures the ability of the model to distinguish between the classes [36]. The score ranges from 0 to 1. The higher the score, the better the model is at predicting the correct class. ROC-AUC plot allows for the visualisation of the trade off between sensitivity and specificity of a classifier. The area under the curve is depicted for each class. The true positive rate of the classifier is plotted against the false positive rate. Class Prediction Error (CPE) plots the total number of training samples per class as a stacked bar chart of total predictions, including false positives and false negatives for each class. To determine if the results obtained by our experiment are statistically significant, the z-test is also conducted. Z-test allows us to compare the raw values obtained by the experiment if the sample size is relatively large. Explanations for the model predictions for the second approach are generated through the LIME framework[3]. Each model implemented in the experiment is considered as a single black-box model. A sparse linear model is learned around the sample for which the explanation is generated.

Table 3. Validation Results for Approach-2 (Feature-based) on Nisha Madhulika's dataset using mBERT

	Algorithm	Accuracy	MCC	Macro-F1	Log loss	Roc-AUC
Last layer	KNN	86.69	0.8450	0.8661	1.1875	0.9744
	SVM-L	87.18	0.8507	0.8711	0.4022	0.9815
	SVM-R	87.02	0.8488	0.8695	0.4097	0.9801
	LR	**87.42**	**0.8535**	**0.8735**	**0.3919**	**0.9820**
	NB-B	86.12	0.8384	0.8609	4.6360	0.9732
	NB-G	86.36	0.8412	0.8639	4.6703	0.9598
Second last layer	KNN	86.04	0.8373	0.8594	1.3740	0.9715
	SVM-L	**87.18**	**0.8506**	**0.8711**	0.4021	0.9817
	SVM-R	87.02	0.8487	0.8695	0.4147	0.9799
	LR	87.02	0.8486	0.8696	**0.3880**	**0.9827**
	NB-B	85.79	0.8347	0.8578	4.6951	0.9745
	NB-G	85.55	0.8319	0.8550	4.7970	0.9696
Sum last 4 layers	KNN	86.12	0.8383	0.8600	1.3388	0.9710
	SVM-L	86.85	0.8469	0.8677	**0.4012**	**0.9817**
	SVM-R	**87.18**	**0.8507**	**0.8711**	0.4116	0.9801
	LR	86.12	0.8382	0.8603	0.4578	0.9789
	NB-B	86.20	0.8394	0.8615	4.5733	0.9737
	NB-G	85.30	0.8290	0.8523	4.9436	0.9663
Concat last 4 layers	KNN	86.20	0.8393	0.8610	1.3116	0.9714
	SVM-L	**87.26**	**0.8516**	**0.8719**	**0.3963**	**0.9824**
	SVM-R	87.02	0.8487	0.8695	0.4006	0.9816
	LR	87.18	0.8506	0.8710	0.4055	0.9818
	NB-B	85.79	0.8347	0.8575	4.8326	0.9531
	NB-G	85.46	0.8310	0.8545	4.9765	0.9327

[3] https://github.com/marcotcr/lime.

Table 4. Validation Results for Approach-2 (Feature-based) on Nisha Madhulika's dataset using RoBERTa

	Algorithm	Accuracy	MCC	Macro-F1	Log loss	Roc-AUC
Last layer	KNN	86.12	0.8382	0.8610	1.2826	0.9723
	SVM-L	85.63	0.8325	0.8562	0.4153	0.9820
	SVM-R	**86.44**	**0.8421**	**0.8648**	0.4328	0.9791
	LR	86.28	0.8401	0.8626	**0.4058**	**0.9826**
	NB-B	85.14	0.8268	0.8504	4.7306	0.9755
	NB-G	85.71	0.8336	0.8577	4.8732	0.9552
Second last layer	KNN	85.87	0.8353	0.8582	1.2672	0.9719
	SVM-L	**86.04**	**0.8373**	**0.8604**	0.4153	0.9810
	SVM-R	85.87	0.8353	0.8586	0.4176	0.9819
	LR	85.79	0.8343	0.8576	**0.4014**	**0.9827**
	NB-B	85.30	0.8287	0.8526	4.8063	0.9749
	NB-G	85.71	0.8335	0.8562	4.8186	0.9663
Sum last 4 layers	KNN	85.79	0.8344	0.8575	1.3580	0.9716
	SVM-L	**86.04**	**0.8373**	**0.8602**	0.4081	0.9819
	SVM-R	85.87	0.8353	0.8585	0.4142	0.9820
	LR	85.87	0.8353	0.8585	**0.4020**	**0.9830**
	NB-B	85.30	0.8287	0.8525	4.7695	0.9756
	NB-G	85.71	0.8335	0.8573	4.8919	0.9574
Concat last 4 layers	KNN	**86.04**	0.8372	**0.8602**	1.2330	0.9729
	SVM-L	85.95	0.8363	0.8595	0.4079	0.9823
	SVM-R	85.95	0.8363	0.8596	0.4087	0.9820
	LR	**86.04**	0.8372	0.8601	**0.4047**	**0.9826**
	NB-B	85.63	0.8325	0.8560	4.9132	0.9517
	NB-G	**86.04**	**0.8373**	0.8595	4.8000	0.9414

5   Results and Analysis

In this section, the results obtained by the two approaches are recorded and analysed.

5.1   Empirical Results

Table 1 and Table 2 display the results for the first approach for Kabita Kitchen's and Nisha Madhulika's datasets, respectively. For the first approach, for Kabita Kitchen's dataset, RoBERTa gives a higher accuracy of 85.06%, MCC of 0.8261 and macro-F1 score of 0.8496. For Nisha Madhulika's channel, RoBERTa gives a higher accuracy of 81.79%, MCC of 0.7877, and macro-F1 score of 0.8176. Thus, RoBERTa outperforms mBERT for both datasets.

For the second approach, the classification results achieved by selecting features from the intermediate layers of mBERT and RoBERTa for Nisha Madhulika's channel are displayed in Table 3 and 4, respectively. For Nisha Madhulika's

Table 5. Validation Results for Approach-2 (Feature-based) on Kabita Kitchen's dataset using mBERT

	Algorithm	Accuracy	MCC	Macro-F1	Log loss	Roc-AUC
Last layer	KNN	**92.65**	**0.9143**	**0.9263**	0.8644	0.9837
	SVM-L	91.59	0.9019	0.9156	0.2706	0.9903
	SVM-R	91.67	0.9028	0.9166	0.2970	0.9871
	LR	92.40	0.9115	0.9237	**0.2585**	**0.9918**
	NB-B	92.57	0.9133	0.9256	2.5033	0.9843
	NB-G	92.40	0.9114	0.9242	2.6221	0.9652
Second last layer	KNN	91.91	0.9058	0.9188	0.8965	0.9832
	SVM-L	92.16	0.9086	0.9213	0.2679	0.9908
	SVM-R	92.24	0.9095	0.9221	0.2685	0.9910
	LR	**92.73**	**0.9152**	**0.9270**	**0.2535**	**0.9924**
	NB-B	91.51	0.9011	0.9149	2.7978	0.9852
	NB-G	91.67	0.9029	0.9168	2.8287	0.9735
Sum last 4 layers	KNN	91.59	0.9020	0.9154	1.0037	0.9811
	SVM-L	**92.32**	**0.9105**	**0.9230**	**0.2625**	**0.9913**
	SVM-R	91.91	0.9057	0.9188	0.2667	0.9905
	LR	**92.32**	**0.9105**	0.9229	0.2629	**0.9913**
	NB-B	91.02	0.8954	0.9099	2.8475	0.9858
	NB-G	91.34	0.8992	0.9135	2.9101	0.9744
Concat last 4 layers	KNN	91.59	0.9019	0.9155	0.9445	0.9824
	SVM-L	91.91	0.9057	0.9188	0.2637	0.9913
	SVM-R	92.08	0.9076	0.9205	0.2654	0.9908
	LR	**92.24**	**0.9095**	**0.9221**	**0.2574**	**0.9919**
	NB-B	91.67	0.9029	0.9165	2.8026	0.9658
	NB-G	91.83	0.9048	0.9184	2.8118	0.9593

channel, the feature-based method achieves the highest accuracy of 87.42% when the features from the last layer were selected and an LR classifier was used. This model also achieves the highest MCC of 0.8535 and highest macro-F1 score of 0.8735. It performs well on other metrics as well, with a log loss of 0.3919 and ROC-AUC score of 0.9820. Thus, we select this model as the best performing model for the dataset. The RoBERTa model gives a comparable performance, with an accuracy of 86.44%, MCC of 0.8421, and macro-F1 of 0.8648 using SVM-R and features from the last layer.

Figure 4 displays the CPE for Nisha Madhulika's dataset for the best performing model (mBERT + LR). It generally performs well on all classes, but has the worst performance on the 'Suggestion or queries' and 'Hybrid' classes. Figure 5 displays the ROC-AUC of mBERT + LR classifier trained on Nisha Madhulika's dataset using features from the last layer. From the figure, we see that the AUC for all classes is >0.96, indicating that the classifier is optimally

trained and performs well on all classes. The best performance is on class 'Suggestion or queries', with an AUC score of 1.
The classification results for the feature-based method for Kabita Kitchen's channel for mBERT and RoBERTa model are displayed in Table 5 and 6, respectively. For Kabita Kitchen's channel, selecting features from the second last layer of mBERT and using LR classifier provides the highest accuracy of 92.73%, MCC of 0.9152, macro-F1 score of 0.9270, Log loss of 0.2535, and ROC-AUC of 0.9924. Thus, on the basis of accuracy, macro-F1, MCC, Log loss, and ROC-AUC score, this is selected as the best performing model. The RoBERTa model gives a comparable accuracy of 92.40%, MCC of 0.9114, macro-F1 of 0.9240, Log-loss of 0.2585, and ROC-AUC score of 0.9916. Based all the evaluation criteria, mBERT gives better contextual representations and is the better performing model. The logistic regression model usually performs the best on all metrics for all vector combinations. The log loss is highest for Naive Bayes classifiers.

Table 6. Validation Results for Approach-2 (Feature-based) on Kabita Kitchen's dataset using RoBERTa

	Algorithm	Accuracy	MCC	Macro-F1	Log loss	Roc-AUC
Last layer	KNN	91.83	0.9048	0.9180	0.9145	0.9831
	SVM-L	91.67	0.9029	0.9165	0.2640	0.9907
	SVM-R	91.91	0.9057	0.9190	0.2733	0.9898
	LR	**92.16**	**0.9086**	**0.9215**	**0.2603**	**0.9909**
	NB-B	91.83	0.9048	0.9181	2.6215	0.9885
	NB-G	91.91	0.9058	0.9189	2.6937	0.9844
Second Last Layer	KNN	91.75	0.9040	0.9172	0.9443	0.9825
	SVM-L	92.08	0.9076	0.9205	0.2740	0.9896
	SVM-R	**92.32**	**0.9105**	**0.9233**	0.2885	0.9883
	LR	**92.32**	**0.9105**	0.9232	**0.2585**	**0.9916**
	NB-B	91.75	0.9039	0.9172	1.9780	0.9895
	NB-G	91.10	0.8965	0.9103	1.7120	0.9909
Sum last 4 layers	KNN	91.59	0.9020	0.9155	0.9482	0.9825
	SVM-L	91.83	0.9047	0.9182	**0.2678**	**0.9905**
	SVM-R	92.00	0.9066	0.9200	0.2882	0.9879
	LR	**92.16**	**0.9086**	**0.9215**	0.2751	0.9903
	NB-B	91.59	0.9019	0.9162	2.7196	0.9880
	NB-G	91.75	0.9038	0.9177	2.7904	0.9802
Concat last 4 layers	KNN	91.75	0.9039	0.9170	0.9949	0.9818
	SVM-L	91.91	0.9057	0.9191	0.2668	0.9906
	SVM-R	92.08	0.9076	0.9207	0.2830	0.9884
	LR	**92.40**	**0.9114**	**0.9240**	**0.2602**	**0.9912**
	NB-B	91.51	0.9012	0.9144	2.5242	0.9883
	NB-G	92.00	0.9068	0.9196	2.7356	0.9693

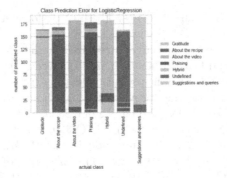

Fig. 4. Class Prediction Error Plot Nisha Madhlika's dataset

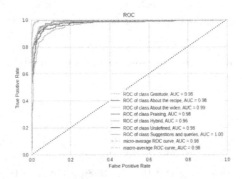

Fig. 5. ROC Curve for Nisha Madhlika's dataset

Figure 6 displays the CPE graph for the mBERT+LR model for Kabita Kitchen's dataset, and it allows us to visualise the incorrect predictions per class. The model seems to perform well on each class, but incorrectly classifies a few instances of class 'Suggestion or queries' as 'Undefined'. Figure 7 depicts the ROC-AUC for Kabita Kitchen's channel, and the AUC for all the classes is >0.98.

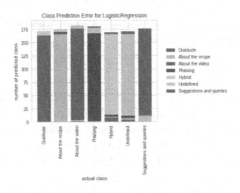

Fig. 6. Class Prediction Error Plot for Kabita Kitchen's Channel

The lowest AUC score is for the class 'Undefined' (0.98), and the best performance is 1.0 for classes 'Gratitude', 'About the recipe', and 'About the video'.

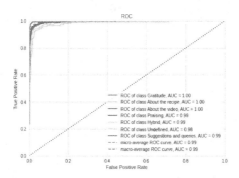

Fig. 7. ROC curve for Kabita Kitchen's Channel

5.2   Statistical Testing

To determine if the results obtained by the experiment are statistically significant, z-test was performed on the 24 results of the second approach for accuracy, macro-F1 and MCC. The null hypothesis for the z-test assumes that there is no significant difference between the means of the results obtained by the mBERT and RoBERTa models.

For Nisha Madhulika's dataset, the p-values for accuracy, macro-F1 and MCC are 6.30e−06, 2.00e−05, and 3.29e−06 respectively. Thus, the hypothesis can be rejected at significance levels 0.01, 0.05, and 0.10. The z-test concludes that there is a significant difference between the results obtained by the two models for this dataset. For Kabita Kitchen's channel, the p-values for accuracy, macro-F1 and MCC are 0.4124, 0.3877, and 0.4188 respectively. Thus, the hypothesis fails to reject at significance levels 0.01, 0.05, and 0.10 for accuracy, macro-F1 and MCC. For this dataset, the z-test concludes that there is no significant difference between the results obtained by the two models.

5.3   Explainability

LIME has been used to explain model predictions of the second approach in Figs. 8, 9, 10, and 11. The prediction probabilities are displayed for the top classes, and the contributing weight of each word towards the respective classes is also displayed along with the sentence. For both the datasets, an example of each an incorrect and correct prediction made by the best performing model has been examined.

Figure 8 displays an explanation for a correct prediction made by the best performing model (mBERT + LR) for Kabita Kitchen's channel on a code-mixed sentence. The code-mixed sentence "Nice mam I will try thanku itni acchi or easy resipes ko share kiya" translates to "Nice ma'am I will try thank you for sharing

114   S. Yadav and A. Kaushik

such good and easy recipes". The model predicts the correct class 'Hybrid' with
high confidence (0.97), and the highest contribution towards the correct prediction is given by 'Nice', 'thanku', and 'easy'. The 'Hybrid' category combines
sentiments such as Gratitude and opinions about the video, thus indicating the
significance of words such as 'Nice' towards the category.

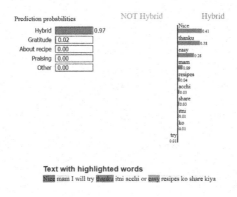

Text with highlighted words
Nice mam I will try thanku itni acchi or easy resipes ko share kiya

Fig. 8. LIME explanation for correct model prediction for Kabita Kitchen's dataset

Figure 9 displays an explanation for an incorrect prediction made by the best
performing model for Kabita Kitchen's channel on a code-mixed sentence. The
statement "Mujhe bhot ache lagi apki respi mene subscribe kardia bhot ache he"
translates to "I really liked your recipe I have subscribed It's very good". The
true class of the sentence is 'About recipe' but the model incorrectly predicted it
is as 'Praising', with the highest weights given to 'apki' (yours) (0.67), 'Mujhe'
(I) (0.16) and 'ache' (good) (0.12). The model incorrectly assumed that this
instance belonged to the class 'Praising' due to the presence of such tokens.

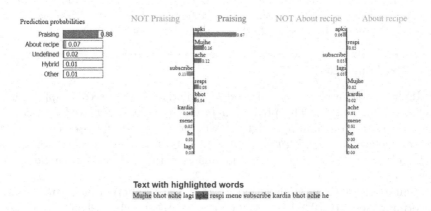

Text with highlighted words
Mujhe bhot ache lagi apki respi mene subscribe kardia bhot ache he

Fig. 9. LIME explanation for incorrect model prediction on Kabita Kitchen's dataset

Figure 10 displays an explanation for an correct prediction made by the best performing model (mBERT + LR) for Nisha Madhulika's channel on a code-mixed sentence. The sentence "Thanks aap itna Achha paratha Banai hai aur aap bahut acchi hai thanks" translates to "Thanks you have made such good parathas and you are very nice thanks." The explanation shows that the models assigns significant weights to 'aap' (you), 'thanks', 'acchi' (nice), etc., which can be logically significant to the class 'Hybrid'.

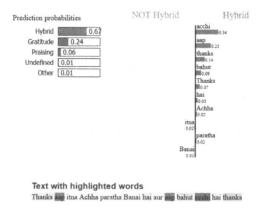

Fig. 10. LIME explanation for correct model prediction on Nisha Madhulika's dataset

Figure 11 displays an explanation for an incorrect prediction made by the best performing model for Nisha Madhulika's channel on a code-mixed sentence. The sentence "bhot Asha aalo vala prantha" translates to "very good potato prantha (flat bread)". The model incorrectly classifies the sentence as 'Undefined', and assigns a relatively small probability to the correct label 'About the recipe'. LIME shows that the model does however assign some weights to 'prantha' (0.02) and 'bhot' (0.03), which are significant for the class 'About the recipe'. Thus, it is evident that using LIME for creating explanations for model predictions provides significant and human-interpretable rationales for model behavior.

6   Discussion

In this section, we discuss our findings with respect to the research questions that were posed and previous work that has been conducted on the dataset.

1. Which Transformer-based model, multilingual BERT or monolingual RoBERTa, provides better results for sentiment analysis on code-mixed Hinglish data?
   For Kabita Kitchen's dataset, RoBERTa provides the higher accuracy of 85.06%, MCC of 0.8261 and macro-F1 score of 0.8496 out of the two models.

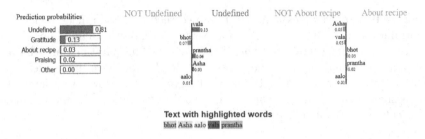

Fig. 11. LIME explanation for incorrect model prediction on Nisha Madhulika's dataset

For Nisha Madhulika's dataset, RoBERTa provides the higher accuracy of 81.79%, MCC of 0.7877, and macro-F1 of 0.8176. Thus, for both datasets in approach-1, RoBERTa outperforms mBERT. The RoBERTa-base model is a monolingual model trained only on English, and could provide an advantage for code-mixed languages. The first approach employed in this study also outperforms the results of the baseline study done by Kaur et al. [4], with an improvement in accuracy of 9.69 points for Kabita Kitchen's dataset and 7.78 points for Nisha Madhulika's dataset.

2. Do the final layers of the models provide accurate sentence-level representations for classification?

For Kabita kitchen's channel, selecting the vector representation of the [CLS] token from the second last layer of mBERT gives the highest accuracy of 92.73% with LR classifier. Compared to the first experimental approach of using a fully-connected classification layer, there is an improvement of 7.67 points in accuracy over using a fine-tuned RoBERTa and 8.16 over using mBERT. For Nisha Madhulika's channel, embeddings from the last layer of mBERT using a LR classifier give the highest accuracy of 87.42%, an improvement of 6.45 points over using a fine-tuned mBERT, and 5.63 points over fine-tuned RoBERTa in the first approach. The scores are a significant improvement over the scores obtained by Kaur et al. [4], where TF-IDF vectorizer and LR classifier provided an accuracy of 74.01% in Nisha Madulika's dataset and 75.37% in Kabita's Kitchen dataset. The methodology also outperforms the approach taken in study [6], where a fine-tuned BERT model was used to extract token embeddings, and sentence-level embeddings were calculated by taking mean of all tokens. For Kabita Kitchen's dataset, the highest accuracy achieved was 76% and for Nisha Madhulika's dataset, the highest accuracy achieved was 72%. However, the methodology used in this study does not outperform the approach used by Donthula et al. [5], where the highest accuracy achieved was 98.53% on Kabita's dataset and 98.48% on Nisha Madhulika's dataset by using count vectorizer and MLP.

3. Are the results obtained by the study statistically significant?

To determine statistical significance, z-test was applied on the accuracy, macro-F1, and MCC scores of Approach-2 for both models. For Nisha Madhulika's dataset, the z-test concluded that the results are statistically significant for significance levels 0.01, 0.05, and 0.10 for model accuracy, macro-F1 score, and MCC. The null hypothesis was rejected and it can be concluded that the results obtained in our study are statistically significant. However, for Kabita Kitchen's dataset, the hypothesis failed to reject for all three significance levels.

4. Are the explanations for classifications provided by the models trustworthy? Using LIME explanations, we can see that the model is using significant features to classify a sentence to a particular class, and is behaving in a coherent manner. The explanations were obtained by manually examining separate predictions. For future experimentation, a human annotated dataset that includes the rationales used for classification, as done by Mathew et al. [19], needs to be compiled and studied so that the explanations provided by LIME can be correctly evaluated and understood.

7   Conclusion and Future Work

In this study, we measured the performance of two transformer-based pre-trained language models, RoBERTa and mBERT, on mix-code Hinglish data. In the first approach, the standard RoBERTA outperforms mBERT on both datasets, resulting in the best accuracy of 85.06% for Kabita's kitchen channel, and 81.79% for Nisha Madhulika's channel. In the second approach, contextual sentence embeddings were extracted from intermediate layers of the two models and machine learning classifiers were implemented. Compared to the baseline study done by Kaur et al. [4], the feature-based approach explored in this study obtains an improvement in accuracy of 17.36 points for Kabita Kitchen's dataset and 13.41 points for Nisha Madhulika's dataset. We can thus safely conclude that the encoder layers of transformer-based language models encode rich contextual information which can be used for downstream NLP tasks. The XAI technique of LIME also generates human-readable explanations for model predictions and highlights some significant patterns. As 'Hinglish' is a under-resourced language, there are not many pre-trained language models, tokenizers, and other NLP toolkits for text processing. Future scope of this study will be to further explore the type of information the pre-trained language model is encoding for the respective datasets. Further analysis of features obtained from transformer-based models could also provide better insight into the model's knowledge and learning capabilities for low-resource languages. Other approaches to exploring explainability of BERT-based models, such as SHAP and model attention weights, can also be studied to understand predictions and improve trust in the model. A larger dataset can also be annotated to introduce rationales to LIME explanations, allowing further understanding of model performance on the 'Hinglish' language.

References

1. YouTube India Statistics. https://www.statista.com/statistics/280685/number-of-monthly-unique-youtube-users/. Accessed 26 July 2022
2. Arora, G.: iNLTK: natural language toolkit for Indic languages. arXiv preprint arXiv:2009.12534 (2020)
3. Jain, K., Deshpande, A., Shridhar, K., Laumann, F., Dash, A.: Indic-transformers: an analysis of transformer language models for Indian languages. arXiv preprint arXiv:2011.02323 (2020)
4. Kaur, G., Kaushik, A., Sharma, S.: Cooking is creating emotion: a study on Hinglish sentiments of YouTube cookery channels using semi-supervised approach. Big Data Cogn. Comput. **3**(3), 37 (2019)
5. Donthula, S.K., Kaushik, A.: Man is what he eats: a research on Hinglish sentiments of YouTube cookery channels using deep learning. Int. J. Recent Technol. Eng. (IJRTE) **8**(2S11), 930–937 (2019)
6. Yadav, S., Kaushik, A., Sharma, S.: Cooking well, with love, is an art: transformers on YouTube Hinglish data. In: 2021 International Conference on Computational Performance Evaluation (ComPE), pp. 836–841. IEEE (2021)
7. Vaswani, A., et al.: Attention is all you need. In: Advances in Neural Information Processing Systems, vol. 30 (2017)
8. Devlin, J., Chang, M.W., Lee, K., Toutanova, K.: BERT: pre-training of deep bidirectional transformers for language understanding. arXiv preprint arXiv:1810.04805 (2018)
9. Polignano, M., Basile, P., De Gemmis, M., Semeraro, G., Basile, V.: ALBERTO: Italian BERT language understanding model for NLP challenging tasks based on tweets. In: 6th Italian Conference on Computational Linguistics, CLiC-it 2019, vol. 2481, pp. 1–6. CEUR (2019)
10. de Vries, W., van Cranenburgh, A., Bisazza, A., Caselli, T., van Noord, G., Nissim, M.: BERTje: a Dutch BERT model. arXiv preprint arXiv:1912.09582 (2019)
11. Lee, S., Jang, H., Baik, Y., Park, S., Shin, H.: KR-BERT: a small-scale Korean-specific language model. arXiv preprint arXiv:2008.03979 (2020)
12. Martin, L., et al.: CamemBERT: a tasty French language model. arXiv preprint arXiv:1911.03894 (2019)
13. Adadi, A., Berrada, M.: Peeking inside the black-box: a survey on explainable artificial intelligence (XAI). IEEE Access **6**, 52138–52160 (2018)
14. Ribeiro, M.T., Singh, S., Guestrin, C.: "why should i trust you?" Explaining the predictions of any classifier. In: Proceedings of the 22nd ACM SIGKDD International Conference on Knowledge Discovery and Data Mining, pp. 1135–1144 (2016)
15. Liu, Y., et al.: RoBERTA: a robustly optimized BERT pretraining approach. arXiv preprint arXiv:1907.11692 (2019)
16. Kabita's Kitchen Cookery Channel. https://www.Youtube.com/channel/CChqsCRFePrP2X897iQkyAA. Accessed 10 July 2022
17. Nisha Madhulika's Cookery Channel. https://www.Youtube.com/user/NishaMadhulika. Accessed 10 July 2022
18. Kaushik, A., Kaur, G.: YouTube cookery channels viewers comments in Hinglish, May 2019. https://doi.org/10.5281/zenodo.2841848
19. Mathew, B., Saha, P., Yimam, S.M., Biemann, C., Goyal, P., Mukherjee, A.: HateXplain: a benchmark dataset for explainable hate speech detection. In: Proceedings of the AAAI Conference on Artificial Intelligence, vol. 35, no. 17, pp. 14867–14875 (2021)

20. Rogers, A., Kovaleva, O., Rumshisky, A.: A primer in BERTology: what we know about how BERT works. Trans. Assoc. Comput. Linguist. **8**, 842–866 (2020)
21. Sang, E.F., De Meulder, F.: Introduction to the CoNLL-2003 shared task: language-independent named entity recognition. arXiv preprint cs/0306050 (2003)
22. Yang, J., Zhao, H.: Deepening hidden representations from pre-trained language models. arXiv preprint arXiv:1911.01940 (2019)
23. Su, T.C., Cheng, H.C.: SesameBERT: attention for anywhere. In: 2020 IEEE 7th International Conference on Data Science and Advanced Analytics (DSAA), pp. 363–369. IEEE (2020)
24. McCoy, R.T., Pavlick, E., Linzen, T.: Right for the wrong reasons: diagnosing syntactic heuristics in natural language inference. arXiv preprint arXiv:1902.01007 (2019)
25. Kazhuparambil, S., Kaushik, A.: Classification of Malayalam-English mix-code comments using current state of art. In: 2020 IEEE International Conference for Innovation in Technology (INOCON), pp. 1–6. IEEE (2020)
26. Patwa, P., et al.: SemEval-2020 task 9: overview of sentiment analysis of code-mixed tweets. In: Proceedings of the Fourteenth Workshop on Semantic Evaluation, pp. 774–790 (2020)
27. Bhange, M., Kasliwal, N.: HinglishNLP at SemEval-2020 task 9: fine-tuned language models for Hinglish sentiment detection. In: Proceedings of the Fourteenth Workshop on Semantic Evaluation, pp. 934–939 (2020)
28. Szczepański, M., Pawlicki, M., Kozik, R., Choraś, M.: New explainability method for BERT-based model in fake news detection. Sci. Rep. **11**(1), 1–13 (2021)
29. BERT Word Embeddings Tutorial. https://mccormickml.com/2019/05/14/BERT-word-embeddings-tutorial/. Accessed 13 July 2022
30. A Visual Guide to Using BERT for the First Time. https://jalammar.github.io/a-visual-guide-to-using-bert-for-the-first-time/. Accessed 13 July 2022
31. Wolf, T., et al.: HuggingFace's transformers: state-of-the-art natural language processing. arXiv preprint arXiv:1910.03771 (2019)
32. Paszke, A., et al.: Pytorch: an imperative style, high-performance deep learning library. In: Wallach, H., Larochelle, H., Beygelzimer, A., d'Alché-Buc, F., Fox, E., Garnett, R. (eds.) Advances in Neural Information Processing Systems, vol. 32, pp. 8024–8035. Curran Associates, Inc. (2019). https://papers.neurips.cc/paper/9015-pytorch-an-imperative-style-high-performance-deep-learning-library.pdf
33. Scikit Learn: Machine Learning in Python. https://scikit-learn.org/stable/. Accessed 25 Oct 2022
34. Shah, S.R., Kaushik, A.: Sentiment analysis on Indian indigenous languages: a review on multilingual opinion mining. arXiv preprint arXiv:1911.12848 (2019)
35. Bishop, C.M., Nasrabadi, N.M.: Pattern Recognition and Machine Learning, vol. 4, no. 4. Springer, New York (2006)
36. Hand, D.J., Till, R.J.: A simple generalisation of the area under the ROC curve for multiple class classification problems. Mach. Learn. **45**(2), 171–186 (2001)

Transformer Based Hope Speech Comment Classification in Code-Mixed Text

Prasanna Kumar Kumaresan[1]([✉]) [iD], Rahul Ponnusamy[2] [iD], Elizabeth Sherly[1] [iD], Sangeetha Sivanesan[3] [iD], and Bharathi Raja Chakravarthi[4] [iD]

[1] Indian Institute of Information Technology and Management-Kerala, Thiruvananthapuram, Kerala, India
kprasannakumar30@gmail.com, sherly@iiitmk.ac.in
[2] Techvantage Analytics, Thiruvananthapuram, Kerala, India
[3] National Institute of Technology, Tiruchirappalli, India
sangeetha@nitt.edu
[4] University of Galway, Galway, Ireland
bharathiraja.asokachakravarthi@universityofgalway.ie

Abstract. Our research aims to describe Natural Language Processing (NLP) tasks aimed at hope speech detection in social media code-mixed comments. Commentaries on social media often violate strict grammar rules and contain code-mixed text written in non-native scripts. Detecting hope speech from these code-mixed sentences will be challenging in three languages: Tamil, English, and Malayalam. First, we remove unnecessary content from noisy texts as a pre-processing and set a baseline for detecting hope speech. Then we implemented pre-trained transformer models and different traditional machine-learning models with feature extraction methods. In the test set, our best configurations achieved macro F1 scores of 0.5498, 0.5447, and 0.7202 for Tamil, English, and Malayalam, while in the development set, we achieved macro F1 scores of 0.5825, 0.4779, and 0.7202 for Tamil, English, and Malayalam.

Keywords: Transformer · Hope speech · Code mixing · Machine learning

1   Introduction

Hope gives people a reason to keep fighting even though human existence is unpredictable. Hope motivates us to remain committed to the goal, which despite its unpredictable nature, is important enough to keep going toward achieving for as long as possible. Facebook, Twitter, Instagram, and YouTube are among the social media platforms used today to express their views and opinions. Marginalized individuals also use these platforms to receive online assistance and support [1–3]. During the pandemic outbreak, people from several parts of the world fear losing loved ones and cannot access essential services such as schools, hospitals, and mental health facilities. Therefore, people turn to online forums to meet

Anand Kumar M et al. (Eds.): SPELLL 2022, CCIS 1802, pp. 120–137, 2023.
https://doi.org/10.1007/978-3-031-33231-9_8

their informational, emotional, and social needs. People can network on social networking sites, feel socially included, and gain a sense of belonging by participating. These factors significantly affect physical and psychological well-being and mental health [4].

Despite these positive features, social media platforms also contain many malicious or harmful posts due to the absence of any governing authority [5,6]. The analysis of social media posts would help to avoid this problem by identifying and controlling the spread of harmful content, using methods such as hate speech detection [7], offensive language detection [8,9], homophobia and transphobia detection [10], and abusive language detection. In addition to their drawbacks, technologies designed to prevent hate speech and offensive language have disadvantages, such as bias in training data, and restricting user expression through policies that prohibit specific modes of expression, thus compromising the principles of Equality, Diversity, and Inclusion. Therefore, we should focus on spreading positively rather than curbing individual indications to address negative comments.

Hope speech refers to any social media comment that is positive, encouraging, reassuring, inclusive, or supportive that inspires and engenders optimism in people's minds. Hope speech detection refers to classifying a given comment into one of the following classes Hope_speech, Non_hope_speech, or None of these languages. A few examples for each label in all three languages are included in Table 1. The English dataset contained monolingual YouTube comments, while Tamil and Malayalam contained code-mixed comments [11]. We implemented the hope speech detection task as a post/comment-level classification task. First, we performed pre-processing steps to normalize the text. Then we extracted the features from the text using TF-IDF and CountVectorizing and performed six traditional Machine Learning models for baseline (Fig. 1). Next, we performed various pre-trained transformer models to detect hope speech on given code-mixed comments. We follow the process to accomplish the mission and classify whether the text is a hope speech or not. We begin by describing the corpora and the related work for this task, analyze the datasets, explain the methodology, discuss the results & evaluation, and conclude.

Table 1. Examples for each labels in all three languages

English	
God gave us a choice is to love, I would die for that kid	Hope_Speech
The Democrats are backed powerful rich people like soros	Non_Hope_Speech
ESTE PSICA"PATA MAS ~ A"N LUCIFERIANO ES HOMBRE TRANS	Not_English
Tamil	
Neega podara vedio nalla iruku ana subtitle vainthuchu ahh yella language papaga	Hope_Speech
Avan matum enkita maatunan... Avana kolla paniduven	Non_Hope_Speech
I can't uninstall my Pubg	Not_Tamil
Malayalam	
ooororutharum avarude ishtam pole jeevikatte .k.	Hope_Speech
Etraem aduthu nilkilae arunae	Non_Hope_Speech
Phoenix contact me give you're mail I'd I hope I can support you sure!	Not_Malayalam

2 Related Work

The first multilingual hope speech dataset for Equality, Diversity, and Inclusion [11] was created by sourcing comments from YouTube. Then Chakravarthi et al. 2021 [10] conducted the LT-EDIEACL-2021 workshop on hope speech detection, highlighting the importance of identifying positive comments on social media. The task proposed in the workshop has promoted research in the NLP field. Recently, Transformer-based approaches also proved adequate for detecting the hope speech. Several models, namely mBert, IndicBERT, and XLM-RoBERTa framework, have been deployed, and the labels have categorized the usage of the output acquired from the final layer of XLM-RoBERTa, and it outperformed other models. The problem of hope speech detection has been approached using character n-grams-based TF-IDF and MuRIL text representations in the dataset [12].

The authors of this paper [13] have compared the different approaches, namely TF-IDF+LR, TF-IDF+SVM, MuRIL+LR, and MuRIL+SVM, for each language. BiLSTM and Dense architectures and the transformer embeddings like BERT, ULMFiT, MuRIL. For the Tamil and Malayalam languages to classify the comments, they implemented mBERT cased with BiLSTM architecture and mBERT uncased with BiLSTM architecture, which outperformed other models, respectively.

Counter-narratives are another approach that has recently attracted researchers' attention [14]. A counter-narrative method was proposed to weigh the true freedom of speech and avoid over-blocking. [15] created and launched a dataset for counter-speech using comments from YouTube. However, the central concept of immediately interfering with textual responses escalates hostility, although it is acceptable for the author to apprehend why their comment/post has been deleted or blocked and favorably alternate their feedback discourse and attitudes. So we flip our studies to locate excellent data consisting of wishes and inspiring activities like hope speech.

IIITSurat@LT-EDI-EACL2022 participated in the hope speech shared task and worked on the English dataset. Their model works in two phases: first, it uses over-sampling techniques to increase the number of samples and make them comparable in the training dataset, followed by a random forest classifier to classify the comments into hope and non-hope categories [5]. SSN_ARMM@LT-EDI-ACL2022 [16] worked on the English, Tamil, Malayalam, and Kannada dataset. They used the IndicBERT, a multilingual model trained on large-scale corpora covering 12 Indian languages. IndicBERT takes a smaller number of parameters and still gives a state-of-the-art performance.

This research paper [17] Carried out a hope speech detection task with various models and found out that the mBERTcased model provided the best results. They employed zero short cross-lingual model transfer to fine-tune the model evaluation. They found out that the degradation of the model performance was due to the freezing of the base layers of the transformer model. Words Worth: Verbal Content and Hirability Impressions research paper [18] focused on YouTube sentiment analysis. The researchers analyzed these data to find trends and found that user sentiments influence real-life events. As a counter-point to hate speech, hope speech can also be defined as a positive message. Comments offensive or harmful to a particular work or individual are considered hate speech. There is a terrible impact on this society as a result of these offensive comments [11].

Other researchers have attempted to use code-mixed to sample hope speech and have used it along with an English language identifier to re-retrieve texts in Romanized Hindi [19]. They developed a classifier based on active learning strategies to support the Rohingya minority community [20]. A study involving a curated analysis of the movie industry's corpus to identify potential biases toward gender, skin color, and gender representation has been conducted [21].

3 Dataset Description

The total number of comments in each language in the dataset is shown in Table 2. These datasets are in three languages Tamil, English, and Malayalam. We found the hope speech dataset from the [11] in code-mixed texts. They collected data from the social media comments on YouTube[1], the most widely used platform to express an opinion about a particular video. They collected data for English on EDI topics, including women in STEM, LGBTQI issues, COVID-19, and Black Lives Matter from YouTube video comments. For Tamil and Malayalam, they collected data from India on YouTube related to LGBTQI issues [22], COVID-19, women in STEM, the Indochina war, and Dravidian affairs [23]. We collected these comments from YouTube with the help of YouTube Comment Scraper[2].

Then annotated the comments with the help of human annotators. Because of our annotation setup, they used Krippendorff's alpha to measure inter-annotator agreement. We split each dataset into training, development, and test sets. These datasets contain only three labels: hope speech and non-hope speech; these labels were common to all three languages [24,25]. But the third label was different, i.e., not Tamil for the Tamil dataset, not English for the English dataset, and not Malayalam for the Malayalam dataset. This non-language label indicates that the YouTube comments do not belong to a specific language. The detailed distribution of datasets in each set and the total number of labels in each dataset are shown in Table 3. The total amount of comments in all three languages is 59,354. In Tamil dataset has 20198, English has 28,451, and Malayalam has 10705 comments from YouTube.

- **Hope speech:** A number of praises are expressed for love, courage, inter-personal skills, beauty, perseverance, forgiveness, tolerance, and future consciousness. Harmony, beauty, and patience are promoted by comments, and people are positively impacted by them.
  For example:- kashtam thaan. irundhaalum muyarchi seivom
  Translation: It is indeed difficult. Let us try it out though.

---

[1] https://www.youtube.com/.
[2] https://github.com/philbot9/youtube-comment-scraper.

Table 2. Dataset Statistics

Language	Number of Comments
Tamil	20198
English	28451
Malayalam	10705

Table 3. No. of comments in each labels for all languages

Languages	Split	Labels	No. of Comments	Total
Tamil	Training	Hope Speech	6327	16160
		Non-Hope Speech	7872	
		Not-Tamil	1961	
	Development	Hope Speech	757	2018
		Non-Hope Speech	998	
		Not-Tamil	263	
	Test	Hope Speech	815	2020
		Non-Hope Speech	946	
		Not-Tamil	259	
English	Training	Hope Speech	1962	22762
		Non-Hope Speech	20778	
		Not-Tamil	22	
	Development	Hope Speech	272	2843
		Non-Hope Speech	2569	
		Not-Tamil	2	
	Test	Hope Speech	250	2846
		Non-Hope Speech	2593	
		Not-Tamil	3	
Malayalam	Training	Hope Speech	1668	8564
		Non-Hope Speech	6205	
		Not-Tamil	691	
	Development	Hope Speech	190	1070
		Non-Hope Speech	784	
		Not-Tamil	96	
	Test	Hope Speech	194	1071
		Non-Hope Speech	776	
		Not-Tamil	101	

– **Non-Hope speech:** Racism, prejudice, attacks on individuals, anti-humanity, and other items that do not inspire hope in readers.
For example:- paambu kari saappittu namma uyirai vaanguranunga
Tanslation: These guys (Chinese) eat snake meat and make our lives miserable

– **Not-English, Not-Malayalam, Not-Tamil:** There are languages other than English, Malayalam, or Tamil in the data set of languages English, Malayalam, and Tamil. For example, comments are posted in the Tamil language in the English data set.
For example:-
Not Tamil : Plz talk slowly **Translation:** Please talk slowly
Not Malayalam : Gd msg. thanks dr. **Translation:** It is a good message. Thanks Doctor.

4 Methodology

Analyzing the nature of text has been one of the central tasks of natural language processing (NLP). The textual analysis divides texts into relevant meanings [26]. There have been many advancements in solving the problem in the domain of NLP. HAlthough a solution exists, it is difficult to express texts in a format that is appropriate for textual analysis due to the wide variety of languages [27].

4.1 Feature Extraction

Term Frequency and Inverse Document Frequency (TF-IDF) are statistical measures assess how relevant a word is to a report in various records. TF-IDF is commonly used in machine learning algorithms, including stop-word removal. It is common for terms like "a, the, an, it" to occur in a sentence, but they do not carry much information.

$$TF - IDF = TF * IDF \tag{1}$$

Term Frequency is possible to determine the frequency of a term by counting the number of occurrences that appears in a document.

$$TF = \frac{number\ of\ times\ the\ term\ appears\ in\ the\ document}{total\ number\ of\ terms\ in\ the\ document} \tag{2}$$

The *Inverse Document Frequency (IDF)*: This metric is generated to represent the relative frequency of a word across documents. A high number takes many words, and it is a highly repetitive type of document. It helps reduce the weight of standard terms within a group of documents. In our work, we did these TF-IDF measures with the help of *SKlearn* packages[3].

$$IDF = \log(\frac{number\ of\ documents\ in\ the\ corpus}{number\ of\ documents\ in\ the\ corpus\ contain\ the\ term}) \tag{3}$$

CountVectorizer: The CountVectorizer tokenizes the text and performs some basic reprocessing. We have removed all punctuation marks and converted all words to lowercase. It was also necessary to develop a vocabulary of known

---

[3] https://scikit-learn.org/.

words, which we will use to encode unseen text in the future. We returned a vector containing the entire speech's length and the number of times each word appears. CountVectorizer is an excellent source of information provided by the scikit-learn library.

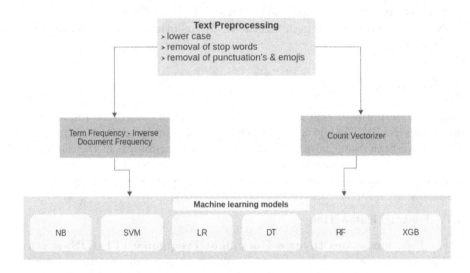

Fig. 1. Flow chart for baseline models

4.2 Machine Learning Model

After extracting features, we performed the machine learning models for classifying the text using the sklearn package. The models that had used are explained one by one below:

Naive Bayes(NB) is a probabilistic model which is simple and fast in predicting the class of tests for data. It is based on the Bayes theorem. In contrast to models such as strategic relapse, Naive Bayes classifiers perform better when autonomy is presumed, and it requires less preparation time. As opposed to a mathematical variable, it performs well when inputs are categorical.

Support Vector Machine (SVM) is a supervised ML algorithm that can be utilized for classification or regression. It uses a kernel method to change your information, and afterward, dependent on these changes, it tracks down an ideal limit between the possible outputs. We executed this model with the scikit-learn library.

Random Forest (RF) assembles various decision trees and combines them to get a more exact and stable forecast. The random forest has similar hyperparameters to a decision tree. Random forest adds extra irregularity to the model while developing the trees, and this is also done with the sklearn package.

A **decision tree (DT)** is a non-parametric model that estimates the target values using decision rules derived from the input vectors' attributes. It is like a tree structure with internal nodes as features, branches as decision points, and leaf nodes as outcomes. Information gain, entropy, and the Gini index build the decision tree. All the variations of the decision tree models are trained with default parameters.

Logistic regression (LR) is used as a classifier to predict the output using linear input combinations. The logistic function is used to indicate the probability of a specific class. The input and the corresponding system determine the result of logistic regression. The likelihood of output is estimated using a memory-based method in which the probability of output p_o, the possibility of the associated input p_i, and the likelihood of the system p_s are all taken into account. As a result, the classifier predicts p_o with $P(p_o /p_i, p_s)$ as a categorical output. We trained the models with default parameter settings such as $C = 1.0$ and kernel $=$' linear' for each data set. The class labels are predicted using the models for our collection of features.

XGBoost is one of the foremost standard ML algorithms recently. No matter the sort of prediction task at hand, regression, or classification. XGBoost is standard to produce better solutions than different ML algorithms. In this problem, we instantiate an XGBoost classifier because this is a classification problem by calling the XGBClassifier() class from the XGBoost library, becoming the classifier to the training set, and constructing predictions at the test set the usage of the familiar.

4.3 Deep Learning Models

Based on our previous analysis of the hope speech task description and task data, we decided to implement transformer models[4] to detect the hope speech. We explained the models one by one below, which are pretrained models for various languages.

BERT: Bidirectional Encoder Representations from Transformers have been published by researchers at Google AI Language [28]. It has created many debates in the Machine Learning community. A crop of state-of-the-art results on various natural language processing tasks has inspired numerous discussions and conclusions. Transformer, a popular attention model, is applied bidirectionally to language modeling as part of BERT's critical technical innovation. This contrasts with previous efforts, which looked at a text sequence from left to right or combined left-to-right and right-to-left training. For this transformer model, we took two models, cased and uncased, for training the dataset.

We fine-tuned our pre-trained BERT (cased and uncased) model to identify hope speech. Considering the sequence of 512 tokens and emitting the representation of a series of hidden vectors, the BERT base model contains 12 layers of encoder blocks and 12 bidirectional self-attention heads [29]. We added an

---

[4] https://huggingface.co/.

output layer to the BERT model to calculate the conditional probability over the output classes, either hope or non-hope.

- **BERT multilingual base model (uncased):** This is a pretrained language model on the top 102 languages, using an MLM objective. It was introduced in [28]. This model is uncased: it does not differentiate between english and English.
- **BERT multilingual base model (cased):** This is a pre-trained model using the exact masked language modeling (MLM) objective on the top 104 languages. It's also introduced in [28]. Case sensitivity is applied to this model: english and English are different.

A **Robustly optimized BERT Pre-training Approach (RoBERTa)** is a modification of BERT. RoBERTa was trained for longer, with larger batches on 1000% more data than BERT. We removed the Next Sentence Prediction task employed in BERT's pre-training, and dynamic masking during training was introduced. The RoBERTa Base model contains 12 transformer blocks, 768 hidden layers, 12 self-attention heads, and 125 million trainable parameters. Similar to the pretrained BERT model, the pretrained RoBERTa model is also cased, making it appropriate for fine-tuning named entity recognition (NER) problems [30].

- **RoBERTa-base** and **RoBERTa-large** follow the BERT architecture but have 125M parameters. The models are case-sensitive: one difference matters between english and English.
- I also used **RoBERTa-large-MultiNLI**, the large-scale multilingual parallel corpus they released in 2017, featured in a Nature article.

XLM-RoBERTa is a pretrained multilingual language model to execute diverse NLP transfer tasks. It's introduced in the paper Unsupervised Crosslingual Representation Learning at Scale [31].

- **XML-RoBERTa-base** and **XML-RoBERTa-large:** These models learn an internal representation of 100 languages which it can use to extract features beneficial for downstream tasks: when you have a dataset of labeled sentences, you could train a preferred classifier for the usage of the components produced through the XLM-RoBERTa model as inputs. There are approximately 125M parameters in the XLM-R model, which has 12 layers and 768 hidden states. A series of up to 512 tokens are fed into the algorithm, and an output representation of the series is generated. For text classification tasks, XLM-R uses the final hidden state h of the first token to represent the whole sequence. As shown in Eq. 4, XLM-R is enhanced with a simple softmax classifier to predict the probability of label c.

$$p(c|h) = softmax(Wh) \qquad (4)$$

By maximizing the log probability of the correct label, we fine-tune all the parameters from XLM-R and W together.

4.4   Approaches

Following is a detailed description of the methodology:

We used YouTube comment posts in code-mixed Tamil, English, and Malayalam languages to find hope speech comments for this research. First, we loaded the data with the help of Panda's library. We had three datasets: training, development, and testing. Models are trained based on training data, validated based on development datasets, and tested based on test datasets. Before introducing the model to the data, we removed punctuation's and emojis and converted them to lowercase text to make sense of the data using machine learning. We did this by creating a user-defined function called remove_punctuation().

Another step involves encoding labels in the datasets within the string. To use the systems, we used a label encoder module from sklearn, which is imported as a preprocessor module. We encoded labels from strings to numbers using the LabelEncoder() function from the Sklearn package and displayed those encoded label values in Table 4. Next, we perform feature extraction, which is crucial for building traditional machine learning models. The features will be extracted as vectors in this step. We used TFIDFVectorizer and CountVectorizer extractions for performing the various machine-learning models from the sklearn package for this step. Both of these extraction processes transform the text into vectors. Compared with the count vectorizer, TF-IDF was a better feature extraction because it focuses on the frequency of words present in the corpus and the importance of those words. By reducing the input dimensions, the model building becomes less complex by removing the less essential comments.

Table 4. Encoded classes for all three languages

Classes	Encoded labels
None_of_these_language	0
Hope_Speech	1
Non-Hope_Speech	2

Afterward, we performed traditional machine learning (ML) models. The preparation of an ML model includes calculations and gathering information. This term refers to a model created using the preparation interaction in machine learning. In addition to forecasts for old data that don't know what to do, we can utilize ML models to do new analyses on unrelated data. We performed machine learning models such as Naive Bayes (NB), Support Vector Machines (SVM), Logistic Regression (LR), Decision Tree (DT), Random Forest (RF), and Extreme Gradient Boosting (XGBoost) with the help of the sklearn package. In Sect. 4.2, those models' definitions are discussed. These models were trained with two feature extractions and tested with the development and test sets. Their results will be addressed in the following section.

These models are set as a baseline model, and we decided to use transformer models. To approach the problem, we used models based on transformer architecture. We have used the huggingface[5] various transformers library for our implementations, the original models' original versions, and their customized versions with different loss functions. We have used BERT multilingual base model (cased), BERT multilingual base model (un-cased), XLM-RoBERTa (base-sized model), and XLM-RoBERTa (large-sized model), RoBERTa base, RoBERTa large, and Roberta-large-mnli models for our implementations. The evaluation of each model's performance in Tamil, English, and Malayalam is discussed in the next section.

5 Results and Evaluation

5.1 Results

According to the tables following, we have tested several different combinations of models that were discussed in the previous section across the datasets of each language. As a measure of evaluation, macro F1 scores are reported. We have used machine learning and transformers as typical models in code-mixed texts across all three datasets, Tamil, English, and Malayalam. These tasks are still crucial when dealing with code-mixed text.

We evaluated traditional machine learning models in the previous section and briefly discussed their average performance. Both feature extraction with traditional ML model predictions gave similar results for all three languages Tamil, English, and Malayalam. Similar results are obtained in both the test and development sets. The mBERT-uncased and RoBERTa-base models performed equally in the Tamil dataset in the test and development set.

Even so, the BERT-cased model provided the most accurate prediction in the development set. BERT-uncased predicted well in the test set for English, but other models did not anticipate the result due to an imbalanced dataset. The BERT case performed well in the development set of the English dataset. The XLM-RoBERTa-base model produced good predictions in the test set and similar results in the development set for the Malayalam dataset. In all three languages, these models provided better predictions. The macro F1 score is used to evaluate these results because it calculates the arithmetic mean of all the per-class F1 scores.

5.2 Evaluations

The performance of each model is calculated with a confusion matrix, precision (P), recall (R), F1-score (F1) of macro and weighted average, and accuracy using a confusion matrix and classification report from sklearn.matrics packages. The evaluation metrics were calculated using true positive (TP), false positive (FP), false negative (FN), and true negative (TN). The best performance of the models was calculated with the macro F1-score for all three languages.

---

[5] https://huggingface.co/transformers/.

Table 5. Results for **Tamil** predicted with **Test set**

Features	Models	Acc	MP	MR	MF1	WP	WR	WF1
TF-IDF	NB	0.4886	0.5899	0.3617	0.2873	0.5560	0.4886	0.3673
	SVM	0.4782	0.5058	0.3566	0.2835	0.5003	0.4782	0.3573
	LR	0.4847	0.5660	0.3600	0.2894	0.5326	0.4847	0.3677
	DT	0.4703	0.4730	0.3517	0.2871	0.4655	0.4703	0.3611
	RF	0.4733	0.4864	0.3554	0.2898	0.4773	0.4733	0.3610
	XGB	0.4817	0.6822	0.3544	0.2586	0.6403	0.4817	0.3325
Count	NB	0.4896	0.5765	0.3634	0.2903	0.5551	0.4896	0.3693
	SVM	0.4772	0.5005	0.3568	0.2846	0.4942	0.4772	0.3568
	LR	0.4856	0.5573	0.3608	0.2903	0.5317	0.4856	0.3689
	DT	0.4708	0.4741	0.3520	0.2873	0.4669	0.4708	0.3614
	RF	0.4752	0.4851	0.3577	0.2918	0.4842	0.4752	0.3621
	XGB	0.4817	0.6585	0.3544	0.2592	0.6260	0.4817	0.3334
RoBERTa	base	0.5693	0.5667	0.6112	**0.5498**	0.5721	0.5693	0.5289
	large	0.5312	0.5087	0.6059	0.4709	0.5247	0.5312	0.4432
	large-mnli	0.5545	0.5380	0.6145	0.5322	0.5419	0.5545	0.5052
XLM-RoBERTa	base	0.5490	0.5231	0.5890	0.5041	0.5234	0.5490	0.4756
	large	0.5421	0.5166	0.5857	0.5134	0.5126	0.5421	0.4869
mBERT	uncased	0.5708	0.5702	0.5759	0.5447	0.5769	0.5708	0.5395
	cased	0.4985	0.4402	0.5613	0.4210	0.4565	0.4985	0.4008

Table 6. Results for **English** predicted with **Test set**

Features	Models	Acc	MP	MR	MF1	WP	WR	WF1
TF-IDF	NB	0.9139	0.5549	0.3488	0.3483	0.8994	0.9139	0.8779
	SVM	0.9100	0.4619	0.3595	0.3669	0.8770	0.9100	0.8809
	LR	0.9157	0.5425	0.3615	0.3707	0.8987	0.9157	0.8844
	DT	0.9041	0.4512	0.3970	0.4129	0.8821	0.9041	0.8897
	RF	0.9097	0.4661	0.3798	0.3957	0.8823	0.9097	0.8880
	XGB	0.9143	0.6078	0.3465	0.3439	0.9129	0.9143	0.8769
Count	NB	0.9132	0.4919	0.3702	0.3838	0.8871	0.9132	0.8867
	SVM	0.9104	0.4639	0.3560	0.3613	0.8768	0.9104	0.8796
	LR	0.9153	0.5151	0.3710	0.3855	0.8934	0.9153	0.8881
	DT	0.8960	0.4328	0.4013	0.4127	0.8786	0.8960	0.8860
	RF	0.9058	0.4521	0.3880	0.4039	0.8807	0.9058	0.8885
	XGB	0.9157	0.6163	0.3519	0.3538	0.9162	0.9157	0.8801
RoBERTa	base	0.0348	0.2816	0.1284	0.0514	0.6917	0.0340	0.0155
	large	0.0562	0.3214	0.2425	0.0387	0.8778	0.0562	0.1044
	large-mnli	0.0394	0.2056	0.3677	0.0620	0.4657	0.0394	0.0168
XLM-RoBERTa	base	0.0358	0.0320	0.2458	0.0518	0.0084	0.0358	0.0136
	large	0.9111	0.3037	0.3333	0.3178	0.8301	0.9111	0.8687
BERT	uncased	0.5708	0.5702	0.5759	**0.5447**	0.5769	0.5708	0.5395
	cased	0.0928	0.3298	0.3991	0.0771	0.8124	0.0928	0.0524

Table 7. Results for **Malayalam** predicted with **Test set**

Features	Models	Acc	MP	MR	MF1	WP	WR	**WF1**
TF-IDF	NB	0.7526	0.8538	0.3998	0.4049	0.7842	0.7526	0.6735
	SVM	0.7563	0.8068	0.4127	0.4264	0.7696	0.7563	0.6826
	LR	0.7628	0.8274	0.4248	0.4450	0.7832	0.7628	0.6943
	DT	0.7628	0.7873	0.4389	0.4638	0.7654	0.7628	0.7041
	RF	0.7619	0.8076	0.4311	0.4549	0.7727	0.7619	0.6976
	XGB	0.7488	0.8177	0.3907	0.3889	0.7727	0.7488	0.6631
Count	NB	0.7582	0.8566	0.4146	0.4296	0.7883	0.7582	0.6853
	SVM	0.7582	0.8073	0.4175	0.4338	0.7709	0.7582	0.6871
	LR	0.7619	0.8306	0.4217	0.4405	0.7843	0.7619	0.6916
	DT	0.7628	0.7891	0.4376	0.4622	0.7660	0.7628	0.7033
	RF	0.7582	0.7829	0.4265	0.4470	0.7600	0.7582	0.6939
	XGB	0.7498	0.8598	0.3908	0.3892	0.7859	0.7498	0.6647
RoBERTa	base	0.7656	0.6419	0.5402	0.5511	0.6966	0.7656	0.7055
	large	0.7087	0.6012	0.4901	0.5230	0.6682	0.7087	0.6793
	large-mnli	0.3968	0.3998	0.4613	0.3386	0.6534	0.3968	0.4493
XLM-RoBERTa	base	0.8086	0.7296	0.7115	**0.7202**	0.8051	0.8086	0.8066
	large	0.7246	0.2415	0.3333	0.2801	0.5250	0.7246	0.6088
BERT	uncased	0.7460	0.6049	0.5307	0.5450	0.6923	0.7460	0.7040
	cased	0.5481	0.5502	0.5159	0.5176	0.6514	0.5481	0.5857

Table 8. Results for **Tamil** predicted with **Dev set**

Features	Models	Acc	MP	MR	MF1	WP	WR	WF1
TF-IDF	NB	0.5129	0.5970	0.3596	0.2888	0.5546	0.5129	0.3904
	SVM	0.5059	0.5311	0.3571	0.2888	0.5162	0.5059	0.3848
	LR	0.5114	0.5514	0.3624	0.2998	0.5317	0.5114	0.3974
	DT	0.5025	0.5153	0.3574	0.2985	0.5003	0.5025	0.3935
	RF	0.5094	0.5477	0.3659	0.3072	0.5283	0.5094	0.3960
	XGB	0.5089	0.6821	0.3533	0.2642	0.6318	0.5089	0.3629
Count	NB	0.5149	0.5856	0.3675	0.3046	0.5530	0.5149	0.3967
	SVM	0.5040	0.5050	0.3573	0.2903	0.5013	0.5040	0.3834
	LR	0.5119	0.5699	0.3655	0.3063	0.5388	0.5119	0.3997
	DT	0.5025	0.5144	0.3574	0.2986	0.4992	0.5025	0.3935
	RF	0.5050	0.5104	0.3623	0.3048	0.5042	0.5050	0.3948
	XGB	0.5084	0.6091	0.3547	0.2677	0.6016	0.5084	0.3636
RoBERTa	base	0.5912	0.6384	0.6189	0.5274	0.6529	0.5912	0.5127
	large	0.3751	0.1250	0.3333	0.1819	0.1407	0.3751	0.2047
	large-mnli	0.5287	0.4046	0.4423	0.3807	0.3465	0.5287	0.3951
XLM-RoBERTa	base	0.5585	0.5545	0.5881	0.4651	0.5828	0.5585	0.4622
	large	0.4945	0.1648	0.3333	0.2206	0.2446	0.4945	0.3273
BERT	uncased	05669	0.5525	0.5592	0.5168	0.5634	0.5669	0.5206
	cased	0.6046	0.5969	0.6200	**0.5825**	0.6079	0.6046	0.5796

Table 9. Results for **English** predicted with **Dev set**

Features	Models	Acc	MP	MR	MF1	WP	WR	WF1
TF-IDF	NB	0.9064	0.5642	0.3464	0.3425	0.8948	0.9064	0.8665
	SVM	0.9061	0.4922	0.3682	0.3799	0.8788	0.9061	0.8767
	LR	0.9057	0.4883	0.3692	0.3813	0.8779	0.9057	0.8769
	DT	0.8952	0.4468	0.3982	0.4129	0.8726	0.8952	0.8807
	RF	0.9029	0.4686	0.3824	0.3985	0.8752	0.9029	0.8804
	XGB	0.9057	0.5687	0.3429	0.3357	0.8953	0.9057	0.8642
Count	NB	0.9033	0.4711	0.3694	0.3813	0.8730	0.9033	0.8758
	SVM	0.9085	0.5117	0.3746	0.3899	0.8858	0.9085	0.8806
	LR	0.9050	0.4807	0.3766	0.3916	0.8774	0.9050	0.8795
	DT	0.8938	0.4472	0.4075	0.4212	0.8750	0.8938	0.8823
	RF	0.9043	0.4766	0.3982	0.4176	0.8810	0.9043	0.8863
	XGB	0.9050	0.5353	0.3415	0.3332	0.8854	0.9050	0.8632
RoBERTa	base	0.0021	0.3405	0.1706	0.0056	0.9056	0.0021	0.0028
	large	0.0007	0.0002	0.3333	0.0005	0.0000	0.0007	0.0000
	large-mnli	0.0060	0.2503	0.1841	0.0220	0.6104	0.0060	0.0075
XLM-RoBERTa	base	0.0148	0.4587	0.1950	0.0496	0.8661	0.0148	0.0266
	large	0.9036	0.3012	0.3333	0.3165	0.8165	0.9036	0.8579
BERT	uncased	0.2082	0.3247	0.2729	0.1492	0.8063	0.2082	0.3268
	cased	0.9205	0.5299	0.4513	**0.4779**	0.9083	0.9205	0.9104

Table 10. Results for **Malayalam** predicted with **Dev set**

Features	Models	Acc	MP	MR	MF1	WP	WR	WF1
TF-IDF	NB	0.7579	0.8063	0.4007	0.4087	0.7724	0.7579	0.6823
	SVM	0.7579	0.7603	0.4159	0.4346	0.7558	0.7579	0.6885
	LR	0.7636	0.8205	0.4194	0.4401	0.7790	0.7636	0.6945
	DT	0.7561	0.7247	0.4284	0.4535	0.7400	0.7561	0.6973
	RF	0.7626	0.7577	0.4287	0.4539	0.7578	0.7626	0.7002
	XGB	0.7514	0.7859	0.3892	0.3890	0.7631	0.7514	0.6672
Count	NB	0.7589	0.7661	0.4169	0.4359	0.7570	0.7589	0.6920
	SVM	0.7570	0.7574	0.4142	0.4318	0.7539	0.7570	0.6868
	LR	0.7617	0.7835	0.4182	0.4377	0.7667	0.7617	0.6941
	DT	0.7570	0.7296	0.4275	0.4522	0.7424	0.7570	0.6970
	RF	0.7589	0.7453	0.4257	0.4498	0.7500	0.7589	0.6964
	XGB	0.7533	0.8165	0.3897	0.3900	0.7737	0.7533	0.6697
RoBERTa	base	0.4645	0.5331	0.5974	0.4922	0.7024	0.4645	0.4975
	large	0.0897	0.0299	0.3333	0.0549	0.0080	0.0897	0.0148
	large-mnli	0.7215	0.5659	0.5483	0.5532	0.6711	0.7215	0.6931
XLM-RoBERTa	base	0.8168	0.7476	0.7101	0.7231	0.8055	0.8168	0.8076
	large	0.7327	0.2442	0.3333	0.2819	0.5369	0.7327	0.6197
BERT	uncased	0.7963	0.7281	0.6129	0.6411	0.7781	0.7963	0.7692
	cased	0.8187	0.7532	0.7248	**0.7378**	0.8124	0.8187	0.8148

There are plenty of evaluation metrics for different ML tasks. We used accuracy, precision, recall, and F1-score (macro and weighted average) metrics to evaluate the classification task. An accuracy metric evaluates how often the classifier can predict accurately. The precision metric describes how many accurately estimated positive events could calculate correctly with our model. Recall explains how many actual positive events can calculate correctly with our model. An F1-Score is calculated by harmonically measuring precision and recall. False positives and false negatives are both evaluated.

Consequently, it performs well on unbalanced datasets. The arithmetic mean of all measures across all classes is used in the macro average. Because this method assigns equal weights to all classes, it is an excellent choice for unbalanced data. A weighted average calculates estimates for each class individually but adds them together based on the level of support.

In the test set of the Tamil dataset, the RoBERTa-base model performed well compared to other models. The macro F1 score of this model is 0.5498. All machine learning models archive low F1 scores with various feature extraction in this XGBoost model with TF-IDF archive 0.2586 macro F1 scores, and this is a minor prediction of this Tamil language in the test set. These values are shown in Table 5. The performance of all other models, like transformer models, gives average results for this test set in the Tamil language. In Table 8, you can see the average output for all models for the development set in Tamil. The mBERT-base model performed well in this set and got 0.5825 macro F1 scores. The last macro F1 score for the development set is the RoBERTa-large model, which fetched 0.1819.

A macro F1 score of 0.5447 in the test set for the mBERT-uncased model was better than the other models on the English dataset. Lastly, RoBERTa-large is predicted to have a macro F1 score of 0.0387. The models didn't predict the classes and didn't give better results because of the data imbalance problem in this dataset. These results are described in Table 6. Next, the mBERT-Case model predicted a 0.4779 macro F1 score for development set in English and shown in Table 9. But the RoBERTa-large model didn't predict this dataset because it contains an imbalanced dataset and gives only a 0.0005 macro F1 score. The performance of other models gave medium results for both the test set and development set.

In the Malayalam dataset, a macro F1 score of 0.7202 was predicted by XLM-RoBERTa-base in the test set and compared to other models gave good results. XLM-RoBERTa-large expected a macro F1 score of 0.2801 in the development set, and this model provides a minor performance among other models. The mBERT-case model gave a macro F1 score of 0.7378 in the development set and predicted well, while the RoBERTa-large model predicted a macro F1 score of 0.0549. The test and development sets are shown in Table 7 and Table 10.

6   Conclusion

We categorized code-mixed comments into Hope-Speech, Non-Hope-Speech, and None of These Languages. We used ML and transformer algorithms to identify hope speech in a code-mixed statement of Dravidian languages. However, the algorithms must predict some classes well, mainly in the English dataset. An imbalance in the data primarily accounts for this. In addition, all models achieve good accuracy, especially in the Malayalam dataset with a 0.7378 macro F1 score. Overall, pre-trained transformer models performed very well. Using the macro F1 score, we predicted the above calculations.

References

1. Wang, A., Singh, A., Michael, J., Hill, F., Levy, O., Bowman, S.: GLUE: a multi-task benchmark and analysis platform for natural language understanding. In: Proceedings of the 2018 EMNLP Workshop BlackboxNLP: Analyzing and Interpreting Neural Networks for NLP, pp. 353–355. Association for Computational Linguistics, Brussels, November 2018
2. Gowen, K., Deschaine, M., Gruttadara, D., Markey, D.: Young adults with mental health conditions and social networking websites: seeking tools to build community. Psychiatr. Rehabil. J. **35**(3), 245 (2012)
3. Yates, A., Cohan, A., Goharian, N.: Depression and self-harm risk assessment in online forums. In: Proceedings of the 2017 Conference on Empirical Methods in Natural Language Processing, pp. 2968–2978. Association for Computational Linguistics, Copenhagen, September 2017
4. Chung, J.E.: Social networking in online support groups for health: how online social networking benefits patients. J. Health Commun. **19**(6), 639–659 (2014)
5. Chakravarthi, B.R., et al.: Overview of the shared task on hope speech detection for equality, diversity, and inclusion. In: Proceedings of the Second Workshop on Language Technology for Equality, Diversity and Inclusion, pp. 378–388 (2022)
6. Priyadharshini, R., et al.: Findings of the shared task on abusive comment detection in Tamil. In: Proceedings of the Second Workshop on Speech and Language Technologies for Dravidian Languages. Association for Computational Linguistics (2022)
7. Schmidt, A., Wiegand, M.: A survey on hate speech detection using natural language processing. In: Proceedings of the Fifth International Workshop on Natural Language Processing for Social Media, 3 April 2017, pp. 1–10. Association for Computational Linguistics, Valencia (2019)
8. Zampieri, M., Malmasi, S., Nakov, P., Rosenthal, S., Farra, N., Kumar, R.: Predicting the type and target of offensive posts in social media. In: Proceedings of the 2019 Conference of the North American Chapter of the Association for Computational Linguistics: Human Language Technologies, Volume 1 (Long and Short Papers), pp. 1415–1420. Association for Computational Linguistics, Minneapolis, June 2019
9. Kumaresan, P.K.: Findings of shared task on offensive language identification in Tamil and Malayalam. In: Forum for Information Retrieval Evaluation, pp. 16–18 (2021)

10. Chakravarthi, B.R., Muralidaran, V.: Findings of the shared task on hope speech detection for equality, diversity, and inclusion. In: Proceedings of the First Workshop on Language Technology for Equality, Diversity and Inclusion, pp. 61–72 (2021)
11. Chakravarthi, B.R.: HopeEDI: a multilingual hope speech detection dataset for equality, diversity, and inclusion. In: Proceedings of the Third Workshop on Computational Modeling of People's Opinions, Personality, and Emotion's in Social Media, pp. 41–53. Association for Computational Linguistics, Barcelona, December 2020
12. Arunima, S., Ramakrishnan, A., Balaji, A., Thenmozhi, D., Senthil Kumar, B.: SSN_DIBERTSITY@LT-EDI-EACL2021: hope speech detection on multilingual YouTube comments via transformer based approach. In: Proceedings of the First Workshop on Language Technology for Equality, Diversity and Inclusion, pp. 92–97 (2021)
13. Dave, B., Bhat, S., Majumder, P.: IRNLP_DAIICT@DravidianLangTech-EACL2021: offensive language identification in Dravidian languages using TF-IDF char n-grams and MuRIL. In: Proceedings of the First Workshop on Speech and Language Technologies for Dravidian Languages, pp. 266–269. Kyiv, Association for Computational Linguistics, April 2021
14. Chung, Y.-L., Kuzmenko, E., Tekiroglu, S.S., Guerini, M.: CONAN - COunter NArratives through nichesourcing: a multilingual dataset of responses to fight online hate speech. In: Proceedings of the 57th Annual Meeting of the Association for Computational Linguistics, pp. 2819–2829. Association for Computational Linguistics, Florence, July 2019
15. Mathew, B., et al.: Thou shalt not hate: countering online hate speech. In: Proceedings of the International AAAI Conference on Web and Social Media, vol. 13, pp. 369–380 (2019)
16. Vijayakumar, P.: SSN_ARMM@ LT-EDI-ACL2022: hope speech detection for equality, diversity, and inclusion using albert model. In: Proceedings of the Second Workshop on Language Technology for Equality, Diversity and Inclusion, pp. 172–176 (2022)
17. Ghanghor, N., Ponnusamy, R., Kumaresan, P.K., Priyadharshini, R., Thavareesan, S., Chakravarthi, B.R.: IIITK@ LT-EDI-EACL2021: hope speech detection for equality, diversity, and inclusion in Tamil, Malayalam and English. In: Proceedings of the First Workshop on Language Technology for Equality, Diversity and Inclusion, pp. 197–203 (2021)
18. Muralidhar, S., Nguyen, L., Gatica-Perez, D.: Words worth: verbal content and hirability impressions in YouTube video resumes. In: Proceedings of the 9th Workshop on Computational Approaches to Subjectivity, Sentiment and Social Media Analysis, pp. 322–327. Association for Computational Linguistics, Brussels, October 2018
19. KhudaBukhsh, A.R., Palakodety, S., Carbonell, J.G.: Harnessing code switching to transcend the linguistic barrier. arXiv preprint arXiv:2001.11258 (2020)
20. Palakodety, S., KhudaBukhsh, A.R., Carbonell, J.G.: Voice for the voiceless: active sampling to detect comments supporting the Rohingyas. In: Proceedings of the AAAI Conference on Artificial Intelligence, vol. 34, pp. 454–462 (2020)
21. Khadilkar, K., KhudaBukhsh, A.R.: An unfair affinity toward fairness: characterizing 70 years of social biases in Bhollywood (student abstract). In: Proceedings of the AAAI Conference on Artificial Intelligence, vol. 35, pp. 15813–15814 (2021)

22. Chakravarthi, B.R., Hande, A., Ponnusamy, R., Kumaresan, P.K., Priyadharshini, R.: How can we detect homophobia and transphobia? Experiments in a multilingual code-mixed setting for social media governance. Int. J. Inf. Manag. Data Insights **2**(2), 100119 (2022)

23. Hande, A., Priyadharshini, R., Chakravarthi, B.R.: KanCMD: Kannada CodeMixed dataset for sentiment analysis and offensive language detection. In: Proceedings of the Third Workshop on Computational Modeling of People's Opinions, Personality, and Emotion's in Social Media, pp. 54–63 (2020)

24. Chakravarthi, B.R.: Hope speech detection in YouTube comments. Soc. Netw. Anal. Min. **12**(1), 1–19 (2022)

25. Bharathi Raja Chakravarthi: Multilingual hope speech detection in English and Dravidian languages. Int. J. Data Sci. Anal. **14**(4), 389–406 (2022)

26. Priyadharshini, R., Chakravarthi, B.R., Vegupatti, M., McCrae, J.P.: Named entity recognition for code-mixed Indian corpus using meta embedding. In: 2020 6th International Conference on Advanced Computing and Communication Systems (ICACCS), pp. 68–72. IEEE (2020)

27. Jose, N., Chakravarthi, B.R., Suryawanshi, S., Sherly, E., McCrae, J.P.: A survey of current datasets for code-switching research. In: 2020 6th International Conference on Advanced Computing and Communication Systems (ICACCS), pp. 136–141. IEEE (2020)

28. Devlin, J., Chang, M.-W., Lee, K., Toutanova, K.: BERT: pre-training of deep bidirectional transformers for language understanding. arXiv preprint arXiv:1810.04805 (2018)

29. Gundapu, S., Mamidi, R.: Transformer based automatic covid-19 fake news detection system. arXiv preprint arXiv:2101.00180 (2021)

30. Lothritz, C., Allix, K., Veiber, L., Klein, J., Assise Bissyande, T.F.D.: Evaluating pretrained transformer-based models on the task of fine-grained named entity recognition. In: Proceedings of the 28th International Conference on Computational Linguistics, pp. 3750–3760 (2020)

31. Conneau, A.: Unsupervised cross-lingual representation learning at scale. arXiv preprint arXiv:1911.02116 (2019)

Paraphrase Detection in Indian Languages Using Deep Learning

Durairaj Thenmozhi[1], C. Jerin Mahibha[2]([✉]), S. Kayalvizhi[1], M. Rakesh[1],
Y. Vivek[1], and V. Poojesshwaran[1]

[1] Sri Sivasubramaniya Nadar College of Engineering, Kalavakkam, India
{theni_d,kayalvizhis}@ssn.edu.in
[2] Meenakshi Sundararajan Engineering College, Chennai, India
jerinmahibha@gmail.com

Abstract. Multiple sentences that reveal the same meaning are considered to be paraphrases. Paraphrases restate a given text, passage or statement using different words in which the original context and the meaning are kept intact. It can be used to expand, clarify or summarize the content of essays, research papers and journals. Semantic identity of sentences are detected during the process of paraphrase detection. Paraphrase detection can be related to different applications, like plagiarism detection, text summarizing, text mining, question answering, and query ranking, in the domain of Natural Language Processing. Effective paraphrase detection could be implemented if the semantics of the language and their interactions are adequately captured. The process of paraphrase detection is considered to be a difficult and challenging task due to the wide range of complex morphological structures and vocabulary that prevails in most of the Indian languages. The approaches that exist for paraphrase detection include machine learning techniques like Multinomial Logistic Regression model and Recursive Auto Encoders, which lacks in hand-crafted feature engineering. The problem could be solved when deep learning approaches are used for paraphrase detection. In the proposed system, the classification of paraphrase, semi-paraphrase and non-paraphrase sentences are implemented using an ensemble of three deep learning algorithms which includes BERT (Bidirectional Encoder Representations from Transformers), USE (Universal Sentence Encoder) and Seq2Seq (Sequence to Sequence). The DPIL corpus has been used for the evaluation of the proposed system and the highest accuracy obtained considering languages Hindi and Punjabi are 85.22% and 85.80% respectively.

Keywords: Paraphrase · Deep learning · Transformer · Sentence Encoder · Sequence to Sequence

1 Introduction

Languages act as a universally preferred means of communication between human beings for sharing and conveying their feelings. Paraphrasing is one of the

Anand Kumar M et al. (Eds.): SPELLL 2022, CCIS 1802, pp. 138–154, 2023.
https://doi.org/10.1007/978-3-031-33231-9_9

semantics of a language in which distinct words are used to render the meaning of a text or passage. Plagiarism detection, text summarizing, text mining, question answering and query ranking are a few areas where a paraphrase detection system can be applied [10]. Plagiarism detection can use paraphrase detection to validate duplication of contents in news articles and research papers. The correctness of answers in a question answering system can be evaluated using a paraphrase detection system as the same answer can be stated in different forms by different people [11].

Consider the two sentences:

சங்கராபுரம் தொகுதியில் போட்டியிடும் ஸ்டாலின் நடைபயணமாக சென்று பிரசாரம் செய்தார்.

தி.மு.க., வேட்பாளர் ஸ்டாலின் போட்டியிடும் சங்கராபுரம் தொகுதியில் சின்ன சேலம் பகுதியில் நடைபயணமாக சென்று ஓட்டு சேகரித்தார்.

The above two sentences are considered as paraphrases as they convey the same meaning.

தஞ்சையில் நம்மாழ்வார் இயற்கை வேளாண்மை மையம் அமைக்கப்படும் என கனிமொழி எம்.பி பேச்சு.

தஞ்சை மாவட்டத்தில் தி.மு.க. மற்றும் கூட்டணி கட்சி வேட்பாளர்களை ஆதரித்து கனிமொழி எம்.பி பிரசாரம் செய்தார்.

The above sentences are non-paraphrase as they convey different meanings even though they have the same subject.

There are several language families spoken by Indians, of which the widely used language families are Indo-Aryan and Dravidian languages. After Papua New Guinea, the world's fourth highest number of languages is found in India[1]. The presence of complex vocabulary is an important feature to be considered while working with most of the Indian languages [17]. Hence, recognition of paraphrases in Indian languages has become a tedious process. Many well-known Indian literature, books and poems have a historical value that can be paraphrased for a better understanding of it. Releasing a book with the same content as a historic valued book has become popular nowadays since there's no copyright for those books, thus by paraphrase detection, content theft can be resolved [12]. There are no available tools for detecting paraphrases in Indian languages. Paraphrase detection for Indian Languages is still a tedious process because of its complex vocabulary. Several works have been done on paraphrase detection for Indian languages using machine learning [5,6] and deep learning [1,2] approaches. However, understanding the contextual meaning of the words in

---

[1] https://www.weforum.org/agenda/2021/03/these-are-the-top-ten-countries-for-linguistic-diversity/.

the language is crucial, which the proposed system attempts to incorporate into the system. Paraphrase detection could be effectively implemented using deep learning algorithms as they capture the contextual meaning along with lexical and semantic meanings to understand the sentences. We combine the advantages of three deep learning algorithms for detecting paraphrases by constructing an ensembled model of the deep learning algorithms and classifying the sentences based on the approach of maximum voting.

The proposed system uses the DPIL [4] corpus to implement paraphrase identification in four Indian languages, which include Tamil, Malayalam, Hindi and Punjabi. Different deep learning algorithms are used in the process of classifying the sentences as paraphrases or not which is further fine tuned as paraphrase, semi-paraphrase or non-paraphrase. The deep learning algorithms used by the proposed system are BERT [14], Seq2Seq [16] and USE [15].

The objective of this work is to implement deep learning techniques to detect paraphrases from sentences and measure the performance of these algorithms for Indian languages. It also intend to build a computational model which is an optimized and adaptable paraphrase detection system with the ability to identify various types of obfuscation during the process of paraphrase identification. The major tasks associated with the work include:

- Study and experimenting new approaches for paraphrase identification in Indian languages.
- Identify the optimized parameters for paraphrase detection models and analyze the performance on different types of obfuscation.
- Propose an ensemble approach for paraphrase identification in Indian languages.

2   Literature Survey

A paraphrase identification method for English had been proposed by D. Thenmozhi and C. Aravindan [7] where the clauses which represent a set of relations and propositions that exist in a text were extracted using a clause extraction engine. The clauses in the text have been determined by taking the negations, inverse relations and semantic roles of sentences into consideration and the conjunctions have also been identified and resolved. Concept score, proposition score, relation scores, and word scores are the features from text that are considered during the extraction of clause-based similarity features. During the identification of a paraphrase, the above features and machine translation metric features are combined. Synset shortest path from Wordnet had been used to compute the semantic relatedness measure for deciding whether a sequence is a paraphrase or not [8]. The approach had used the distance between two words in the sentences to identify the semantic identities between them and it had been evaluated against Microsoft Research Paraphrase Corpus, which had shown better results compared to other semantic similarity approaches. Unsupervised deep learning technique had also been proposed for paraphrase detection which had used Recursive Auto Encoders (RAE) [2]. Parse trees had been constructed using the parsed data and unfolded RAE had been used for training. The unfolding Recursive Auto Encoder had been used on each node of the parse tree to compute phrase embedding vectors. Generation of a similarity matrix had also been done using the vector generated from RAE, based on which paraphrase detection had been implemented. Deep learning algorithms like Recursive Auto Encoders (RAE's) and dynamic pooling had been used by Socher et al. [9] for paraphrase detection in the English language. They had used the Microsoft Research paraphrase corpus (MRPC) in which each sentence pair had been parsed and embeddings had been computed for each node in the parse trees and a similarity matrix had been constructed comparing the embedding vectors for all nodes within the parse trees. Dynamic pooling had been used to convert a variable size similarity matrix for each sentence pair to a fixed sized matrix. To decide on a paraphrase, the resultant matrix had been passed to the softmax activation function.

Paraphrase detection in the language Tamil had been implemented using Long-Short Term Memory (LSTM) neural networks by Senthil Kumar et al. [1]. The model used NMT architecture for the prediction of class labels, which had been supported by different layers like embedding layer, encoders, Bi-LSTM layers as decoders and attention mechanisms on top of the decoders. A paraphrase detection model that had been trained with sentence pair similarity metrics that include both lexical and semantic level similarities, like cosine similarity, word overlap exact match and n-gram based similarity had been implemented using the Multinomial Logistic Regression model [5]. The evaluation metrics that had been used for analysing the performance of this system was the F1 measure which had shown better performance scores for languages like Punjabi and Hindi. The performance score for Tamil and Malayalam languages had been found to be relatively low and the semantic complexities that exist in the vocabulary of these languages had been stated as a cause of the low score. Paraphrase detection had been implemented by unfolding Recursive Auto Encoders (RAEs), which represents a deep learning technique making use of a syntax tree representation for phrases from which feature vectors are generated by Mahalakshmi et al. [2]. Shallow parsers had been used to parse the Tamil sentences. The Recursive Auto Encoder (RAEs) have been used to receive good representations at each and every inner node of the parse tree. Deciding whether the two sentences are paraphrases is determined using the concept of minimal tree matching, applied over the two parse trees that had been generated. Classification had been implemented using Probabilistic Neural Networks (PNNs) by Sandip Sarkar et al. [6] in which feature extraction had been done using lexical features like Jaccard similarity, length normalized edit distance and cosine similarity. Paraphrase detection in few Indian languages had been performed by Saikh et al. [3] which had determined the similarity using vector-based (cosine similarity, dice similarity), lexical-based (unigram matching with respect to sentence1 and sentence2) and set-based (Jaccard, overlap, and harmonic) measures. An end to end encoder-decoder model had been used to analyze and classify the paraphrased sentences in the Tamil language which had used a deep neural network using LSTM, GRU units and gNMT with an attention mechanism [13] and the F1-measure had been found to be increased by 0.5%.

The above discussed methods use lexical, syntactic and semantic similarity features which are considered to be traditional similarity measures and are associated with large memory requirements and vocabulary of the languages. The proposed model attempts to use pre-trained models to reduce this overhead using BERT, Seq2Seq and USE models. Algorithms like BERT perform better as they capture not only the semantic meaning but also the contextual meaning as embedding is done from both right to left and left to right of the sentences.

3 Methodology

The proposed system uses three models, namely BERT, Seq2Seq and USE to detect paraphrases from the input sentences. The models fall under the category of deep learning algorithms for which Recurrent Neural Network (RNN) forms the base. Four languages, namely Tamil, Punjabi, Malayalam and Hindi, are used for testing the model and the sentences are labelled as paraphrase, non-paraphrase or semi-paraphrase. The execution of these models provides the associated probability scores as the output. Based on the confidence scores, ensembling of the models is carried out which implements the process of classification using the highest confidence score of the predictions.

3.1 System Architecture

The proposed system uses three different models, namely Seq2Seq model, Bidirectional Encoder Representations from Transformers (BERT) model and Universal Sentence Encoder (USE) model for the process of identifying paraphrases from the dataset. Figure 1 depicts the proposed system's general architecture. The preprocessed data is given as input to the three models that provide a probability scores for the predictions. Each model's result will be a class label, based on the individual predictions' confidence scores. On using the ensembled classification algorithm, the output is considered to be the label that corresponds to the prediction, with the highest confidence score.

3.2 System Description

The different approaches used by the proposed system and the techniques behind the models are detailed in this section. The proposed system uses three models namely BERT, USE AND Seq2Seq for implementing the process of detecting paraphrases from sentence pairs.

Seq2Seq Model. The Seq2Seq model [16] learns the target sequence conditioned on the source sequence in which the sequences of n words are mapped with a target label. Due to the categorical nature, the retrieval of word representations is based on the source and target embedding. The architecture of the

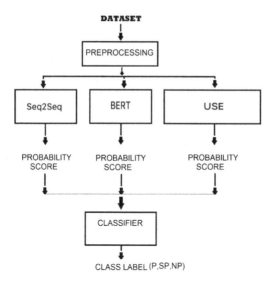

Fig. 1. System architecture

Seq2Seq model is represented in Fig. 2. The components of the Seq2Seq model include an embedding layer, encoder, decoder and a projection layer. The embedding layer generates word embedding for both the input sequence and the label. For each of the languages considered, a vocabulary of size V is selected. All the other words are assigned as an "unknown" token with the same embedding.

Several recurrent units like LSTM and GRU are stacked to form an encoder, which collects information from each input sequence that is passed during forward propagation. The hidden states h_i are computed using the formula:

$$h_t = f(W^{(hh)}h_{t-1} + W^{(hx)}x_t)$$

The recurrent neural network is represented by the above formula which shows that the previous hidden state $h_{(t-1)}$ and the input vector x_t are provided with appropriate weights. Information for all input elements is encapsulated in a vector which assists the decoder in making accurate predictions.

Decoder is a combination of multiple recurrent units and y_t represents the output predicted by each unit at time t. The hidden state from the previous unit acts as the input for each of the recurrent units, based on which its own hidden state and output are determined. Any hidden state h_i is computed using the formula:

$$h_t = f(W^{(hh)}h_{t-1})$$

The next state is computed using the previous hidden state, and the output y_t at time step t is computed using the formula:

$$h_t = Softmax(W^s h_t)$$

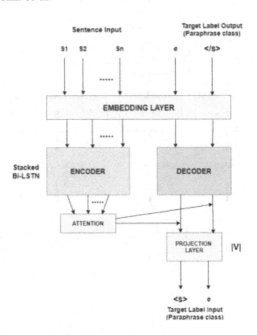

Fig. 2. Seq2Seq architecture

The hidden state at the current time step and their respective weight $W(S)$ are used to compute the output. The final output is determined by the probability vector that is generated using the Softmax activation function.

BERT Model. BERT [14] is a fine tuned representation model that provides better performance on tasks which considers both sentence level and token level representations. It is found to outperform many task-specific architectures and the BERT architecture is shown in Fig. 3. The BERT algorithm (Bidirectional Encoder Representations from Transformers) takes the nuances of the context into consideration to interpret the meaning of sentences. To retrieve the contextual relation from the given text, it makes use of a transformer and 15% of the input words are masked during this approach. In its vanilla form, the input text is read using an encoder and a decoder does the prediction process. During the pretraining stage of the BERT model, unlabelled data is used for training the model and during the finetuning stage, pre-trained parameters are used for model initialization, which are then fine tuned using labeled data from the downstream tasks.

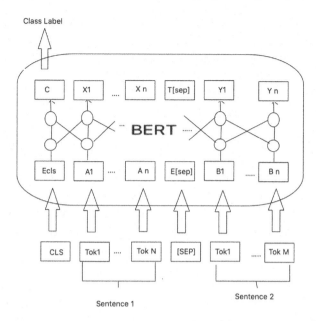

Fig. 3. BERT architecture

Universal Sentence Encoder (USE) Model. The Universal Sentence Encoder [15] implements tasks associated with the domain of natural language processing, like text classification, semantic similarity, and clustering, by encoding text into high-dimensional vectors. Training is implemented using both transformer encoder and Deep Averaging Network (DAN), which represents the two variants of USE and these show trade-offs in terms of accuracy and computational resource requirements. The accuracy associated with the transformer architecture is high but the model complexity and resource consumption are also on the higher side, whereas efficient inference is aimed by DAN with slightly reduced accuracy. The sentence embeddings are constructed using an encoded subgraph by the transformer model. The Deep Averaging Network (DAN) generates sentence embeddings by passing the average of the input embeddings for words and bi-grams through a feed forward deep neural network. Universal Sentence Encoder is capable of training a classifier with 1.5 million data at the embedding level. A deep learning model can use the Universal Sentence Encoder as an embedding layer and classification could be implemented by identifying semantically similar sentences.

3.3 Dataset

The dataset from DPIL@FIRE2016 [4] has been used for experimental purposes, which provides paraphrase dataset in four Indian languages, namely Tamil, Malayalam, Hindi and Punjabi. The first task is to classify the sentences as paraphrases(P) or non-paraphrases(NP). The second task is associated with the classification of the sentences into three categories, namely paraphrases(P), non-paraphrases(NP) and semi-paraphrases(SP). The sentences from news articles[2] are used in the evaluation dataset. The distribution of data for different languages in the training and test dataset is provided in Table 1.

Table 1. Data Distribution

Task No	Language/ No.of instances	Tamil	Malayalam	Hindi	Punjabi
1	Training Data	2500	2500	2500	1700
	Test Data	900	900	900	500
2	Training Data	3500	3500	3500	2200
	Test Data	1400	1400	1400	750

The training dataset of Task1 for Tamil, Malayalam and Hindi had 2500 instances each and Punjabi had 1700 instances. The test data for the same task had 900 instances for languages Tamil, Malayalam and Hindi while Punjabi had 500 instances. Considering Task2, each of the languages Tamil, Malayalam and Hindi had 3500 instances and Punjabi had 2200 instances in the training dataset, while the test dataset for Tamil, Malayalam and Hindi had 1400 instances each and Punjabi had 750 instances. The XML representation of data was used with both training and test datasets. A sample of the training data is given below:

```
<Paraphrase pID="TAM0009">

    <Sentence1>அரசு ஊழியர்களுக்கு வழங்குவது போல் சாலை
பணியாளர்களுக்கும் வங்கிகள் மூலம் சம்பளம் பட்டுவாடா.

    </Sentence1>

    <Sentence2>சாலைப்பணியாளர்களுக்கு    வங்கிகள்    மூலம்
சம்பளம் என தமிழக அரசு அறிவித்துள்ளது.</Sentence2>

    <Class>P</Class>

</Paraphrase>
```

4   Implementation

This section provides an insight into the preprocessing mechanisms, and the workflow associated with the proposed system. The formats of the training and test data required by each of the algorithms are also discussed.

---

[2] http://nlp.amrita.edu/dpil_cen/.

Data Preprocessing. In the proposed system, datasets from four Indian languages are used for training and testing the model. XML and Xlsx file formats are used by the training and test dataset respectively. As a tab separated variable format is required by the proposed algorithms, extraction and conversion of data from the XML file formats needs to be implemented. After the training dataset is obtained, the development dataset is created by extracting 20% of the instances from the training dataset. The extracted data is converted to the format as required by the respective algorithms.

4.1 BERT

The data in the training and the test dataset are stored using the same format which is given below

ID   label   placeholder   sentence1<eol >sentence2

Sample instances from the training dataset are given below:

TAM0131 1 a பாவங்கள் போக்கும் காயத்ரி மந்திர சுலோகம். <eol>காயத்ரி மந்திரம் ஜெபித்து வர பாபங்கள் விலகும்.

TAM1083 2 a அரியானா சட்டசபை கூடியது.<eol>அரியானா மாநிலத்தின் 13வது சட்டசபை கூட்டம் இன்று கூடியது.

TAM2128 0 a மோடியிடம் நான் கேட்க விரும்புகிறேன்.<eol>டெல்லி அரசை மோடி செயல்படவிடாமல் தடுக்கிறார்.

Sample instances from the test dataset are given below:

1 2 a மின் கம்பத்தில் ஆம்னி பஸ் மோதி குழந்தை உள்பட 3 பேர் பலி.<eol>3 பேர் பஸ் மோதி பலியானார்கள்.

2 1 a அப்துல்கலாம் அவர்கள் அனைவரையும் கனவு காணச் சொல்கிறார்<eol>கனவு காணுங்கள் என அப்துல்கலாம் கூறுகிறார்

4 1 a இடி எனும் இசை முழங்கிட வரும் மழை எனும் மகள் <eol>மழைமகள் இடி இசை முழங்கிட வருவாள்

The text from the training dataset is loaded and fragmented into tokens and token ids are assigned to each of the tokens. Using the methods of padding and truncation, all the sentences are converted into sentences with a fixed length. The padding token and the normal tokens are distinguished using attention masks. On proving the input data, training of both the pre-trained BERT model and the additional classification layer are performed on the specific task. The parameters associated with the 'bert-base-uncased' version of the pretrained model includes 12-layers with 768 hidden layers, 12 heads and 110M parameters. The model is pretrained on cased text on top of 104 languages with the largest Wikipedias. Training parameters used by the model include a batch size of 32, a learning rate of 2e-5 and the number of epochs used is 4. The instances of the training dataset are used for the training of the model developed. It is tested using the test data which returns logits and the associated probabilities are obtained using the Softmax activation function.

4.2 Seq2Seq

The pre-processing of the data is implemented using the XML parser to make the model understand the dataset. The unique words from the training, development and test dataset are saved into the file which serves as a dictionary for the training model. Separate directories are used for saving the results and checkpoints. The RNN model is used for training the dataset, and it stores the past values and gives the new input to the next layer along with the past value for better predictions. Evaluation of the performance of the model is done by computing the accuracy of the results of the prediction.

4.3 USE

The dataframes are used to represent the contents of the raw text file, and as numerical values are used to denote the label column, categorical type is associated with it. During the training phase, validation of the model's performance is done at the end of each epoch using the test dataset. After training for 10 epochs, the validation result showed the highest accuracy around 50–60%. Training of the model and saving the corresponding weights into a file, is followed by the process of predictions on a new set of sentence pairs. Comparison of the predicted and the true labels is carried out for calculating the performance scores, like f1-score, accuracy, precision and recall. The format of the data required by the USE model is

label : sentence1 <eol >sentence2

Sample instances used by this model are given below:

SP: கேரளா லாட்டரியில் அரசு ஊழியருக்கு ரூ.4 கோடி பரிசு.<eol>கேரளா, அரசு ஊழியருக்கு லாட்டரியில் பரிசு.

NP: திருக்குறள் மிகவும் பழமை வாய்ந்த நூல்.<eol>அனைவராலும் போற்றப்படும் நூல் ஆகும்.

NP: பாதுகாப்பு படை தரப்பில் ஒரு வீரர் பலியானார்.<eol>4 வீரர்கள் காயமடைந்தனர்.

4.4 Ensembled Model

The confidence scores that are obtained from the three models during predictions, are used to implement an ensembled model. The accuracy obtained from the BERT, Seq2Seq and USE algorithms individually is improved by combining all the three into a single model using an ensembled approach. The probability of predictions from the individual models is stored and the highest confidence score from the three models is retrieved for a corresponding sentence pair. The result is derived as paraphrase or non-paraphrase depending on the prediction corresponding to the identified highest confidence value. For a sequence considering Task 1, when predictions are made using BERT, the scores obtained were 0.12 for P and 0.88 for NP, predictions using seq2seq, provided a score of 0.67 for P and 0.33 for NP, and USE predictions provided a score of 0.11 for P and 0.89 for NP. Comparing the scores it could be found that the score on using USE algorithm has a highest value for NP compared to the other scores. So the given sentence is classified as a Non-paraphrase class.

5   Experimental Results

This section summarizes the prediction statistics corresponding to both the tasks considering the languages Tamil, Malayalam, Hindi and Punjabi. This is done for all the three models and the ensembled model which uses the confidence scores to make the predictions.

5.1   Prediction Results

The statistics on category wise data and predictions for each task considering different languages using the four different models are explained in this section. Based on the correct number of predictions, the accuracy is computed using the formula:

Accuracy = (No of correct paraphrase detected / total no of sentences)* 100

5.2   Task 1

The dataset provided for implementing Task 1 had a total of 2500 instances in the training dataset of which 1000 instances were under the paraphrase category and 1500 instances were under the non-paraphrase category for languages Tamil, Malayalam and Hindi. Considering the language Punjabi, there were 1700 instances under the training dataset with 1000 instances under the paraphrase category and 700 under the non-paraphrase category. Considering the test dataset, the languages Tamil, Malayalam and Hindi had 900 instances, of which 400 were paraphrases and 500 instances were non-paraphrases. For the Punjabi language, there were 250 instances under each category.

The BERT algorithm resulted with 526 true predictions and 374 false predictions for the Tamil dataset, 589 true predictions and 311 false predictions for the Malayalam dataset, 765 true predictions and 135 false predictions for the Hindi dataset and 428 true predictions and 72 false predictions for the Punjabi dataset. On implementing the Seq2Seq model for the same task, the number of true predictions and false predictions were 474 and 426 for the Tamil dataset, 522 and 378 for the Malayalam dataset, 500 and 400 for the Hindi data set, 250 and 250 for the Punjabi dataset. The USE algorithm when used for paraphrase detection, the Tamil dataset provided 486 true predictions and 414 false predictions, the Malayalam dataset provided 505 true predictions and 395 false predictions, the Hindi dataset provided 504 true predictions and 396 false predictions and the Punjabi dataset provided 291 true predictions and 209 false predictions. Considering the language Tamil, the Ensembled model had made 526 correct predictions. Similarly considering the language Malayalam, 590 predictions were right among the 900 predictions. For the language Hindi, out of 900 predictions, 767 predictions were correct and 429 correct predictions were made for the language Punjabi. The prediction distribution can be visualized from Fig. 4.

The accuracy associated with all the above models is represented by Table 2. It can be found that, considering the language Tamil, the accuracy obtained

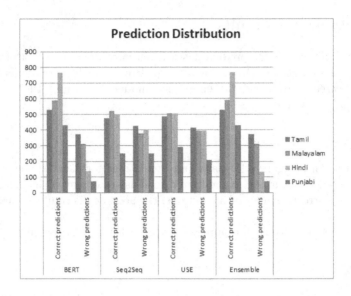

Fig. 4. Distribution of predictions(Task 1)

is 58.44%, 52.66%, 54% and 58.44% using BERT, Seq2Seq, Use and Ensembled models respectively. For language Malayalam, the accuracy provided by the BERT model is 65.44%, the Seq2Seq model is 58%, the USE model is 56.11% and the Ensembled model is 65.55%. It was found that the language Hindi had obtained an accuracy of 85% using the BERT model, 55.55% using the Seq2Seq model, 56% using the USE model and 85.22% using the Ensembled model. The models using BERT, Seq2Seq, USE and Ensembled approaches had achieved an accuracy of 81.6%, 50%, 58.2% and 85.8% respectively on the Punjabi dataset.

Table 2. Model Accuracy(Task 1)

Language	BERT	Seq2seq	USE	Ensembled
Tamil	58.44%	54.00%	52.66%	44.57%
Malayalam	65.55%	56.11%	57.99%	65.55%
Hindi	85.22%	59.22%	55.55%	85.22%
Punjabi	85.80%	58.19%	50.00%	85.8%

5.3 Task 2

There were a total of 3500 instances in the training dataset for Task2, of which 1000 instances were paraphrases, 1500 were non-paraphrases and 1000 were semi-paraphrases considering the languages Tamil, Malayalam and Hindi. For the

Punjabi language there were 2200 instances in the training dataset with 700 paraphrases, 1000 non-paraphrases and 500 semi-paraphrases. Considering the test dataset, the languages Tamil, Malayalam and Hindi had 1400 instances of which 400 were paraphrases, 500 were non-paraphrases and 500 instances were semi-paraphrases. For the Punjabi language there were 250 instances under each category.

The BERT model had provided 629, 807, 800 and 487 correct predictions for the languages Tamil, Malayalam, Hindi and Punjabi respectively. The correct predictions provided by the Seq2Seq model for Tamil, Malayalam, Hindi and Punjabi were 694, 499, 476 and 250 respectively. The USE model provided 308 correct predictions for Tamil, 501 correct predictions for Malayalam, 484 correct predictions for Hindi and 275 correct predictions for the Punjabi language. The number of correct predictions using the Ensembled model were 624, 794, 783 and 473 for languages Tamil, Malayalam, Hindi and Punjabi respectively. This is represented by Fig. 5. From the predictions, the accuracy of the different

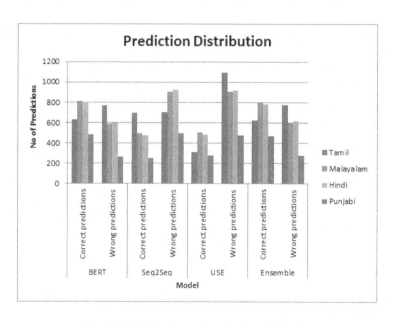

Fig. 5. Distribution of predictions(Task 2)

Table 3. Model Accuracy(Task 2)

Language	BERT	Seq2seq	USE	Ensembled
Tamil	44.92%	49.57%	22%	44.57%
Malayalam	57.64%	35.64%	35.78%	56.71%
Hindi	57.14%	34%	34.42%	55.92%
Punjabi	64.93%	33.33%	36.66%	63.06%

models is calculated and tabulated in Table 3. It can be found that, considering the language Tamil, the accuracy obtained is 44.92%, 49.57%, 22% and 44.57% using BERT, Seq2Seq, Use and Ensembled models respectively. For the language Malayalam the accuracy provided by the BERT model is 57.64%, the Seq2Seq model is 35.64%, the USE model is 35.78% and the Ensembled model is 56.71%. It was found that the language Hindi had obtained an accuracy of 57.14% using the BERT model, 34% using the Seq2Seq model, 34.42% using the USE model and 55.92% using the Ensembled model. The models using BERT, Seq2Seq, USE and Ensembled approaches had achieved an accuracy of 64.93%, 33.33%, 36.66% and 63.06% respectively on the Punjabi dataset.

5.4   Comparison of Algorithms

The paraphrase detection models show a low performance in languages Tamil and Malayalam when compared with the languages Hindi and Punjabi and the tables Table 3 and Table 3 represent this. The complex vocabulary that exists in Tamil and Malayalam languages is considered as one of the reasons. As the contextual meaning associated with the sentences can be understood by BERT, the performance of BERT is better compared to other algorithms. It is also evident from the tables that the ensembled model has produced better accuracy than the individual models.

5.5   Performance Comparison

The results obtained by different paraphrase detection models for Indian languages have been tabulated in Table 4. Senthil Kumar et al. [1] had used LSTM and reported an accuracy of 65.2%. Mahalakshmi et al. [2] had represented feature vectors using RAE for Tamil paraphrase detection and have reported accuracy of 50%. Using encoder-Decoder Neural network [13] for paraphrase detection in Tamil has resulted in an accuracy of 75.04% for Task1 and 75.42%

Table 4. Performance Comparison

Language/ Methodology	Task	Tamil	Malayalam	Hindi	Punjabi
Mahalakshmi etal. [2]	Task1	50%	-	-	-
Senthil Kumar etal. [1]	Task1	65.20%	-	-	-
Saikh et al. [3]	Task1	57.55%	59%	82.22%	95.20
	Task2	55.07%	42.21%	68.57%	88.6%
Senthil Kumar etal. [13]	Task1	75.04%	-	-	-
	Task2	75.42%	-	-	-
Proposed Model	Task1	58.44%	65.55%	85.22%	85.80%
	Task2	44.57%	56.71%	55.92%	63.06%

for Task2. The proposed system has performed better than Mahalakshmi et al. [2] methodology. The system also has performed better than the proposed machine learning approach of Saikh et al. [3] for Tamil, Malayalam, and Hindi languages. The proposed system has improved the accuracy of Hindi by 2% and Malayalam by 6.55%.

5.6   Error Analysis

The system encountered a greater number of new words that were not found even once in the training dataset and some words had occurred only one or two times. The complex nature in terms of the structure and vocabulary of Tamil and Malayalam languages has led to a reduction in prediction accuracy. In the pair of sentences below, the words that do not occur even once in the training data are listed and are assigned with the UNK token. This has also led to the false prediction where a paraphrase gets predicted as a non-paraphrase.

ஆசைக்கும் பேராசைக்கும் சண்டை நடந்தால் அதில் பேராசைதான் ஜெயிக்கும்<ஊ0l>பேராசையே ஜெயிக்கும், ஆசைக்கும் பேராசைக்கும் சண்டை நடந்தால்

ஆசைக்கும், பேராசைக்கும், ஜெயிக்கும்

6   Conclusion

The proposed system uses BERT, Seq2Seq, and USE algorithms to identify whether a given pair of sentences are paraphrases of each other. The implementation of the system is carried out as two subtasks, of which the first task identifies whether the given sentence pair is a paraphrase or not. The second task further categorises the sentence pair as a paraphrase, semi-paraphrase or non-paraphrase. Based on the requirements of the algorithms, data preprocessing is carried out and generation of vocabulary files is done. Predictions are made on the basis of the probability scores obtained as output from the algorithms and the score values are used to do the ensembling process. The proposed system has achieved an accuracy of 85.22% and 85.80% for the first task, considering the languages Hindi and Punjabi, respectively. The confidence values of BERT are higher than other models and this has an impact on the model performance which is found to be equivalent to that of BERT. It is also observed that there is a reduction in the accuracy of predictions on increasing the size of dataset. In future, the sentences for the USE and Seq2Seq models can be modified to incorporate character embedding as well. An extension of the work can be done for cross-lingual paraphrase detection, considering more Indian languages.

References

1. Senthil Kumar, B., Thenmozhi, D., Aravindan, C., Kayalvizhi, S.: Tamil Paraphrase Detection using Long-Short Term Memory Networks. In: Proceedings of Tamil Internet Conference-TIC2019, pp. 4–10, Chennai, India (2019)

2. Mahalakshmi, S., Anand Kumar, M., Soman, K.P.: Paraphrase detection for Tamil language using deep learning algorithm : Int. J. Appl. Eng. Res. **10**(17), 13929–13934 (2015)
3. Saikh, T., Naskar, S.K., Bandyopadhyay, V.: JU_NLP@ DPIL-FIRE2016: Paraphrase Detection in Indian Languages-A Machine Learning Approach : FIRE (Working Notes), pp. 275–278 (2016)
4. Anand Kumar, M., Singh, S., Kavirajan, B., Soman, K.P.: Shared task on detecting paraphrases in indian languages (dpil): an overview. In: Majumder, P., Mitra, M., Mehta, P., Sankhavara, J. (eds.) FIRE 2016. LNCS, vol. 10478, pp. 128–140. Springer, Cham (2018). https://doi.org/10.1007/978-3-319-73606-8_10
5. Sarkar, K.: KS_JU@ DPIL-FIRE2016: Detecting Paraphrases in Indian Languages Using Multinomial Logistic Regression Model : arXiv preprint arXiv:1612.08171 (2016)
6. Sarkar, S., Saha, S., Bentham, J., Pakray, P., Das, D., Gelbukh, A.: NLP-NITMZ@ DPIL-FIRE2016: Language Independent Paraphrases Detection, FIRE (Working Notes), pp. 256–259 (2016)
7. Thenmozhi, D., Aravindan, C.: Paraphrase identification by using clause-based similarity features and machine translation metrics. Comput. J. Oxford University Press **59**(9), 1289–1302 (2016)
8. Lee, J.C., Cheah, Yu-N.: Paraphrase detection using semantic relatedness based on Synset Shortest Path in WordNet. In: 2016 International Conference on Advanced Informatics: Concepts, Theory and Application (ICAICTA), IEEE, pp. 1–5 (2016)
9. Socher, R., Huang, E., Pennin, J., Manning, C.D., Andrew, N.: Dynamic Pooling and Unfolding Recursive Autoencoders for Paraphrase Detection. In: Advances in Neural Information Processing Systems, vol. 24 (2011)
10. Agarwal, B., Ramampiaro, H., Langseth, H., Ruocco, M.: A deep network model for paraphrase detection in short text messages. Inform. Process. Manage. Elsevier **54**(6), 922–937 (2018)
11. Shen, Y., Rong, W., Sun, Z., Ouyang, Y., Xiong, Z.: Question/answer matching for CQA system via combining lexical and sequential information. In: Twenty-Ninth AAAI Conference on Artificial Intelligence (2015)
12. Gelbukh, A.: Plagiarism Detection Through Paraphrase Recognition : Instituto Politécnico Nacional (2018)
13. Senthil Kumar, B., Thenmozhi, D., Kayalvizhi, S.: Tamil paraphrase detection using encoder-decoder neural networks. In: Chandrabose, A., Furbach, U., Ghosh, A., Kumar M., A. (eds.) ICCIDS 2020. IAICT, vol. 578, pp. 30–42. Springer, Tamil paraphrase detection using encoder-decoder neural networks (2020). https://doi.org/10.1007/978-3-030-63467-4_3
14. Devlin, J., Chang, M.W., Lee, K., Toutanova, K.: BERT: Pre-training of Deep Bidirectional Transformers for Language Understanding : CoRR, http://arxiv.org/abs/1810.04805, dblp computer science bibliography, vol. : abs/1810.04805 (2018)
15. Cer, D.: Universal Sentence Encoder: 10.48550/ARXIV.1803.11175, https://arxiv.org/abs/1803.11175 arXiv (2018)
16. Sutskever, I., Vinyals, O., Le, Q.V.: Sequence to Sequence Learning with Neural Networks : 10.48550/ARXIV.1409.3215, https://arxiv.org/abs/1409.3215, arXiv (2014)
17. Thapa, S., Adhikari, S., Mishra, S.: Review of text summarization in indian regional languages. In: Abraham, A., Castillo, O., Virmani, D. (eds.) Proceedings of 3rd International Conference on Computing Informatics and Networks. LNNS, vol. 167, pp. 23–32. Springer, Singapore (2021). https://doi.org/10.1007/978-981-15-9712-1_3

Opinion Classification on Code-mixed Tamil Language

S. Divya$^{(\boxtimes)}$ (iD), N. Sripriya$^{(\boxtimes)}$, Daphne Evangelin, and G. Saai Sindhoora

Department of Information Technology, Sri Sivasubramaniya Nadar College of Engineering, Chennai, Tamilnadu, India
divya_stephenson@yahoo.com, sripriyan@ssn.edu.in

Abstract. User Sentiment Analysis (SA) is an interesting application of Natural Language Processing (NLP) to analyze the opinions of an individual. The user's opinion is beneficial to the public, business organizations, movie producers etc. to take valid decisions and enhance it. Few sentiments are incorrectly interpreted due to context errors such as multi-polarity. People belonging to multilingual communities utilize multiple regional languages for communication and thus social media platform enabled the users to express their ideas in mixed languages. The user opinions posted as a mixture of two or more language is known as code-mixed data. It is quiet challenging to handle such code-mixed data as it contains colloquial vocabulary and is difficult to interpret the context in mixed languages. This proposed system focuses on this issue by analyzing the efficiency several word embedding techniques in the generation of contextual representation of words. To evaluate the performance of various embedding techniques, the representations generated are given as input to a standard machine learning technique for sentiment classification. The efficiency of several embedding algorithm is analyzed by classifying the code-mixed data based on its representation. This analysis is carried out on Dravidian Code-mixed FIRE 2020 Tamil dataset which contains review comments collected from YouTube. The evaluation proves that the transformer model generates effective representations and the positive labels are efficiently identified with the F1 score of 0.75. The representations generated by various embedding algorithms are fed as input to several classification algorithms and the accuracy of the models are estimated. From the result, it is derived that IndicBERT generates semantically efficient representations and thus facilitates in achieving greater classification accuracy.

Keywords: Sentiment Analysis · Natural Language Processing · Social Media Platform

1 Introduction

1.1 Sentiment Analysis

Sentiment Analysis supports in identify the opinion, thought, judgement of an individual about system. Various text collected from forums such as tweets, posts, comments, and

Anand Kumar M et al. (Eds.): SPELLL 2022, CCIS 1802, pp. 155–168, 2023.
https://doi.org/10.1007/978-3-031-33231-9_10

reviews are analyzed and the consolidated output is generated. Sentiment analysis can be performed at various levels such as sentence, document, or on specific feature. Due to the massive exposure in the number of online media and people accessing to express their opinions or attitudes on diverse subjects over the past few decades [1].

There exist several online social media platforms and messaging tools that have been very popular to facilitate users to generate and observe information about films, politics, products, trading surveys, etc. Such content archive users' judgement, mostly positive or negative and few being neutral. Sentiment Analysis (SA) contributes in the analysis of people's appreciation and feelings towards several entities that are introduced to them.

1.2 Sentiment Analysis on Code-mixed Language

As a result of a massive enhancement of social media, the facility for users to convey or communicate their opinions became feasible. Since most of the social media sites provide and user-friendly strategy for the users to post their opinion in their native language. Thus, the users opt to post their opinions as a mixture of languages. This pattern of collaborating two languages in the user's linguistics has led to coining of two terms: code-switching and code-mixing. The tendency of switching within two or more language in the same speech is termed as Code-Switching. Code-Mixing refers to the combination of language-specific units such as tokens, phrases, sentences, sub-tokens and morphemes of one language into an annotation of another language [2]. Code-mixed is a tend to frame scripts by using more than one language to share the user's opinion on social media. This combines multiple languages to create a linguistic that consists of elements in a contextually understandable manner. In a community of bilingual community, Code-mixing is very common among speakers. Now a days, English is projected as the language of repute and standard, the embedding of lexicon, tokens and phrases from English language with Tamil became very gradual. Due to the influence of English online, code-mixed Tamil-English (Tanglish) [3] sentences are mostly written in Roman script. Dravidian code-mixed languages, such as Tamil, Malayalam are increasingly used by people in social media. This facilitates the users to post their opinion in their native language.

Since the number of non-English and multilingual users accessing social media has drastically increased, the focus in identifying the user sentiment from the content posted by the user also drastically increased. This led to the necessity for analyzing the individual's emotion that are expressed as comments in code-mixed language. The code-mixed data has wide application areas such as Machine Translation (MT), Text Summarization, Mixed Script Information Retrieval (MSIR), Identification of Language, Opinion analysis, etc.

Our objective of this work is to facilitate the effective identification of the sentiment on code-mixed Tamil sentences. This is done by generating contextual representation of each input token followed by classification is performed using a standard Machine Learning (ML) model. Since accurate classification depends on the effective representation of input, various embedding techniques are used to create representation and the classification accuracy is evaluated by applying them on a standard machine learning technique. The organization of this paper is as follows. Sect. 1 describes the domain knowledge and the objective. Section 2 details the background of sentiment analysis.

Section 3 presents the design of the proposed system with the description of each module and Sect. 4 details the tools and technologies used for the implementation of the system. The result of the proposed model is discussed in Sect. 5 and Sect. 6 concludes the paper.

2 Literature Review

Sentiment Analysis supports in understanding the opinion of audience towards a content. This user opinion facilitates in improvising the task such as recommendation systems towards satisfying the users.

2.1 Sentiment Analysis on Mono Lingual Data

The term "Sentiment Analysis" was introduced by Nasukawa et al. [4] but research has been carried out to some extend by linguistics people before the year 2000. In the beginning of the twenty-first century, this task was a challenging task in NLP stream. This task was not just restricted to computer science but also reached various other fields. In 2007, the task of opinion analysis was implemented in the field of management studies to obtain product price [5]. Then, Sentiment analysis task was carried out on social media content, in 2012, Federico Neri et al. made a sentiment analysis study on Facebook posts about newscasts [6]. Liu et al. identified three levels at which the opinion classification could be applied on the input text [7]. Those three are document level, sentence level, and entity level. After a point of time, various techniques have been analyzed and implemented to all these levels of processing. Several Machine learning models have been applied and has achieved greater performance in sentimental analysis task for the monolingual data. Sajeetha et al. have reviewed on sentiment analysis in Tamil texts. By using SVM classifier, they achieved 75% [8]. The technique is effective to analyze the sentiment for monolingual data. This paper contributes to analyzing the sentiments on code-mixed data.

2.2 Sentiment Analysis on Code-Mixed Data

Code-mixing is recently a critical research area in the field of opinion classification and transliteration. Processing of code-mixed data in order to exatract its context is quiet challenging. Dinakar Sitaram et al. had analyzed much for the processing of Hindi-English code-mixed data [9]. Code-mixed data requires a huge pre-processing step compared to monolingual data. Nithya et al. proposed deep neural network model for the analysis of low-resource languages and had applied a lot of pre-processing techniques that suits well to code-mixed linguistics [10]. Due to the existence of very small number of data, training is done partially and thus the accuracy of the classification model is minimal. Bharathi Raja Chakravarthy et al. have proposed the process of creating the corpus and defining polarities for code-mixed Tamil-English text [11].

Anita Saroj et al. applied BERT_BASE model for emotion analysis on low-resourceCode-mixed Tamil data and Malayalam-English code-mixed languages. They achieved an F-score of 0.59 for English-Tamil code mixed data [14]. Kalavani et al. have done research to identify the sentiment message polarity from code-mixed Tamil and Malayalam code-mixed social media comments using the ULM fit framework and achieved F-1 score of 0.6 for both code-mixed languages [12]. This led to a challenge of imbalance in the code-mixed dataset. Srinivasan et al. used sampling techniques to detect sentiments on code-mixed dataset that are imbalanced and the performance of the model is compared with various machine learning techniques using F1- Score [13].

In addition to sentiment analysis on code-mixed data, Bharathi Raja Chakravarthy et al. have defined corpus for low-resource languages on the task of analyzing the sentiments and finding if the input has offensive context or not. They have used multi-lingual models for sentiment analysis [15].

It is challenging to process code-mixed data for the generation of contextual representations. To effectively process this kind of data, various embedding algorithms are applied on the input data and the classification is performed. The representations from several embedding techniques are given as input to a standard machine learning technique namely eXtreme Gradient Boosting (XGBoost) and the classification accuracy is evaluated. As XGboost is efficient in many applications and have majorly dominated in many competitions, this algorithm is chosen to evaluate the effectiveness of embedding techniques. The embedding algorithm that generates effective representation is chosen and is integrated with several classification and the efficiency of the models are estimated.

3 Methodology

3.1 Data Description

The dataset utilized for the evaluation of the proposed sentiment analysis model in processing the code-mixed Tamil data is provided by the organizers of the Dravidian Code-Mix FIRE 2020 task. The dataset contains the user comments collected from the social media and the labels that represent the polarity of each data. The data in the dataset are in Tamil code-mixed language. The polarities in the dataset and a sample for each label from the dataset is shown in Table 1.

Table 1. Tamil Annotated YouTube Comments

Text	Labels
Trailer yae rombe interesting a iruku… Vera level trailer…	Positive
Ayyayyo. Sruthihassan. ellame poch	Negative
it not vijay hair.,., hair setup paaa	Mixed_feelings
2018 la intha teaser a paathavanga like pannunga	Unknown_state
Ye Kya kardi kangna ne…..?	Not_Tamil

The dataset comprises of 35,657 training data, 3,963 validation data and 4,403 test data collected from YouTube comments and is presented without labels. Table 2 shows the polarity-wise specification of YouTube comments that are in Tamil-English code-mixed language.

Table 2. Dataset - YouTube Comments

Category	Train	Test
Positive	20070	2257
Negative	4271	480
Mixed_feelings	4020	438
Unknown_state	5629	611
Not_Tamil	1666	176

3.2 System Design

The proposed mode is mainly focused in effectively identifying the sentiment of the code-mixed Tamil sentences by generating a contextual representation of each token in the input. These contextual representations are fed into a standard machine learning approach to classify them into five diverse polarities such as positive, negative, mixed-feelings, unknown state, and not Tamil. Architecture of the proposed system is shown in Fig. 1. Initially, the input data is pre-processed as it contains noise data such as hashtags, special characters, punctuation marks, and emojis. Initially, the numerical representation is generated for the input text. This identifies the features of the input that contributes to the effective prediction of class labels using machine learning algorithms. Word embedding represents a word by a numeric vector of a fixed dimension.

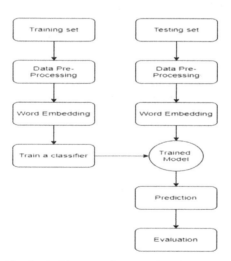

Fig. 1. Architecture of Proposed methodology

The representations generated by the word embeddings are given as input into a classification model. The performances of several embedding algorithms are evaluated on Dravidian Code-mixed FIRE 2020 Tamil dataset. The classification accuracy of the machine learning integrated with various embedding algorithms are analyzed to estimate the efficiency of each embedding techniques.

3.3 Data Pre-processing

Data pre-processing is a initial step in any Natural Language Processing task as it plays a major role in standardizing the input. Pre-processing is necessary in any task as it helps in removing noise from the input data that will facilitate in representing the classes with its specific features. This is necessary as the presence of the noise in the input diminishes its efficiency. Pre-processing contributes to the extraction of contextual information from the text. NLTK and regex libraries are used for pre-processing the corpus. Pre-processing stage executes the following steps:

Removal of Emojis
An idea or emotion that are present in a message can be represented visually as emojis that are included in a text message. All emojis are removed because they are noise data.

Removal of Punctuations, Symbols and Numbers
Generally, sentences are written with punctuations that are used in writing to separate sentences and their constituents. These symbols are helpful in explaining the meaning of the text. Users in social media platform use punctuations and their placement randomly to defy the linguistical conventions. Punctuations are eliminated because these symbols do not support in the contribution of contextual information during processing.

Removal of Hashtags and URLs
Hashtags and URLs don't add meaningful context to the sentence. To yield good results, hashtags and URLs are removed from the data.

Removal of Stop Words
Sentences generally include few irrelevant words that are used while speaking and those are named as stop words. To reduce the processing time, stop words are removed from the data.

Tokenization
An attempt to break each token in a sentence into a list of words is termed as tokenization. This step is a vital as it provides more information about a contextual essence of a particular text. The sample data being pre-processed and the output derived is shown in Table 3.

Table 3. Sample text after the removal of punctuation

Text	Token
Sample text after the removal of punctuation	
it not vijay hair,,,, hair setup paaa	vijay hair hair setup paaa
vera level… pakka blockbuster for sure…:)…	vera level pakka blockbuster for sure
Sample text after the removal of hashtags and urls	
Ending Vera level da deii #GetRajinified	Ending Vera level da deii
vera level… #str #aravindhsamy #VJS #arunvijay	vera level
Sample for tokenization	
I love you ajith very I like	[I, love, you, ajith, very, I, like]
Arjun sir kaaga poi padam pakelam	[Arjun, sir, kaage, poi, padam, pakelam]

3.4 Word Embedding

A technique for representing each word or sentence in the document is called Embedding. Word Embedding generates a numeric vector for each input word in a lower-dimensional space. Words that convey similar meanings have a similar representation. Precisely, extraction of features from the input is known as embeddings. These representations can be fed into a machine learning model to classify them. These extracted features hold syntactical and semantic information. The proposed work analyzed five such word embeddings as TF-IDF [16], Word2Vec [17], CountVectorizer [18] and transformer models such as BERT [19, 20] and IndicBERT [21].

3.4.1 TF-IDF

TF-IDF is a statistical measure that assigns weight for each token in the input. The term frequency (TF) frequency of word occurrence in a document whereas, Inverse Document Frequency (IDF) specifies in the increase of weights for words that are not frequent but reducing the weight for unimportant words that appear very frequently.

$$TF = \frac{No.\ of\ times\ word\ w\ occured}{Total\ no.\ of\ words\ in\ the\ documents}$$

$$IDF(w) = log[\frac{No.\ of\ Documents}{No.\ of\ Documents\ containing\ word\ w}]$$

3.4.2 Word2Vec

A Deep Learning model named Word2vec is coined by Google to capture the meaning of words easier and faster to pre-process given plain text input. A corpus of huge size comprising documents from various platforms are fed as input to this approach. The vector space with a greater number of dimensions is given as output. Each input token is given a unique vector placed in the vector space.

3.4.3   CountVectorizer

CountVectorizer is a flexible tool given by the sci-kit-learn library in Python. Based on the frequency of each word in the input text, every text will be transformed into a vector. This approach will be useful in the presence of many such texts, in which each word has to be converted into vectors.

3.4.4   BERT

BERT stands for Bi-directional Encoder Representations from Transformers. This is a deep learning model which has a contextual connectivity between every output element and every input element Its weights are dynamically estimated based on those connection. It is a transformer-based model that can read input from both directions simultaneously and is thus termed as bidirectionality.

The BERT model is pretrained with Masked Language Model (MLM) in which it is trained to hide a token in a sentence and then tries to predict the hidden word(masked) based context of the sentence Another task in which the BERT model is trained is Next Sentence Prediction which tries to predict whether two given sentences are contextually related or not. BERT is a pre-trained model that uses only an unlabeled, plain text corpus (namely the English Wikipedia).

Label prediction is performed by appending a classification layer over the encoder output. This multiplies the output vectors by the embedding matrix, changing them into the vocabulary dimension, and estimating the probability of each word in the vocabulary with any softmax activation function. Multi-lingual BERT is pre-trained with 104 languages with the largest Wikipedia with an objective of Masked Language Modelling (MLM) objective. It is designed in a way to pre-train by using unlabeled text and can then be fine-tuned by incorporating the last layer. This work focusses on exploring the task of how the classification of code-mixed data into their corresponding sentiment categories are performed.

IndicBERT is a BERT model pre-trained exclusively in 12 major Indian languages. The pre-training of this model is performed on a corpus of around 9 billion tokens which comprises 549M Tamil tokens. IndicBERT has comparatively fewer parameters than every other multilingual model (BERT, XLM-R, etc.) but still manages to give a state-of-the-art performance on various tasks and achieves performance better than these models. IndicBert has the capacity to handle 12 diverse languages such as Assamese, Bengali, English, Gujarati, Hindi, Kannada, Malayalam, Marathi, Oriya, Punjabi, Tamil, and Telugu.

3.5   Machine Learning Approach

The numerical representation of the pre-processed text is fed as input to the classification algorithms to predict the sentiments. Two challenges that can prevail while applying ML algorithms to any data is, to find the appropriate word embedding technique and to find a suitable classification algorithm. Identification of suitable word embedding techniques facilitates in the generation of contextual numerical representation and thus contributes to the effective classification of sentiments. This work focusses in classifying the input sentences based on its sentiments using a gradient based classification algorithm named,

XGBoost [21]. All the classification algorithms are applied for each word embedding and the results are evaluated separately.

3.5.1 XGBoost

XGBoost stands for e**X**treme **G**radient **B**oosting. This model is an implementation of Gradient Boosted Decision Trees. In gradient boosting, each predictor validates the error made by its predecessor. Instead of tweaking the weights of the training instances, each predictor is trained with the help of the residual errors of the predecessor as labels. XGboost implementation incorporates built-in cross-validation method, which faciliatates the algorithm to prevent overfitting in the absence of huge dataset. It can perform regression, classification, grading and certain prediction problems defined by the user.

This work focuses on the analysis of various word embedding techniques in the generation of contextual representations that are fed as input to a standard classification model. The efficiency of each model in the identification of each label are evaluated.

4 Performance Evaluation

The sentiment analysis model is implemented in python with the use of Scikit-learn, NLTK, Genism and Transformers packages. The input sentence taken from the dataset posted in Dravidian CodeMix-FIRE2021 is pre-processed and is given as input to various embedding models (TF-IDF, Word2Vec, CountVectorizer, Indic BERT). The intermediate representations generated by various models are fed as input to a classification model. The accuracy of various embedding models integrated with variety of classification models are analyzed.

4.1 Evaluation Metrics

The performance of the model is evaluated using various metrics and the formula for those evaluation metrics is shown in the following equation:

- Recall is calculated by finding the ratio of correctly predicted sentence with the overall observation in the original class.

$$Recall = \frac{True\ Positive}{(True\ Positive + False\ Negatives)}$$

- Precision is estimated by calculating the ratio of correctly predicted sentences with the total predicted sentences.

$$Recall = \frac{True\ Positive}{(True\ Positive + False\ Positives)}$$

- F1 Score is calculated as the weighted average of precision and recall.

$$F1\ Score = 2(\frac{Precision * Recall}{Precision + Recall})$$

- Accuracy is the level of acceptance between the actual label and the absolute label.

$$Accuracy = \frac{No.\ of\ correctly\ classified\ comments}{Total\ No.\ of\ comments\ in\ the\ corpus} \times 100$$

The classification report for various embedding models integrated with several classification algorithm is shown in the table below.

Table 4. Precision Recall and F1- score of **TF-IDF.**

Model	Class Labels	Precision	Recall	F1-score
XGBoost	Positive	0.57	0.92	0.70
	Negative	0.08	0.02	0.04
	Mixed Feelings	0.24	0.02	0.03
	Unknown State	0.14	0.02	0.04
	Not Tamil	0.08	0.04	0.05
Accuracy				42%

Table 5. Precision Recall and F1- score of **Word2Vec.**

Models	Class Labels	Precision	Recall	F1-score
XGBoost	Positive	0.63	0.18	0.28
	Negative	0.13	0.65	0.22
	Mixed Feelings	0.13	0.12	0.13
	Unknown State	0.14	0.12	0.13
	Not Tamil	0.00	0.00	0.00
Accuracy				47%

Table 6. Precision Recall and F1- score of **CountVectorizer.**

Model	Class Labels	Precision	Recall	F1-score
XGBoost	Positive	0.57	0.84	0.68
	Negative	0.05	0.03	0.04
	Mixed Feelings	0.15	0.00	0.01
	Unknown State	0.24	0.09	0.13
	Not Tamil	0.04	0.02	0.02
Accuracy				47%

Table 7. Precision Recall and F1- score of **BERT.**

Model	Class Labels	Precision	Recall	F1-score
XGBoost	Positive	0.63	0.93	0.75
	Negative	0.39	0.16	0.22
	Mixed Feelings	0.34	0.10	0.16
	Unknown State	0.47	0.21	0.29
	Not Tamil	0.77	0.35	0.48
Accuracy				52%

Table 8. Precision Recall and F1- score of **IndicBERT.**

Model	Class Labels	Precision	Recall	F1-score
XGBoost	Positive	0.64	0.93	0.75
	Negative	0.35	0.11	0.17
	Mixed Feelings	0.33	0.11	0.16
	Unknown State	0.43	0.18	0.26
	Not Tamil	0.77	0.36	0.49
Accuracy				58%

While analyzing the classification accuracy of XGBoost with various embedding algorithms, the efficiency of the representations can be determined. The above given tables represent the precision, recall, and F1-score for the five classes, namely positive, negative, mixed_feelings, unknown_state, and not-Tamil classified by XGBoost classifier. Among all the models, highest F1-Score (0.75) is achieved by the Transformer model (IndicBERT) when classifying the positive samples. While considering this measure, it is concluded that the representations generated by the IndicBERT are efficient.

5   Results and Discussions

The classification accuracy of various embedding techniques integrated with XGBoost algorithm is compared and the results are tabulated in Tables 4, 5, 6, 7, 8, and 9. This comparison concludes that the embeddings generated by IndicBERT is effective and thus lead to efficient classification. From the above comparison, it is evident that the prediction of Negative, Mixed Feelings and Unknown State labels are comparatively less. This is due to the imbalance distribution of dataset. From Table 2, it is evident that out of 35,657 sentences 56% belong to the Positive class while the other sentiment classes are relatively low. The precision, recall, and F-measure scores are higher for the Positive class compared to other classes.

In addition to XGBoost, the representations generated by Transformer models and other embedding models are given as input to various classification algorithms and the accuracy is determined. The performance of several classification algorithm integrated with Transformers models are evaluated and is tabulated in Table 9.

Various Machine Learning Techniques:

- Random Forest

Random forest is a Supervised Machine Learning Algorithm that can solve Classification and Regression problems. This ensemble classifier makes prediction by embedding different decision trees that are trained on datasets of the similar size in the training set, called bootstraps. This is created by applying random resampling on the training set itself. After the tree construction, a set of bootstraps, that does nor incorporate any record from the actual dataset is a test set. The error rate while performing classification on all the test sets is the out-of-bag estimate of the generalization error.

Moreover, has certain significant characteristic like, an intrinsic feature selection step that are applied before the classification task to suppress the variables' space by assigning value to each feature. RF follows certain constraints for tree generation, appending of tree, testing itself and post-processing. This model ensures being robust to overfitting.

- Decision Tree

Decision tree is effective model for classification and prediction. This develops models of classification in the aspect of a tree structure. A dataset fragmented into subsets now when associated decision tree is mutually built at the same time. The tree with decision nodes and leaf nodes is the final product. The leaves in the tree determine the classification labels. After sequentially selecting compensative decisions, each node is fragmented iteratively. Finally, specific constraints are defined by the for the identification of result.

- Multi-nomial Naive Bayes

Multi-nomial Naive Bayes algorithm is a type of probabilistic learning method that is often applied in Natural Language Processing (NLP). MNB is suitable for the classification of discrete features. In general, multinomial distribution necessitates the number of integer feature. Multi-nomial Naive Bayes is a Bayesian classifier that functions on assumption of naiveness between features. This assumption specifies that each input is independent and is thus unrealistic for real data. On the other hand, this model simplifies various complex tasks and meets the requirement of the user. The Naïve Bayes classifier is evaluated on distributed data, that are derived from Bayes Theorem that identifies the probability of a next event while given with a currently observed event.

From the above table it is evident that the accuracy of various classification algorithm integrated with Transformer models achieves greater accuracy than other embedding algorithms. While analyzing the performance recorded in Table 9, it is concluded that the representation generated by IndicBERT is efficient and thus greater achieves greater accuracy.

Table 9. Performance of several embedding and classification models.

Embedding Model	Classification Algorithm	Accuracy
BERT	Random Forest	56%
	Decision Tree	51%
	Multinomial Naïve Bayes	55%
IndicBert	Random Forest	55%
	Decision Tree	51%
	Multinomial Naïve Bayes	56%
TF-IDF	Random Forest	39%
	Decision Tree	40%
	Multinomial Naïve Bayes	44%
Word2Vec	Random Forest	42%
	Decision Tree	41%
	Multinomial Naïve Bayes	40%
CountVectorizer	Random Forest	45%
	Decision Tree	42%
	Multinomial Naïve Bayes	47%

6 Conclusion

Various real-world applications like user opinion analysis and recommendation systems are necessarily applied on text collected from various social media platforms. The proposed work performs sentiment analysis on Tamil code-mixed data by generating a better representation of the tokens using Transformer models namely BERT and IndicBERT. These representations are given as input to several machine learning techniques to evaluate its efficiency. This concludes that the transformer model generates semantical representation and achieves greater accuracy. Also, the positive labels are effectively identified with the maximum F1 Score of 0.75.

References

1. Mandl, T., Modha, S., Kumar, A.M., Chakravarthi, B.R.: Overview of the hasoc track at fire 2020: hate speech and offensive language identification in Tamil, Malayalam, Hindi, English and German. In: Forum for Information Retrieval Evaluation, pp. 29–32 (2020)
2. Myers-Scotton, C.: Duelling languages: Grammatical structure in codeswitching, Oxford University Press (1997)
3. Chakravarthi, B.R., Muralidaran, V., Priyadharshini, R., McCrae, J.P.: Corpus creation for sentiment analysis in code-mixed Tamil-English text, in: Proceedings of the 1st Joint Workshop on Spoken Language Technologies for Under-resourced languages (SLTU) and Collaboration and Computing for Under-Resourced Languages (CCURL), pp. 202–210. European

Language Resources association, Marseille, France (2020). https://www.aclweb.org/anthol
ogy/2020.sltu-1.28

4. Nasukawa, T., et al.: Sentiment analysis: capturing favorability using natural language
   processing. In: Proceedings of the 2nd International Conference on Knowledge Capture,
   pp. 70–77 (2003). https://doi.org/10.1016/j.knosys.2016.08.012

5. Archak, N., et al.: Deriving the pricing power of product features by mining consumer reviews.
   deriving the pricing power of product features by mining consumer reviews. Manage.Sci.
   57(8), 1485–1509 (2011). http://dx.doi.org/https://doi.org/10.1287/mnsc.1110.1370

6. Neri, F., et al.: Sentiment Analysis on Social Media. In: 2012 IEEE/ACM International
   Conference on Advances in Social Networks Analysis and Mining (2012)

7. Liu, B.: Sentiment analysis and opinion mining. Synth. Lect. Hum. Lang. Technol. **5**, 1–167
   (2012)

8. Thavareesan, S., et al.: Review on sentiment analysis in tamil texts. JSc EUSL(2018), vol. 9,
   no. 2, pp. 1–18, e- ISSN: 2602-9030 (2018)

9. Sitaram, D., et al.: Sentiment analysis of mixed language employing Hindi – English code
   switching. In: International Conference on Machine Learning and Cybernetics (ICMLC),
   pp. 271–276 (2015)

10. Nithya, K., et al.: Deep learning based analysis on code-mixed tamil text for sentiment classi-
    fication with pre-trained ULMFiT. In: Proceedings of the Sixth International Conference on
    Computing Methodologies and Communication (ICCMC 2022) IEEE Xplore Part Number:
    CFP22K25-ART; ISBN: 978-1-6654-1028-1 (2022)

11. Chakravarthi, B.R., et al.: DravidianCodeMix: sentiment analysis and offensive language
    identification dataset for Dravidian languages in code-mixed text. Lang. Resources Eval.
    56(3), 765–806 (2022). https://doi.org/10.1007/s10579-022-09583-7

12. Kalaivani, A., et al.: Dravidian-CodeMix-FIRE2020: sentiment code-mixed text classifica-
    tion in Tamil and Malayalam using ULMFiT. In: CEUR Workshop Proceedings, vol. 2826,
    pp. 528–534 (2020)

13. Srinivasan, R., et al.: Sentimental analysis from imbalanced code-mixed data using machine
    learning approaches. Distrib Parallel Databases (2021)

14. Anita, S., Pal, S.: Sentiment Analysis on Multilingual Code Mixing Text Using BERT-BASE"
    participation of IRLab@IIT(BHU) in Dravidian-CodeMix and HASOC tasks of FIRE2020
    (2020)

15. Chakravarthi, B.R., et al.: Corpus creation for sentiment analysis in code-mixed Tamil-English
    text". In: Proceedings of the 1st Joint Workshop on Spoken Language Technologies for
    Under-resourced languages (SLTU) and Collaboration and Computing for Under-Resourced
    Languages (CCURL), pp. 202–210. European Language Resources association, Marseille,
    France. (2020)

16. Aizawa, A.: An information-theoretic perspective of tf–idf measures. Inf. Process. Manage.
    39(1), 45–65 (2003)

17. Mikolov, T., Chen, K., Corrado, G., Dean, J.: Efficient estimation of word representations in
    vector space, arXiv preprint arXiv:1301.3781 (2013)

18. Patel, A., Meehan, K.: Fake news detection on reddit utilising CountVectorizer and term
    frequency-inverse document frequency with logistic regression, MultinominalNB and support
    vector machine. In: 2021 32nd Irish Signals and Systems Conference (ISSC), pp. 1–6. IEEE
    (2021)

19. Devlin, J., Chang, M.W., Lee, K., Toutanova, K.: Bert: Pre-training of deep bidirectional
    transformers for language understanding. arXiv preprint arXiv:1810.04805 (2018)

20. Kannan, R.R., Rajalakshmi, R., Kumar, L.: IndicBERT based approach for Sentiment Analysis
    on Code-Mixed Tamil Tweets (2021)

21. Chen, T., et al.: Xgboost: extreme gradient boosting. R package version 0.4-2, **1**(4), 1–4
    (2015)

Analyzing Tamil News Tweets in the Context of Topic Identification

Brigil Justin[1] and Dhivya Chinnappa[2](✉)

[1] St. Xavier's Catholic College of Engineering,
Chunkankadai, Nagercoil, Tamil Nadu, India
brigil.justin@gmail.com
[2] Thomson Reuters,
Minnesota, USA
dhivya.infant@gmail.com

Abstract This paper introduces a Tamil News dataset extracted from Tamil tweets. First, a keyword-based distant supervision technique is followed to label the topic of the tweets, and an extensive corpus analysis is provided. Next, a binary classification approach is used to identify the topic of a given tweet. The paper then presents results from multiple traditional baseline machine learning models. Finally, the limitations of the work are discussed.

Keywords: Tamil News · Tamil social media · Tamil topic classification · Tamil News dataset · Tamil tweets.

1 Introduction

One of the six classical languages of India, Tamil is known for its versatility. From Sangam literature to the popular Gana songs, Tamil can adapt to the changing lives of Tamil speakers. Tamil enthusiasts have taken several measures to protect and cherish the richness of Tamil. Be it the multitude of Tamil schools across the world in non-Tamil speaking countries or the translation of Tamil literature to foreign languages, Tamil lives. With the progress in communication and technology, Tamil also progresses.

Consider the famous Tamil novel *Ponniyin Selvan* written by Kalki Krishnamurthy in the 1950s. Though the novel is historical fiction, the author strove hard to bring the history of Chozhas through the print media by conducting extensive research in India and Srilanka. The novel has been read by generations since then, letting everyone imagine the world of Chozhas in their way. Thus the cultural heritage was passed on to the upcoming generations through print media. The novel has now taken a new form into a video-audio movie adapting to the current technology. This evolution of Tamil opens up new research opportunities to enhance the lives of Tamilians and the language itself.

The oldest record of Tamil printing dates back to 1578[1]. Tamils have always shown keen interest in reading journals, as shown by the successful circulation

---

[1] thehindu.com

Ⓒ The Author(s), under exclusive license to Springer Nature Switzerland AG 2023
Anand Kumar M et al. (Eds.): SPELLL 2022, CCIS 1802, pp. 169–182, 2023.
https://doi.org/10.1007/978-3-031-33231-9_11

Table 1. Twitter handles of Tamil News channels used in extracting the News tweets

@PTTVOnlineNews, @polimernews, @sunnewstamil, @news7tamil, @ThanthiTV, @News18TamilNadu, @dinakaranonline, @JuniorVikatan, @bbctamil, @dinamalarweb, @tamilnews24711, @tamilnewsSL, @maalaimalar, @NDTVTamil, @GlobalPoorani, @Kalaignarnews, @rajnewstamil, @AsianetNewsTM, @DDNewsChennai, @NewsfirstTamil, @TamilMintNews, @SamayamTamil, @toptamilnews, @tamil7news, @tamilnewsbbc, @ibctamilnews1, @KathirNews, @KinTVNews

of the oldest Tamil Newspaper *Swadesamitran* from 1882 to 1985. Since then, there have been several News Papers and magazines that have circulated among the Tamilians.

With the advent of Television, several 24*7 Tamil News channels are actively watched by millions of Tamilians across the world. These popular news channels and newspapers have set their foot in social media, especially on Twitter, targeting the next generation of Tamils. In this paper, we target these tweets from reliable, popular Tamil News sources, either in print, TV, or both.

The contributions of this paper are three-fold. First, we present the most famous Tamil News social media [2] corpus, with more than 200,000 tweets. Second, we identify the topics of the tweets using distant supervision, annotating more than 100,000 tweets. Finally, we present strong baseline results using traditional machine learning models and compare their performance. We also provide ideas about using our corpus and suggest machine learning models that offer better performance.

2 Related Work

Topic identification is a long-studied work in Natural Language Processing. The work done in Tamil topic identification, specifically on New data, however, is limited. In this section, we discuss the relevant Tamil topic classification tasks.

Anusha et al.[1] work with social media texts to identify topics from social media. They extract texts from multiple social media, including Facebook, Youtube, and Twitter. They compare the results of several machine learning algorithms. Selvi et al.[5] work with Tamil, Hindi, and Telugu news articles to categorize articles based on their topic. They use NB, CNN, and SVM and compare the results. Ramraj et al.[3] work with Tamil News to identify a topic. They do not focus on social media but rather work with News articles. They note that CNN with pre-trained word embeddings performs better than traditional machine learning algorithms with TFIDF vectors. Nivedha and Sairam work with tweets to classify if a tweet belongs to the category *health* or not. They compare CART, and Naive Bayes approaches to achieve the same.

Unlike these topic identification works, we strictly work with News data extracting tweets from reliable news sources. We also remove all tweets in English

---

[2] Available at https://github.com/BrigilJustin/Tamil-News-Tweets

Table 2. Topics and definitions of each category used in the corpus.

Topic	Definition
Politics	Tweets that include opinions, events, involving political parties and political party leaders
Entertain-ment	Tweets that include updates about movies, TV series, short films and web series
Medical	Tweets mostly about COVID-19 and other diseases
Sports	Tweets about sports events and sports people
Weather	Tweets about weather updates
Religion	Tweets about religious events and places of worship
Other	All tweets that were not included in one of the topics defined above. These tweets usually are about a specific rare event.

and ensure our tweets are strictly in Tamil. To the best of our knowledge, we present the largest Tamil News social media corpus (>200,000 tweets) and present distantly supervised topic categories to more than 100,000 tweets.

Several works involve classifying Tamil social media text. Subramanian et al.[6] work on identifying offensive language from Tamil YouTube comments. Chakravarthi et al.[2] work on identifying and detecting abusive YouTube comments in Tamil. Reshma et al. [4] present supervised methods for domain classification.

3   Corpus Creation

3.1   Extracting Tweets

We create a Tamil News tweets corpus following three steps. First, we manually identify the Twitter handles of popular Tamil News channels and Tamil Newspapers. These include the Twitter handles of media like Dhinathanthi, Puthiyathalaimurai, Sun News, etc. Second, we collect all recent 3,500 tweets from these handles. Finally, we removed all tweets that included words other than Tamil. Following this method, we downloaded tweets at three different points in time. Initially, we extracted tweets in November 2021, then in February 2022, and finally in September 2022. We used the [3]Tweepy python package to extract the tweets. We present the Twitter handles of the news sources in Table 1. Note that most Twitter handles belong to Tamil news accounts in India and Srilanka. This ensures that our dataset is not only diverse in terms of the news source but also in terms of the time and geographical location.

After removing duplicates, we end up with 2,01,698 tweets. Thus we present a new of Tamil News tweets extracted from several reliable News sources.

---

[3] https://docs.tweepy.org/en/stable/

Table 3. Keywords used in labeling the tweets per topic

Topic	Keywords
Politics	திமுக, அதிமுக , பாஜக, தேமுதிக, அமமுக, தொகுதி, பாமக, விசிக, வேட்பாளர், தமாகா,கூட்டணி, தேர்த, அரசியல், முதல்வர், மக்களாட்சி, ஆட்சி, கூட்டாட்சி, அரசு, வேட்புமனு, நாடாளுமன்ற, கட்சி, வாக்கு, எம்.பி., எம்.எல்.ஏ.,அமைச்ச, அரசியல், பேரணி, வெளிநடப்பு, உள்ளாட்சி, கூட்டாட்சி, சுயாட்சி, உட்கட்சி, எதிர்க்கட்சி, எதிர்க்கட்சி, கலவரம், தர்ணா, ஊராட்சி, எம்.ஜி.ஆ, சீமான், குடியரசு, மநீம, து.தலைவர், மு.க., பிரதம
Entertainment	நடி, ரீமேக், பாட, இலக்கிய, திரை, படத், பட, இசை, நடன, சினிமா, கதை, கவிதை, கட்டுரை, இலக்கிய
Medical	கொரோனா, கரோனா, மருத்து, மருந்து, தடுப்பூசி, சிகிச்சை, ஊசி, வைத்தி, நோய், நோயாளி, செவிலிய, பரிசோதனை,மருந்த, அறுவை, சிகிச்சை
Sports	விளையா, கிரிக்கெட், டெஸ்ட் மேட், ஹாக்கி, வீரர், வீராங்கனை, மைதான, உடற்பயிற்சி, ஊக்க, பதக்க
Weather	வெள்ள, மழை, வெயில், புயல், வானிலை, காற்று, காற்றி, பெருவெள்ள, கொந்தளிப், சுனாமி, நிலநடுக், எரிமலை
Religion	தெய்வ, மத, திருவிழா, பூஜை, பக்தர், தரிசனம், கோவில், கோயில், பூசை, சர்ச், மசூதி, இந்து, முஸ்லீம், கிறிஸ்த்தவ, பாதிரியா, ஆயர், அருட்பணி, போப், மதகுரு

3.2   Generating Labels Through Keyword-Based Distant Supervision

We intend to label the tweets using distant supervision following a keyword-based approach. To accomplish this, we investigated the tweets manually, looking for topics. After several iterations of reading the tweets and based on world knowledge, we ended up with six news topics. We present the labels and their definitions in Table 2. Note that the category *Other* might include tweets that belong to one of the other categories and is a limitation of our approach.

After deciding on the labels, we curated a set of keywords that belonged to a specific topic. These keywords are either complete words or a lemma corresponding to a specific topic. The list of keywords corresponding to each category is present in Table 3. Since Tamil is an agglutinative language, we keep lemmas as keywords rather than words whenever possible. The keywords are chosen by native Tamil speakers accustomed to Tamil news. However, we would like to note that the set of keywords we use is limited and may not be complete.

Table 4. Statistics of the Tamil News tweets corpus

No. tweets	2,01,698
No. tweets assigned at least one topic	1,05,550
No. tweets assigned two topics	18,735
No. tweets assigned 3 topics or more	1,701
No. words	19,03,969
Vocabulary size	1,86,243 words
Length of an average tweet	9 words
Length of the longest tweet	22 words
Length of the shortest tweet	1 word

We argue that it is nearly impossible to identify all keywords associated with a specific category manually.

For every keyword corresponding to a specific topic, we check if the keyword is present in the chosen tweet. If the keyword is present, the tweet is assigned the topic the keyword belongs. Following this approach, we create a Tamil topic identification corpus on Tamil News tweets. We present examples of our corpus in Table 5. Note that this approach might assign more than one topic to a single tweet.

We decided to follow a keyword-based distant supervision approach for tweet labeling for two reasons. (i) News tweets are generally cleaner than tweets by individuals. Since our dataset includes tweets only from reliable news accounts, we found that the tweets convey the intended information precisely. Most tweets are straightforward and talk about the concerned news. Thus a keyword-based distant supervision approach is a sufficient starting point for labeling the tweets. (ii) Topic classification is relatively straightforward, and manual labeling is expensive. Generating a corpus manually labeling more than 200,000 tweets is time-consuming and monetarily expensive. The distance supervision method in this paper helps build a large corpus of Tamil tweets more simply. To ensure our dataset was of the desired quality, we examined 300 random tweets to verify if the labels were correct. We found our tweets are correct 96% of the time. Refer to Table 10 for examples of incorrect tweets.

4   Corpus Analysis

We present the statistics of our corpus in Table 4. Our corpus includes a total pf 2,01,698 unique tweets extracted from multiple reliable sources across the years 2021 and 2022, and also across different geographical locations. More than 50% (10,5550) of the tweets in our corpus receives at least one of the topic labels we chose. There are 18,735 tweets that includes at least two topics. There are 1,701 tweets that belong at least 3 topic categories. Our corpus includes a total of 19, 03, 969 words with a vocabulary size of 1,86,23 words. The average length of a tweet is 9 words, whereas the maximum length of the tweet is 22 words and the minimum length of a tweet is 1 word. We present the distribution of the length

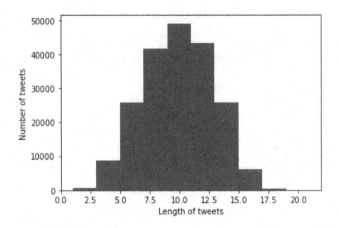

Fig. 1. Length of tweets versus the number of Tamil News tweets

of the tweets in Fig. 1. The X-axis corresponds to the length of the tweets and the Y-axis corresponds to the number of tweets.

We present example for each topic in Table 5. Example 1 talks about a political event where the Chief Minister M.K.Stalin honors the statue of Periyar. This is clearly a political event and is triggered by the keyword முதல்வர். Hence the topic of this tweet is *Politics*. In example 2, actor M.S. Baskar provides an opinion that Cinema industry will never let down hardworking people. This tweets talks about the movie industry and belongs to the category *Entertainment*. The keyword associated with the topic here is நடி. The lemma நடி in the word நடிகர் indicates that this tweet belongs to the category *Entertainment*. Example 3 talks about a government initiative where the Government conducts camps across the state of Tamil Nadu in response to increasing seasonal diseases. The associated keyword here is நோய் and hence receives the topic *Medical*. In example 4, the Minister Meinaathan talks about the magnificent field to be set for the upcoming Jallikattu event. Jallikattu is a traditional sport event involving bulls usually celebrated during the Tamil festival Pongal. The keyword that triggered the label *Sports* in this tweet is மைதானம். Tweet 5 is a weather update warning fishermen about the chances of heavy rain in the upcoming days. The associated keyword is மழை. In example 6, the tweet talks about a cultural fest in Tanjore temple regarding International Tourist Day. Since this tweet talks about an event in Tanjore temple, this receives the label *Religion*. The associated keyword is திருவிழா.

Table 6 presents examples where a tweet is assigned more than one topic. In example 1 the tweet talks about the permission granted for Jallikattu by the Government and that the bullfighters are required to produce a COVID negative certificate. Since the tweet talks about a Government (political) decision made for a sporting event during COVID times, it receives the topics *Politics, Medical, and Sports*. Example 2 talks about an accident that happened to actress and political leader Mrs. Kushboo. Clearly, the tweet gets categorized as *Politics,*

Table 5. Example tweets per topic and their English translation

	Topic	Example	Keyword	English translation
1	Politics	பெரியார் சிலைக்கு முதல்வர் முகஸ்டாலின் மரியாதை. இன்றைய லைவ் அப்டேட்ஸ்	முதல்வர்	Chief Minister honored Periyar's statue. Today's live updates
2	Entertainment	உண்மையாக உழைத்தால் சினிமா என்றும் கைவிடாது - நடிகர் எம். எஸ். பாஸ்கர்	சினிமா, நடிகர்	Cinema will never let down someone who truly works hard. Actor M.S. Baskar
3	Medical	அதிகரிக்கும் சீசனல் நோய்கள்: அரசு சார்பில் மாநிலம் முழுவதும் இன்று சிறப்ப முகாம்	நோய்	Increasing seasonal diseases: Government conducts special camps across the state today
4	Sports	பிரமாண்டமாக அமையவுள்ள ஜல்லிக்கட்டு மைதானம் - அமைச்சர் மெய்யநாதன்	ஜல்லிக்கட்டு மைதானம்	Magnificient field to be built for Jallikattu - Minister Meiyyanaathan
5	Weather	தமிழகத்தில் 5 நாட்களுக்கு மழை வாய்ப்பு - மீனவர்களுக்கு எச்சரிக்கை!	மழை	Chances of rain for 5 days in Tamil Nadu - Fisherman warned
6	Religion	உலக சுற்றுலா தினத்தையொட்டி தஞ்சை பெரிய கோவிலில் கலாச்சார திருவிழா	கோவிலில், திருவிழா	Cultural fest in Thanjavur temple in regards to International Tourist Day.
7	Other	பதப்படுத்தப்பட்ட உணவுகளை விரும்பி உண்பவரா? இந்த பக்கவிளைவுகள் கட்டாயம் உண்டு!	*none*	Do you enjoy processed foods? These side-effects are for sure.

Entertainment, and Medical. In tweet 3, the Deputy Chief Minister wishes a movie actor, and thus the tweet is categorized as *Politics and Entertainment.* Similarly, the last tweet talks about a bomb blast involving a political leader who they were later hospitalized. This event categorizes the tweet to *Politics and Medical.*

Table 7 presents the number of tweets in each topic. The category *Politics* includes the most tweets, totaling 58,446 tweets. The category *Religion* includes 20,883 tweets and receives the next position. Following that, the category *Entertainment* has 19,346 tweets, followed by the categories *Medical* and *Sports* with 17,177 tweets and 5,102 tweets, respectively. The category *Weather* has

Table 6. Tamil news tweets with at least two topics

	Tamil Tweet	English translated tweet	N.	Topics
1	ஜல்லிக்கட்டிற்கு அனுமதி: ஜல்லிக்கட்டு நடத்த தமிழக அரசு அனுமதி அளித்துள்ளது, மாடுபிடி வீரர்களுக்கு கொரோனா நெகடிவ் சான்றிதழ் அவசியம்	Jallikaatu Permitted:Tamil Nadu government has granted permission for Jallikattu. Bull fighters should produce Corona negative certificate	3	*Politics, Medical, Sports*
2	மதுராந்தகம் அருகே நடிகையும் பாஜக பிரமுகருமான குஷ்பு சென்ற கார் கண்டெய்னர் லாரி மீது மோதி விபத்து, இதில் குஷ்புவிற்கு லேசான காயம் ஏற்பட்டுள்ளதாக தகவல்	Actress and BJP personnel Kushboo met with an accident in Madhuraanthakam. She is mildly wounded.	3	*Politics, Entertainment, Medical*
3	நடிகர் அஜித்திற்கு துணை முதல்வர் ஓபன்னீர்செல்வம் வாழ்த்து	Deputy Chief Minister wishes actor Ajith	2	*Politics, Entertainment*
4	மேற்கு வங்க தொழிலாளர் நலத்துறை அமைச்சர் மீது வெடிகுண்டு வீச்சு மருத்துவமனையில் அனுமதி	Bomb blast on West Bengal labourer welfare minister admitted in hospital after	2	*Politics, Medical*

Table 7. Counts per topic category in the Tamil news tweets corpus

Topic	Frequency
Politics	58,446
Entertainment	19,346
Medical	17,177
Sports	5,102
Weather	5,053
Religion	20,883
Other	96,148

the least number of tweets (5,053). There are 96,148 tweets belonging to the *Other* category. Note that the tweets belonging to the *Other* might belong to one of the other categories. We leave assigning tweets from the *Other* category to one of the predefined categories for future work.

Figure 4 presents the wordcloud of the most frequent words in each topic. It is interesting to note that the word cloud includes words that are not part of the chosen keywords. For instance, தமிழக is not a keyword for the *Politics* category, and இந்திய is not a keyword for the *Sports* category.

Fig. 2. Wordcloud generated from each topic category. The top three word clouds belong to the categories *Political, Entertainment, Medical* (from left to right), and the bottom three-word clouds belong to the categories *Sports, Weather, Religion* (left to right)

5 Experiments and Results

We formulate the topic identification problem as a binary classification problem classifying if a tweet belongs to a specific category. Since the dataset is highly imbalanced and our goal is to present multiple baseline models for the task, we follow a simple approach and build models for each label separately. We describe the experimental setup and then discuss the results of each algorithm described in the experimental setup.

5.1 Experiments

We build multiple classifiers that take as input the TF-IDF features of each tweet using traditional machine learning algorithms. To generate the TF-IDF features we build the IDF vectors using all data in the train dataset, and generate TF-IDF vectors for each word. We use these TF-IDF features and work with popular traditional machine learning algorithms, including K-Nearest Neighbors, Naive Bayes, tree-based classifiers, and logistic regression.

  We do an 80:20 split on our data and stratify the splits based on the labels used in the classification. That is, for classifying if a tweet belongs to the *Politics* category, we generated a stratified train-test split based on the labels. We use

178   B. Justin and D. Chinnappa

Table 8. Results from the binary classifier for topic classification for the topics *Politics, Entertainment* and *Medical*

		Politics			Entertainment			Medical		
		P	R	F1	P	R	F1	P	R	F1
KNN	Yes	0.73	0.70	0.72	0.94	0.27	0.42	0.90	0.37	0.52
	No	0.88	0.89	0.89	0.93	1.00	0.96	0.94	1.00	0.97
Naive Bayes	Yes	0.92	0.28	0.43	0.98	0.03	0.06	0.88	0.02	0.04
	No	0.77	0.99	0.87	0.91	1.00	0.95	0.92	1.00	0.96
Log. reg.	Yes	0.80	0.85	**0.82**	0.83	0.60	**0.69**	0.73	0.59	**0.65**
	No	0.94	0.91	0.92	0.96	0.99	0.97	0.96	0.98	0.97
Decision tree	Yes	0.77	0.81	0.79	0.63	0.66	0.64	0.58	0.62	0.60
	No	0.92	0.90	0.91	0.96	0.96	0.96	0.96	0.96	0.96
Random forest	Yes	0.90	0.75	**0.82**	0.97	0.52	0.68	0.91	0.42	0.58
	No	0.91	0.96	0.93	0.95	1.00	0.97	0.95	1.00	0.97
Ada boost	Yes	0.83	0.71	0.76	0.87	0.53	0.66	0.74	0.38	0.50
	No	0.89	0.94	0.91	0.95	0.99	0.97	0.94	0.99	0.97
XGboost	Yes	0.88	0.70	0.78	0.96	0.51	0.66	0.86	0.31	0.46
	No	0.89	0.96	0.92	0.95	1.00	0.97	0.94	1.00	0.97

the 80% for training and test on the remaining 20%. The TF-IDF features for the test data are also generated using the IDF features of the train data.

K-Nearest Neighbor

For KNN, we set the number of nearest neighbors to 50. We use *uniform* weights and set the leaf size to 30.

Naive Bayes

We use the multinomial naive Bayes classifier setting the smoothing parameter alpha to 1. We learn based on the class's prior probabilities to predict if the tweet belongs to a specific category.

Logistic Regression

For logistic regression, we use the *l2* regularization parameter and use the *lbgs* solver.

Decision Tree

For the decision tree, we use the Gini impurity loss function and the maximum depth of the tree to be 8. We do not set any class weights and pick the *best* splitter used in the sklearn implementation.

Random Forest

For the random forest classifier, we set the number of estimators to 100 and set the maximum depth to 8. Similar to the decision tree algorithm, we use the *best* splitter.

Ada Boost

For the ada boost algorithm, we set the number of estimators to 50 and the learning rate to 1.

XGBoost

For the XGboost algorithm, we follow the parameters similar to other tree-based classifiers setting the depth to 8.

Table 9. Results from the binary classifier for topic classification for the topics *Sports*, *Weather* and *Religion*

		Sports			Weather			Religion		
		P	R	F1	P	R	F1	P	R	F1
KNN	Yes	0.91	0.17	0.29	0.94	0.45	0.61	0.95	0.22	0.36
	No	0.98	1.00	0.99	0.99	1.00	0.99	0.92	1.00	0.96
Naive Bayes	Yes	0.00	0.00	0.00	1.00	0.05	0.09	0.94	0.00	0.01
	No	0.97	1.00	0.99	0.98	1.00	0.99	0.90	1.00	0.95
Log. reg.	Yes	0.75	0.55	**0.64**	0.94	0.63	**0.76**	0.96	0.79	**0.86**
	No	0.99	1.00	0.99	0.99	1.00	0.99	0.98	1.00	0.99
Decision tree	Yes	0.60	0.56	0.58	0.77	0.71	0.74	0.84	0.85	0.84
	No	0.99	0.99	0.99	0.99	0.99	0.99	0.98	0.98	0.98
Random forest	Yes	0.90	0.41	0.56	0.98	0.59	0.73	0.99	0.77	**0.86**
	No	0.98	1.00	0.99	0.99	1.00	0.99	0.97	1.00	0.99
Ada boost	Yes	0.72	0.50	0.59	0.94	0.63	0.75	0.97	0.77	**0.86**
	No	0.99	0.99	0.99	0.99	1.00	0.99	0.97	0.77	0.86
XGboost	Yes	0.79	0.55	**0.65**	0.99	0.61	0.75	0.99	0.76	**0.86**
	No	0.99	1.00	0.99	0.99	1.00	0.99	0.97	1.00	0.99

5.2   Results

We present the results for the topics *Politics*, *Entertainment*, and *Medical* in Table 8 and the results for the topics *Sports*, *Weather* and *Religion* in Table 9.

Regarding the label *Politics*, the highest performance is achieved using the logistic regression classifier and the random forest classifier, receiving an F1 score of 0.82. The highest precision is achieved using the Naive Bayes algorithm (0.92), and the highest recall is achieved using the logistic regression classifier (0.85).

In the case of the label *entertainment*, the highest performance is achieved using the random forest classifier with 0.68 F1. While Naive Bayes achieves the highest precision (0.98), the recall is very poor (0.03). The highest recall, however, is obtained using the decision tree classifier (0.66).

For the label *Medical*, the best F1 is achieved using the logistic regression classifier (0.66). Random forest achieves the highest precision (0.91), and decision tree achieves the highest recall (0.62)

Considering the label *Sports*, the highest performance is achieved by the XGboost classifier with an F1 of 0.65. The KNN algorithm achieves the highest precision (0.91), and the decision tree algorithm achieves the highest recall (0.56).

In the case of the *Weather* label, the highest F1 is achieved using the logistic regression classifier (0.76). Naive Bayes is able to get full precision, but the recall is very poor (0.05). The best recall is achieved using the decision tree classifier (0.71).

Finally, for the label *Religion*, the best F1 (0.86) is achieved using logistic regression and most tree-based classifiers, including random forest, ada boost, and XGboost. Random forest receives the highest precision of 0.99, and the highest recall is achieved using the decision tree (0.85).

Table 10. Example tweets where the assigned topic is wrong.

N.	Tweet	Wrong label	Keyword
1	த்ரிஷா, ஐஸ்வர்யா ராயுடன் இசைப்புயல் ஏ.ஆர் ரகுமான்	Weather	புயல்
2	மோதலில் முடிந்த வாக்குவாதம்... ஊடகத்தினரை தாக்கிய நடிகை தமன்னாவின் பாதுகாவலர்கள்?	Politics	வாக்கு
3	சங்கரன்கோவில் அருகே தீண்டாமை - போலீசார் விசாரணை	Religion	கோவில்
4	களைகட்டிய பீர் திருவிழா... திகட்ட திகட்ட பீர் குடித்து...உற்சாக வெள்ளத்தில் மிதந்த மக்கள்	Religion, Weather	திருவிழா, வெள்ள
5	வெம்பக்கோட்டை அகழ்வாராய்ச்சி : சங்கு வளையல்கள், செப்பு காசு, சுடுமண் முத்திரை கண்டெடுப்பு	Entertainment	திரை

6   Limitations and Future Work

In this section, we discuss the limitations of our approach. First, we point out the issues in our dataset. Table 10 presents examples of a few mistakes in our dataset.

In example 1, musician A.R.Rahman's title புயல், literally translated to the musical storm, categorizes the tweet to *Weather*. However, the tweet is incorrect and unrelated to the *Weather* category. In example 2, the word வாக்கு triggers the category *Politics*. While வாக்கு means *vote* in English வாக்குவாதம் means *argument*. The label of this tweet hence is incorrect. In the third tweet, the word கோவில் miscategorizes the tweet to the topic *Religion*. கோவில் refers to places of worship like a temple or a church. However, in this context, கோவில் is part of the place சங்கரன்கோவில் and does not mean a place of worship. Tweet 4 talks about a beer feast. The word திருவிழா meaning feast (usually used in the context of religion) incorrectly categorizes the tweet as *Religion*. Similarly, the word வெள்ளம் refers to flood, incorrectly categorizing the tweet as *Weather*. In this context, the term வெள்ள is metaphorically used as people were immersed in a flood of excitement. Finally, in the last example, the keyword திரை incorrectly classifies the tweet as *Entertainment*. திரை means screen and is the lemma for the words திரைப்படம், திரையரங்கு, வெள்ளித்திரை (movie, theatre, silver screen) that belong to the category *Entertainment*. However, in this case, முத்திரை refers to the emblem, and hence the chosen category is incorrect. We attribute these inconsistencies in our dataset to the richness of the Tamil language. Linguistic aspects like Word Sense Disambiguation, polysemy, and metaphors contribute to these inconsistencies.

To achieve a clean gold topic labeled social media dataset, we could use the current dataset as silver data and annotate it on top of it. For instance, if a tweet has at least two keywords belonging to a specific category, we can be confident the tweet belongs to a particular category. If a tweet has keywords from different topics, we should introspect to understand the category of the tweet. Thus a human-in-the-loop approach could help generate high-quality datasets.

Next, we work only with traditional machine learning approaches and do not use neural networks or transformer-based models. While we tried to fine-tune transformer-based models for topic classification, it took longer than expected to train due to the large size of our dataset. We will experiment with neural networks in our future work.

7   Conclusion

In this paper, we present the largest ever Tamil social media News corpus to the best of our knowledge. We follow a distant supervision technic using keywords to generate labels for each tweet in the data. Each tweet is categorized into *Politics, Entertainment, Medical, Sports, Weather, Religion* or *Other*. We present a detailed corpus analysis of the dataset and present statistics of various attributes associated with the dataset. Then we formulate a binary classification problem to identify if a tweet belongs to a certain category or not. We experiment on multiple traditional machine learning classifiers and compare their results. Finally, we identify the limitations of our approach and present ideas for future work.

References

1. Anusha, M., Kumar S, S., Kp, S.: Deep Learning-Based Topic Categorization of Tamil Social Media Text Content, pp. 829–844 (06 2022). https://doi.org/10.1007/978-981-19-0840-8_64
2. Chakravarthi, B.R., et al.: Overview of the shared task on homophobia and transphobia detection in social media comments. In: Proceedings of the Second Workshop on Language Technology for Equality, Diversity and Inclusion, pp. 369–377. Association for Computational Linguistics, Dublin, Ireland (May 2022). https://doi.org/10.18653/v1/2022.ltedi-1.57. https://aclanthology.org/2022.ltedi-1.57
3. Ramraj, S., Arthi, R., Murugan, S., Julie, M.: Topic categorization of tamil news articles using pretrained word2vec embeddings with convolutional neural network. In: 2020 International Conference on Computational Intelligence for Smart Power System and Sustainable Energy (CISPSSE), pp. 1–4 (2020). https://doi.org/10.1109/CISPSSE49931.2020.9212248
4. Reshma, U., Hb, B.G., Kumar, M., Kp, S.: Supervised methods for domain classification of tamil documents. ARPN J. Eng. Appl. Sci. **10**, 3702–3707 (01 2015)

5. Selvi, C., N, I., L, L.S., S, N.: Topic categorization of tamil news articles. In: 2022 International Conference on Computer Communication and Informatics (ICCCI), pp. 1–6 (2022). https://doi.org/10.1109/ICCCI54379.2022.9741061
6. Subramanian, M., et al.: Offensive language detection in tamil youtube comments by adapters and cross-domain knowledge transfer. Comput. Speech Lang. **76**, 101404 (2022). https://doi.org/10.1016/j.csl.2022.101404. https://www.sciencedirect.com/science/article/pii/S0885230822000407

Textual Entailment Recognition with Semantic Features from Empirical Text Representation

Md Shajalal[1,6(✉)], Md. Atabuzzaman[2,3], Maksuda Bilkis Baby[3], Md. Rezaul Karim[1,5], and Alexander Boden[1,4]

[1] Fraunhofer Institute for Applied Information Technology FIT, Sankt Augustin, Germany
md.shajalal@fit.fraunhofer.de
[2] Bangladesh University of Engineering and Technology, Dhaka, Bangladesh
[3] Hajee Mohammad Danesh Science and Technology University, Dinajpur, Bangladesh
[4] Bonn-Rhein-Sieg University of Applied Science, Sankt Augustin, Germany
[5] RWTH Aachen University, Aachen, Germany
[6] University of Siegen, Siegen, Germany

Abstract. Textual entailment recognition is one of the basic natural language understanding (NLU) tasks. Understanding the meaning of sentences is a prerequisite before applying any natural language processing (NLP) techniques to automatically recognize the textual entailment. A text entails a hypothesis if and only if the true meaning and intent of the hypothesis follows the text. Classical approaches generally utilize the feature value of each word from word embedding to represent the sentences. In this paper, we propose a new framework to identify the textual entailment relationship between text and hypothesis, thereby introducing a new semantic feature focusing on empirical threshold-based semantic text representation. We employ an element-wise Manhattan distance vector-based feature that can identify the semantic entailment relationship between the text-hypothesis pair. We carried out several experiments on a benchmark entailment classification (SICK-RTE) dataset. We train several machine learning (ML) algorithms applying both semantic and lexical features to classify the text-hypothesis pair as entailment, neutral, or contradiction. Our empirical sentence representation technique enriches the semantic information of the texts and hypotheses found to be more efficient than the classical ones. In the end, our approach significantly outperforms known methods in understanding the meaning of the sentences for the textual entailment classification task.

Keywords: Textual entailment · Semantic representation · Word embedding · Machine learning · NLP

© The Author(s), under exclusive license to Springer Nature Switzerland AG 2023
Anand Kumar M et al. (Eds.): SPELLL 2022, CCIS 1802, pp. 183–195, 2023.
https://doi.org/10.1007/978-3-031-33231-9_12

1   Introduction

Recognizing Textual Entailment (RTE) is one of the basics of natural language understanding (NLU) and NLU is a subclass of natural language processing (NLP) tasks. Textual entailment is the relationship between two texts where one text fragment, referred to as *'Hypothesis (H)'* can be inferred from another text fragment, referred to as *'Text (T)'* [1,2]. In other words, Text T entails Hypothesis H, if hypothesis H is considered to be true according to the corresponding text T's context [1]. Let's consider a text-hypothesis pair to illustrate an example of an entailment relationship. Suppose *"A mother is feeding milk to a baby"* is a particular text T and *"A baby is drinking milk"* is a hypothesis H. We see that the hypothesis H is a true statement that can easily be inferred from the corresponding text T. Let's consider another hypothesis H, *"A man is eating rice"*. For the same text fragment T, we can see that there is no entailment relationship between T and H, referred neutral. The identification of entailment relationship has a significant impact in different NLP applications that include question answering, text summarization, machine translation, information extraction, information retrieval etc. [2,3].

Since the first PASCAL challenge [1] for recognizing textual entailment to date [4,5], different machine learning approaches have been proposed by the research community. The proposed approaches tried to employ supervised machine learning (ML) techniques using different underlying lexical, syntactic, and semantic features of the text-hypothesis pair. Recently, deep learning-based approaches including LSTM (Long Short Term Memory) based encoder-decoder [4], CNN (Convolutional Neural Network), BERT [6], Attention based encoder-decoder [5] and Transfer Learning [7] are being applied to detect the entailment relationship between the text-hypothesis pair. Almost all methods utilized the semantic information of the text-hypothesis pair by representing them as semantic vectors.

For doing so, classical approaches employ a high-dimensional vector for representing each word returned from the pre-trained word-embedding model. For sentence representation, the classical approach also applies the average over the vectors for each word. Atabuzzaman et al. [8] employed a sentence representation technique with the help of a threshold that selects/discards specific features of a word's vector before the arithmetic average. The findings indicated improvements in identifying textual similarity. Inspired by their threshold-based technique in representing text employing word embedding, we also hypothesize that some values of a particular word's vector might impact negatively on overall sentence representation. Because they will be passed through an arithmetic average function. Moreover, the arithmetic average suffers from a sampling fluctuation problem, i.e., affected by extremely large/small values. Considering this intuition, we observed that the elements of the words' vectors relevant to already present ones in the semantic vectors of the text-hypothesis pair, can be eliminated to get a better semantic representation. Following this observation, we apply a threshold-based empirical text representation technique considering the mean and standard deviation of the words' vectors.

Applying the threshold-based semantic sentence representation, the text and hypothesis are represented by two real-valued high-dimensional vectors. Then we introduce an element-wise Manhattan distance vector (EMDV) between vectors for text and hypothesis to have semantic representation for the text-hypothesis pair. This EMDV vector is directly employed as a feature vector to ML algorithms to identify the entailment relationship of the text-hypothesis pair. In addition, we introduce another feature by calculating the absolute average of the element-wise Manhattan distance vector of the text-hypothesis pair. In turn, we extract several handcrafted lexical and semantic features including Bag-of-Words (BoW) based similarity score, the Jaccard similarity score (JAC), and semantic similarity based on BERT for the corresponding text-hypothesis pair. To classify the text-hypothesis pair, we also apply multiple machine learning classifiers that use different textual features including our introduced ones. Then the ensemble of the ML algorithms with the majority voting technique is employed that provides the final entailment relationship for the corresponding text-hypothesis pair. To validate the performance of our method, a wide range of experiments are carried out on a benchmark SICK-RTE dataset. The experimental results on the benchmark textual entailment classification dataset achieved efficient performance to recognize different textual entailment relations. The results also demonstrated that our approach outperforms some state-of-the-art methods.

The rest of the paper is organized as follows: Section 2 presents some related works on RTE. Then our method is discussed in Sect. 3. The details of the experiments with their results are presented in Sect. 4. Finally, Sect. 5 presents the conclusion with the future direction.

2   Related Work

With the first PASCAL challenge, textual entailment recognition has gained considerable attention of the research community [1]. Several research groups participated in this challenge. But most of the methods applied lexical features (i.e., word-overlapping) with ML algorithms to recognize entailment relation [1]. Several RTE challenges have been organized and some methods with promising performance on different downstream tasks are proposed [9–15]. Malakasiotis et al. [16] proposed a method employing the string matching-based lexical and shallow syntactic features with support vector machine (SVM). Four distance-based features with SVM are also employed [17]. The features include edit distance, distance in WordNet, and longest common substring between texts.

Similarly, Pakray et al. [18] applied multiple lexical features including Word-Net based unigram match, bigram match, longest common sub-sequence, skip-gram, stemming, and named entity matching. Finally, they applied SVM classifiers with introducing lexical and syntactic similarity. Basak et al. [19] visualized the text and hypothesis leveraging directed networks (dependency graphs), with nodes denoting words or phrases and edges denoting connections between nodes. The entailment relationship is then identified by matching the graphs' with vertex and edge substitution. Recently, Renjit et al. [20] determined entailment relationship of a low resourced language using different semantic and syntactic features such as bigram, tfidf and different types of similarity score with ML algorithms. Similarly, Liu et al. [21] combined different features with ML approaches for Chinese language. Some other methods made use of bag-of-words, word-overlapping, logic-based reasoning, lexical entailment, ML-based methods, and graph matching to recognize textual entailment [22].

Bowman et al. [23] introduced a Stanford Natural Language Inference corpus (SNLI) dataset consists of labeled sentence pairs that can be used as a benchmark in NLP tasks. This is a very large entailment (inference) dataset that provides the opportunity for researchers to apply deep learning-based approaches to identify the entailment relation between text and hypothesis. Therefore, different deep learning-based approaches including BERT [6], and Transfer Learning [7] are being applied to RTE. All the methods either used lexical or semantic features. But our proposed method uses both the lexical and semantic features including element-wise Manhattan distance vector (EMDV), an average of EMDV, BoW, Jaccard similarity, and semantic textual similarity to recognize entailment.

3   Proposed Approach

This section presents our framework to recognize textual entailment (RTE) using the semantic information of the Text-Hypothesis (T-H) pair. The high-level overview of our method is presented in Fig. 1. After applying different preprocessing techniques to have a better textual representation that is supposed to eventually boost the performance. In this phase, punctuation marks are removed, and the stopwords are also eliminated (except for negative words such as no, not, etc.). Here, a stopword is a word that has very little influence on the meaning of the sentence (i.g. a, an, the, and, or, etc.). After that, a tokenizer is utilized to split the sentence into a list of words. Then, we apply a lemmatizer to get the base form of the words.

3.1   Empirical Text Representation

The semantic information of a word is represented as a vector. The elements of the vector are real numbers that represent the contextual meaning of that word. By using the word-embedding, the semantic vectors of the words can be obtained. Almost all classical approaches apply arithmetic average using the words' semantic vectors to get the semantic information of the sentences. But all the values of the words' semantic vector might not be important to express the meaning of the text-hypothesis pair in the form of vectors. We hypothesize that some values of a particular vector of a word might impact negatively since they will be passed through an arithmetic average function.

Let T and H be the input text and hypothesis, respectively. We first apply empirical sentence representation using Algorithm 1 to represent the sentence that provides better semantic information [8]. From the first two statements, the function named $preprocess(T)$ returns the lists of preprocessed words T_p and H_p for corresponding text T and hypothesis H, respectively. After that, a

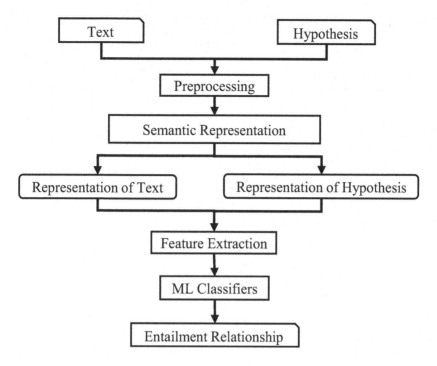

Fig. 1. Overview diagram for recognising textual entailment

vector of size K with the initial value of zeros is taken (statement 3). Then a function ($get\_Semantic\_Info()$) returns the semantic representation applying our threshold-based empirical representation (statement 4–21).

In the function, the words which are available in the word2vec model's vocabulary are considered for further actions. In the representation, the first word of the text is added with vec_S as it is, without considering any condition or automated threshold. We found with empirical experiments that some elements from the word's vector might provide a negative bias in the arithmetic average. By ignoring those, the sentence can be represented as a semantic vector omitting sampling fluctuation. Therefore, we attempt to study the sentence intent information by employing an automated threshold (α) on the semantic elements of the words. We hypothesize that, if a certain element in index i has not a significant absolute difference with the average of feature value in the same index i in the sentence S, the representation might lose some contextual information, adding irrelevant semantics. To filter those irrelevant elements, we apply the empirical threshold α using mean and standard deviation as $\alpha = \bar{x} + \sigma$. The elements of the word are added after employing the threshold to get the semantic information of the sentence.

Algorithm 1. Semantic information of T-H pair based on an automated threshold of words semantic representation [8]

Require: Text (T) and Hypothesis (H) pair and Word-embedding models (word2vec)
Ensure: Semantic information of Text (T) and Hypothesis (H)
1: $T_p \Leftarrow preprocess(T)$ ▷ List of words of Text
2: $H_p \Leftarrow preprocess(H)$ ▷ List of words of Hypothesis
3: $vec\_S \Leftarrow [0, 0, ..., 0]$
4: **function** $get\_Semantic\_Info(Sent)$
5:     **for** each $word \in Sent$ **do**
6:         **if** $word \in word2vec.vocab$ **then**
7:             $x \Leftarrow word2vec[word]$ ▷ Vector representation of the word
8:             $\bar{x} \Leftarrow Mean(x)$
9:             $\sigma \Leftarrow Standard\_Deviation(x)$
10:            $\alpha \Leftarrow \bar{x} + \sigma$
11:            $k \Leftarrow 0$
12:            **while** $k < length(x)$ **do**
13:                **if** $abs(vec\_S[k] - x[k]) \geq \alpha$ **then**
14:                    $vec\_S[k] \Leftarrow add(vec\_S[k], x[k])$
15:                **end if**
16:                $k + +$
17:            **end while**
18:        **end if**
19:    **end for**
20:    $return\ vec\_S$
21: **end function**
22: $v\_T \Leftarrow get\_Semantic\_Info(T_p)$ ▷ Semantic information of Text
23: $v\_H \Leftarrow get\_Semantic\_Info(H_p)$ ▷ Semantic information of Hypothesis

---

3.2   Feature Extraction of Text-Hypothesis Pair

Besides the empirical semantic text representation technique, we also extract different features to capture the relationship between text and hypothesis. The reminder of this section presents detail about extracted features.

Element-Wise Manhattan Distance Vector (EMDV). The empirical threshold based text representation returns the semantic real-valued vectors v_T and v_H for text and hypothesis, respectively. Our primary intuition to recognize the entailment relationship is that, the smaller the difference between text and hypothesis the larger the chance of entailment between them. Therefore we apply the Manhattan distance function to compute the element-wise Manhattan distance vector $EMDV = v_T - v_H$ where each element is the difference between the corresponding elements of the vectors for T and H, respectively.

Average of EMDV. The EMDV provides a real-valued Manhattan distance vector for the text-hypothesis pair. Applying the average over the summation of the absolute difference between text v_T and hypothesis v_H representations, we can calculate the average of EMDV which is a scaler value corresponding to the text-hypothesis pair. This can be calculated as following:

$$Sum_{EMDV} = \frac{1}{k} \sum_{i}^{k} abs(v_{T_i} - v_{H_i}), \tag{1}$$

where k is the dimension of the vector. v_{T_i} and v_{H_i} are the i-th elements of the text and hypothesis, respectively.

Jaccard Similarity Score (JAC). Jaccard similarity assesses the similarity of the text-hypothesis pair (T-H) to determine which words are common and which are unique. It is calculated by no. of common words present in the pair divided by no. of total words present in the sentence pair. This can be represented in set notation as the ratio of intersection $(T \cap H)$ and union $(T \cup H)$ of two sentences.

$$JAC(T, H) = \frac{T \cap H}{T \cup H} \tag{2}$$

where $(T \cap H)$ indicates the number of words shared between both sentences and $(T \cup H)$ provides the total number of words in both sentences (shared and un-shared). The Jaccard similarity will be 0 if the two sentences don't share any values and 1 if the two sentences are identical.

Bag-of-Words Based Similarity (BoW). BoW is the vector representation where the dimension of the vector is the number of unique words exist in the text and the value of the vector is the frequency of the words. Suppose, Bag-of-Words based vectors for text and hypothesis are obtained as $[1, 0, 2, 0, 4, 0, 0, 0, 1, 1]$ and $[0, 2, 0, 1, 4, 3, 0, 1, 2, 1]$ for T and H, respectively. Then cosine similarity [8] is applied on these vectors to compute the similarity score.

BERT-Based Semantic Similarity Score (STS). Inspired by one of the prior works [24] on semantic textual similarity, we applied several semantic similarity methods. To compute the semantic textual similarity score (STS), pre-trained BERT word embedding is employed. Using the BERT word embedding, the T and H are represented as semantic vectors adding the words' vectors one by one. Then the cosine similarity between the vectors for text and hypothesis is considered as the STS score.

4   Experiments Results

This section presents the details about the dataset, evaluation metrics, experimental setup, and performance analysis compared with known related works.

4.1 Dataset

We applied our method to a benchmark entailment recognition dataset named SICK-RTE [25]. This is an English dataset consisting of almost 10K English Text-Hypothesis (T-H) pairs exhibiting a variety of lexical, syntactic, and semantic phenomena. Each text-hypothesis pair is annotated as either **Neutral**, **Entailment** or **Contradiction** which are used as ground truth. Among 10k text-hypothesis pairs 5595 are annotated as Neutral, 2821 as Entailment, and 1424 as Contradiction. Table 1 presents some text-hypothesis pairs with corresponding entailment relations.

Table 1. Examples of Text-Hypothesis pair from SICK-RTE dataset

Text (T)	Hypothesis (H)	Relationship
Two dogs are fighting	Two dogs are wrestling and hugging.	Neutral
A person in a black jacket is doing tricks on a motorbike	A man in a black jacket is doing tricks on a motorbike.	Entailment
Two dogs are wrestling and hugging	There is no dog wrestling and hugging.	Contradiction
A woman selling bamboo sticks talking to two men on a loading dock	There are at least three people on a loading dock.	Entailment
A woman selling bamboo sticks talking to two men on a loading dock	A woman is selling bamboo sticks to help provide for her family.	Neutral
A woman selling bamboo sticks talking to two men on a loading dock	A woman is not taking money for any of her sticks	Contradiction

We make use of the pre-trained BERT word-embedding model and pre-trained word-embedding model (word2vec) trained on the Google news corpus. The dimension of each word vector is $k = 300$ and $k = 768$ for word2vec and BERT, respectively. We evaluate the performance of our methods in terms of classification accuracy.

4.2 Experimental Settings

To evaluate the performance of our approach, several experiments have been carried out on the SICK-RTE dataset. To explore the effectiveness of empirical threshold-based semantic text representation, we designed experiments employing Algorithm 1 and element-wise Manhattan distance vector. The text and hypothesis are first represented by empirical text representation Algorithm 1. Then we apply the element-wise Manhattan distance between semantic representations of text and hypothesis. This setting referred to EMDV with empirical text representation, $EMDV\_ETR$. The second setting denoted by

$EMDV\_without\_ETR$, is similar to the previous setting but here we have not applied the empirical threshold-based representation technique. Rather we used classical text representation with averaging vector.

To demonstrate the performance of our handcrafted features along with threshold-based semantic representation technique, we carried out experiments applying features with Algorithm 1. Here we applied our four handcrafted features namely, *Average of EMDV, JAC, BoW*, and *STS* to classify the entailment relationship between text and hypothesis. The average of EMDV is calculated over the text and hypothesis representations by Algorithm 1. This setting is referred to as *handcrafted features with empirical text representation* HF_ETR. To demonstrate the impact of Algorithm 1, we applied a similar experiment with the handcrafted features where *Average of EMDV* is calculated from the classical representation of the text and hypothesis, not applying Algorithm 1. This setting is denoted as $HF\_without\_ETR$.

For all settings, we employed several classification algorithms including support vector machine with RBF kernel, K-nearest neighbors, random forest, and naive Bayes. Finally, the ensemble result considering the majority voting of the ML algorithms is also considered. To do the experiments 75% data are used in training and the rest are used as testing data.

Table 2. Performance of ML models based on EMDV

Algorithm	Features	Accuracy
SVM_rbf	$EMDV\_ETR$	0.66
	$EMDV\_without\_ETR$	0.58
KNN	$EMDV\_ETR$	**0.67**
	$EMDV\_without\_ETR$	**0.57**
R.Forest	$EMDV\_ETR$	0.62
	$EMDV\_without\_ETR$	0.58
Naive Bayes	$EMDV\_ETR$	0.66
	$EMDV\_without\_ETR$	0.58
Ensemble	$EMDV\_ETR$	0.66
	$EMDV\_without\_ETR$	0.58

4.3   Performance Analysis of Entailment Recognition

Table 2 demonstrates the performance of different ML algorithms to recognize entailment relation with element-wise Manhattan distance vector-based features ($EMDV\_ETR$). Here we also reported the performance of the EMDV feature vector without applying Algorithm 1, ($EMDV\_without\_ETR$). This table illustrates that the KNN classifier achieved better performance than other ML algorithms to detect entailment relationship using $EMDV$ representation. The table also demonstrates how the element-wise distance-based feature vector from threshold-based semantic representation helps the ML models to recognize different entailment labels.

Table 3. Confusion matrix for ensemble learning with EMDV and threshold

(a) With threshold

	Neutral	Entail	Contradict
Neutral	**1135**	193	17
Entail	328	**370**	37
Contradict	96	155	**129**

(b) Without threshold

	Neutral	Entail	Contradict
Neutral	**1407**	15	0
Entail	674	**13**	0
Contradict	344	7	0

For a better understanding of the impact of the our introduced features, we present Table 3 comprising the confusion matrixes of the ensemble methods considering the element-wise EMDV vector with and without the proposed sentence representation algorithm. Table 3a shows that the ensemble method can detect neutral, entailment, and contradiction T-H pair. But Table 3b reflects that without the proposed representation ML algorithms are not able to recognize the contradiction relationship between text and hypothesis and only can detect a few entailment relations. This also signifies the impact of our proposed feature with threshold-based sentence representation.

Table 4. Performance of ML models based on handcrafted features

Algorithm	Features	Accuracy
SVM_rbf	HF_ETR	0.80
	$HF\_without\_ETR$	0.78
KNN	HF_ETR	0.81
	$HF\_without\_ETR$	0.79
R.Forest	HF_ETR	0.81
	$HF\_without\_ETR$	0.78
Naive Bayes	HF_ETR	0.74
	$HF\_without\_ETR$	0.73
Ensemble	HF_ETR	**0.81**
	$HF\_without\_ETR$	**0.79**

Table 4 presents the performance of different ML algorithms to recognize entailment with semantic and lexical features including our proposed average of EMDV feature (Eq. (1)). The table reflects that when all the features are combined, all the classifiers are showing better performance with the average of EMDV feature (Eq. (1)) than without threshold-based text representation. This also consistently demonstrates that the proposed average of the EMDV feature can capture a better entailment relationship than other classical features. Table 5 presents the confusion matrixes of the ensemble models with different features' combinations. Both tables show that with all the features considering the proposed semantic representation, the ensemble method can classify different text-hypothesis pairs more accurately than classical semantic representation. This also concludes the performance consistency.

Table 5. Confusion matrix for ensemble learning with handcrafted features

(a) With threshold

	Neutral	Entail	Contradict
Neutral	**1225**	138	16
Entail	177	**523**	8
Contradict	108	23	**242**

(b) Without threshold

	Neutral	Entail	Contradict
Neutral	**1252**	149	25
Entail	191	**479**	14
Contradict	124	15	**211**

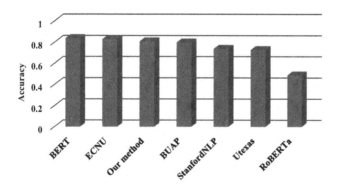

Fig. 2. Performance comparison of our proposed method in terms of Accuracy on the SICK-RTE dataset.

4.4 Comparative Analysis

Figure 2 shows the comparison of different known prior related works with our method on the SICK-RTE dataset. BUAP [26] employed a language model with different features including sentence's syntactic and negation features to classify text-hypothesis pairs as entailment, neutral, and contradiction. Utexas [26] used sentence composition and phrase composition features with negation and vector semantic model to recognize the entailment relationship. These two models employed different features and neural network models but still, our method outperformed them. Our proposed features with an empirical threshold-based sentence representation algorithm can capture better semantic entailment relationships. Different feature engineering method with deep learning is employed for

RTE task by ECNU [27]. BERT (Finetuned) [27] applied bidirectional encoder representation of sentences pair. Though our method does not outperform ECNU and BERT(Finetuned), the performance difference compared to them is subtle and hence performed effectively.

5   Conclusion with Future Direction

This paper presents a novel method to recognize textual entailment by introducing new features based on element-wise Manhattan distance vector employing empirical semantic sentence representation technique. To extract the semantic representation of the text-hypothesis pair, an empirical threshold-based algorithm is employed. The algorithm eliminates the unnecessary elements of the words' vectors and extracts the semantic information from the text-hypothesis pair. Then various ML algorithms are employed with the extracted semantic information along with several lexical and semantic features. The experimental results indicate the efficiency in identifying textual entailment relationships between text-hypothesis pairs. In summary, the performance of different experimental settings with multiple classifiers was consistent and outperformed some know-related works.

In the future, it would be interesting to apply deep learning-based method using the element-wise Manhattan distance vector to recognize text entailment.

References

1. Dagan, I., Glickman, O., Magnini, B.: The PASCAL recognising textual entailment challenge. In: Quiñonero-Candela, J., Dagan, I., Magnini, B., d'Alché-Buc, F. (eds.) MLCW 2005. LNCS (LNAI), vol. 3944, pp. 177–190. Springer, Heidelberg (2006). https://doi.org/10.1007/11736790_9
2. Sharma, N., Sharma, R., Biswas, K.K.: Recognizing textual entailment using dependency analysis and machine learning. In: Proceedings of the 2015 Conference of the North American Chapter of the Association for Computational Linguistics: Student Research Workshop, pp. 147–153 (2015)
3. Almarwani, N., Diab, M.: Arabic textual entailment with word embeddings. In: Proceedings of the Third Arabic Natural Language Processing Workshop, pp. 185–190 (2017)
4. Kiros, R., et al.: Skip-thought vectors. arXiv preprint arXiv:1506.06726 (2015)
5. Vaswani, A. et al.: Attention is all you need. arXiv preprint arXiv:1706.03762 (2017)
6. Devlin, J., Chang, M.-W., Lee, K., Toutanova, K:. Bert: Pre-training of deep bidirectional transformers for language understanding. arXiv preprint arXiv:1810.04805 (2018)
7. Conneau, A., Kiela, D., Schwenk, H., Barrault, L., Bordes, A.: Supervised learning of universal sentence representations from natural language inference data. arXiv preprint arXiv:1705.02364 (2017)
8. Atabuzzaman, M., Shajalal, M., Aono, M.: Semantic representation of sentences employing an automated threshold. In: 2021 Joint 10th International Conference on Informatics, Electronics & Vision (ICIEV) and 2021 5th International Conference on Imaging, Vision and Pattern Recognition (icIVPR), pp. 1–6. IEEE (2021)

9. Bar Haim, R., et al.: The second pascal recognising textual entailment challenge. In: Proceedings of the Second PASCAL Challenges Workshop on Recognising Textual Entailment, vol. 7 (2006)

10. Giampiccolo, D., Magnini, B., Dagan, I., B Dolan, W.: The third pascal recognizing textual entailment challenge. In: Proceedings of the ACL-PASCAL workshop on textual entailment and paraphrasing, pp. 1–9 (2007)

11. Giampiccolo, D., Dang, H.T., Magnini, B., Dagan, I., Cabrio, E., Dolan, B.: The fourth pascal recognizing textual entailment challenge. In TAC, Citeseer (2008)

12. Bentivogli, L., Clark, P., Dagan, I., Giampiccolo, D.: The fifth pascal recognizing textual entailment challenge. In: TAC (2009)

13. Bentivogli, L., Clark, P., Dagan, I., Giampiccolo, D.: The Seventh Pascal Recognizing Textual Entailment Challenge. In TAC, Citeseer (2011)

14. Dzikovska, M.O., et al.: Semeval-2013 task 7: The joint student response analysis and 8th recognizing textual entailment challenge. Technical report, NORTH TEXAS STATE UNIV DENTON (2013)

15. Paramasivam, A., Jaya Nirmala, S.: A survey on textual entailment based question answering. J. King Saud Univ.-Comput. Inform. Sci. **34**(10), 9644–9653 (2021)

16. Malakasiotis, P., Androutsopoulos, I.: Learning textual entailment using svms and string similarity measures. In: Proceedings of the ACL-PASCAL Workshop on Textual Entailment and Paraphrasing, pp. 42–47 (2007)

17. Julio Javier Castillo and Laura Alonso Alemany: An Approach Using Named Entities for Recognizing Textual Entailment. In TAC, Citeseer (2008)

18. Pakray, P., Bandyopadhyay, S., Gelbukh, A.F.: Lexical based two-way rte system at rte-5. In: TAC (2009)

19. Basak, R., Naskar, S.K., Pakray, P., Gelbukh, A.: Recognizing textual entailment by soft dependency tree matching. Computación y Sistemas, **19**(4), 685–700 (2015)

20. Renjit, S., Sumam, M.I.: Feature based entailment recognition for malayalam language texts. Int. J. Adv. Comput. Sci. Appl. **13**(2) (2022)

21. Liu, M., Zhang, L., Huijun, H., Nie, L., Dai, J.: A classification model for semantic entailment recognition with feature combination. Neurocomputing **208**, 127–135 (2016)

22. Ghuge, S., Bhattacharya, A.: Survey in textual entailment. Center for Indian Language Technology, retrieved on April (2014)

23. Bowman, S.R., Angeli, G., Potts, C., Manning, C.D.: A large annotated corpus for learning natural language inference. arXiv preprint arXiv:1508.05326 (2015)

24. Shajalal, Md., Aono, M.: Semantic textual similarity between sentences using bilingual word semantics. Prog. Artif. Intell. **8**(2), 263–272 (2019). https://doi.org/10.1007/s13748-019-00180-4

25. MMarelli, M., Menini, S., Baroni, M., Bentivogli, L., Bernardi, R., Zamparelli, R.: A sick cure for the evaluation of compositional distributional semantic models. In: Proceedings of the Ninth International Conference on Language Resources and Evaluation (LREC'14), pp. 216–223 (2014)

26. Bentivogli, L., Bernardi, R., Marelli, M., Menini, S., Baroni, M., Zamparelli, R.: Sick through the semeval glasses. lesson learned from the evaluation of compositional distributional semantic models on full sentences through semantic relatedness and textual entailment. Lang. Resources Eval. **50**(1), 95–124, 2016

27. Shin, T., Razeghi, Y., Logan IV, R.L., Wallace, E., Singh, S. Autoprompt: Eliciting knowledge from language models with automatically generated prompts. arXiv preprint arXiv:2010.15980 (2020)

Impact of Transformers on Multilingual Fake News Detection for Tamil and Malayalam

Ramakrishnalyer LekshmiAmmal Hariharan$^{(\boxtimes)}$ (iD)
and Madasamy Anand Kumar (iD)

Department of Information Technology, National Institute of Technology Karnataka,
Surathkal, India
{hariharanrl.197it003,m_anandkumar}@nitk.edu.in

Abstract. Due to the availability of the technology stack for implementing state of the art neural networks, fake news or fake information classification problems have attracted many researchers working on Natural Language Processing, machine learning, and deep learning. Currently, most works on fake news detection are available in English, which has confined its widespread usability outside the English-speaking population. As far as multilingual content is considered, the fake news classification in low-resource languages is challenging due to the unavailability of enough annotated corpus. In this work, we have studied and analyzed the impact of different transformer-based models like multilingual BERT, XLMRoBERTa, and MuRIL for the dataset created (translated) as a part of this research on multilingual low-resource fake news classification. We have done various experiments, including language-specific and different models, to see the impact of the models. We also offer the multilingual dataset in Tamil and Malayalam, which are from multiple domains that could be useful for research in this direction. We have made the datasets and code available in Github (https://github.com/hariharanrl/Multilingual_Fake_News).

Keywords: Fake News · XLM-RoBERTa · M-BERT · Low-Resource

1 Introduction

Nowadays, a wide range of information is available and flooded in social media. The main issue is that it will be hard for the public to distinguish between genuine and fake information. In the recent past, we can see that the amount of fake information generated on the internet is significantly growing and leading as the primary source of misinformation. Moreover, the important thing is that fake or unauthentic information will spread quickly. The echo chamber effect also impacts the users in social media, which only gives information that the users like in their chamber or reflects their views [4]. Social media users are subject to confirmation bias, the tendency to search for, interpret, favor, and recall information that confirms or supports one's prior beliefs [4].

Anand Kumar M et al. (Eds.): SPELLL 2022, CCIS 1802, pp. 196–208, 2023.
https://doi.org/10.1007/978-3-031-33231-9_13

The literature shows that the fake news or information spreads faster than the genuine ones [17]. The main reason behind this is the users tend to share or retweet the information which are typically unauthentic and the same happens with those who see this information first. As per the news[1] during the 2014 US presendential campaign, the fake news had more engagement than the top legitimate news stories.

We can see that there is significant research [3,9,12] and advancements in the area of tackling the problem of fake news in social media as well as the internet, and most of them are dedicated to curbing misinformation in general [20,21]. However, most of the times these systems are developed to address to a particular or specific language which are rich in resource like English. In the case of multilingual system we have [14] which presents a multilingual corpus and debunks which contains text, tag, images and videos for searching and leveraging the content. In [6,7] have worked on identifying fake news detection for a long document using an Ensemble method and a Window based method; both were on English data. A discourse patterns in multilingual corpora is studied in [16] using Rhetorical Structure Theory framework and have created a multilingual deceptive corpus.

FEVER (Fact Extraction and VERification) [15] is focused on Wikipedia data for fact verification and claims against textual sources. A multilingual fake news dataset which is focused on Covid-19 related news released by [11] collected from various fack-checked articles from 92 different fact-checking websites. There are few system which could handle multiple languages. But when it comes to low-resource languages like Tamil, Malayalam and most of the Indian languages we don't have significant amount of research being done, due to lack of data and resource restrictions to access the data. We have few datasets like [11] which we discussed above and [13] is multilingual data repository (13 languages) based of fake news incidents in India collected from social media and are fact-checked. When we see into the details, we have Tamil datasets available from many resources but Malayalam is less.

1.1 Motivation and Contribution

Misinformation or Fake information is one of the interesting research areas in the field of natural language processing. Due to wide reach of technologies like Artificial Intelligence, Machine Learning and Deep Learning and due to the availability of datasets, has attracted attention of researchers and developers. While coming to multilingual misinformation we have been less explored. As fake news is serious threat to the society, we have introduced a dataset in two low-resource languages (Tamil and Malayalam) and build a model for these. The contributions are listed as follows.

- We have used Google Translate [19] to translate news items from Fake-NewsAMT and Celebrity Fake which are used in [1] into two low resource

---

[1] https://www.buzzfeednews.com/article/craigsilverman/viral-fake-election-news-out performed-real-news-on-facebook.

languages (Tamil and Malayalam). Thus we create a novel dataset for multilingual fake news classification employing two additional low-resource languages.
- We propose to analyze the impact of the different transformer-based models on this multilingual fake news classification data.

2   Multilingual Fake News Dataset Description

Most of the fake news datasets available are monolingual in nature. The recent developed datasets are also released mainly in English alone. We also have some of the data available in Hindi but not much in Tamil and Malayalam especially for fake news detection. To address this issue connecting to multilingual annotated data we created fake news dataset consisting of data from various domain for two low resource languages namely Tamil and Malayalam.

We obtain the Fake News dataset from [1] which had the translated version of the dataset from [10], where authors crowdsourced 240 pieces of legitimate news from variety of news websites mainly from United States. The dataset is released in English containing news from mainly six domains (sports, entertainment, politics, technology, and education).

The dataset obtained from FakeNewsAMT and Celebrity Fake News in English was translated into Tamil and Malayalam using Google Machine Translation (Fig. 1) which gives a total of 1188 news items per language whose examples are statistics are shown in Table 1.

Table 1. Dataset Description

Language	Dataset	# of samples	Fake	Legit
English	Train	1188	579	609
	Test	772	401	371
Tamil	Train	1188	579	609
	Test	772	401	371
Malayalam	Train	1188	579	609
	Test	772	401	371

The dataset after being collected and translated are to be annotated for which we used the original annotated fake news dataset in English [10]. Some examples from dataset are given in Table 2.

3   Methodology

In this section we will be discussing about the methodologies adopted for our fake news detection model.

Bidirectional Encoder Representations from Transformers (BERT) [2] is the model we will use in this work. BERT is a transformer model which can attend to different positions of the input sequence to get a representation by different

Table 2. Examples of Original (English) and Translated (Tamil and Malayalam) Dataset

Label	Language	Topic and News
Fake	English	Topic: Elvis Costello Blasts Kanyne Over Album Re Release
		News: In an interview with BBC 6 Costello commented that the very idea of Kanyne attempting to redo Sir Paul McCartney's work was as disgusting as a dirty nappy and just as appealing. ... Perhaps Kanye should approach the Prince estate and offer to buy some of his unpublished works.
	Tamil	Topic (translated): ஆல்பம் மறு வெளியீட்டில் எல்விஸ் காஸ்டெல்லோ கேனை வெடிக்கிறார்
		News (translated): பிபிசி 6 க்கு அளித்த பேட்டியில் காஸ்டெல்லோ, சர் பால் மெக்கார்ட்னியின் வேலையை மீண்டும் செய்ய முயற்சிக்கும் கேனின் யோசனையே ஒரு அழுக்கு நாப்பியைப் போல அருவருப்பானது .... ஒருவரால் மட்டுமே அந்த சாதனையை செய்ய முடியும் அல்லது முயற்சிக்க வேண்டும். ஒருவேளை கன்யே பிரின்ஸ் தோட்டத்தை அணுகி, அவருடைய வெளியிடப்படாத சில படைப்புகளை வாங்க முன்வர வேண்டும்.
		Topic (transliterated): Ālpam maṟu veḷiyīṭṭil elvis kāsṭellō kēṉai veṭikkiṟār
		News (transliterated): Pipici 6 kku aḷitta pēṭṭiyil kāsṭellō, car pāl mekkārṭṉiyiṉ vēlaiyai mīṇṭum ceyya muyaṟcikkum kēṉiṉ yōcaṉaiyē oru aḻukku nāppiyaip pōla aruvuruppāṉatu.... Oruvarāl maṭṭumē anta cātaṉaiyai ceyya muṭiyum allatu muyaṟcikka vēṇṭum. Oruvēḷai kaṉyē pirins tōṭṭattai aṇuki, avaruṭaiya veḷiyiṭappaṭāta cila paṭaippukaḷai vānka muṉvara vēṇṭum.
	Malayalam	Topic (translated): ആൽബം റീ റിലീസിനെശേഷം എൽവിസ് കോസ്റ്റെല്ലോ കാനിൻ പൊട്ടിത്തെറിച്ച
		News (translated): ബിബിസി 6-ന് നൽകിയ അഭിമുഖത്തിൽ കോസ്റ്റെല്ലോ അഭിപ്രായപ്പെട്ടത്, സർ പോൾ മക്കാർട്ട്നിയുടെ സൃഷ്ടികൾ വീണ്ടും ചെയ്യാൻ കെയ്ൻ ശ്രമിച്ചുവെന്ന ആശയം തന്നെ ഒരു വൃത്തികെട്ട നാപ്പി പോലെ വെറുപ്പുളവാക്കുന്നതും ആകർഷകവുമാണെന്ന്. ഏവേഴ്സ് ഇൻ ദി ഡേർട്ട് മക്കാർട്ട്നിയുടെ സൃഷ്ടികളിലെ ഏറ്റവും മികച്ച ആൽബങ്ങളിലൊന്നാണെങ്കിലും, ... ഒരുപക്ഷ കാനി പ്രിൻസ് എസ്റ്റേറ്റിനെ സമീപിച്ച് അദ്ദേഹത്തിന്റെ പ്രസിദ്ധീകരിക്കാത്ത ചില കൃതികൾ വാങ്ങാൻ വാഗ്ദാനം ചെയ്യേക്കാം
		Topic (transliterated): ālbam ṟī ṟilīsinuśēṣam elvis kēāsṟṟellēā kānin peāṭṭitteṟiccu
		News (transliterated): bibisi 6-n nalkiya abhimukhattil kēāsṟṟellēā abhiprāyappeṭṭat, sar pēāḷ makkārṭṭniyuṭe sṛṣṭikaḷ vīṇṭum ceyyān keyn śramiccuvenna āśayam tanne oru vṛttikeṭṭa nāppi pēāle veṟuppuḷavākkunnatum ākarṣakavumāṇenn. phlavēḷs in di ḍērṭṭ makkārṭṭniyuṭe sṛṣṭikaḷile ēṟṟavum mikacca ālbaṅṅaḷileānnāṇeṅkilum, ... orupakṣē kāni prins esṟṟēṟṟine samīpicc addēhattinṟe prasid'dhīkarikkātta cila krtikaḷ vānnān vāgdānam ceytēkkām

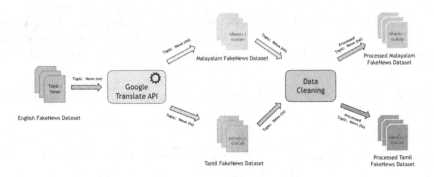

Fig. 1. Dataset Creation Flow Diagram.

heads with the help of multi-head self-attention and can learn long-range dependencies using stacks of self-attention layers. BERT produces state-of-the-art results in many natural language understanding tasks, including the General Language Understanding Evaluation (GLUE) [18] benchmark. We have used a multilingual variant of BERT (M-BERT) and XLMRoBERTa [8], an improved version of BERT. Google's MuRIL [5] is another BERT-based model; a multilingual language model built explicitly for Indian languages. MuRIL is trained on augmented text corpora with translated and transliterated document pairs that serve as cross-lingual signals in training.

The architecture for our model is shown in Fig. 2. As mentioned earlier we used M-BERT, XLM-RoBERTa and MuRIL as models and they all have similar kind of method to process the input data. The description for each of the layer is explained below. The general architecture for transformer based models and there input is given in Figs. 3 and 4 respectively. The general architecture is same for all the models and the only difference is how the sentence is being tokenized and fed to the model. The Fig. 4 shows how the sentence is being tokenized and given as input in the case of M-BERT model. In the case of XLM-RoBERTa the subword splitting is little different and it uses $< s >$ and $< /s >$ instead of [CLS] and [SEP] for sentence begin and end.

Tokenizer: We have appended the topic and news of the dataset to get an entire sentence as input, which is separated with a full stop and space (". "). This entire sentence is tokenized according to the underlying model before giving as input. We use the tokenizers provided by hugging face library[2] which tokenizes according to the model.

---

[2] https://huggingface.co/docs/tokenizers/python/latest/.

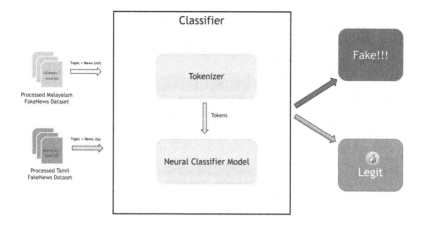

Fig. 2. Proposed Model Architecture.

Neural Classifier Model: This phase uses the particular model we will be deploying to build our classification model. We have used three transformer-based models like M-BERT, XLM-RoBERTa and MuRIL.

M-BERT is a 12-layered transformed-based architecture with 12 multiheaded self attention heads which helps in attention based contextual embeddings and account for long-range dependencies. Tokenization is done particular to the underlying transformer model an example of how tokenization is done for M-BERT is shown in Fig. 4. The tokenized input is fed into this layer and the final hidden state is retrieved from the last layer which is given to the classification layer as shown in Fig. 3. The classification layers takes the input from the last hidden layer and the softmax function gives us the final label probabilities.

XLM-RoBERTa is a multilingual RoBERTa model, an improved version of BERT, and pre-trained on 2.5 TB of filtered CommonCrawl data containing 100 languages. The RoBERTa model is trained on the Masked Language Modeling (MLM) objective, which takes a sentence and randomly masks 15% of the words in the input, then run the entire masked sentence through the model to predict the masked words. The main difference between RoBERTa and BERT is that they use dynamic masking patterns which different masking strategies.

MuRIL is also a BERT model pre-trained on 17 Indian languages and their transliterated counterparts. The model uses similar paradigms for training as BERT with few modifications like translation and transliteration of segment pairs and keeping a different exponent value for upsampling. They trained on monolingual data too, which are publicly available corpora from Wikipedia and CommonCrawl.

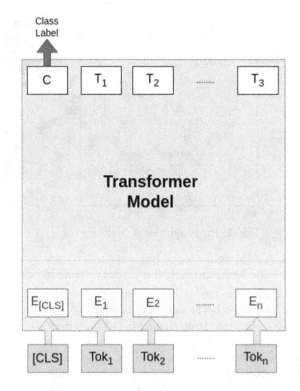

Fig. 3. Transformer-based Model Architecture.

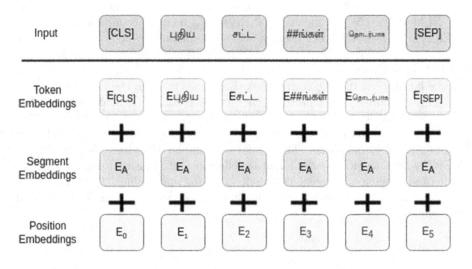

Fig. 4. Input for M-BERT Model.

Table 3. Example on English, Malayalam and Tamil

Topic and News	True Label	Predicted Label
Elon Musk creates Neuralink brain electrode firm. Tesla chief executive Elon Musk has launched Neuralink a start-up which aims to develop technology that connects our brains to computers. A report from the Wall Street Journal later confirmed in a tweet by Mr Musk said the company was in its very early stages and registered as a "medical research" firm. The company will develop so-called "neural lace" technology which would implant tiny electrodes into the brain. The technique could be used to improve memory or give humans added artificial intelligence.	LEGIT	FAKE
ഇലോൺ മസ്ക് ന്യൂറലിങ്ക് ബ്രെയിൻ ഇലക്ട്രോഡ് ഫേം ഉണ്ടാക്കുന്നു. ടെസ്‌ല ചീഫ് എക്‌സിക്യൂട്ടിവ് എലോൺ മസ്ക് നമ്മുടെ തലച്ചോറിനെ കമ്പ്യൂട്ടറുമായി ബന്ധിപ്പിക്കുന്ന സാങ്കേതികവിദ്യ വികസിപ്പിക്കാൻ ലക്ഷ്യമിട്ടുള്ള ന്യൂറലിങ്ക് എന്ന സ്റ്റാർട്ടപ്പ് ആരംഭിച്ചു. വാൾ സ്ട്രീറ്റ് ജേണലിൽ നിന്നുള്ള റിപ്പോർട്ട് പിന്നീട് മസ്കിന്റെ ട്വീറ്റിൽ സ്ഥിരീകരിച്ചു, കമ്പനി അതിന്റെ പ്രാരംഭ ഘട്ടത്തിലാണെന്നും ഒരു; മെഡിക്കൽ റിസർച്ച്; സ്ഥാപനമായി രജിസ്റ്റർ ചെയ്തിട്ടുണ്ടെന്നും പറഞ്ഞു. തലച്ചോറിലേക്ക് ചെറിയ ഇലക്ട്രോഡുകൾ സ്ഥാപിക്കുന്ന ;ന്യൂറൽ ലേസ്; സാങ്കേതികവിദ്യ കമ്പനി വികസിപ്പിക്കും. മെമ്മറി മെച്ചപ്പെടുത്തുന്നതിനോ മനുഷ്യർക്ക് ആർട്ടിഫിഷ്യൽ ഇന്റലിജൻസ് നൽകുന്നതിനോ ഈ സാങ്കേതികവിദ്യ ഉപയോഗിക്കാം.	LEGIT	LEGIT
எலோன் மஸ்க் நியூராலிங்க் மூளை மின்முனை நிறுவனத்தை உருவாக்குகிறார். டெஸ்லாவின் தலைமை நிர்வாகி எலோன் மஸ்க், நமது மூளையை கணினிகளுடன் இணைக்கும் தொழில்நுட்பத்தை மேம்படுத்தும் நோக்கில் நியூராலிங்க் என்ற ஸ்டார்ட்-அப்பை அறிமுகப்படுத்தியுள்ளார். வோல் ஸ்ட்ரீட் ஜேர்னலின் அறிக்கை பின்னர் திரு மஸ்க் ஒரு ட்வீட்டில் உறுதிப்படுத்தியது, நிறுவனம் அதன் ஆரம்ப கட்டத்தில் இருப்பதாகவும், ;மருத்துவ ஆராய்ச்சி; நிறுவனமாக பதிவு செய்ததாகவும் கூறினார். நிறுவனம் ; நரம்பியல் சரிகை; என்று அழைக்கப்படும் தொழில்நுட்பத்தை உருவாக்கும், இது மூளையில் சிறிய மின்முனைகளை பொருத்துகிறது. இந்த நுட்பம் நினைவகத்தை மேம்படுத்த அல்லது மனிதர்களுக்கு செயற்கை நுண்ணறிவை சேர்க்க பயன்படுத்தப்படலாம்.	LEGIT	LEGIT

3.1 Experimental Setup

We have initialized the weights of corresponding transformer-based models BERT or MuRIL or RoBERTa. For the experiments we used a learning rate of $3e^{-5}$ and maximum sequence length of 512 which signifies the length of tokens a sequence can contain in it. We run all training for 10 epochs (increasing the number of epochs is possible but the model's validation loss is getting saturated before itself) using a batch size of 16 and with a call back on validation loss. All the experiments are done on the NVIDIA Tesla V100 16 GB GPU environment.

Table 4. Misclassified Examples

Topic and News	True Label	Predicted Label
How a Red State City Fell in Love With Muslim Immigrants. Every week hosts Dan Moss and Scott Lanman bring you a jargon-free dive into the stories that drive the global economy....	LEGIT	FAKE
എങ്ങനെയാണ് ഒരു റെഡ് സ്റ്റേറ്റ് സിറ്റി മുസ്ലീം കടിയേറ്റക്കാരുമായി പ്രണയത്തിലായത്.എല്ലാ ആഴ്ചയും ആതിഥേയരായ ഡാൻ മോസും സ്കോട്ട് ലാൻമാനും ആഗോള സമ്പദ്‌വ്യവസ്ഥയെ നയിക്കുന്ന കഥകളിലേക്ക് ഒരു പദപ്രയോഗങ്ങളില്ലാതെ മുഴുകന്നു....	LEGIT	FAKE
ஒரு சிவப்பு மாநில நகரம் முஸ்லீம் குடியேறியவர்களை எப்படி காதலித்தது.ஒவ்வொரு வாரமும் தொகுப்பாளர்கள் டான் மோஸ் மற்றும் ஸ்காட் லான்மன், உலகப் பொருளாதாரத்தை இயக்கும் கதைகளில் வாசகங்கள் இல்லாத முழுக்கை உங்களுக்குக் கொண்டு வருகிறார்கள்....	LEGIT	FAKE

4 Results and Discussions

In this section we will be discussing about the results of multi-lingual fake news classification model. The Table 6 shows the results of our proposed model for both Tamil and Malayalam Dataset. We can see that XLMRoBERTa model works well for both Tamil and Malayalam languages. Though MuRIL is a model which is trained explicitly on Indian languages it was not able to surpass the results by XLMRoBERTa but it came almost close to M-BERT model. The downside in the result could be because of the translation happened, we can see the example given in Table 2 where the sentence translated in Malayalam have a similar meaning but in the case of Tamil it is diverting and making it not meaningful. On overall we can say that XLMRoBERTa performed better for both Tamil and Malayalam eventhough there where some problems with the translated data.

The results of the English dataset which we have used to translate is given in Table 5. Here we can see that BERT and RoBERTa models perform close to each other, but the BERT model has the upper hand. MuRIL could not perform; maybe it was pre-trained specifically for Indian languages.

We will discuss how the results have impacted different languages. We have considered the model with the best result, as shown in the above tables, for comparing the examples of predictions. In most cases, Fake news content was predicted as 'FAKE', but we could see that for some news for different languages,

Table 5. Results of different models on English Dataset

Language	Model	Class	Precision	Recall	F1-Score
English	MuRIL	FAKE	0.8661	0.7581	0.8085
		LEGIT	0.7696	0.8733	0.8182
		OVERALL	0.8178	0.8157	0.8133
	XLMRoBERTa	FAKE	0.9275	0.8928	0.9098
		LEGIT	0.8886	0.9245	0.9062
		OVERALL	0.9080	0.9086	0.9080
	M-BERT	FAKE	0.9071	0.9252	0.9160
		LEGIT	0.9174	0.8976	0.9074
		OVERALL	0.9122	0.9114	**0.9117**

the prediction went wrong, as shown in Table 3. The interesting finding is that the same news content is predicted as legitimate for Tamil and Malayalam languages, but for English, it is predicted as fake.

Table 6. Results of different models

Language	Model	Class	Precision	Recall	F1-Score
Tamil	MuRIL	FAKE	0.8929	0.7481	0.8141
		LEGIT	0.7683	0.9030	0.8302
		OVERALL	0.8306	0.8255	0.8222
	XLMRoBERTa	FAKE	0.8518	0.8454	0.8486
		LEGIT	0.8342	0.8410	0.8376
		OVERALL	0.8430	0.8432	**0.8431**
	M-BERT	FAKE	0.8000	0.8778	0.8371
		LEGIT	0.8524	0.7628	0.8051
		OVERALL	0.8262	0.8203	0.8211
Malayalam	MuRIL	FAKE	0.8810	0.7756	0.8249
		LEGIT	0.7852	0.8868	0.8329
		OVERALL	0.8331	0.8312	0.8289
	XLMRoBERTa	FAKE	0.8753	0.7880	0.8294
		LEGIT	0.7932	0.8787	0.8338
		OVERALL	0.8343	0.8334	**0.8316**
	M-BERT	FAKE	0.8154	0.8703	0.8420
		LEGIT	0.8488	0.7871	0.8168
		OVERALL	0.8321	0.8287	0.8294

206 R. L. Hariharan and M. Anand Kumar

Now we will see some misclassified examples predicted the same for all three languages, as given in Table 4. Here we can see that the same news content is predicted in all the languages as 'FAKE' though they are legitimate news. The reason for contradicted prediction may be because of words in the content contributing to some of the news being labeled 'FAKE'. Overall we could tell that the models we used were almost performing well though one of them had the upper hand. Moreover, in this work, we have mainly focused on dataset creation and have not done much to fine-tune the models. If we could do language-specific fine-tuning and some analysis on the discernment of data, we could improve the model performance even more. The Ensembling technique could also be used with more models and thereby get improved performance.

5 Conclusion and Future Works

In this work we have developed a Multilingual Fake news detection system. We have proposed a multilingual dataset which is from multiple domains consisting two low resource languages Tamil and Malayalam. We propose a baseline model for multilingual fake news detection in the low-resource settings. Our proposed model which is trained on language based data will be able to give predictions when its fed with directly without the need of explicit translation. In future we would like to extend further this research by incorporating more number news articles of low-resource language and trained on wide variety of domains as well as generic datasets. Moreover, we would examine the possibility of different transformer-based models and an ensemble strategy to develop a model with a more satisfactory prediction. We would further investigate the issues of translation which causes the wrong prediction for the news sentence, which could be because of the difference in meaning. We would explore the possibility of multimodality in the case of multilingual fake news detection, a less explored region.

References

1. De, A., Bandyopadhyay, D., Gain, B., Ekbal, A.: A transformer-based approach to multilingual fake news detection in low-resource languages. ACM Trans. Asian Low-Resour. Lang. Inf. Process. **21**(1), 1–20 (2022). https://doi.org/10.1145/3472619
2. Devlin, J., Chang, M.W., Lee, K., Toutanova, K.: BERT: pre-training of deep bidirectional transformers for language understanding. In: Proceedings of the 2019 Conference of the North American Chapter of the Association for Computational Linguistics: Human Language Technologies. vol. 1 (Long and Short Papers), Minneapolis, Minnesota, pp. 4171–4186. Association for Computational Linguistics (Jun 2019). https://doi.org/10.18653/v1/N19-1423, https://aclanthology.org/N19-1423
3. Hanselowski, A., et al.: A retrospective analysis of the fake news challenge stance-detection task. In: Proceedings of the 27th International Conference on Computational Linguistics, Santa Fe, New Mexico, USA, pp. 1859–1874. Association for Computational Linguistics (Aug 2018). https://aclanthology.org/C18-1158

4. Hayes, D.: Political Science Quarterly. **124**(3), 560–562 (2009). http://www.jstor.org/stable/25655715

5. Khanuja, S., et al.: MuRIL: multilingual representations for indian languages. arXiv preprint arXiv:2103.10730 (2021)

6. LekshmiAmmal, H.R., Madasamy, A.K.: NITK_NLP at checkThat! 2021: Ensemble transformer model for fake news classification. In: CLEF (Working Notes), pp. 603–611 (2021)

7. LekshmiAmmal, H.R., Madasamy, A.K.: NITK-IT NLP at checkthat! 2022: Window based approach for fake news detection using transformers (2022)

8. Liu, Y., et al.: RoBERTa: A robustly optimized BERT pretraining approach. arXiv preprint arXiv:1907.11692 (2019)

9. Mehta, D., Dwivedi, A., Patra, A., Anand Kumar, M.: A transformer-based architecture for fake news classification. Soc. Netw. Anal. Min. **11**(1), 1–12 (2021)

10. Pérez-Rosas, V., Kleinberg, B., Lefevre, A., Mihalcea, R.: Automatic detection of fake news. In: Proceedings of the 27th International Conference on Computational Linguistics, Santa Fe, New Mexico, USA, pp. 3391–3401. Association for Computational Linguistics (Aug 2018). https://aclanthology.org/C18-1287

11. Shahi, G.K., Nandini, D.: FakeCOVID-A multilingual cross-domain fact check news dataset for COVID-19

12. Shu, K., Sliva, A., Wang, S., Tang, J., Liu, H.: Fake news detection on social media: a data mining perspective. ACM SIGKDD Explor. Newslett. **19**(1), 22–36 (2017)

13. Singhal, S., Shah, R.R., Kumaraguru, P.: FactDrill: a data repository of fact-checked social media content to study fake news incidents in India. In: Proceedings of the International AAAI Conference on Web and Social Media. vol. 16(1), pp. 1322–1331 (May 2022). https://doi.org/10.1609/icwsm.v16i1.19384, https://ojs.aaai.org/index.php/ICWSM/article/view/19384

14. Tagarev, A., Bozhanova, K., Nikolova-Koleva, I., Ivanov, I.: Tackling multilinguality and internationality in fake news. In: Proceedings of the International Conference on Recent Advances in Natural Language Processing (RANLP 2021), pp. 1380–1386. INCOMA Ltd., Held Online (Sep 2021). https://aclanthology.org/2021.ranlp-1.154

15. Thorne, J., Vlachos, A., Christodoulopoulos, C., Mittal, A.: FEVER: a large-scale dataset for fact extraction and VERification. In: Proceedings of the 2018 Conference of the North American Chapter of the Association for Computational Linguistics: Human Language Technologies. Vol. 1 (Long Papers), New Orleans, Louisiana, pp. 809–819. Association for Computational Linguistics (Jun 2018). https://doi.org/10.18653/v1/N18-1074, https://aclanthology.org/N18-1074

16. Vargas, F., Benevenuto, F., Pardo, T.: Toward discourse-aware models for multilingual fake news detection. In: Proceedings of the Student Research Workshop Associated with RANLP 2021, pp. 210–218. INCOMA Ltd., Online (Sep 2021). https://aclanthology.org/2021.ranlp-srw.29

17. Vosoughi, S., Roy, D., Aral, S.: The spread of true and false news online. Science **359**(6380), 1146–1151 (2018). https://doi.org/10.1126/science.aap9559, https://www.science.org/doi/abs/10.1126/science.aap9559

18. Wang, A., Singh, A., Michael, J., Hill, F., Levy, O., Bowman, S.R.: GLUE: a multi-task benchmark and analysis platform for natural language understanding. arXiv preprint arXiv:1804.07461 (2018)

19. Wu, Y., et al.: Google's neural machine translation system: Bridging the gap between human and machine translation (2016). https://doi.org/10.48550/ARXIV.1609.08144, https://arxiv.org/abs/1609.08144

20. Zhang, X., Ghorbani, A.A.: An overview of online fake news: characterization, detection, and discussion. Inf. Process. Manage. **57**(2), 102025 (2020). https://doi.org/10.1016/j.ipm.2019.03.004, https://www.sciencedirect.com/science/article/pii/S0306457318306794

21. Zhou, X., Zafarani, R.: A survey of fake news: fundamental theories, detection methods, and opportunities. ACM Comput. Surv. **53**(5) (sep 2020). https://doi.org/10.1145/3395046, https://doi.org/10.1145/3395046

Development of Multi-lingual Models for Detecting Hope Speech Texts from Social Media Comments

Malliga Subramanian[1](✉), Ramya Chinnasamy[1], Prasanna Kumar Kumaresan[2], Vasanth Palanikumar[3], Madhoora Mohan[3], and Kogilavani Shanmugavadivel[1]

[1] Kongu Engineering College, Perudurai, Erode, Tamil Nadu, India
mallinishanth72@gmail.com
[2] Indian Institute of Information Technology and Management-Kerala, Kazhakkoottam, India
[3] Chennai Institute of Technology, Chennai, Tamil Nadu, India

Abstract. Comments on social media can be written in any number of languages, and many of them may also be written in languages with few resources. Hope Speech comments are kind expressions that support or critique a viewpoint without offending the individual or the community. On the other hand, non-hope speech is made up of harsh, mocking, or demotivating words. Since the Covid-19 pandemic, the need for positive reinforcement on the internet has made the field of natural language processing pay more attention to hope speech detection. Hope speech detection looks for words and phrases in social media comments that make people feel good. In this paper, an attempt to share content on these platforms that is positive and helpful is made. The models that are based on transformers to figure out whether a social media comment is "hope speech" or "non-hope speech" has been used. The objective of this work is to find the "hope speech" comments in YouTube datasets that were made as part of the "LT-EDI-ACL 2022: Hope Speech Detection for Equality, Diversity, and Inclusion" shared task. The shared task dataset was suggested in five different languages: Malayalam, Tamil, English, Spanish, and Kannada. The model based on a transformer was used as both a fine-tuner and an adapter transformer. In the end, adapters and fine-tuners do the same thing, but adapters add layers to the main model that has already been trained and freeze the weights of those layers. This study shows that models that are based on adapters do better than models that are fine-tuned. The proposed model classifies the Tamil dataset with an accuracy of 51.7% and the English dataset with an accuracy of 92.1%, which is the highest among all the datasets.

Keywords: Hope Speech · Transformer model · Fine-tuner · Adapter

1 Introduction

Users provide content for social networks. Individuals may start their own blogs, update them with their own ideas on a topic, and include media such as videos or photos. Real-time interaction is another distinguishing feature of social media. These features let social media users express themselves freely and anonymously. Due to the platform's

Anand Kumar M et al. (Eds.): SPELLL 2022, CCIS 1802, pp. 209–219, 2023.
https://doi.org/10.1007/978-3-031-33231-9_14

accessibility and lack of identification verification standards, it has been used to a greater extent [1]. It is undeniable that social media has changed how internet users communicate and go about their daily basis [2]. With so much information at their fingertips, users of social media platforms like YouTube, Facebook, and Twitter are increasingly vocal about their beliefs, which often take the form of remarks that can be interpreted as hate speech or as being otherwise harmful [3, 4]. Unfortunately, cyberbullying is not the only kind of online harassment in which certain persons or groups are targeted by those who use these sites to promote harmful or destructive behavior [5]. With the goal of avoiding content and maintaining healthy social media, most social media analyses focus on identifying negative content such as hate speech, abusive language, fake news, etc. [19]. However, there is a dearth of research on the use of social media analytics to find optimistic content like encouragement and inspiration.

The dissemination of harmful information has the capacity to provoke, legitimate, and spread feelings of hostility, resentment, and prejudice against the targeted users who intend to receive it. In light of the fact that doing so would constitute a violation of the user's right to free speech, erasing comments of this nature was never a practical possibility. In point of fact, it would encourage him or her to continue making statements like that in the future [6]. As a result of this, this work aims to encourage positivity and hope by assisting people in discovering and sharing information that is optimistic and uplifting online in an effort to cultivate a society that is more welcoming and inclusive.

Because of this, the number of marginalized people around the world who are looking for assistance and support online has considerably increased. In recent years, several forms of online assistance, such as social media networks (SMN), online blogs, and online support groups (OSG), have gained widespread popularity. Therefore, researchers are attempting to construct a computational model that can locate information that is uplifting and encouraging across various social media platforms.

Researchers working in the field of Natural Language Processing (NLP) have recently become interested in the automatic detection of hope-speech [7, 8]. Linguists, computer scientists, and psychologists now have more opportunities than ever to delve deeply into many types of human expression, such as anger, grief, joy, and love, thanks to the platforms provided by social media [9–11]. Methods based on machine learning (ML) and deep learning (DL) have been applied in an effort to solve the challenge of hope speech recognition. Due to the fact that they are able to handle dependencies between input and output with both attention and recurrence, transformers have garnered an enormous amount of popularity over the past few years. As a consequence of this, numerous NLP tasks have been developed utilizing transformer-based models to achieve state-of-the-art performance [12].

However, the majority of research efforts are focused on the English language, which limits the classification power in other languages such as Tamil, Kannada, Malayalam, and so on where there are fewer resources available. In this study, an effort is made to create a BERT (Bidirectional Encoder Representations from Transformers) transformer-based model for the purpose of classifying the comments and texts that were collected in five different languages, including English, Tamil, Malayalam, Kannada, and Spanish. The following is a list of the most important contributions made by this research:

1. Developed a multilingual BERT-based transformer model to extract word embeddings in English, Tamil, Spanish, Kannada, and Malayalam to identify the hope speech comments.
2. Integrated adapter modules into the proposed model to reduce the training parameters.
3. Transliterated the English comments, which are present in Tamil, Malayalam, and Kannada datasets
4. Evaluated how well the models work with the datasets in five languages.

The rest of the article is organized as follows: Sect. 2 provides a concise summary of the efforts that were concentrated on categorizing the hope speech comments. In Sect. 3, a comprehensive report on the datasets and the preprocessing methods that were used on these datasets is presented. Section 3 also provides an explanation of the developed models as well as their approach. In Sect. 4, an analysis of the results of the experiments as well as the results of the experiments themselves are described. Section 5 concludes the work by providing a summary of the study as well as the possible extensions of the study.

2 Literature Survey

A review of the attempts to identify hope speech text is presented in this section. As transformers and pretrained language models have grown in popularity, deep learning techniques are now the mainstay of contemporary solutions for recognizing hope speech remarks. Over the past few years, the organization of and participation in shared tasks has become more popular in NLP.

In the second workshop on Language Technology for Equality, Diversity, and Inclusion (LT-EDI-2022), Chakravarthi et al. released a shared task [13] on hope speech detection for Tamil, Malayalam, Kannada, English, and Spanish languages in 2022. The authors summarized the systems submitted by the shared task participants and provided a full description of the datasets. This task is intended to motivate researchers to tackle issues with hope speech identification and draw attention to the need for greater study into identifying and disseminating the hope speech texts in languages with limited resources. A new method for automatically discovering conflict-neutral web content was developed by Palakodety et al. [16]. Polyglot word embeddings, an approach that requires minimal human annotation, were utilized by the authors.

Zhao and Tao [14] performed a classification challenge utilizing the XLM-RoBERTa model as the foundation, extracting features and merging 12 layers of output with an embedding layer. The NLTK tool was used to clean up the training comments in the datasets. This made it simpler to identify useful features and reduce noise during model training. Additionally, Stratified-K-Fold is employed to improve the training data. Huang and Bai [15] recommended utilizing XLM-RoBERTa in conjunction with Term Frequency-Inverse Document Frequency (TF-IDF) to extract the features. The authors of the work [15] used TF-IDF to weight the output of the last layer of XLM-RoBERTa in order to get a weighted output. Chen and Kong et al. [16] built a model to recognize hopeful speech using a pre-trained ALBERT model. The authors picked ALBERT because it has fewer parameters and requires less time and memory to train. Using K-fold cross-validation on the training dataset, this study enhanced results and generated an F1 score of 93% for the English dataset. Ghanghor et al. [17] utilized monolingual models based on (cased and uncased) BERT, multilingual-cased BERT, XLMRoberta, and IndicBERT models for the construction of systems to recognize hope speech comments presented in [13]. The aforementioned models have been enhanced by utilizing both the original and customized versions of the datasets. Using the shared task [13], Praveenkumar et al. [18] attempted to classify comments as "Hope speech" or "Non-hope speech". These authors used ALBERT for their work, which employs the pre-trained language model BERT.

Hossain et al. [19] developed a model using cross-lingual contextual word embeddings (i.e. transformers) to distinguish hopeful speech from codemixed data in English, Tamil, and Malayalam. They then carried out extensive tests to see which approaches worked best. According to the findings of this study [19], transformer-based models outperform machine and deep learning methods.

Hande et al. [20] produced the English-Kannada KanHope speech dataset and compared the results of numerous experiments to benchmark the dataset. The dataset consists of 6,176 user-generated comments from YouTube that were manually tagged and are in code-mixed Kannada. This work also introduced DC-BERT4HOPE, a dual-channel model that uses the English translation of KanHope for further training to support hope speech detection [20]. With this approach, a weighted F1-score of 0.756 is obtained.

A stacked encoder architecture and language-independent cross-lingual word embeddings were used by Sundar et al. [21]. They also carried out an empirical investigation and contrasted the proposed models with the traditional, transformer, and transfer learning approaches. The suggested model outperforms the alternatives, according to a k-fold paired t-test that was also run. In this approach, Tamil and Malayalam datasets received F1 scores of 0.61 and 0.85, respectively.

In summary, most attempts toward the hopeful speech detection made use of transformer models. The transformer model is a novel architecture in NLP that facilitates the management of long-range dependencies while solving sequence-to-sequence problems. When attempting to determine what its inputs and outputs are, it does not make use of sequence-aligned RNNs or convolution. Instead, it relies solely on the self-attention mechanism. Therefore, the models that are based on precisely tuned transformers have a higher degree of accuracy. Although a significant amount of work has been done on hope speech recognition with highly refined transformer models, the adapter-based models have not yet been put to the test. Adapters carry out the same functions as fine-tuning, but they do so by adding layers to a pre-trained model and modifying the weights of these new layers while leaving the weights of the pre-trained model unchanged. In other words, adapters perform the same tasks as fine-tuning, but they do so in a different way. Because of this, adapters are far more effective than fine-tuning in saving both time and space. Based on our examination of the relevant research, we are aware of no work classifies hope speech texts using an adapter-based transformer model; nonetheless utilizing such models will result in the work being more successful. As a result, in this work, the transformer model is extended with an adapter and evaluated how effectively it functions.

3 Proposed Methodology

The proposed method has 2 phases namely preprocessing and model construction to put a given text into one of two categories: "Hope" or "Not Hope.". Below are descriptions of the steps for pre-processing and building the model.

3.1 Preprocessing

In this study, hope speech texts have been identified from YouTube comments and postings that provide encouragement, assurance, advice, inspiration, and insight. In the second workshop on Language Technology for Equality, Diversity, and Inclusion, Chakravarthi et al. released a shared task [T1] on hope speech recognition for Tamil, Malayalam, Kannada, English, and Spanish languages. The texts were taken from social media, and they contain characters such as URLs, hashtags, and others. The noise and undesirable characters must be eliminated from the raw, unstructured text data before the text is mined in order to produce relevant features that could aid in classifying the comments. To prepare the data, the following processes have been taken:

Getting Rid of Emojis. Emojis and emoticons are used in the text communications in the dataset. They can be fully eliminated or changed to a textual word. Instead, their textual equivalents have been utilized in this study.

Removing All Punctuation, Numerals, and Non-Tamil Text. The extra white space, punctuation like!,?, etc., and numerals have been removed in addition to removing non-Tamil texts. These characters make it easier to read, but they are not helpful for determining a person's point of view. Duplicate comments have also been removed.

Transliteration. A word written in one language is said to be transliterated when it is written using the alphabet of a different language. As the Tamil, Malayalam, and Kannada datasets contain the comments in English, the AI4Bharat Indic-Transliteration engine [22], which covers 21 main Indian languages, is used for transliterating the comments written in English. People who are not familiar with a language's alphabet will find it a little easier to understand when it is transliterated. Table 1 provides a transliteration example.

Table 1. Example for Transliteration

Thalaivare..neengale inum one plus mobile vachu-rukinga...adha udachurunga	Tamil comments transliterated in English
தலைவரேநீங்களே இனும் ஒனே பிளஸ் மொபைல் வச்சுருகிங்க...அதா உடச்சுருங்க	Tamil

3.2 Model Construction

In this work, the pre-trained mBERT models to classify the hope speech comments and fine-tuned the model to learn the weights for the new dataset has been trained. In addition, adapter modules have also been integrated into the layers of mBERT model. The details are presented below:

mBERT – Fine-Tuned. Multilingual BERT (mBERT), which supports 104 languages, was released alongside BERT. The approach is quite straightforward: it consists primarily of BERT trained on text from multiple languages. It was specifically trained on Wikipedia articles with a shared vocabulary across all languages. The number of comments was few in some languages and high is some languages. Such cases have been oversampled and undersampled to overcome the content imbalance on Wikipedia. Due to the fact that mBERT contains sentence representations for 104 languages, it is beneficial for a variety of multilingual activities. mBERT model is used to classify the dataset, which comprises five different languages. mBERT can function as a language and label classifier [23] and it is used label classification in this work. mBERT model parameters have been used for fine-tuned on the target task data sets. A standard fine-tuning model takes the weights from a pre-trained network and modifies them so that they are appropriate for a downstream task. This is necessary since each of these tasks requires a unique set of weights. To put it another way, the parameters are updated alongside each new task. If lower layers of the network are shared by numerous tasks, fine-tuning may be able to boost the efficiency of the parameters.

mBERT – Adapter-Based. In the context of transfer learning for NLP, parameter inefficiency occurs when an entirely new model needs to be built for every downstream task and the number of parameters accumulates to an unacceptable level. Because of this, it is necessary to apply previously gained knowledge to a different endeavor without first training the complete model. Houslby et al. [24] recommended the use of transfer learning in conjunction with adapter modules as an alternative. The use of adapter modules results in a model that is both compact and extensible. Adapter modules increase the efficiency of the trainable parameters by simply adding a few of them for each task. Additionally, as new tasks are introduced, the previously trained parameters do not need to be revisited. Adapters [24] add new bottleneck modules that are fine-tuned for the specified task and are contained within the transformer layers of the pre-trained network. For the purpose of classifying the hope speech using the pre-trained mBERT model, the adapter modules have been integrated in the proposed study.

4 Experimental Settings, Results and Findings

This section discusses about how the training process for the experiments was set up, including how the hyperparameters were chosen and how the evaluation metrics were used to compare how well the models worked. Due of concerns about power consumption and the need for high-performance hardware, we ran the proposed models on a Graphical Processing Unit (GPU). Table 2 shows the hyperparameters tuned for this work. The search space of these hyperparameters include a set of values. For instance, the batch size tested include 16, 32, 64, and 128. After a set of trails, the values shown in Table 2 is found to give optimized results.

Table 2. Hyperparameters and their values

Hyperparameters	Search Space	Without Adapters	With Adapters
Batch size	16,32,64,128	16	64
Learning rate	1e−2,1e−3,1e−4,1e−5	1e−4	1e−4
Batch size for training	16,32,64,128	16	64
Batch size for evaluation	16,32,64,128	16	32

4.1 Experimental Results

For finetuning the weights of the pre-trained mBERT have been inherited and a classification layer has been added on the top of the model. The entire model is retrained on the downstream task. The results of finetuned models are shown in Table 3.

Table 3. Results of fine-tuned mBERT model

Language	mBERT		
	Accuracy	Precision	F1-score
Malayalam	0.869	0.683	0.6631
Kannada	0.7357	0.5871	0.6124
Spanish	0.709	0.6994	0.7159
English	0.9234	0.5888	0.5155
Tamil	0.506	0.492	0.413

To validate that adapter yield compact, performant, models, we test on the hope speech dataset undertaken. The results are presented in Table 4.

For a classification task, the predicted outcomes can be summarized using a confusion matrix. In a confusion matrix, each row represents a true class and each column represents a predicted class. The confusion matrices obtained for the adapter-based mBERT model for all the five languages are depicted in the Fig. 1. For instance, 398 hope speech Tamil comments have been classified correctly by the adapter-based models. But, 413 instances have been misclassified as "Hope Speech". But, the misclassification rate is comparatively low for the comments in other languages.

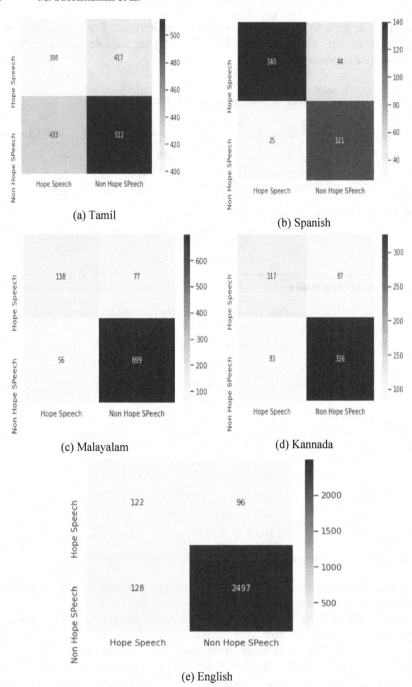

(a) Tamil

(b) Spanish

(c) Malayalam

(d) Kannada

(e) English

Fig. 1. Confusion Matrices for Adapter-based mBERT model

Table 4. Results of Adapter-based mBERT model

Language	mBERT		
	Accuracy	Precision	F1-score
Malayalam	0.863	0.901	0.913
Kannada	0.723	0.789	0.793
Spanish	0.791	0.733	0.778
English	0.921	0.963	0.957
Tamil	0.517	0.551	0.546

4.2 Findings and Discussions

The performance of the developed models has been evaluated using the metrics namely accuracy, precision, and F1 score, and the results were presented in Sect. 4.1. From Fig. 1, it can be seen that adapter-based models give high accuracy for English datasets and lowest for Tamil datasets. Since, Tamil has a dearth of word embeddings because to its low level of resource availability, developing a Tamil word embedding considering the morphological, semantic and syntactic relationships would help to solve this issue. For English, the best word embeddings and pretrained models are available. So, the results are found to be appreciable. This is same for other languages too. Figure 2 compares the performance of fine-tuned and adapter-based mBERT models. As the datasets are

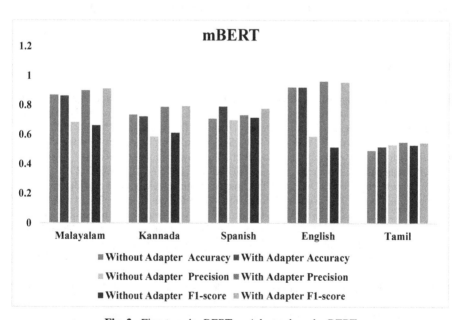

Fig. 2. Fine-tuned mBERT vs Adapter-based mBERT

not balanced, accuracy alone is not a good measure of evaluation for the proposed classification models. so, other metrics have been used to evaluate the

In contrast to the transformer model based on adapters, it is also found that the number of trainable parameters for the fine-tuned model is enormous. For adapter-based models, just 3(%) of the parameters or less must be trained, which is almost as much as or more than that of fully trained models. In addition, when analyzing the reason for the poor performance of the proposed models against the Tamil dataset, it is found that the imbalance in the distribution of the classes is one of the reasons.

5   Conclusion and Future Work

Users of social networking sites leave comments on various kinds of posts to express their thoughts, accomplishments, successes, and failures. Positive comments definitely increase confidence and occasionally inspire people to be resilient in strange circumstances. An adapter-based transformer model was proposed in this study to identify hope speech comments on social media platforms using multilingual corpora. For classifying the hope speech texts, two models have been developed using pre-trained mBERT, a multilingual transformer model. The developed models have been fine-tuned for the corpora under consideration and further, adapters have been integrated into the transformer layers, which require training of a small number of parameters. It is found that adapter-based models outperform fine-tuned models with less number of training parameters and increased performance. In further work, it is planned to address the issue of class imbalance in an effective manner by enhancing the dataset. In addition to this, transformer models such as RoBERTa, XLNet, and Albert amongst others for a more accurate hope speech detection will also be investigated.

References

1. Balouchzahi, F., Aparna, B., Shashirekha, H.: MUCS@ DravidianLangTech-EACL2021: COOLI-code-mixing offensive language identification. In: Proceedings of the First Workshop on Speech and Language Technologies for Dravidian Languages, pp. 323–329 (2021)
2. Jose, N., Chakravarthi, B.R., Suryawanshi, S., Sherly, E., McCrae, J.P.: A survey of current datasets for code-switching research. In: 2020 6th International Conference on Advanced Computing and Communication Systems (ICACCS), pp. 136–141. IEEE (2020)
3. Chakravarthi, B.R., et al.: Overview of the track on sentiment analysis for dravidian languages in code-mixed text. In: Forum for Information Retrieval Evaluation, pp. 21–24 (2020)
4. Mandl, T., Modha, S., Kumar, M.A., Chakravarthi, B.R.: Overview of the hasoc track at fire 2020: Hate speech and offensive language identification in tamil, malayalam, hindi, english and german. In: Forum for Information Retrieval Evaluation, pp. 29–32 (2020)
5. Abaido, G.M.: Cyberbullying on social media platforms among university students in the United Arab Emirates. Int. J. Adolesc. Youth **25**(1), 407–420 (2020)
6. Yasaswini, K., Puranik, K., Hande, A., Priyadharshini, R., Thavareesan, S., Chakravarthi, B.R.: IIITT@ DravidianLangTech-EACL2021: Transfer learning for offensive language detection in Dravidian languages. In: Proceedings of the First Workshop on Speech and Language Technologies for Dravidian Languages, pp. 187–194 (2021)

7. Chakravarthi, B.R.: HopeEDI: a multilingual hope speech detection dataset for equality, diversity, and inclusion. In: Proceedings of the Third Workshop on Computational Modeling of People's Opinions, Personality, and Emotion's in Social Media, pp. 41–53 (2020)
8. Chakravarthi, B.R., Muralidaran, V.: Findings of the shared task on hope speech detection for equality, diversity, and inclusion. In: Proceedings of the First Workshop on Language Technology for Equality, Diversity and Inclusion, pp. 61–72 (2021)
9. Chakravarthi, B.R., et al.: Dataset for identification of homophobia and transophobia in multilingual YouTube comments, arXiv preprint arXiv:2109.00227 (2021)
10. Ashraf, N., Rafiq, A., Butt, S., Shehzad, H.M.F., Sidorov, G., Gelbukh, A.: YouTube based religious hate speech and extremism detection dataset with machine learning baselines. J. Intell. Fuzzy Syst. no. Preprint, 1–9 (2022)
11. Sampath, A., et al.: Findings of the shared task on Emotion Analysis in Tamil. In: Proceedings of the Second Workshop on Speech and Language Technologies for Dravidian Languages, pp. 279–285 (2022)
12. Chen, B., et al.: Transformer-based language model fine-tuning methods for COVID-19 fake news detection. In: Chakraborty, T., Shu, K., Bernard, H.R., Liu, H., Akhtar, M.S. (eds.) CONSTRAINT 2021. CCIS, vol. 1402, pp. 83–92. Springer, Cham (2021). https://doi.org/10.1007/978-3-030-73696-5_9
13. Shared Task on Hope Speech Detection for Equality, Diversity, and Inclusion (English, Tamil, Spanish, Kannada, and Malayalam) at LT-EDI (2022). https://competitions.codalab.org/competitions/36393
14. Zhao, Y., Tao, X.: ZYJ@ LT-EDI-EACL2021: XLM-RoBERTa-based model with attention for hope speech detection. In: Proceedings of the First Workshop on Language Technology for Equality, Diversity and Inclusion, pp. 118–121 (2021)
15. Huang, B., Bai, Y.: TEAM HUB@ LT-EDI-EACL2021: hope speech detection based on pre-trained language model. In: Proceedings of the First Workshop on Language Technology for Equality, Diversity and Inclusion, pp. 122–127 (2021)
16. Chen, S., Kong, B.: cs_english@ LT-EDI-EACL2021: Hope speech detection based on fine-tuning ALBERT model. In: Proceedings of the First Workshop on Language Technology for Equality, Diversity and Inclusion, pp. 128–131 (2021)
17. Ghanghor, N., Ponnusamy, R., Kumaresan, P.K., Priyadharshini, R., Thavareesan, S., Chakravarthi, B.R.: IIITK@ LT-EDI-EACL2021: Hope speech detection for equality, diversity, and inclusion in Tamil, Malayalam and English. In: Proceedings of the First Workshop on Language Technology for Equality, Diversity and Inclusion, pp. 197–203 (2021)
18. Vijayakumar, P., et al.: SSN_ARMM@ LT-EDI-ACL2022: hope speech detection for equality, diversity, and inclusion using ALBERT model. In: Proceedings of the Second Workshop on Language Technology for Equality, Diversity and Inclusion, pp. 172–176 (2022)
19. Hossain, E., Sharif, O., Hoque, M.M.: NLP-CUET@ LT-EDI-EACL2021: multilingual code-mixed hope speech detection using cross-lingual representation learner. arXiv preprint arXiv:2103.00464 (2021)
20. Hande, A., Priyadharshini, R., Sampath, A., Thamburaj, K.P., Chandran, P., Chakravarthi, B.R.: Hope speech detection in under-resourced kannada language. arXiv preprint arXiv:2108.04616 (2021)
21. Sundar, A., Ramakrishnan, A., Balaji, A., Durairaj, T.: hope speech detection for dravidian languages using cross-lingual embeddings with stacked encoder architecture. SN Comput. Sci. 3(1), 1–15 (2021). https://doi.org/10.1007/s42979-021-00943-8
22. https://pypi.org/project/ai4bharat-transliteration/
23. Tanti, M., van der Plas, L., Borg, C., Gatt, A.: On the Language-specificity of Multilingual BERT and the Impact of Fine-tuning. arXiv preprint arXiv:2109.06935 (2021)
24. Houlsby, N., et al.: Parameter-efficient transfer learning for NLP. In: International Conference on Machine Learning, 2019: PMLR, pp. 2790–2799 (2019)

Transfer Learning Based Youtube Toxic Comments Identification

S. Santhiya[✉] ⓘ, P. Jayadharshini ⓘ, and S. V. Kogilavani ⓘ

Department of Artificial Intelligence, Kongu Engineering College, Perundurai 638060, India
jayadharshini.ai@kongu.edu

Abstract. Online users are negatively affected by the spread of offensive content on social media sites. A fear, dislike, unease, or distrust of lesbian, gay, bisexual, or transgender persons is known as homophobia or transphobia. Homophobic/transphobic speech, which can be summed up as bigotry directed towards LGBT+ people, has grown to be a significant problem in recent years. The major social problem of online homopho- bia/transphobia threatens to eliminate equity, diversification, and acceptance while also making online places toxic and unwelcoming for LGBT+ people. It is found to be sensitive subject and untrained crowd sourced annotators have trouble in identifying homophobia due to cultural and other preconceptions. As a result, annotators had been educated and provided them with thorough annotation standards. 15,141 multilingual annotated comments make up the dataset. The proposed work identifies the best Machine Learning Classifier with BERT embedding model for the Code-Mixed Dravidian Languages in order to identify the toxic languages directed towards LGBTQ+ individuals. Adaboost classifier outperforms other three classifiers in terms of accuracy.

Keywords: Dravidian languages · Code-Mixed Language · BERT · Mixed-Feelings · Machine Learning Classifiers

1 Introduction

In the digital age, social media is crucial for online communication because it enables users to publish content, share it with others, and voice their opinions whenever they want. NLP academics have access to a large amount of data that allows them to tackle more difficult, enduring issues like comprehending, analyzing, and tracking user actions toward particular topics or events. Additionally, the rapid development of deep learning-based NLP and the enormous volume of user-generated content that is readily available online, particularly on social media, offer reliable and effective methods to analyses users' behaviors. Such tactics can be employed for purposes like acquiring data for affective behavior research or sexism detection. Online, there are many unpleasant statements, including those that are sexist, homophobic, racist, and racial slurs, as well as threats and insults that are directed at particular people or organizations. The proliferation of

Supported by organization x.

online content has made it a serious issue for online communities. Online profanity has been noted as a global phenomenon that has spread over social media sites like Facebook, YouTube, and Twitter during the past ten years [1]. It is even more disturbing for vulnerable Lesbian, Gay, Bisexual, Transgender, and other (LGBT+) individuals. LGBT+ people endure violence, injustice, suffering, and sometimes even assassination because of what they love, how they appear, or who they are. The Internet has, however, given everyone the ability to significantly influence the lives of other people by utilizing some of its distinctive features, such as anonymity. Homophobic and transphobic content attacks the LGBT+ individuals frequently. LGBT+ individuals who seek support online experience abuse or assault, which has a serious negative impact on their mental health [2, 3]. An original study on the automatic detection of homophobic and transphobic content on social media for LGBT+ groups, particularly among Tamil people. English, Tamil, and code-mixed Tamil English are all included in the datasets. The Codemixed dataset includes symbols, tags, punctuation and symbols. Stop words and tag were used for preprocessing to clean the data. First work, consist of five classes. They are Mixed feeling, Neutral, Positive, Negative and unknown state. Second work consist of three classes namely homophobic, transphobic, and non-anti-LGBT+ content labels. Embedding technique namely BERT embedding has been used for both the proposed work. Models are built with BERT embedding using following Classifiers. Ada Boost classifier, Logistic Regression Classifier, K-Nearest Neighbor Classifier, Random Forest Classifier. Word embedding features from the BERT vectorized the text for both the task A and task B. The classifiers are used after vectorizing the text to build the models.

2 Related Work

The use of ict infrastructure, particularly social media, has altered how individuals connect with one another and communicate on a global scale as a result of the widespread usage of social media apps. As an illustration, the popular networking sites site YouTube allows users to build their own profiles, upload videos, and leave comments. Numerous individuals may view each video or comment due to "liking" and "sharing" strategies, offering cyberbullies a simple opportunity to disseminate offensive or unwelcome information about their victims. A Platform [4, 5] has been provided for antisocial behaviors like racism, sexism, homophobia, and transphobia. Later, Code-mixed datasets [6, 7] were in scarce in terms of quantity, size, and accessibility. Gender bias in NLP [6] has been actively mitigated for the English language using several techniques. The studies examined [8, 9] gender discrimination not only for English language and also for other language including French and other languages. One of the first experiments on Tamil abusive language recognition was carried out in 2020 by HASOC Dravidian CodeMix [10, 11]. A Tamil dataset of disgusting comments was created and supplied to the shared task's participants afterwards, as reported by Dravidian LangTech [12]. Social media activity in local languages with mixed codes has dramatically expanded over the past several years as a result of cheaper internet and more people using smartphones. A significant amount of these exchanges are contributed by the 215 million speakers of Dravidian languages (4, many of whom are multilingual with English because it is India's national language). The examination of code-mixed text in Dravidian languages is hence becoming more and more necessary. The majority of current research on offensive language detection and sentiment analysis has been done on social media platforms using high resource languages. Empathy and offensiveness can be predicted by models that have been trained on such rich monolingual data. However, because bilingual people use social media more regularly, a system trained some under code mixed data is necessary.

3 Proposed System

Dataset Description. The dataset gathered by the organizers consists of 15,141 YouTube comments from different languages that have been categorized as homophobic, transphobic, or non-anti-LGBT+ content. In a multilingual culture, code-mixing is a common occurrence, and the writings that result from it are occasionally written in scripts that are not native to the speaker's language [23]. Systems trained on monolingual data struggle with code-mixed material because it is challenging to switch codes at lexical and syntactic levels in the text. The Common Task uses text that is code-mixed in Dravidian languages - A introduces a fresh corpus of unmatched quality for sentiment analysis (Tamil, English, Tamil- English). Task - B, which is shared, addresses homophobia and transphobia. The goal of detection is to isolate non-anti-LGBT+ content and homophobic, transphobic, and other offensive language from the corpus [24]. The destructive rhetoric used against LGBTQ+ people is known as "hate speech," and it includes both homophobia and transphobia.

Homophobic Language. It as a specific type of gender-based harassment statement that includes the practice of derogatory terms such as "fag," "homo," or "that's so gay" in reference to anyone who identify as gay, lesbian, bisexual, queer, or gender non-conforming [13, 14]. A posture of hatred against homosexuals, male or female is the most popular definition of homophobia [15]. Lesbophobia, gayphobia, and biphobia are three families of phobias that target various target groups. However, there is a distinction between general and specific homophobia.

Transphobic Language. Although there are minute differences, the reader may wonder why homophobia and transphobia shouldn't be included together. Contrary to popular belief, transphobia and homophobia [16] are not the same. A person who was given the gender of a woman at birth but now identifies as a man is an example of a heterosexual person. Nowadays, a lot of transgender persons refer to their gender identity in the present tense rather than their gender at birth by using the terminology of sexual orientation. Teenage transgender people face much greater marginalization and lack access to resources than their LGB counterparts in a number of different nations throughout the world. Given that numerous laws intended to protect LGB people do not include protections related to gender uniqueness or appearance [17, 18]. People who are transphobic may or may not also be homophobic. They may be homosexual or straight. In India, transgender persons have a constitutional basis because of mythology and their affiliations to Hindu gods, they must be accorded particular treatment. LGBQ individuals, however, are unable to be married in India. In Tamil Nadu, the word "homophobia" is forbidden than their LGB colleagues in some global regions. People who are transphobic may or may not also be homophobic. They may be homosexual or straight. LGBQ individuals, however, are unable to be married in India. In Tamil Nadu, the word "homophobia" is forbidden.

Non-LGBT+hating Material. Information that is not anti-LGBT+ can be divided into three categories, all of which are crucial for the study of homophobia and transphobia. The toxic online disinhibition and a lack of empathy [3] are linked to homophobic/transphobic cyberbullying. Second, by examining non-anti-LGBT+ remarks, Development of preventative and interventionary programs aid in changing the online behaviors and opinions of social media users.

3.1 Models

Word Embedding –BERT Model. A method for minimizing the amount of elements in the input is feature selection. Variety of feature extraction approaches are employed with word embedding such as BERT in the proposed work. BERT uses masked language models to enable pretrained deep bidirectional interpretations.

BERT embedding is word embedding that generates vectors depend on both the sentence's context and the word's meaning [19]. The universal language model BERT generates a summarised word vectors at the inter- and intra level. By using bidirectional self-attention transformers, BERT, as opposed to static, non-contextualized word embedding, captures both short- and long-span contextual dependency in the input text. The [CLS] token and [SEP] token are concatenated at the beginning and end of the sentence after it has been initially tokenized in the BERT embedding, respectively. Then, each token has a 768-byte embedding created for it (Figs. 1 and 2).

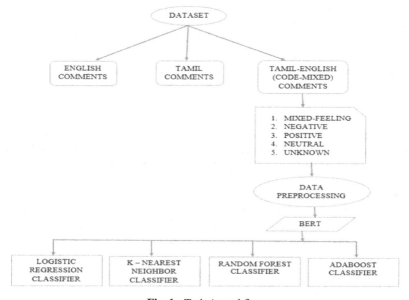

Fig. 1. Task A workflow

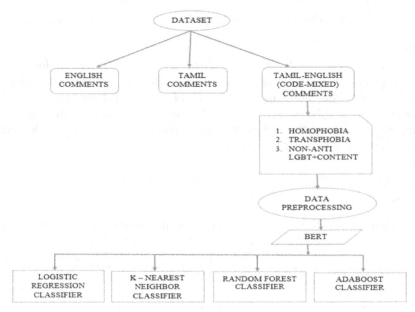

Fig. 2. Task B workflow

3.2 Classifiers

Logistic Regression One of the core machine learning algorithms is LR, a probabilistic classifier used for the purpose of classifying data. In essence, it is the logistic function-based transformed a linear regression style. In order to determine the class probability, it first accepts legitimate data as input, increases each by a load, and then delivers the generated summation to the nonlinear function, also known as the logistic function [20]. To predict the result, the classifier uses linear combinations of input. The logistic function is used to predict the likelihood of the specific class. The outcome of a logistic regression depends on the input and the associated system. Given that neural pathways can be seen as a collection of several LR classifications, logistic regression and neural networks have a tight link. As opposed to the operational classifier Nave Bayes, LR is a computational method. LR is clearly more resistant to correlated features [21] but Nave Bayes keeps strict restrictions on conditional independence. It indicates that the weight W will be distributed among the features as W1, W2, and W3, respectively, when there are numerous features, such as F1, F2, and F3, that are positively correlated.

Random Forest. As an ensemble classifier, random forest uses bootstraps, which are samples drawn at random from the training set, to construct its predictions. Bootstraps are a group of different decision trees that have all been trained using training datasets that are the same size as the training set. Following the construction of a tree, a set of bootstraps is used as the test set, which omits any particular record from the baseline dataset (out-of-bag (OOB) samples). The classification error rate across all test sets is the OOB estimate of the predictive performance. RF showed substantial advantages over other systems in managing extremely nonlinearly connected data, noise tolerance, adjustment easiness, and the capability for efficient massively parallel processing. Another crucial element that RF offers is an intrinsic feature selection step that is used before the classification task in order to condense the space of variables by assigning a value to each feature's relevance. In comparison to other machine learning algorithms, for tree structures, tree pairing, identity, and comment, RF follows specific guidelines. Additionally, it is resistant to overloading and is considered to be more stable when outliers are present and in very high-dimensional parameter spaces. With the same properties as DT, RF model has been assessed.

K-Nearest Neighbor. The classification task is where KNN is most frequently utilized, while it can also be used for regression problems. The KNN algorithm maintains all available data and categorizes new data points based on similarities. It suggests that as fresh data arrives; it can be easily categorized using the KNN algorithm into a suitable category. The KNN approach places the new case in the category that most closely resembles the categories that are currently accessible because it expects that the new incoming data will be linked to the existing examples. KNN is a quasi method [22]. Since it makes no assumptions about the underlying data, Because it saves the dataset and performs an operation on it when classifying data, this method is frequently referred to as a sloppy learner's algorithm rather than automatically recognizing from the training set. KNN method only retains the dataset during training; as new data is encountered, it sorts it into groups that are fairly similar to the present dataset. Applying consistent weights, KNN has been employed for classification with 3, 4, and 9 neighbors.

AdaBoost Classifier. AdaBoost derives its feature importance from the feature importance that its base classifier provides. The average feature importance provided by each Decision Tree, assuming you utilize one as your base classifier, determines how important a feature is to AdaBoost. It is very similar to the widespread method of assessing feature relevance by looking at a forest of trees. It takes advantage of the fact that a bigger proportion of input samples generate final predictions as a result of features identified at the top of the tree, and expected fraction may be used to calculate the relative relevance of a feature. Adaptive Boosting, often known as AdaBoost algorithm, is a Boosting method used as an Ensemble Method in Machine Learning. It is known as adaptive boosting because each instance receives a new set of weights, with higher weights given to examples that were mistakenly categorized. As the input parameters are not jointly optimized, Adaboost is less susceptible to overfitting. Adaboost can be used to increase the accuracy of weak classifiers. Adaboost is now used to categories text and graphics instead of binary classification issues.

4   Performance Evaluation

Precision, recall, F1-score, Support and Accuracy results from tests using the BERT Embedding model which displayed are machine learning classifiers for sentiment classification and identifying inappropriate language. The table describes the metrics (precision, recall, and F1-score) are annually calculated for each class, then combined using a macro-average. As a result, the statistic does not take into consideration the property of misclassification and treats all classes equally. A weighted sum employs metrics from each class, like a macro average does, but its contribution to the average is weighted based on how many examples are available for that class (Tables 1, 2, 3, 4, 5 and Figs. 3, 4).

Table 1. BERT Embedding using Logistic Regression Classifier

Class	Precision	Recall	F1 Score	Support
Mixed - Emotions	0.25	0.04	0.07	52
Negative	0.55	0.51	0.53	131
Positive	0.65	0.80	0.72	321
Neutral	0.61	0.67	0.64	110
Unknown	0.47	0.26	0.34	69
Mac	0.57	0.46	0.46	691
Weighted	0.58	0.61	0.58	

Table 2. BERT Embedding using K-Nearest Neighbor Classifier

Class	Precision	Recall	F1 Score	Support
Mixed - Emotions	0.32	0.13	0.19	52
Negative	0.58	0.52	0.55	139
Positive	0.66	0.86	0.72	321
Neutral	0.61	0.65	0.63	110
Unknown	0.56	0.32	0.41	69
Mac	0.55	0.48	0.50	691
Weighted	0.60	0.62	0.60	

Table 3. BERT Embedding using Random Forest Classifier

Class	Precision	Recall	F1 Score	Support
Mixed - Emotions	0.25	0.12	0.16	52
Negative	0.48	0.42	0.44	139
Positive	0.60	0.78	0.68	321
Neutral	0.58	0.51	0.54	110

(continued)

Table 3. (*continued*)

Class	Precision	Recall	F1 Score	Support
Unknown	0.43	0.22	0.29	69
Mac	0.47	0.41	0.42	691
Weighted	0.53	0.56	0.53	

Table 4. BERT Embedding using AdaBoost Classifier

Class	Precision	Recall	F1 Score	Support
Mixed - Emotions	0.22	0.10	0.13	52
Negative	0.58	0.47	0.52	139
Positive	0.65	0.78	0.71	321
Neutral	0.58	0.56	0.57	110
Unknown	0.38	0.33	0.35	69
Mac	0.48	0.45	0.46	691
Weighted	0.57	0.59	0.57	

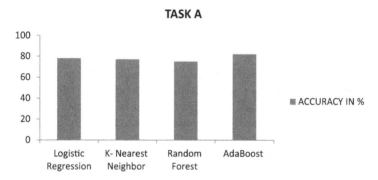

Fig. 3. Evaluation of Different Classifier with BERT Embedding for Task A

Table. 5. BERT Embedding using Different Classifiers for 3 Class Dataset

Classifier	Pmac	Rmac	F1mac	Pw	Rw	F1w
Logistic Regression	0.61	0.36	0.38	0.84	0.89	0.85
K – Nearest Neighbor	0.49	0.52	0.50	0.85	0.83	0.84

(*continued*)

Table. 5. (*continued*)

Classifier	Pmac	Rmac	F1mac	Pw	Rw	F1w
Random Forest	0.49	0.60	0.52	0.87	0.81	0.83
AdaBoost	0.62	0.38	0.39	0.85	0.88	0.85

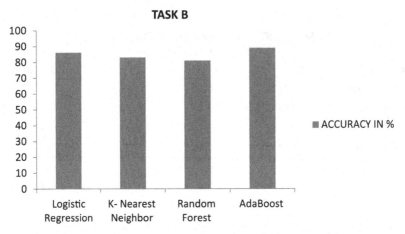

Fig. 4. Evaluation of Different Classifier with BERT Embedding for Task B

5   Conclusion

The work includes a dataset with elevated, trained evaluation of homophobic and transphobic content from linguistic YouTube comments. Many efforts to detect umbrella hate speech have not focused on detecting homophobia and transphobia. In a dataset of English and Tamil-language YouTube comments, Efficiency of big transformer-based pre-trained models has been tested to identify homophobia and transphobia. The final dataset is trivial in comparison to other labelled data used for other classification. The findings of the experiments showed that multilingual BERT, which had not previously been exposed to code mixing, excelled in both language challenges and the code-mixed test. From the above analysis, AdaBoost Classifier gives the better accuracy in place of detecting the toxic languages which is offensive towards Homophobia and Transphobia individuals using BERT Model. Future options for the work include building the dataset for more Dravidian languages. By crawling and annotating more social media data sets, Tamil dataset have to expanded significantly. To enhance the performance of the classifiers, it is intended to investigate semi-supervised and incremental methods. Additionally, it is decided to investigate the relationship between sarcasm and anti-LGBT+ comments as our manual analysis revealed that many of these comments are ironic.

References

1. Gao, Z., Yada, S., Wakamiya, S., Aramaki, E.: Offensive language detection on video live streaming chat. In: Proceedings of the 28th International Conference on Computational Linguistics, pp. 1936–1940, Barcelona, Spain (Online). International Committee on Computational Linguistics (2020)
2. McConnell, E.A., Clifford, A., Korpak, A.K., Phillips, G., Birkett, M.: Identity, victimization, and support: Facebook experiences and mental health among lgbtq youth. Comput. Hum. Behav. **76**, 237–244 (2017). https://doi.org/10.10007/1234567890
3. Wright, M.F., Wachs, S.: Does empathy and toxic online disinhibition moderate the longitudinal association between witnessing and perpetrating homophobic cyberbullying? Int. J. Bully. Prevent. **3**(1) (2021)
4. Diefendorf, S., Bridges, T.: On the enduring relationship between masculinity and homophobia. Sexualities **23**(7), 1264–1284 (2020)
5. Larimore, S., Kennedy, I., Haskett, B., Arseniev Koehler, A.: Reconsidering annotator disagreement about racist language: Noise or signal? In: Proceedings of the Ninth International Workshop on Natural Language Processing for Social Media, pp. 81–90, Online. Association for Computational Linguistics (2021)
6. Ranjan, P., Raja, B., Priyadharshini, R., Balabantaray, R.C.: A comparative study on code-mixed data of Indian social media vs formal text. In: 2016 2nd International Conference on Contemporary Computing and Informatics (IC3I), pp. 608–611 (2016). https://doi.org/10.1109/IC3I.2016.7918035
7. Jose, N., Chakravarthi, B.R., Suryawanshi, S., Sherly, E., McCrae, J.P.A.: survey of current datasets for code-switching research. In: 2020 6th International Conference on Advanced Computing Communication Systems (ICACCS) (2020)
8. Vanmassenhove, E., Hardmeier, C., Way, A.: Getting gender right in neural machine translation. In: Proceedings of the 2018 Conference on Empirical Methods in Natural Language Processing, pp. 3003–3008. Brussels, Belgium. Association for Computational Linguistics (2018)
9. Prates, M.O.R., Avelar, P.H., Lamb, L.C.: Assessing gender bias in machine translation: a case study with google translate. Neural Comput. Appl. **32**(10), 6363–6381 (2020)
10. Chakravarthi, B.R.: HopeEDI: a multilingual hope speech detection dataset for equality, diversity, and inclusion. In: Proceedings of the Third Workshop on Computational Modeling of People's Opinions, Personality, and Emotion's in Social Media, pp.41–53. Barcelona, Spain (Online). Association for Computational Linguistics (2020)
11. Mandl, T., Modha, S., Kumar, M.A., Chakravarthi, B.R.: Overview of the HASOC Track at FIRE 2020: hate speech and offensive language identification in Tamil, Malayalam, Hindi, English and German. In: Forum for Information Retrieval Evaluation pp. 29–32. Association for Computing Machinery, New York, NY, USA, FIRE 2020 (2020). https://doi.org/10.1145/3441501.3441517
12. Chakravarthi, B.R., et al.: Findings of the shared task on offensive language identification in Tamil, Malayalam, and Kannada. In: Proceedings of the First Workshop on Speech and Language Technologies for Dravidian Languages, pp. 133–145. Kyiv. Association for Computational Linguistics (2021)
13. Meyer, E.J.: Gendered harassment in secondary schools: understanding teachers'(non) Interventions. Gender Educ. **20**(6), 555–570
14. Poteat, V.P., Rivers, I.: The use of homophobic language across bullying roles during adolescence. J. Appl. Develop. Psychol. **31**(2), 166–172 (2008)
15. Fra¨ıss´e, C., Barrientos, J.: The concept of homophobia: a psychosocial perspective. Sexologies **25**(4), e65–e69 (2016)

16. Graham, R., Berkowitz, B., Blum, R., Bockting, W., Bradford, J., de Vries, B., Makadon, H.: The health of lesbian, gay, bisexual, and transgender people: building a foundation for better understanding, vol. 10, p. 13128. Institute of Medicine, Washington, DC (2011)

17. McGuire, J.K., Anderson, C.R., Toomey, R.B., Russell, S.T.: School climate for transgender youth: a mixed method investigation of student experiences and school responses. J. Youth Adolesc. **39**(10), 1175–1188 (2010)

18. Hatchel, T., Valido, A., De Pedro, K.T., Huang, Y., Espelage, D.L.: Minority stress among transgender adolescents: the role of peer victimization, school belonging, and ethnicity. J. Child Fam. Stud. **28**(9), 2467–2476 (2019)

19. Devlin, J., Chang, M.-W., Lee, K., Toutanova, K.: BERT: Pre-training of deep bidirectional transformers for language understanding. In: Proceedings of the 2019 Conference of the North American Chapter of the Association for Computational Linguistics: Human Language Technologies, Volume 1 (Long and Short Papers), pp. 4171–4186. Minneapolis, Minnesota. Association for Computational Linguistics (2019)

20. Shah, K., Patel, H., Sanghvi, D., Shah, M.: A comparative analysis of logistic regression, random forest and KNN models for the text classification. Augment. Hum. Res. **5**(1), 1–16 (2020)

21. Jin, S., Pedersen, T.: Duluth UROP at SemEval-2018 task 2: Multilingual emoji prediction with ensemble learning and oversampling. In: Proceedings of The 12th International Workshop on Semantic Evaluation, Association for Computational Linguistics, New Orleans, Louisiana, pp. 482–485 (2018). https://doi.org/10.18653/v1/S18-1077, https://www.aclweb.org/anthology/S18-1077

22. Nongmeikapam, K., Kumar, W., Singh, M.P.: Exploring an efficient handwritten Manipuri meetei-mayek character recognition using gradient feature extractor and cosine distance based multiclass k-nearest neighbor classifier. In: Proceedings of the 14th International Conference on Natural Language Processing (ICON-2017), pp. 328–337. NLP Association of India, Kolkata, India (2017). https://www.aclweb.org/anthology/W17-7541

23. Chakravarthi, B.R., et al.: Dravidiancodemix: Sentiment analysis and offensive language identification dataset for Dravidian languages in code-mixed text. Lang. Resources Evalu. 1–42 (2022)

24. Stakic, I.: Homophobia and hate speech in Serbian public discourse: how nationalist myths and stereotypes influence prejudices against the LGBT minority. Master's thesis, Universitetet (2011)

Contextual Analysis of Tamil Proverbs for Automatic Meaning Extraction

Anita Ramalingam$^{(\boxtimes)}$ ⓘ and Subalalitha Chinnaudayar Navaneethakrishnan ⓘ

Department of Computing Technologies, SRM Institute of Science and Technology,
Kattankulathur 603 203, India
{anitar,subalaln}@srmist.edu.in

Abstract. The Tamil proverbs are treasure of Tamil language, as they are crisp and easy to remember the advice, awareness and knowledge embedded in it. The current Tamil generation does not know the cultural values of proverbs as they are oral and passed on from one generation to the other by word of mouth. Many Tamil proverbs are misunderstood by the global society and explanation is not known for vast amount of Tamil proverbs. The Tamil proverbs have many nuggets hidden, which need to be explored for the goodness of the society. There is no state of the art technique to extract the meaning of the Tamil proverbs till now. In the proposed research, the proverb dataset is created and the meanings of the Tamil proverbs are automatically extracted by contextual analysis. This work is evaluated with the precision, recall and F1-score and achieved 92% of precision, 87% of recall and 89% of F1-Score.

Keywords: Tamil proverb · Bidirectional Encoder Representations from Transformers (BERT) · Sentence Scoring · Meaning Extraction · Word Embedding · Sentence Embedding

1 Introduction

Tamil is an ancient language which is 4000–4500 years old, has transformed to a greater extent, in terms of both script and speech. Tamil has two kinds of literatures, such as, written Tamil literature and oral Tamil literature. Written Tamil literatures are written and preserved within a grammatical structure with the author's name. But oral literature does not have a specific author. Oral literature is followed in a country, in a particular region, in urban areas, in rural areas, without being written down. Since it is an unwritten literature, its author cannot be specified. Some of the Oral Tamil literature are Narrative stories, story songs, fairy tales, mythological stories, nursery rhymes for children, sports songs, professional songs, sowing songs, planting songs, harvest songs, wedding songs, Themmangu songs, Oppari songs, Maradi Songs, Gummi Songs, Udukkadi Songs, Villu Songs, Proverbs, Sayings, and Greetings. In the proposed research, the oral Tamil literature, proverbs are considered for computational analysis.

The Tamil language has many valuable proverbs, which are passed on from one generation to other. The current Tamil generation is unaware of many of these proverbs

Anand Kumar M et al. (Eds.): SPELLL 2022, CCIS 1802, pp. 231–243, 2023.
https://doi.org/10.1007/978-3-031-33231-9_16

and even if aware of few of them, they are misinterpreted and are used in the wrong contexts. Explanation of many proverbs are not available on the web but many have been used in stories and essays. The correct description and the meaning of these proverbs need to be automatically extracted from the contexts in which the proverbs are uttered. This will help making the global Tamil society aware of the proverbs. This work lays a foundation for automatic extraction of meaning for the Tamil proverbs using contextual analysis.

Tamil proverbs contain valuable information that can serve as a guide to even today's modern culture. Tamil proverb demonstrates that it is both a historical treasure and a solution provider for every element of life. When they are accessed on World Wide Web, its hidden valuable information will reach the global society. This is possible only if the Tamil proverbs are computationally analyzed. The contributions of this research is twofold:

1. Data set creation
2. Retrieving description from the context of the text using word and sentence embeddings.

The structure of the paper is organized as follows: Sect. 2 describes about BERT model. Section 3 presents the literature survey. Section 4 explains the proposed work. The result and discussions are given in Sect. 5. Section 6 explains about the conclusion.

2 Background

This section describes about Bidirectional Encoder Representations from Transformers (BERT) model. BERT makes use of Transformer, an attention mechanism that learns contextual relations between words or sub-words in a text [1]. BERT multilingual base model [2] is used in this research, which is a pretrained model on the top 104 languages. It is used to extract features from text data, such as word and sentence embedding vectors [3]. It has one input layer and 12 hidden layers.

Word embedding refers to a group of language modelling and feature learning approaches used in NLP to map words or phrases from a vocabulary to real-number vectors. It can recognize a word's context in a document, its semantic and syntactic similarities, and its relationship to other words, etc. BERT has an advantage over models like Word2Vec in that, while each word in Word2Vec has a fixed representation regardless of the context in which it appears, BERT generates word representations that are dynamically informed by the words around them.

Example 1

1. "நூலைப் போல சேலை தாயைப் போல பிள்ளை. (Nūlaip pōla cēlai tāyaip pōla piḷḷai)."
2. "நூல் கற்றவனே மேலவன். (Nūl karravaṉē mēlavaṉ)."

For the given two Tamil proverbs in Example 1, Word2Vec would create the same word embedding for the word "நூல் (Nūl)", however in BERT, the word embedding for "நூல் (Nūl)"ūl)" in the first proverb would be different from the second proverb.

3 Related Works

The literature survey has been done on the Tamil language and Literature, and sentence scoring approach, since the proposed work relies on these.

3.1 Works Related to Tamil Language and Literature

This section examines computational works carried out on Tamil language and literature. The search engine for the Thirukkural was proposed by Elanchezhiyan et al. [4], which retrieves couplets based on concepts, expanded query terms, and keywords. The evaluation metric was MAP, which received a score of 0.83. Using a rule-based method and context-free grammar to establish the rules, Madhavan et al. [5] categorized Tamil poems into four protocols termed "Paa." Tamil poems were parsed, an intermediate representation was constructed, and the poems were then divided into four groups. They were able to reach a categorization accuracy of 90%. Sridevi and Subashini [6] used a probabilistic neural network to classify 11th century Tamil handwritten writings. Before the classification, lines, words, characters segmentation and feature extraction were done using syntactic features. A total of 500 characters were used in the testing, with accuracy serving as the evaluation criterion and achieved 80.52% of accuracy.

Subalalitha and Ranjani [7] adopted a concept called Suthras, which can be found in the Tamil grammar text Nannool as well as in Sanskrit literature, for a crisp depiction of texts. They aimed to determine the semantic indices of Tamil documents by combining these notions with current text processing techniques such as RST and universal networking language. As features, the most frequent terms and synonyms were selected. Their dataset consisted of 1000 tourism-related Tamil documents, which were scored with 0.7 using the MAP measure. Prasath et al. [8] proposed a cross-language IR approach for a given user query in another language. A corpus-driven query suggestion approach for re-ranking was used on Tamil and English news collections of the Forum for Information Retrieval Evaluation (FIRE) corpora, with precision as the evaluation metric. Subalalitha and Anita [9] proposed a page ranking algorithm based on discourse relations, to retrieve web pages. The RST was applied to ascertain semantic relations between web pages, as well as hyperlinks in the web pages. In all, 500 Tamil and 50 English tourism web pages were tested, using precision as the evaluation metric.

Giridharan et al. [10] proposed a scheme to retrieve information from ancient Tamil texts inscribed in temples, and after that transform the epigraphy into current Tamil digital texts, along with their meaning. The Brahmi database was used as a dataset, and accuracy of 84.57% obtained. Sankaralingam et al. [11] put forward a methodology for IR for Tamil texts, using ontology to convert ontological structures into visual representations that aid retrieval. Lexical and semantic relations such as homonymy, synonymy, antonymy, and meronymy were used on their 50000-word general domain dataset. Thenmozhi and Aravindan [12] suggested an ontology-based cross-lingual IR system. Tamil queries were translated into English and the relevant documents were retrieved in English. Ambiguity was eliminated from Tamil and English queries with word-sense disambiguation and ontology, respectively. A Tamil-English bilingual dictionary, a Tamil morphological analyzer, and a named entity database were used to translate Tamil queries into English. Their methodology was evaluated for the agricultural domain, with precision as the evaluation metric.

Subalalitha and Poovammal [13] used the Naïve Bayes machine learning approach to create an automatic bilingual dictionary for the Thirukkural. They used G. U. Pope's English translation and commentary [14], as well as Dr. Solomon Pappaiya and Dr. M. Varadharajan's Tamil explanations [15]. They used precision as a metric for evaluation and received a score of 70%. Subalalitha [16] proposed an information extraction strategy for Kurunthogai, a Tamil literary work. Information was extracted from food, fauna, flora, waterbodies, vessels, verb unigrams, noun unigrams, adverb-verb bigrams, and adjective-noun bigrams. N-grams were extracted using a Tamil morphological analyzer. The author scored 88.8% using precision as the evaluation measure. Clustering of Thirukkural couplets based on discourse connectives was proposed by Anita and Subalalitha [17]. The machine learning algorithm used was K-means clustering. Cluster purity, Rand index, precision, recall, and F-score were used as evaluation metrics, resulting in 79% purity, 92% overall Rand index, 79% precision, 80% recall, and a 79% F-score.

A rule-based method for creating a discourse parser for the Thirukkural was proposed by Anita and Subalalitha [18]. Discourse connectives have been used as the features. The authors have used K-means machine learning algorithm for clustering the Thirukkural couplets. Cluster purity, Rand index, precision, recall and F-score were used as evaluation metrics and achieved 79% purity, 92% overall Rand index, 79% precision, 80% recall and 79% F-score. Saravanan [19] proposed a cluster-based Tamil document retrieval system using semantic indexing. The K-means algorithm was used on a dataset taken from the Tamil Language Consortium Repository. The author used F1-score as an evaluation metric and obtained 60%. A Tamil-English code switched sentiment annotated corpus was created by Bharathi et al. [20]. They have collected 15,744 YouTube comments for creating the dataset. Various machine learning and deep learning algorithms were used for determining the sentiments from YouTube posts. The authors have evaluated their work by using precision, recall and F1-score metrics.

A classification of troll meme was proposed by Suryawanshi and Chakravarthi [21] in Tamil language. They have used deep learning models for classification. The authors have used TamilMemes dataset. They have evaluated their work with the evaluation metric F1-score and obtained 55%. A discourse-based information retrieval system for the Tamil literary texts such as, Thirukkural and Naladiyar was proposed by Anita and Subalalitha [22]. The discourse structure was constructed and discourse-based inverted indexing, searching and ranking were performed for information retrieval. The work is compared with the Google search and keyword-based search. Mean Average Precision (MAP) was used to evaluate their work and achieved 89%. Tamil handwritten character recognition was proposed by Vinotheni et al. [23]. The authors have used modified convolution neural network model for this work. They have collected the dataset from various schools. They have evaluated their work with accuracy and obtained 97.07%.

Anita and Subalalitha [24] classified the Thirukkural into ten new categories called superclasses. The classifier was trained using Multinomial Naïve Bayes algorithm. Each superclass was further classified into two subcategories based on the didactic information. The proposed classification framework was evaluated using precision, recall and F-score metrics and achieved an overall F-score of 82.33% and a comparison analysis has been done with the Support Vector Machine, Logistic Regression and Random Forest algorithms. An IR system was built on top of the proposed system and the performance comparison has been done with the Google search and a locally built keyword search. The proposed classification framework has achieved a mean average precision score of 89%. Anita and Subalalitha [25] surveyed an automatic semantic interpretation framework for Tamil literary texts using discourse parsing by giving works on discourse parsing, text classification, discourse-based clustering and information retrieval, and Tamil language and Tamil literatures.

3.2 Works Related to Sentence Scoring Approach

This section explains about sentence scoring approach, summarization and selecting sentences from the context, since the proposed work relies on these approaches. Deoras et al. [26] proposed re-scoring strategy for capturing longer distance dependencies on English texts. Recurrent Neural Network model was used. English Broadcast News corpus was used as a dataset. Li et al. [27] proposed graph based sentence ranking method for summarization on English texts. They used TAC 2008 and 2009 benchmark datasets. They evaluated their work with Recall-Oriented Understudy for Gisting Evaluation (ROUGE). Ferreira et al. [28] used sentence scoring method for extractive text summarization on English texts. They performed assessment of 15 algorithms. They used three datasets, namely, CNN, Blog summarization and SUMMAC. They used ROUGE for evaluation.

Mikolov et al. [29] proposed efficient estimation of word representations in vector space on English texts and have done word similarity task. They used Recurrent Neural Net language model, and Feed forward Neural Network language model for their work. They used Google News corpus for training. They evaluated their work with accuracy. Vural et al. [30] proposed unsupervised sentimental analysis of movie reviews in Turkish language. They have extracted the sentences from the texts for sentiment analysis. They obtained data from a movie website, Beyazperde. They evaluated their work with accuracy. Ferreira et al. [31] proposed multi-document summarization using sentence clustering algorithm on English texts. They used DUC 2002 as a dataset for testing performance of their system. They calculated F-measure as evaluation metric.

Mesnil et al. [32] proposed sentimental analysis of movie reviews in English. They have done ensemble of generative and discriminative techniques. They compared their work with several machine learning algorithms. IMDB movie reviews was used as a dataset. Accuracy was used as evaluation metric. Van Britsom et al. [33] used data merging techniques for multi-document summarization on English texts. They used DUC2002 and DUC2005 as datasets. They evaluated their work with precision, recall and F1-score. Extractive text summarization was proposed by Babar and Patil [34] utilizing a Fuzzy logic Extraction method and Latent Semantic Analysis. They used a total of ten datasets. As evaluation measures, precision, recall, and F1-score were used.

Ren et al. [35] suggested a contextual relation based summarization neural network model for extractive text summarization on English texts. DUC2001, DUC2002, DUC2004, DUC2005, DUC2006, and DUC2007 were the datasets used. For the evaluation, the authors used the F1-score. Lee et al. [36] proposed the extractive text summarization by using sentence scoring, integer linear programming and title driven models. DUC01 and DUC02 were used as datasets. They used ROUGE as evaluation metric. Zhou et al. [37] extracted important sentences using sentence scoring approach for extractive document summarization. The recurrent neural network model and pre trained model, namely Bidirectional Encoder Representations from Transformers (BERT), were used on two datasets namely CNN/Daily Mail dataset and New York Times dataset for evaluating their work. They used ROUGE as evaluation metric. Annamoradnejad and Zoghi [3] proposed identification of humor in short text. The BERT model was used to generate sentence embedding in the given text. The authors have created the in house dataset with 200k short text. Their work was evaluated using F1-score and achieved 98.2%.

It can be observed that the sentence scoring was used in expository (essay type) texts. The English text follows Subject-Verb-Object (SVO) pattern. The proposed work processes Tamil texts along with the proverbs. Tamil expository texts follow both SVO and Subject-Object-Verb (SOV) pattern. Tamil proverbs on the other side neither follow SVO nor follow SOV pattern. Tamil is a free word order language and also Tamil texts are relatively rich in morphological variants. These challenges make processing of Tamil proverbs more difficult than processing the expository texts. The proposed work generate the description of Tamil proverbs automatically from the contexts in the text.

4 Proposed Work

4.1 Dataset Creation

Tamil proverb is a kind of oral Tamil literature. So the proverb dataset is created by collecting the proverbs from World Wide Web, stories, essays, etc. The meaning for some proverbs are directly appeared. Whereas some proverbs do not contain the meaning. Some proverbs are used in stories, essays and longer texts. That longer texts are also included in the dataset for finding the meaning of the unknown proverbs.

The dataset consists of 400 proverbs with explicit meaning, 400 longer texts which contains proverbs, and 200 proverbs with no meaning. The meaning of the proverbs are extracted from the longer texts using BERT's word embeddings and sentence embeddings.

4.2 Meaning Extraction for Tamil Proverbs

The automatic meaning of Tamil proverbs is extracted using BERT's word embeddings and sentence embeddings. Figure 1 depicts the proposed work's architecture diagram. The Tamil proverb is taken as input from the user. If the proverb's meaning is present in the dataset explicitly, it can be extracted directly. If the proverb's meaning is not given explicitly, it might be appeared in longer text. When the proverb appears in the middle of a text, context analysis is required to determine its meaning. BERT model's word

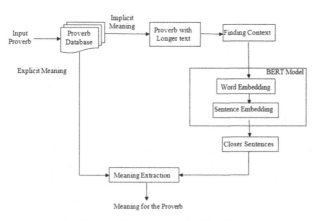

Fig. 1. Architecture Diagram for the Meaning Extraction

and sentence embeddings are used for finding the closer sentences in the context of the proverb, and the closer sentences are used for extracting the meaning of the proverb.

The proverb database is searched for the input Tamil proverb. If it has explicit meaning, it is extracted. Since the proverb given in Example 2 has the direct meaning in the proverb dataset, it is extracted directly.

Example 2

Tamil Proverb: அகத்தின் அழகு முகத்தில் தெரியும். **English Transliteration:** Akattiṉ aḻaku mukattil teriyum. **Output:** **Extracted Tamil Meaning:** ஒருவன் மனத்தில் நினைப்பதை அவன் முகமே காட்டிவிடும். **English Transliteration:** Oruvaṉ maṉattil niṉaippatai avaṉ mukamē kāṭṭiviṭum. **English Explanation:** His face shows what a person thinks in his mind.

If the input Tamil proverb is appeared in some other longer texts in the proverb dataset, such as stories, essays or in the explanation of other proverbs. In Example 3, the proverb P1 does not have a Tamil explanation in the proverb dataset. It is present in another proverb P2's description. The meaning of P1 is derived from P2's description.

Though the proverb may appear anywhere in the text, the proverb's meaning is assumed to be present in the preceding and succeeding sentences of the proverb. Hence the context from which the meaning is to be extracted is comprised of five sentences preceding the proverb and five sentences following the proverb. Example 3 shows the context which is chosen from the description of proverb P2. It contains the 10 sentences and the proverb.

Word embedding is created for all the words in the context. Each word has 768 dimensions of vectors. An easy method for obtaining a single vector for our entire sentence is to average the second to last hidden layer of each token, resulting in a single 768-length vector. Thus the sentence vector is generated for the 11 sentences: 1 Tamil proverb sentence, 5 preceding sentences and 5 succeeding sentences. The sentence vectors for the 11 sentences of context in Example 3 are created.

Then the sentence similarity is found by using cosine similarity. The cosine similarity is calculated between the vector of proverb and the vectors of the surrounding sentences. The closer sentences are identified based on the cosine similarity. The proverb's meaning is then extracted from the closer sentence. In Example 3, the sentence similarity for all the sentences in the context and the proverb are calculated. Since the sentence "ஒவ்வொரு எலியும் தனக்குத் தேவையானதை விட ஐந்து மடங்கு தானியத்தை அள்ளிக் கொண்டு செல்லுமாம்.' (Ovvoru eliyum taṉakkut tēvaiyāṉatai viṭa aintu maṭaṅku tāviyattai aḷḷik koṇṭu cellumām - Each rat can carry five times more grain than it needs)" has the high score, this sentence is extracted as meaning.

Example 3

P1:

Tamil Proverb:
அறுப்புக்காலத்தில் எலிக்கு ஐந்து பெண்சாதி.

English Transliteration:
Aṟuppuk kālattil elikku aintu peṇcāti.

P2:

Tamil Proverb:
ஆனைக்கு ஒரு காலம் வந்தால் பூனைக்கும் ஒரு காலம் வரும்.

English Transliteration:
Āṉaikku oru kālam vantāl pūṉaikkum oru kālam varum

Context:
யானைகளைக் கொண்டு கதிரடித்த பின்னர், பிரிந்த நெல்மணிகளைத் தனியாக எடுத்துத் தானியக்
கிடங்குகளில் சேமித்து வைத்திருப்பர். இப்போது தான் சிக்கல் துவங்குகிறது. சேமித்து
வைக்கப்பட்டுள்ள இந்த நெல்மணிகளைக் குறிவைத்து எலிகளின் பட்டாளம் படையெடுக்கத்
துவங்குகின்றது. ஒவ்வொரு எலியும் தனக்குத் தேவையானதை விட ஐந்து மடங்கு தானியத்தை
அள்ளிக் கொண்டு செல்லுமாம். இதனடிப்படையில் தான், "அறுப்புக் காலத்தில் எலிக்கு ஐந்து
பெண்சாதி"
என்ற பழமொழியே எழுந்தது எனலாம். கூட்டம் கூட்டமாக இவை புகுந்து நெல்மணிகளைத் திருடிக்
கொண்டு செல்வதை அப்படியே விட்டுவிட்டால், கிடங்கையே காலி செய்து விடும். எனவே இந்த
எலிகளைக் கூண்டோடு ஒழிக்க, பூனைகளைக் கொண்டுவந்து தானியக் கிடங்குக்குள் வைப்பர்.
பூனைகளும் கிடங்கிற்குள் வருகின்ற எலிகளை வேட்டையாடித் தின்றுவிடும்.
இவ்வாறாக கதிரடிக்கும் காலத்தில் யானையின் உதவியும் சேமிக்கும் காலத்தில் பூனையின் உதவியும்
மனிதருக்குத் தேவைப்பட்டது.

Output:
Tamil Proverb:
அறுப்புக்காலத்தில் எலிக்கு ஐந்து பெண்சாதி.

Extracted Tamil Meaning:
ஒவ்வொரு எலியும் தனக்குத் தேவையானதை விட ஐந்து மடங்கு தானியத்தை அள்ளிக் கொண்டு
செல்லுமாம்.

English Transliteration:
Ovvoru eliyum taṉakkut tēvaiyāṉatai viṭa aintu maṭaṅku tāṉiyattai aḷḷik koṇṭu cellumām.

English Explanation:
Each rat can carry five times more grain than it needs.

Meaning Extraction Algorithm for the proposed work is given below.

Meaning Extraction Algorithm

Input: Tamil proverbs

Output: Extraction of meaning for the proverbs in Tamil

   1. Get proverb from user, P1

   2. Match with the dataset

   3. if P1 has explicit meaning

              retrieve that meaning for P1

   4. else if P1 is the subpart of another text P2

       4.1. Let P1 as sentence i, Si

       4.2. Select sentences from contexts, Si-5, Si-4, Si-3,Si-2,Si-1 and Si+1,Si+2, Si+3, Si+4, Si+5

       4.3. Find the word embedding and sentence embedding of the sentences using BERT multilingual base model.

       4.4. Find the similarity of the sentences using cosine similarity and choose the closer sentence

       4.5. Generate meaning of the proverb P1 from the closer sentence

---

5 Result and Discussion

The proposed method is tested with 1000 Tamil proverbs. The explanation for 400 Tamil proverbs are given by the proposed system directly. 400 Tamil proverbs are used in the description of other texts. The meaning for these proverbs are extracted using concepts of BERT multilingual base model. The precision, recall, and F1-score metrics are used to evaluate this work. Equations (1), (2), and (3) are used to calculate precision, recall, and F1-score values and shown in Table 1. The value of the variable, C, is calculated using human judgment. About three domain experts have calculated these metrics, and the average has been taken and presented in Tables 1.

$$\text{Precision (P)} = \frac{\text{Number of meaning of the proverbs correctly extracted, (C)}}{\text{Number of meaning of the proverbs extracted, (M)}} \quad (1)$$

$$\text{Recall (R)} = \frac{\text{Number of meaning of the proverbs correctly extracted, (C)}}{\text{Number of relevant meaning of the proverbs present, (N)}} \quad (2)$$

$$\text{F1-Score (F)} \frac{2PR}{P + R} \quad (3)$$

Some of the texts which contains the meaning of the proverb are long and also the context size chosen is five. The relevant meaning for the proverb may have appeared outside the context. The correct meaning can never be extracted if there are no closer sentences found. This is the reason for the resulting precision and recall.

The model is compared with the RoBERTa model embeddings and the comparison graph is given in Fig. 2. The F1-scores of BERT and RoBERTa are compared and it shows that the BERT model gives the good F1-score.

Table 1. Precision, Recall and F1-score for the proposed method

Number of Proverbs (N)	Correctly Extracted (C)	Extracted (M)	Precision P = C/M (%)	Recall R = C/N (%)	F1-score F = $\frac{2PR}{P+R}$ (%)
800	694	755	91.9	86.7	89.2

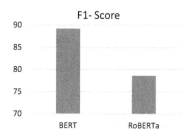

Fig. 2. Comparison of BERT and RoBERTa models

6 Conclusions

Tamil proverbs were coined on the experiences of earlier Tamil speaking generations. Most of the Tamil proverbs are metaphors and the current generation may misunderstand its real meaning behind. This experiment lays the groundwork for attaining automatic meaning extraction for unknown Tamil proverbs by semantic analysis of the stories, essays etc., that contain the proverbs. A transfer learning approach, BERT has been used for this purpose and achieved 92% of precision, 87% of recall and 89% of F1-Score. This work can be further used by many Natural Language Processing applications, such as, Information Retrieval System, Summary Generation System, and Question Answering System.

References

1. Devlin, J., Chang, M.W., Lee, K., Toutanova, K.: BERT: Pre-training of Deep Bidirectional Transformers for Language Understanding. arXiv preprint arXiv:1810.04805, 2018
2. Tsai, H., Riesa, J., Johnson, M., Arivazhagan, N., Li, X., Archer, A.: Small and Practical BERT Models for Sequence Labeling. arXiv preprint arXiv:1909.00100 (2019)
3. Annamoradnejad, I., Zoghi, G.: Colbert: Using BERT Sentence Embedding for Humor Detection. arXiv preprint arXiv:2004.12765 (2020)
4. Elanchezhiyan, K., Geetha, T.V., Ranjani, P., Karky, M.: Kuralagam - Concept Relation based Search Engine for Thirukkural. In: Tamil Internet Conference, pp. 19–23. University of Pennsylvania, Philadelphia, USA (2011)
5. Madhavan, K.V., Nagarajan, S., Sridhar, R.: Rule based classification of tamil poems. Int. J. Inform. Educ. Technol. **2**(2), 156 (2012)
6. Sridevi, N., Subashini, P.: Optimized framework for classification of 11th century handwritten ancient tamil scripts using computational intelligence. Int. J. Comput. Sci. **2**(2), 14–23 (2013)

7. Subalalitha, C.N., Ranjani, P.: A unique indexing technique for discourse structures. J. Intell. Syst. **23**(3), 231–243 (2014)
8. Prasath, R., Sarkar, S., O'Reilly, P.: improving cross language information retrieval using corpus based query suggestion approach. In: Gelbukh, A. (ed.) CICLing 2015. LNCS, vol. 9042, pp. 448–457. Springer, Cham (2015). https://doi.org/10.1007/978-3-319-18117-2_33
9. Subalalitha, C.N., Anita, R.: An approach to page ranking based on discourse structures. J. Commun. Softw. Syst. **12**(4), 195–200 (2016)
10. Giridharan, R., Vellingiriraj, E.K., Balasubramanie, P.: Identification of tamil ancient characters and information retrieval from temple epigraphy using image zoning. In: 2016 International Conference on Recent Trends in Information Technology (ICRTIT), pp. 1–7. IEEE (2016)
11. Sankaralingam, C., Rajendran, S., Kavirajan, B., Kumar, M.A., Soman, K.P.: Onto-thesaurus for tamil language: ontology based intelligent system for information retrieval. In: 2017 International Conference on Advances in Computing, Communications and Informatics (ICACCI), p. 2396. IEEE (2017)
12. Thenmozhi, D., Aravindan, C.: Ontology-based tamil-english cross-lingual information retrieval system. Sādhanā **43**(10), 1–14 (2018)
13. Subalalitha, C.N., Poovammal, E.: Automatic Bilingual Dictionary Construction for Tirukural. Appl. Artific. Intell. **32**(6), 558–567 (2018)
14. Project Madurai (2002). https://www.projectmadurai.org/pm_etexts/pdf/pm0153.pdf
15. Thirukkural, 15 May 2010. https://thirukkural.gokulnath.com/#/thirukkuralchapters/1/thiruk kurals
16. Subalalitha, C.N.: Information extraction framework for kurunthogai. Sādhanā **44**(7), 1–6 (2019)
17. Anita, R., Subalalitha, C.N.: An approach to cluster Tamil literatures using discourse connectives. In: 2019 IEEE 1st International Conference on Energy, Systems and Information Processing (ICESIP), pp. 1–4. IEEE (2019)
18. Anita, R., Subalalitha, C.N.: Building discourse parser for Thirukkural. In: Proceedings of the 16th International Conference on Natural Language Processing, pp. 18–25 (2019)
19. Saravanan, M.S.: Semantic document clustering based indexing for tamil language information retrieval system. J. Critical Rev. **7**(14), 2999–3007 (2020)
20. Chakravarthi, B.R., Muralidaran, V., Priyadharshini, R., McCrae, J.P.: Corpus creation for sentiment analysis in code-mixed tamil-english text. In: Proceedings of the 1st Joint Workshop on Spoken Language Technologies for Under-resourced languages (SLTU) and Collaboration and Computing for Under-Resourced Languages (CCURL), pp. 202–210. European Language Resources Association, Marseille, France (2020)
21. Suryawanshi, S., Chakravarthi, B.R.: Findings of the shared task on troll meme classification in tamil. In: Proceedings of the First Workshop on Speech and Language Technologies for Dravidian Languages, pp. 126–132 (2021)
22. Ramalingam, A., Navaneethakrish, S.C.: A discourse-based information retrieval for Tamil literary texts. J. Inform. Commun. Technol. **20** (2021). https://doi.org/10.32890/jict2021. 20.3.4
23. Vinotheni, C., Lakshmana Pandian, S., Lakshmi, G.: Modified convolutional neural network of tamil character recognition. In: Tripathy, A., Sarkar, M., Sahoo, J., Li, KC., Chinara, S. (eds.) Advances in Distributed Computing and Machine Learning. LNNS, vol. 127. Springer, Singapore (2021). https://doi.org/10.1007/978-981-15-4218-3_46
24. Ramalingam, A., Navaneethakrishnan, S.C.: A Novel classification framework for the Thirukkural for building an efficient search system. J. Intell. Fuzzy Syst. **42**(3), 2397–2408 (2021)
25. Ramalingam, A., Navaneethakrishnan, S.C.: An analysis on semantic interpretation of tamil literary texts. J. Mobile Multimedia **18**(3), 661–682 (2022)

26. Deoras, A., Mikolov, T., Church, K.: A fast re-scoring strategy to capture long-distance dependencies. In: Proceedings of the 2011 Conference on Empirical Methods in Natural Language Processing, pp. 1116–1127 (2011)
27. Li, X., Du, L., Shen, Y.D.: Update summarization via graph-based sentence ranking. IEEE Trans. Knowl. Data Eng. **25**(5), 1162–1174 (2012)
28. Ferreira, R., et al.: Assessing sentence scoring techniques for extractive text summarization. Expert Syst. Appl. **40**(14), 5755–5764 (2013)
29. Mikolov, T., Chen, K., Corrado, G., Dean, J.: Efficient Estimation of Word Representations in Vector Space. arXiv preprint arXiv:1301.3781 (2013)
30. Vural, A.G., Cambazoglu, B.B., Senkul, P., Tokgoz, Z.O.: A framework for sentiment analysis in turkish: application to polarity detection of movie reviews in Turkish. In: Gelenbe, E., Lent, R. (eds.) Computer and Information Sciences III: 27th International Symposium on Computer and Information Sciences, pp. 437–445. Springer London, London (2013). https://doi.org/10.1007/978-1-4471-4594-3_45
31. Ferreira, R., et al.: A multi-document summarization system based on statistics and linguistic treatment. Expert Syst. Appl. **41**(13), 5780–5787 (2014)
32. Mesnil, G., Mikolov, T., Ranzato, M.A., Bengio, Y.: Ensemble of Generative and Discriminative Techniques for Sentiment Analysis of Movie Reviews. arXiv preprint arXiv:1412.5335 (2014)
33. Van Britsom, D., Bronselaer, A., De Tre, G.: Using data merging techniques for generating multidocument summarizations. IEEE Trans. Fuzzy Syst. **23**(3), 576–592 (2014)
34. Babar, S.A., Patil, P.D.: Improving performance of text summarization. Procedia Comput. Sci. **46**, 354–363 (2015)
35. Ren, P., Chen, Z., Ren, Z., Wei, F., Ma, J., de Rijke, M.: Leveraging contextual sentence relations for extractive summarization using a neural attention model. In: Proceedings of the 40th International ACM SIGIR Conference on Research and Development in Information Retrieval, pp. 95–104 (2017)
36. Lee, D., Verma, R., Das, A., Mukherjee, A.: Experiments in Extractive Summarization: Integer Linear Programming, Term/Sentence Scoring, and Title-driven Models. arXiv preprint arXiv:2008.00140 (2020)
37. Zhou, Q., Yang, N., Wei, F., Huang, S., Zhou, M., Zhao, T.: A joint sentence scoring and selection framework for neural extractive document summarization. IEEE/ACM Trans. Audio, Speech, Language Process. **28**, 671–681 (2020)

Question Answering System for Tamil Using Deep Learning

Betina Antony[1]([✉])[ID] and NR Rejin Paul[2]

[1] Computer Engineering, Central Polytechnic College,
Taramani, Chennai 600113, TN, India
betinaantony@gmail.com
[2] Department of Computer Science and Engineering, RMKCET, Puduvoyal,
Thiruvallur 601206, TN, India
rejinpaulcse@rmkcet.ac.in

Abstract. Tamil, a Dravidian language family member, is widely spoken in numerous Indian states. But languages like Tamil, are underrepresented on the web. Many NLP models perform worse with these languages when compared to English, the effects of which lead to subpar experiences in many web applications for most of the users. The number of Tamil websites has grown and continues to expand. Tamil newspapers, periodicals, and e-journals are examples. Therefore Tamil Question Answering System will be beneficial to many people who are in the rural areas and also for those who prefer our native Tamil Language. This paper aims to create a Question Answering System in Tamil using deep learning techniques, starting from question processing through an interface, retrieving the relevant context for the given question and finally the answer is displayed after appropriate processing. The model is evaluated using a manually created test dataset and the metrics are analyzed.

Keywords: Question Answering System · Deep Learning · BERT · Natural Language Processing

1 Introduction

Many current information retrieval systems are specifically built for users who are unfamiliar with document collecting, document representation, and the usage of Boolean operators. The following are the primary requirements for these systems: first, enters a full-text information retrieval system, which is a system that automatically indexes every word in a document. Second, the system rates the retrieved documents based on their likelihood of being relevant to the user. Third, the technology allows for the automated reformulation of the search statement in response to user feedback. Search engines, on the other hand, obtain the entire page, leaving the extraction of the real information necessary to answer the question to the user. As a result, answering the user's natural language query utilizing information from the relevant document of a collection of papers or the relevant websites is a crucial demand for many users. In other words, consumers want

Anand Kumar M et al. (Eds.): SPELLL 2022, CCIS 1802, pp. 244–252, 2023.
https://doi.org/10.1007/978-3-031-33231-9_17

a system that can retrieve quick replies to natural language inquiries. The construction of such a system based on documents retrieved through search engines is an important issue of research in the natural language processing field, and significant work has been done in the field of Question Answering systems in recent years by many researchers.

Although modern algorithms, particularly deep learning-based algorithms, have made significant progress in text and picture categorization, they have yet to handle problems that require logical thinking. The question-answering problem is a good example. There has recently been some development in this subject with the advent of memory and attention-based architectures. However, with the ongoing development, there is much more room for improvement. The analysis of possible deep learning algorithms for question answering has been completed in this project.

A question-answering system often requires an analytical grasp of the query as well as background information inquiries. According to the diverse sources of background knowledge, it may be split into document-based question answering and knowledge-based question answering. The previous challenge is known as machine reading comprehension. The computer must search for answers to questions from a specific context depending on the questions' comprehension.

This project's study focuses on tackling a factoid type QA challenge in Tamil. Because of the morphological diversity of the language and the lack of capitalization in proper nouns, designing the QA System for Tamil is a difficult undertaking. This project presents numerous strategies for each phase of the QA system process for Tamil-like natural languages. Language processing methods developed for the English language have not proved helpful for other languages. This fact compels us to investigate the Tamil language's distinctive features. Using the identified distinctive traits, current methodologies may be adjusted to apply to the Tamil language.

2 Related Works

Various ways for producing Question Answering Systems, beginning with fundamental NLP, have been addressed [3]. They also investigated the algorithm-based technique for improved outcomes, and this research eventually leads to the newly presented Deep Learning approaches. The implementation details and numerous adjustments in these algorithms that resulted in improved outcomes were also explained. The suggested models were tested on twenty tasks from Facebook's babI dataset. A mixed-language online question-answering system has been introduced. This system also analyses the user's mixed-language question and provides an answer, as well as a strategy for decoding English mixed with three different Indian languages: Telugu, Tamil, and Hindi [4]. To lessen data complexity, they are converting the code mixed terms into English. Following this, featuring is applied to them. Deep learning methods such as Recurrent Neural Network (RNN) and Hierarchical Attention Network (HAN) are utilized for question categorization. The confusion matrix is a statistic used to evaluate

RNN and HAN. This system is supported by the internet. In the future, it may be utilized to gather additional code-mixed questions and forecast answer data using this improvised approach.

A probabilistic quasi-synchronous language has been constructed, from which replies may be created by matching with the query using a loose-but-predictable syntactic transformation [6]. Work has been done to provide a unique probabilistic strategy to capture context alignment [5]. This study employs tree-edit operation methods on dependency parse trees to facilitate comprehension of broader contexts. The system was designed to perform the matching procedure with the fewest edit sequences from the dependency parse trees [7]. This allows you to quickly match the question and response phrases. Work has been done on feature engineering-based approaches that incorporate a Support Vector Machine with tree kernels into the process of discriminate tree-edit feature extraction [2]. Furthermore, several external resources can aid in improving response selection performance. The models artificially aggregated the numerous lexical-semantic properties estimated by Word-Net. The semantic significance of the relevant terms between inquiry and response phrases can be used to match them [1]. Although non-Deep Learning methods have achieved good performance for the task of answer selection, they are unable to deal with multi-language answer selection problems, which may be inefficient because non-DL answer selection methods always require a significant amount of handcraft effort and knowledge. To calculate the vectored representation of questions and answers, Convolution Neural Networks were utilized instead of typical bag-of-words. They began by applying deep learning to a Knowledge-Based QA system [8]. This mostly addresses single-relationship questions, which are prevalent on many community websites. "Who is India's president?" is an example of such a query. as well as "Who founded the sport of cricket?" They used a semantic-based CNN architecture (CNNSM) to train two alternative mapping models: The first model connects a query mention to an entity in the knowledge base, whereas the second model translates a relation pattern to a relation.

3   System Architecture

This section introduces the QA system's "Retriever-Reader" design, as seen in Fig. 1. Retriever is used to retrieve relevant papers related to a particular topic and may be seen as an Information retrieval system, whereas Reader seeks to conclude the final answer from the obtained materials. They are two essential components of a contemporary question-answering system. Furthermore, some other modules, denoted by dashed lines, can be incorporated into a QA system, such as Document Pre-processing, which filters and re-ranks reviewed documents in a fine-grained manner to select the most relevant ones and Answer Post-processing, which determines the final answer among multiple answer candidates. To make our statements more understandable, we present a current QA system in this Retriever-Reader form.

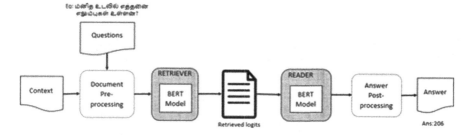

Fig. 1. Architecture of Question Answering System

3.1   Modules

Document Pre-processing. Pre-processing data is one of the challenging parts of the overall system. Text inputs need to be transformed to numerical tokens and arranged in the form of Tensors before feeding as input to the model. The pre-processing transformations are implemented by using various libraries present in the model (Fig. 2).

- Removing punctuation - In order to retrieve relevant information, full stops, commas, and other punctuation are unnecessary. As a result, these are isolated from the context and inquiry of the user.
- Truncation - Truncation is a part of stemming which broadens our search to include various word endings and spellings.
- Stemming - Words can appear in different conjugations (அவர்கள், அவர்). As they may well appear in different forms within in a document, such words are reduced to a base form.
- Padding - Padding is done to make all the inputs in the similar size. Since every sentence in the text has not the same number of words, padding is done. If a sentence is longer then we can drop some words.
- Tagging entities - Entities are names that are frequently extremely relevant to the question. These are included in the query.
- Removing stopwords - Stopwords are regularly used words that have no bearing on the text. Articles such as 'இந்த','இது','என' . As a result, these terms are filtered out.
- Striding - Stride refers to how many characters you want to move forward after the first character is retrieved. The value of stride is set to 1 by default.
- Offset Mapping - The offset mapping returns a tuple specifying the start and end positions of the token in relation to the original token.

Retriever. A retriever is in charge of locating appropriate replies to the user's query. To begin, it attempts to extract the important phrases from the query. It then employs these to get suitable solutions. Questions and contexts are encoded in the same vector space by the retriever model. Retrievers assist the Reader

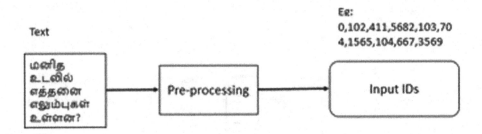

Fig. 2. Pre-processing

in narrowing the scope to smaller chunks of text where a specific query may be answered (Fig. 3). They employ some straightforward but quick algorithms. To handle a huge number of contexts, we can utilise algorithms like TF-IDF or BM25, as well as embedding-based techniques. Various Natural Language Processing (NLP) approaches are employed to convert a user's inquiry into the type of query that the retriever can process. These retriever phases aid in the creation of a query, which is subsequently sent to the text store. The retriever collects relevant documents connected to the query and forwards them to the reader in order to derive a response to the user's question.

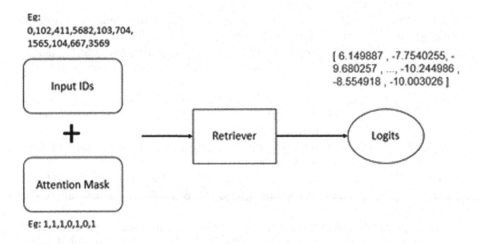

Fig. 3. Retriever

Reader. A Reader searches over the retrieved logits returned by retrievers to find the best replies. With its start and finish positions, the reader assists the question answering system in extracting the response span from the context (Fig. 4. They employ strong yet time-consuming deep learning algorithms. Deep learning models such as BERT, Roberta, and XLMRoBERTa were trained on SQuAD-like problems using Transformers. The Reader takes numerous passages as input and delivers probabilistic replies. A reader must derive a response from the documents he or she gets. It attempts to grasp both the query and the context using a proper language model and extracts the best relevant answer from the situation.

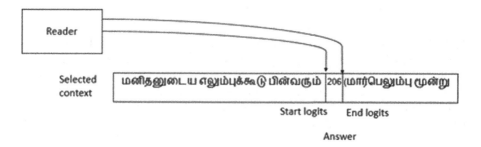

Fig. 4. Reader

Answer Post-processing. Post-processes convert the logits whose similarity values match with the question to answers that are present in the original contexts. These are the base post processing functions for models that only return start and end logits.

4   Experiment and Results

4.1   Datasets

The Dataset is taken from the following sources (Table 1)

Table 1. Datasets

Dataset	No. of Data Entries	Language
Chaii	1114	Tamil and Hindi
MLQA	5425	Hindi
XQuAD	1190	Hindi
SQuAD	4768	Tamil

Chaii. The chaii-Hindi and Tamil Question Answering dataset has been used for building a system for Question Answering for Tamil. This dataset is constructed from wikipedia articles. It contains a total of 1,114 data entries. Among which there are 764 data entries in Hindi and 364 entries in Tamil. Only the Tamil data entries has been used for building the Question Answering System.

MLQA. Multilingual Question Answering (MLQA) is a benchmark dataset for assessing cross-lingual question-answering ability. MLQA is made up of over 5K extractive QA cases (12K in English) in SQuAD format across seven languages: German, Spanish, English, Arabic, Hindi, Vietnamese, Hindi, and Simplified Chinese. MLQA is very parallel, with QA instances running in parallel across four distinct languages on average.

XQuAD. The Cross-lingual Question Answering Dataset, abbreviated as XQuAD, is a benchmark dataset for assessing cross-lingual question-answering efficiency. The dataset includes 240 sections and 1190 question-answer combinations from the SQuAD v1.1 development set, as well as their translations into 10 languages: German, Vietnamese, Greek, Thai, Chinese, Russian, Turkish, Arabic, Spanish, and Hindi. As a consequence, the dataset is parallel in all 11 languages.

SQuAD. The Stanford Question Answering Dataset is abbreviated as a squad. The SQuAD consists of a set of question-answer pairs extracted from Wikipedia articles. The right answers to questions in SQuAD can be any sequence of tokens in the provided text. Because questions and answers are generated by humans via crowdsourcing. SQuAD v1.1 has 107,785 question-answer pairs spread across 536 articles.

4.2 Models Used

4.3 BERT

BERT, or Bidirectional Encoder Representations from Transformers, is a natural language processing machine learning technique. BERT uses surrounding words in the given text to establish context. Thus, it is a context based model. The BERT framework was first trained using Wikipedia material. With question and answer datasets, this model may be fine-tuned even further. BERT is a deep learning model in which every output element is related to every input element and the weightings between them are determined dynamically depending on their relationship. BERT is designed to read text in both directions at once and this feature is called bidirectionality. BERT model uses this property to pre-train for NLP tasks such as Masked Language Modeling and Next Sentence Prediction. Nowadays, BERT is preferred over other models for question answering system because it has better model performance over other methods. It can process larger amount of texts and language and is a good option to use pre-trained models (transfer learning). It also has capabilities to fine tune your data to a specific language context. In few cases, BERT can even be applied directly to the data with no further training and still deliver a high performance.

4.4   XLM-RoBERTa

XLM-RoBERTa or Cross-lingual language Model is a multilingual version of RoBERTa that can outperform other multilingual models. In 100 languages, on 2.5 TB of filtered CommonCrawl data, XLM-R was pre-trained. XLM is a Transformer-based architecture that has been pre-trained to achieve one of three language modeling goals:

- Translation Language Modeling - It is a new translation language model which is used for improving cross-lingual pre-training.
- Casual Language Modeling - A model that aids in determining the likelihood of a word based on the preceding words in a phrase.
- Masked Language modeling - It masks one or more words in a phrase and instructs the model to predict those masked words by providing the remaining words in the sentence.

Roberta is a self-supervised transformers model that was trained on a big corpus. This implies it was trained on raw texts solely, with no human labeling (thus its ability to handle a large amount of publicly available data), and then used an automated procedure to build inputs and labels from those texts. Conneau et al. presented it in their work Unsupervised Cross-lingual Representation Learning at Scale.

4.5   Results

In this paper, we have created a machine comprehensive question answering system for the Tamil Language. We have used 5770 QA instances for training and 112 QA instances for testing. We have calculated the evaluation scores on two different datasets (Table 2). For Squad Dataset, the system gave better results than chaii dataset. This is because the model was trained completely on Tamil instances whereas in chaii dataset, the instances were in both Hindi and Tamil.

Table 2. Evaluation Scores

Dataset	Exact Match	F1 score
squad_translated_tamil	72.59	81.84
chaii_test_data	57.14	62.25

In some cases, the answer generated is wrong as the pattern matching in the question can't find the exact tokenized context part. This is because, after striding, the context is split into several parts according to the striding max length. The given question is mapped in the context of two parts and the context with maximum similarity is retrieved. However, the exact answer does not fall in either part of the mapped context but into a pattern much before that and hence they cannot be mapped. One way of addressing this problem is by increasing the striding length which may, in turn, need higher computational resources. On the other hand, although the answer extracted is correct. It deviates from the original answer due to the grammatical incorrectness of the answer. This in turn leads to a drop in the EM score and Jaccard similarity. The drawback can be addressed by performing a set of post-processing operations to grammatically match the answer to the question asked.

5 Conclusion

A Model for a Question answering system for Tamil was designed by tackling the barrier of the morphological rich nature of the language. Today, assuming you have data, you can quickly create a solution that takes advantage of the most current advances in NLU while using little to no rule-based approaches. Voice assistants built utilize open-domain solutions with text generation for replies are the most visible example of today's QA systems. Single-domain systems that do extractive QA are also gaining interest, although their use cases are far more limited. Furthermore, as high-performance language models become more available outside of "big tech," we may expect to see more QA systems in our daily lives.

References

1. He, H., Lin, J.: Pairwise word interaction modeling with deep neural networks for semantic similarity measurement. In: Proceedings of the 2016 Conference of the North American Chapter of the Association for Computational Linguistics: Human Language Technologies, pp. 937–948 (2016)
2. Severyn, A., Moschitti, A.: Automatic feature engineering for answer selection and extraction. In: Proceedings of the 2013 Conference on Empirical Methods in Natural Language Processing, pp. 458–467 (2013)
3. Sharma, Y., Gupta, S.: Deep learning approaches for question answering system. Procedia Comput. Sci. **132**, 785–794 (2018)
4. Thara, S., Sampath, E., Reddy, P., et al.: Code mixed question answering challenge using deep learning methods. In: 2020 5th International Conference on Communication and Electronics Systems (ICCES), pp. 1331–1337. IEEE (2020)
5. Wang, M., Manning, C.D.: Probabilistic tree-edit models with structured latent variables for textual entailment and question answering. In: Proceedings of the 23rd International Conference on Computational Linguistics (Coling 2010), pp. 1164–1172 (2010)
6. Wang, M., Smith, N.A., Mitamura, T.: What is the jeopardy model? A quasi-synchronous grammar for QA. In: Proceedings of the 2007 Joint Conference on Empirical Methods in Natural Language Processing and Computational Natural Language Learning (EMNLP-CoNLL), pp. 22–32 (2007)
7. Yao, X., Van Durme, B., Callison-Burch, C., Clark, P.: Answer extraction as sequence tagging with tree edit distance. In: Proceedings of the 2013 Conference of the North American Chapter of the Association for Computational Linguistics: Human Language Technologies, pp. 858–867 (2013)
8. Yih, W.t., He, X., Meek, C.: Semantic parsing for single-relation question answering. In: Proceedings of the 52nd Annual Meeting of the Association for Computational Linguistics (Volume 2: Short Papers), pp. 643–648 (2014)

Exploring the Opportunities and Challenges in Contributing to Tamil Wikimedia

Subalalitha Chinnaudayar Navaneethakrishnan[1]($\boxtimes$) ⓘ, Sathiyaraj Thangasamy[2] ⓘ,
Nithya R[3] ⓘ, Info-farmer[4], and Neechalkaran[5]

[1] SRM Institute of Science and Technology, SRM Nagar, Kattankulathur, Chengelpet 603203,
India
subalaln@srmist.edu.in
[2] Srikrishna Aditya College of Arts and Sciences, Coimbatore 641042, India
[3] Tamil Wikimedian, Coimbatore 641016, India
[4] Tamil Wikimedian, Salem 620001, India
[5] Tamil Wikimedian, Chennai, India

Abstract. The term "Wikipedia" is one of the most frequent words that pop up in
the minds of all the academicians and the researchers across the globe as it serves
to be one of the most important data sources. Wikipedia is one of the projects of
"Wikimedia". The Wikimedia project includes Wikipedia, Wikinews, Wikisource,
Wikibooks, Wikiquote, and Wikidata. All these projects are successfully done and
still being enhanced by the consistent efforts of volunteers from all parts of the
world. This article elucidates the experiences of such volunteers, Info-Farmer
and Neechalkaran who have been contributing to the Tamil Wikimedia projects
for more than 12 years. This article focusses on bringing out the challenges and
problems faced by most of Tamil Wikimedia contributors who are called, "Tamil
Wikimedians". The article also insists about the benefits of being part of Tamil
Wikimedia. The prime aim of this article is to encourage more volunteers to
contribute to Tamil Wikimedia.

Keywords: Wikimedia · Wikipedia · Wikidata · Infofarmer · Wikicontributions ·
tamilWikimedia

1 Wikimedia Project- an Introduction

Jimmy Wales established the Wikimedia Foundation in 2003 in St. Petersburg, Florida,
as a nonprofit organization to support projects like Wikipedia, Wiktionary, and other
crowdsourced Wikis that had previously been hosted by Wales's for-profit business,
Bomis [1]. Wikimedia generates most of the funds through millions of small contributions made by Wikipedia readers, which are gathered via email campaigns and annual
fundraising banners posted on Wikipedia. Grants from different tech firms and charitable
organizations supplement these.

Anand Kumar M et al. (Eds.): SPELLL 2022, CCIS 1802, pp. 253–262, 2023.
https://doi.org/10.1007/978-3-031-33231-9_18

Over the course of its existence, the foundation has expanded quickly. It had approximately 550 employees and contractors by 2021, annual sales of over US$160 million, annual expenses of over US$110 million, and a growing endowment that in June 2021 exceeded US$100 million. Wikimedia is a global movement whose mission is to bring free educational content to the world. Wikimedia works to create a society in which every single person can freely share in the totality of knowledge through a variety of projects, chapters, and the support system of the nonprofit Wikimedia Foundation. "To enable and engage people across the world to gather and generate educational information under a free license or in the public domain, and to communicate it efficiently and internationally," is the purpose of the Wikimedia foundation [2].

The Foundation offers the organizational and technical framework necessary for members of the public to create multilingual Wiki material in order to fulfil this purpose. The content on the Wikis is not created or edited by the Foundation. The Foundation works with a global network of volunteers and connected groups, including Wikimedia chapters, thematic organizations, user groups, and other partners, and pledges in its mission statement to make helpful material from its projects freely accessible on the internet forever.

The "strategic direction" of the Wikimedia Foundation, created in 2017 for the next 15 years, is that by 2030, "the Wikimedia Foundation will become the core infrastructure of the ecosystem of free knowledge". The Attribution and Share-alike Creative Commons licenses, version 3.0, govern the redistribution of content on the majority of Wikimedia project websites. 11 Wikis owned and run by the foundation have content that is created and maintained by unpaid volunteers. Contributions are open to the public, and creating a named user account is not required. These Wikis adhere to the free content model, with knowledge distribution as their primary objective. Apart from Wikipedia, there are numerous Wikimedia projects such as, Wiktionary which is an online dictionary and thesaurus, Wiki books, an open source book collections, Wiki quotes that aggregates quotations, Wiki source which is a digital library, Wikidata is operating as a language server for more than 357 languages contributed by people around the globe and provides an open platform to upload knowledge which becomes an important resource in libraries across the world. [3–5].Wiki commons that is resource for multimedia files etc. [1, 6, 7]. These open source repositories are indeed a treasure to pull data to build AI enabled applications.

Since the Wikimedia is contributed by humongous people around the globe, there exit many challenges for the Wikimedia foundation in maintaining the quality of the content. The contributions come from both registered and anonymous users. In order to keep track of quality content, trust models have been suggested by researchers [8]. Also [3] discusses about various factors that influences the contributions like the Government policies in that particular country, the internet structures and the norms, people's preferred languages, the culture etc. This paper tries to narrow down this to a particular language, Tamil and makes an attempt to bring out the opportunities and challenges by the Tamil contributors spread across the globe.

The rest of the paper is organized as follows. Section 2 describes about the Tamil Wikimedia project and the veteran contributors, Sect. 3 briefs about the opportunities and Sect. 4 describes the challenges faced the Tamil contributors and finally Sect. 5 gives the conclusion.

2 Tamil Wikimedia Project

Tamil language is one of the oldest languages that belongs to the Dravidian family of languages and is the 19th most spoken language in the world. Tamil literatures has a great history of spanning for more than 2000 years [9]. Kudos to the Tamil Wikimedia community who are spread world-wide and yet have contributed to almost all Wikimedia projects. For instance, Tamil Wikipedia has more than 20,000 registered users and ranks 5th in India and 69th in the world based on the count of articles in Wikipedia [10]. This stands as one of the strong reasons behind the numerous research and applications that has emerged in Tamil computing which is on par with the state of the art in the field of Natural Language processing. Though contributors are spread world-wide, 94.3% of the Tamil Wiki contributors are from India, 4.3% are from Sri Lanka and the rest from the other countries. The beauty of Wikimedia is that anyone with passion to contribute can be part of it. Tamil Wikimedia is mostly contributed by students. The contributions also come from women that are in career breaks and also from retired people. Not only Wikipedia, Tamil Wikimedia also covers all the flavors of it like Tamil Wiktionary, Tamil Wikiquotes, Tamil Wikidata, Tamil Wikicommons, Tamil Wikisource and Tamil Wikibooks

An example of how Tamil Wiktionary looks like is given below. A word, its meaning, usage and references are given by the contributors. The below example shows Tamil Wiktionary information for the Tamil letter, " அ". Though it is a Tamil letter, it has its own beautiful meanings.

பொருள்

(பெ)அ

1) தமிழின்   முதல்   எழுத்து;   தமிழ் உயிரெழுத்துகளில் முதல் உயிரெழுத்து

2) எட்டு என்னும் எண்ணின் தமிழியக் குறியீடு

3) அழகு

4) அந்த என்னும் சுட்டு (எ.கா. அப்பறவை, அக்கருவி)

5) எதிர்மறை   முன்னொட்டு,   ஆரியமொழிச்சொற்களை எதிர்மறையாக்க வழங்குவது; இடைச்சொல்

6) ஓர் அசைச்சொல் (எ.கா.)(பெயரெச்ச விகுதியாக) => தன்வழிய காளை (சீவக சிந்தாமணி-494)

7) ஓர் இரக்கக் குறிப்பு (எ.கா.) 'அஆ கீழே கொட்டி விட்டதே '

8) ஆறாம்வேற்றுமை உருபுகளுள் ஒன்று. (எ.கா.) என கைகள்

9) அ∴கான்

10) சிவன்

11)திருமால்

12)சாரியை

மொழிபெயர்ப்புகள்

- ஆங்கிலம்

    1) the first tamil vowel

    2) eight the letter printed without the loop at the top

    3) beauty

    4) pref. to nouns, expressing remoteness

    5) placing அ before some words, leads to the **opposite** words

    6) a euphony

    7) ah! expressing pity

    8) the tamil grammatical term

    9) a synonym for the first letter

    10) the (hindu gods) namely siva

    11) the (hindu gods) namely vishnu

    12)auxiliary, component particles employed in the formation of the two classes of verbs

- இந்தி- இதே ஒலியை உடைய இந்தியின் முதலெழுத்து - அ

விளக்கம்

ஆதிகால ஒலியிலிருந்து பெற்ற அ என்னும் எதிர்மறை முன்னொட்டைச் சொற்களுக்கு முன்னே சேர்த்தால் எதிர்மறைப் பொருள் கிடைக்கும். இது ஏறக்குறைய அருந்தமிழ்ச்சொற்களை எதிர்மறையாக்க மட்டுமே அதிகமாக வழங்குவது; சில எடுத்துக்காட்டுகளைக் கீழே காணலாம்.

1 நீதி	1 அநீதி	2 சைவம்	2 அசைவம்	3 சுத்தம்	3 அசுத்தம்	4 தர்மம்	4 அதர்மம்

பயன்பாடு

1. அ என்பது தமிழ் நெடுங்கணக்கில் முதல் உயிரெழுத்து.

(இலக்கணப் பயன்பாடு)

அ என்பது, ஒரு பெயர்ச்சொல், அசைச்சொல், மற்றும் குறில் ஆக அமைகிறது.

(இலக்கியப் பயன்பாடு

அ என்ற சொல்லில் தொடங்கும் திருக்குறள்கள், மொத்தம் = 156. இது தமிழ் அரிச்சுவடியில் அடங்கும், அடிப்படைக் குறியீடாகும்.

சான்றுகள் ---அ--- DDSA பதிப்பு + அகரமுதலி + தமிழ் தமிழ் அகராதி + வாணி தொகுப்பகராதி கழகத் தமிழ் கையகராதி. + க்ரியாவின் தற்காலத் தமிழகராதி

2.1 Veteren Tamil Wikimedia Contributors

Tamil Wikimedia has witnessed many contributors who have been part of it for more than a decade. The details of these veteran contributors are given in this link https://tinyurl.com/2feb37e3. Many of these contributors have also become trainers and they conduct training programs, hackathons and conferences to encourage more contributors. Guruleninn, Info-farmer, Nandhini Kandhasamy, CR Selvakumar, Neechalkaran, NSE_Mahalingam_VNR, Sivakosaran, Fahimrazick and Sridhar_G are few of the trainers who have taken great initiatives in encouraging the next generation to involve more in Tamil Wikimedia project and keep the chain going.

2.2 Being Part of Tamil Wikimedia

To be a contributor in Wikimedia, no previous experience is needed. One can contribute by writing new articles or new information. They can also improve the existing articles and information on Wikimedia by editing. People who are good coding can also contribute to Wikimedia by building open-source tools and APIs. These codes can help writers and editors to contribute to Wikimedia with much ease and also to build API which can pull data from the Tamil Wikimedia which can further be used to build many benchmark datasets for various tasks such as Machine Translations, text to speech, text classification etc. A Python code written by Info- Farmer in Tami for formatting text in shown below.

```
import பைவிக்கிமூலம்,time,re
```

கீழ்கண்ட பக்கங்களில் மட்டும் இந்த நிரலானாது இயங்கும். அடடவணைப் பெயரினையும், பக்கங்களையும் சரிபார்.

##மாற்றம் செய்யப்படவுள்ள மின்னூலின் பெயரை, மேற்கோள் குறிகளுக்கு அடுத்து, இடைவெளி இல்லாமல் இடுக.

```
அட்டவணை = 'சிரிக்க சிந்திக்க சிறுவர் கதைகள்'
# மொத்தம் = 125 பக்கங்கள் https://ta.Wikisource.org/s/swv

தொடக்கயெண் = 48

முடிவெண் = 49
```

---------------- மாறிலிகளை, அமைத்துக் கொள்கிறேன் ----------------------------

```
பைவிழூ = பைவிக்கிமூலம்

விளைவிடு = print

கோடிடு = பைவிழூ.கோடிடு(எண்ணிக்கை=40)

தொடக்கமுடிவெண்நொடி =
பைவிழூ.தொடக்கமுடிவெண்நொடி(தொடக்கயெ
ண்,முடிவெண்,60)

விளைவிடு(தொடக்கமுடிவெண்நொடி)
```

தேவையானப் பக்கங்களை, பைத்தான் பட்டியலாக மாற்றிக் கொள்கிறேன்.

```
பக்கப்பட்டி =
பைவிழூ.பக்கப்பெயரெழுது(அட்டவணை,தொடக்
கயெண்,முடிவெண்)

for பக்கம் in பக்கப்பட்டி: ## பக்கப்பட்டியில் இருந்து,
மாற்றம் செய்ய, ஒவ்வொரு பக்கமாக எடுக்கிறேன்.
```

```
உரலி = பைவிழ்.உரலியிடு(பக்கம்)

பக்கத்தரவு = உரலி.text

விளைவிடு (கோடிடு + '\n' + str(உரலி) + '\n' + கோடிடு
+ '\n')

if '<center>' in பக்கத்தரவு:

    பக்கத்தரவுபுதிது    =    பக்கத்தரவு.replace('<cen-
ter>','{{center|').replace('</center>','}}')

    உரலி.text = பக்கத்தரவுபுதிது

    உரலி.save('<center> என்ற வழக்கொழிந்த குறியீடு
மாற்றப்பட்டது.')

else:

விளைவிடு
```

The volunteers can also seek the help of veteran editors in tea house. In tea house, the veteran contributors will answer the contributors' queries and help them feel comfortable with their contributions. This link https://Wikimediafoundation.org/participate/ has necessary data about Wikimedia foundation which will help us to adapt to our language.

3   Opportunities in Tamil Wikimedia

The contributors get the wonderful opportunity of being part of world largest multilingual encyclopedia. The Wikimedia foundation provides three types of funding opportunities to those who contribute to Wikimedia namely, Rapid Fund, Conference and Event Fund and general support fund [11]. Rapid funds are given to individuals who take initiatives that are completed quickly and done at low-cost by individuals, teams, or organisations working on Wikimedia projects. Event funds are given to support for organizing local, regional, and topical conferences that bring together Wikimedians for experience sharing, skill building, and networking, including funding, and general support fund is given to people, teams, or affiliates who have created bigger projects, programmes, or a strategic plan that needs ongoing funding over time to be successful. Tamil Wikimedians can get funding by contacting appropriate contact persons who are allocated region wise. Further information can be obtained from https://meta.Wikimedia.org/Wiki/Grants:Reg ions/South_Asia.

Though these funding schemes are applicable to the Tamil Wikimedians who have been working consistently for longtime, the student volunteers may readily get the benefit out of being part of Tamil Wikimedia by getting internships and take part in Hackathons veteran Tamil Wikimedia contributors host internship programs and Wikimedia hackathons. Many former contributors have been competitive exam aspirants as well. The student contributors can get the opportunity to interact with them and the students can enrich their soft skills as they will be interacting in workshops and conferences with veteran Tamil Wikimedians and also with fellow- student Tamil Wikimedians. Students get access to all contents of Wikimedia including multimedia files those who have the goal of becoming a programmer there is a lot of scope for them to learn and gain experience as it is an open source tool [12, 13, 14, 15]. Furthermore, they can get a chance to win in Google summer code, as Wikimedia foundation is one of the partners. Also, the opportunity provided by the Wikimedia does not have a bias towards any gender and it fits with Tamil Wikimedia too [16].

4 Challenges in Tamil Wikimedia

Though there have been tremendous contributions coming from Tamil Wikimedians, still there are challenges that when solved can significantly increase the contributions in Tamil Wikimedia to a greater extent [17, 18]. The Tamil Wikimedia project needs more publicity as many are still unaware of this project. Many tools that can make the contribution easier are either unaffordable or not available to Tamil Wikimedians. Also, the lack of awareness of the existing tools is one of the reasons for low participations. Tamil Wikimedians at time face difficulties while coining terms for new technological concepts, dealing with various Tamil dialects and Tamil transliterations. Also, most of the Government data and references works are not in unicode format. So the contributors are unable to cite from online resources. Many formatting issues exist in Tamil like when working with texts that are in double columns using OCR.

Apart from these the ratio between the contributors and editors has huge variation, (i.e.) the contributors are coming mostly from India and Sri Lanka, while the editors are coming from rest of the world. Adding to this as the users are from diverse culture, country and setting up common policy is difficult and following up with the content vandalism from anonymous users, paid users become a daunting task. However, the veteran Tamil Wikimedians are constantly taking efforts to overcome these issues by publicizing more by conducting more events, workshops and conferences and reaching out to the government to seek support for sorting out the prevailing challenges.

5 Conclusion and Future Scope

This article is an attempt to create an awareness about Tamil Wikimedia project and the opportunities and challenges involved in it based on the experiences shared by Info-Farmer and Neechalkaran, who are one of the veteran contributors to Tamil Wikimedia projects. Also, this article aims to encourage more contributors for Tamil Wikimedia projects and get benefitted. The next generation computational research and developments (R &D) in Tamil language mainly rely on the open-source data repositories like Wikimedia. The more contributions to these projects will strengthen such R & D attempts. We hope this article creates a huge positive vibe resulting in many voluntary contributions to Tamil Wikimedia projects.

The Wikimedia foundation has many futuristic goals like giving recognitions to the contributors apart from monetary benefits which may attract more academic collaborations by forming reputation systems [19]. Wikimedia foundation is also planning to host collaborative databases and more tools which may have more flexibility in contributing and editing.

References

1. Redi, M., Gerlach, M., Johnson, I., Morgan, J, Zia, L.: A taxonomy of knowledge gaps for Wikimedia projects (second draft). arXiv preprint arXiv:2008.12314 (2020)
2. Konieczny, P.: Wikis and Wikipedia as a teaching tool: five years late. First Monday 17(9) (2012)
3. Konieczny, P.: Macro-level differences in participation in sharing economy: factors affecting contributions to the collective intelligence wikipedia platform across different Asian Countries. Asian J. Soc. Sci. 48(1–2), 115–149 (2020)
4. Allison-Cassin, S., et al.: ARL white paper on Wikidata: Opportunities and recommendations (2019)
5. Fenoll, C., Cummings, J., Tramullas, J., Hinojo, À.: Opportunities for Public Libraries and Wikipedia (2016)
6. Dobusch, L., Kapeller, J.: Open strategy-making with crowds and communities: comparing wikimedia and creative commons. Long Range Plann. 51(4), 561–579 (2018)
7. Menking, A., Rangarajan, V., Gilbert, M.: Sharing small pieces of the world Increasing and broadening participation in wikimedia commons. In: Proceedings of the 14th International Symposium on Open Collaboration, pp. 1–12 (2018)
8. Javanmardi, S., Ganjisaffar, Y., Lopes, C., Baldi, P.: User contribution and trust in Wikipedia. In: 5th International Conference on Collaborative Computing: Networking, Applications and Work sharing, pp. 1–6 (2009)
9. Sivanantham, R., Seran, M.: Keeladi: An Urban Settlement of Sangam Age on the Banks of River Vaigai. Department of Archaeology, Government of Tamil Nadu, Chennai, India (2019)
10. Vasudevan, T.V.: Indian language wikipedias: a comparison study. Int. J. 93 (2015)
11. Tamil Wiki grants. https://meta.Wikimedia.org/Wiki/Grants:Programs/Wikimedia_Community_Fund/Acquisition_of_missing_pages_and_books_of_Nationalised_books,_Wikisource_workshops_and_a_GLAM_activity_in_TamilNadu/Report
12. Wiki Tools. https://tools.wmflabs.org/hay/directory/
13. Wiki commons. https://commons.Wikimedia.org/Wiki/File:Wikimedia_logo_family_few-Tamil-simple-explanations-ta.svg
14. Tamil Wiki commons, Tamil Wiktionary. https://commons.Wikimedia.org/Wiki/File:0_Introduction_to_Wikipedia_projects_by_Tamil.webm
15. Koteeswaran, B.M.: Bridging the Gender Gap (2021)
16. Tamil Wikisource. https://ta.Wikisource.org/s/9z0e
17. Wiki guide. https://ta.Wikisource.org/s/agii
18. User Experiences, :Info-farmer https://ta.Wikisource.org/s/41e
19. Future of Wikimedia. https://meta.Wikimedia.org/Wiki/The_future_of_Wikipedia

Speech Technologies

Early Alzheimer Detection Through Speech Analysis and Vision Transformer Approach

G. Pranav$^{(\boxtimes)}$, K. Varsha, and K. S. Gayathri

Information Technology Sri Sivasubramaniya Nadar College of Engineering affiliated to Anna University Kalavakkam, Chennai 603110, India
pranav292005@gmail.com

Abstract. Alzheimer's disease is a brain disorder which slowly destroys and deteriorates memory and thinking abilities and, eventually, the ability to carry out the basic tasks. Early diagnostic of Alzheimer's's disease can avail the patient with high probability of cure with minimal cost. The cost required for detection of Alzheimer's is quite high for common people. Therefore diagnosation of Alzheimer from spontaneous speech proves to be a feasible and convenient method as it can be done at home. This paper implements Log Mel Spectrograms with vision transformer deep learning classifier approach to differentiate the Alzheimer group and control group. The vision transformer uses a transformer like architecture over the patches of the image in order to classify the images. Extensive analysis done over the Pitt corpus dataset with the help of the proposed approach, demonstrates the efficiency of Vision Transformer and log mel spectrogram approach over the MFCC and random forest classifier approach.

1 Introduction

Worldwide, around 55 million people have been diagnosed with Alzheimer Disease (AD). It is a neurodegenerative disease, as it becomes worse with time. The symptoms are explicitly noticed only at a later stage. In the starting stage minor changes occur in the brain that are unnoticeable to the person affected [1]. The main risk factor for AD is age, and therefore its highest incidence is amongst the elderly. Dementia is more common as people grow older but it is not a normal part of ageing. The proportion of older people in the population is increasing in every country. An early diagnosis can help the patients as well as their families to make the right decisions at the right time. If detected at an earlier stage, the degeneration can be halted with appropriate treatment. Drug and non-drug treatment can be potentially effective only if it is diagnosed early.

The Traditional method of diagnosing dementia is through MR1 scan and PET scan. The traditional methods have proven to be time consuming and cost ineffective [2]. Therefore researchers worldwide are trying to find efficient approaches for early detection. The radioactive elements used in PET scans are often short-lived. But they might cause some impediments especially to pregnant

Anand Kumar M et al. (Eds.): SPELLL 2022, CCIS 1802, pp. 265–276, 2023.
https://doi.org/10.1007/978-3-031-33231-9_19

patients. It is a new procedure which is quite extravagant compared to other forms of medical imaging. It requires a cyclotron which is an expensive and extravagant machine used to create radioisotopes that are used to produce the radioactive rays required for imaging and thus is a very expensive treatment. Magnetic Resonance Imaging scans, also known as an MRI, are used to ascertain tumours and strokes that can lead to the diagnosis of dementia. They play a vital part in dementia research because they help us to analyse how different types of dementia affect the brain. MRI scans take significantly longer time to acquire than CT and patient solace can be an issue. Acquisition of MRI image is noisy.

Because dementia damages brain cells, a symptom named aphasia is experienced by patients. A dementia person loses the ability to speak and to understand speech. As the time passes by, it becomes harder to remember words and interpret what others are saying. With the help of speech techniques such as memory regurgitation and visual speech perception, dementia can be diagnosed. Dementia patients find it hard to explain about something. They have difficulty in using words and framing sentences. They make grammatical mistakes and jumble up words. By examining the speech it is more effective to identify dementia. This seems to be a less time consuming and feasible method.

The audio data is used to categorise AD and NON-AD patients by extracting acoustic features from speech. The feature extraction from the audio data requires some expertise. Few have converted audio data into mel spectrograms and r Mel-frequency Cepstral Coefficients (MFCCs) [3,4]. As the next step they have trained the data with the help of traditional classifiers like random forest [5]. MFCCs and random forest model have shown excellence in many domains but failed to do so in AD and NON-AD classification. The drawback of using MFCC to extract features is its sensitivity to noise because of its dependence on the spectral form. To address this limitation, Log Mel spectrogram and Vision trans- former classifier is used. As most sounds humans hear are concentrated in very small frequency ranges, log mel spectrogram is used for better feature extraction. Vision Transform classifier is robust against blockages. ViT shows a shape bias that is quite comparable to human judgement.

Our contributions can be summarised as follows:

- Speech of patients is used to classify dementia and non dementia groups.
- The images split into multiple patches of the same height and width. And MLP network and a layer is used to convert the images into patches. These patches are used for better feature extraction.
- Converting audio files into log Mel spectrograms. Converting the log mel spectrograms to patches. Features are extracted from the patches and ViT classifier is used to classify AD and NON AD.
- Log Mel Spectrograms + ViT classifier gives better accuracy than MFCC + Random forest.

2   Related Work

Although memory loss is the most prominent sign of AD (Alzheimer's Disease), language impairment may also be a significant indicator. Amen bidani [5] employed DCNN (Deep Convolutional Neural Network) and Transfer Learning models to identify and categorise MRI (Magnetic Resonance Imaging) brain images from the OASIS dataset that were indicative of dementia. Feature extraction from these MRI pictures was not particularly efficient, and test data accuracy was low. Ahmed et al [6] found that the majority of patients displayed substantial alterations in connected speech output.

In a study of 486 AD patients, Weiner et al. [7] found a significant correlation between dementia severity and semantic fluency. Thomas et al. [8] classified spontaneous speech samples from 95 AD patients and an unspecified number of controls by treating the problem as an authorship attribution task and utilising an N-grams model. The highest and most accurate discrimination between patients with severe AD and controls was 94.5%, whereas the best and most accurate discrimination between patients with moderate AD and controls was 75.3%. In their research, they indicated that closed-class terms were highly revealing. Sharmila Nasreen et al. [9] used disfluency characteristics and interactional features as classification criteria. The CCcorpus dataset was utilised. Interactional characteristics were more accurate than disfluency features. LR and MLP were first used with the aforementioned characteristics. Since accuracy was low, SVM was used for classification.

R'mani Haulcy et al. [10] found that audio classifiers trained on ComParE openSMILE features outperformed those trained on x-vectors and i-vectors taken from VoxCeleb and Pitt data. To identify and diagnose dementia illness, Carlos M. et al. [11] used both DCNN (Deep Convolutional Neural Network) and Transfer Learning models. The results demonstrated that the DCNN model significantly improved the accuracy of dementia diagnosis. Jochen Weiner et al. [12] found that the transcription quality of an ASR system is a good single feature and that the features taken from automated transcriptions perform similarly to or slightly better than the features extracted from hand transcriptions. Chongua Xue et al. [13] compared a hierarchical neural network with an attention mechanism trained on language properties to three acoustic-based systems: (Bag-of-Audio-Words (BoAW)), a Siamese Network, and a Convolutional Neural Network (CNN). The findings demonstrated that the linguistic approach is superior to the acoustical systems. The audio recordings were classified using them.

The above employed methods have not been very efficient in classifying AD and NON AD as they had problems in feature extraction and in classification. Vision transformer seems to be a better model has it has better feature extraction and classification capabilities.

3   Proposed Vision Transformer Approach for Alzheimer Detection

The proposed vision transformer approach for dementia detection is presented in the Fig. 1.

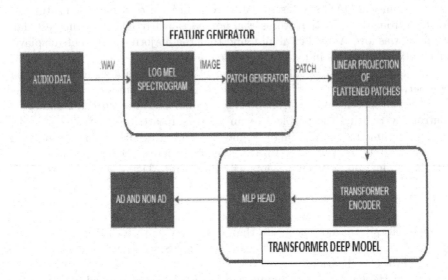

Fig. 1. Vision Transformer approach for Alzheimer detection

3.1   Log Mel Spectogram

The audio files belonging to dementia and control groups are converted to log mel spectrograms which are processed and then fed into the classifier. The primary step involved behind log mel spectrogram is to apply a fourier transform as it converts time domain to frequency domain. As a part of the next step, Pre Emphasis is carried out to increase the magnitude of energy in the higher frequency. A Mel Spectrogram makes two important changes. It uses the Mel Scale instead of Frequency on the y-axis. It uses the Decibel Scale instead of Amplitude to indicate colours. The logarithmic compression is applied on mel spectrograms as shown in Eq. 1.

$$f(x) = log(aX + B) \tag{1}$$

where X is the mel spectrogram matrix (Fig. 2).

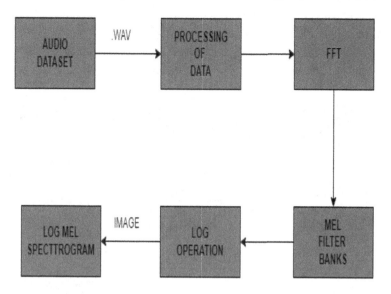

Fig. 2. Conversion of audio data into Log Mel spectrogram

3.2 Vision Transformer Deep Learning Model

Vision transformer (ViT) is a transformer that learns by measuring the relationship between input token pairs. The patches of images are used as input tokens. This can be done either in association with a convolutional network or by replacing some components of convolutional networks. As a part of the first step the hyper parameters such as learning rate and decaying weight are defined. The log mel spectrograms are converted into patches in order to feed it as input to the Vision transformer classifier. The images split into multiple patches of the same height and width. The location of a patch in the picture is inserted together with the encoded vector and sent into the transformer encoder network, which is virtually identical to the one responsible for text input processing. Multiple blocks make up the ViT encoder, with each block including three key processing elements: Layer Norm, Multi-head Attention Network (MSP), and Multi-Layer Perceptrons (MLP). Layer Norm keeps the training process on track and allows the model to adjust to the differences between training photos. MSP is a network tasked with generating attention maps based on embedded visual tokens. These attention maps assist the network in concentrating on the features of the audio which are extracted from log mel spectrogram. The notion of attention maps is identical to that described in classic computer vision literature (e.g. saliency maps and alpha-matting). MLP is a two-layer classification network featuring GELU (Gaussian Error Linear Unit) as its last layer. As the transformer's output, the final MLP block, also known as the MLP head, is employed. Softmax may offer categorization labels when applied to this output (i.e. classification of dementia and non dementia patients) (Fig. 3).

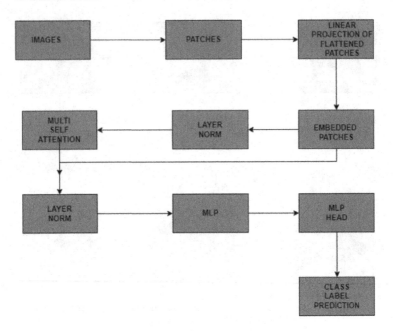

Fig. 3. Vision Transformer architecture

4   MFCC and Random Forest Approach for Alzheimer Detection

4.1   MFCC

Raw audio signal as input to the model is inefficient since the audio signal will include a great deal of noise. Observations indicate that extracting features from the audio signal and applying them as input to the basic model would result in much higher accuracy than sending raw audio signal as input. Coefficients of the MFCC represent the rate variations in the various spectrum bands.

If a cepstral coefficient has a positive value, the majority of spectral energy is concentrated in low-frequency areas. Negative cepstral coefficients indicate that the majority of spectral energy is focused at high frequencies. In order to forecast audio labelling, the mean of these values is transformed into an array and provided as input to the network. The MFCC procedure for extracting features consists of six phases. In the first stage, the signal is divided into brief time frames. Then, windowing is done to primarily decrease spectral leakage. Instead of a rectangular window, Hamming/Hanning windows are used to split the signal so that high-frequency noise is not produced. Using the DFT transform, the signal from the time domain is transformed to the frequency domain. The mel scale converts the real frequency to the perceived frequency by humans. The formula for mapping is given in Eq. 2 (Fig. 4) .

$$mel(f) = 1127ln(1 + f/700) \qquad (2)$$

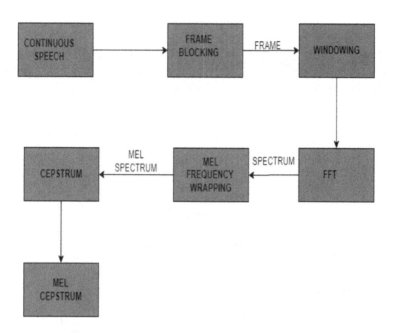

Fig. 4. MFCC architecture

Random Forest Approach. Random forest belongs to the category of ensemble learning. Ensemble learning algorithm comprises more than one algorithm of the same kind. Random forest combines the output of multiple decision trees to reach a single result. Random forest algorithms have three main hyperparameters. The hyperparameters are node size, the number of trees, and the number of features sampled. These hyper parameters need to be set before training. From the data set few audio are randomly selected as test data. More diverse data is added to the data set to reduce the correlations among the data set. For a classification task, a majority vote will give the predicted class (Fig. 5).

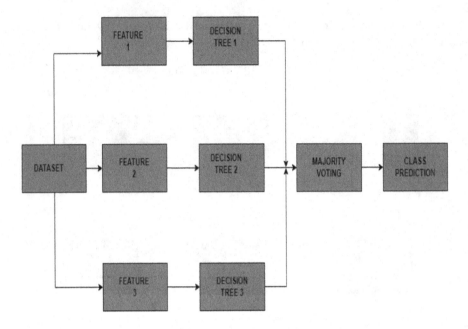

Fig. 5. Random Forest architecture

5   Experimental Analysis

The Cookie Theft picture of Pitt corpus [12] is used by doctors to detect spatial and visual abnormalities and identify issues with speech and fluency.

5.1   Experimental Setup

Dataset. The Pitt Corpus contains data elicited through the following tasks: the Cookie Theft stimulus picture description for AD and non-AD groups. AD group consists of 99 people and non AD consists of 194 people. Train and test data are split in the 80:20 ratio. Train data set consists of 233 audio files and test data consists of 60 audio files.

Libraries. Library used are Pil stands for Python Imaging Library. It is used for image processing. It has so many functions which is used for working on images. In this paper, Image module in PIL is used which provides a class with the same name to represent a PIL image. NUMPY stands for numeric python. Its used for working with arrays. It has a lot of mathematical functions such as linear algebra routines, fourier transform etc. The array function in NUMPY is used to convert input to an array. Cv2 is the latest version of opencv library in python. CV2 functions are used to perform all operations related to images. It helps in manipulation of images such as read and write an image, converting a colour images to grey image. Tensorflow is used for numerical operations using data flow diagrams which makes learning faster and easier. It performs various tasks focused on training and inference of deep neural networks. As tensorflow uses graph framework, it can be executed on multiple CPUs or GPUs and even mobile operating system.

Hyperparameters. The learning rate is a parameter that determines how quickly or slowly a model learns. The learning rate is set to 0.0020. Weight decay is a regularisation technique that is used to regularise the size of the weights of certain parameters in machine learning models and is initialised to 0.001. Batch size is a term used in machine learning and refers to the number of training examples utilised in one iteration. The batch size in vit + patch model is 256. Epochs are defined as the total number of iterations for training the machine learning model with all the training data in one cycle. The model is run for 50 epochs. The image is resized to 72. Size of the patches to be extracted from images is 6. There are eight transformer layers in this model. The size of the transformer layers are set according to the projection. The parameters were hypertuned with different values and the above mentioned values yield the optimal accuracy.

5.2 Experimental Analysis

The audio files belonging to Alzheimer detection and control group were converted into Log Mel spectrogram for better feature extraction. The features extracted from this spectrogram is fed into the vision transformer. The Fig. 6 shown depicts the Log Mel Spectrogram of an audio file. The Log mel spectrogram were converted into patches of equal size and stride equal to that of patch size. The Fig. 7 shown below is a patch of a Log Mel spectrogram.

5.3 Metrics

The output of binary classification is divided into four groups based on whether the anticipated label matches the actual label. True positive, true negative, false positive, and false negative are the four classifications. Recall score, accuracy score, and F1 score are used metrics that are derived based on these criteria. Recall is the total number of positive instances that our model accurately predicted. The F1 score is defined as the average of accuracy and recall. The F1-score is a statistical measure of the model's precision. The accuracy score is the ratio of the total of all forecasts' true positives and true negatives. It is a measure of the model's precision.

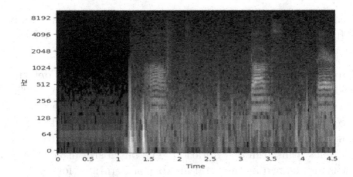

Fig. 6. Log Mel Spectrogram of an audio sample

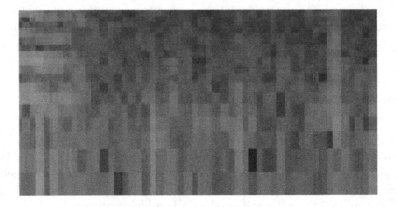

Fig. 7. Patch of Log Mel Spectrogram

5.4 Experimental Results

The proposed approach is compared with a traditional approach of extracting features from the speech signal. The model using mfcc and random forest classification algorithms gave an accuracy score of 0.75, F1 score of 0.8571 and recall score of 0.875. The model which used Mel log spectrogram and Vision transformer gave an accuracy score of 0.857, F1 score of 0.923 and recall score of 1. Based on the above presented results, the Vision transformer model is efficient when compared to the Random forest model. The model also gives an accuracy of 85.71% on test data. The novelty of this approach lies in attempting to model speech data as visual data using Vision transformer, and this technique is capable of capturing all of the intricate relationships in the spectrogram to discriminate and control audio data. It has shown a high degree of accuracy in comparison to other models. Thus, it is observed that the proposed Vision Transformer approach is efficient to model the dementia detection system as it captures the intrinsic features of audio spectrogram to model the early dementia detection system (Table 1).

Table 1. Comparative study on Vision Transformer and Random Forest approach

MODEL	ACCURACY SCORE	F1 SCORE	RECALL SCORE
MFCC+RANDOM FOREST	0.75	0.8571	0.875
LOG MEL SPECTROGRAM+ViT	0.857	0.923	1

6 Conclusion

The Multi-Head Attention in Vision Transformer concentrates only on the significant part of the image. It has better performance/compute trade off compared to random forest classifier. Random forest tends to overfit on prediction. Vision Transform classifier is robust against blockages. ViT shows a shape bias that is quite comparable to human judgement. Log Mel Spectrogram is often good to get the Deep Neural Network to learn complex representations. Log Mel spectrogram based model outperforms the MFCC based model. A Cross model can be built with the idea of detecting Alzheimer detection from speech and transcripts by merging ViT and BERT model. Accuracy of vision transformer should be improved on test data. Different and unique audio files are given as input to vision transformer for better and improved learning of the model. Other feature extraction techniques can be employed to improve accuracy. Scaling analytics along with Vit can make machine learning algorithms work better so that they can be applied at a larger scale than before without compromising accuracy and performance.

References

1. Abel, S., Huber, W., Dell, G.S.: Connectionist diagnosis of lexical disorders in aphasia. Aphasiology **23**, 1353–1378 (2009). https://doi.org/10.1080/02687030903022203
2. Zayats, V., Tran, T., Wright, R., Mansfield, C., Ostendorf, M.: Disfluencies and human speech transcription errors. Graz. arXiv [preprint] (2019). https://doi.org/10.21437/Interspeech.2019-3134
3. Balagopalan, A., Eyre, B., Robin, J., Rudzicz, F., Novikova, J.: Comparing pretrained and feature-based models for prediction of Alzheimer's disease based on speech. Front. Aging Neurosci. **27**(13), 635945 (2021). https://doi.org/10.3389/fnagi.2021.635945
4. Liu, N., Luo, K., Yuan, Z., Chen, Y.: A transfer learning method for detecting Alzheimer's disease based on speech and natural language processing. Front. Publ. Health **13**(10), 772592 (2022). https://doi.org/10.3389/fpubh.2022.772592
5. Addlesee, A., Eshghi, A., Konstas, I.: Current challenges in spoken dialogue systems and why they are critical for those living with dementia. arXiv preprint arXiv:1909.06644 (2019)
6. Wang, J., Wang, Y.H.: A neuropsychological study of linguistic disorder in Alzheimer's disease. Chin. Mental Health J. **5**, 263–5 (1999)
7. Roshanzamir, A., Aghajan, H., Soleymani Baghshah, M.: Transformer-based deep neural network language models for Alzheimer's disease risk assessment from targeted speech. BMC Med. Inform. Decis. Making (2021)

8. Kourtis, L.C., Regele, O.B., Wright, J.M., Jones, G.B.: Digital biomarkers for Alzheimer's disease: the mobile/wearable devices opportunity. NPJ Digit. Med. **2**, 9 (2019)
9. Weiner, J., Engelbart, M., Schultz, T.: Manual and automatic transcriptions in dementia detection from speech (2017)
10. Goodglass, H., Kaplan, E.: The Boston diagnostic aphasia examination (1983)
11. Bidani, A., Gouider, M.S., Traveso, C..M.: Dementia detection and classification from MRI images using deep neural networks and transfer learning. Published in IWANN12 (2019)
12. https://dementia.talkbank.org/access/English/Pitt.html

Multimodal Data Analysis

Active Contour Segmentation and Deep Learning Based Hand Gesture Recognition System for Deaf and Dumb People

A. Parvathy, R. Sriranjani, M. Meenalochani, N. Hemavathi[✉],
and G. Balasubramanian

SASTRA Deemed to Be University, Thanjavur, TamilNadu, India
nuhemasen@gmail.com

Abstract. Sign language facilitates hearing and speech impaired individuals to communicate with other members of the society. However, there are only few trained interpreters available for effective communication through sign language. Hence, an assistive system is mandate and hand gesture recognition system is one such technique. In this system, the hand gesture is captured by the camera and is fed to recognition system. The system involves segmentation and recognition based on trained images. To attain this, the image is segmented through skin, k-Means, edge detection and active contour methods and their quality metrics such as mean square error, root mean square error, signal to noise ratio, peak signal to noise ratio and normalized cross correlation are compared. From the results, it is inferred that the active contour based segmentation yield high quality segmentation. Further, active contour based segmented image is given as input to the deep learning algorithm to predict hand gesture. Furthermore, the generated text is converted to speech using in-built system speaker module.

Keywords: Deaf and dumb people · Hand gesture recognition · Image segmentation · Image extraction · Deep learning and speech synthesis

1 Introduction

Of the world's population, 15% of them suffer from disabilities. In India, 26% of the total population is affected with hearing and speaking disabilities. The deaf people cannot interact with the normal people without a sign language interpreter. Various forms of sign language are ISL (Indian Sign Language), ASL (American Sign Language), BSL (British Sign Language) etc. But, very few instructors/translators are available when compared to other countries which cause a major lack of communication between the normal people and the challenged ones. Even though lot of wearables such as gloves and wrist watch are available, it is not cost efficient and comfortable enough to deracinate the communication gap. Hence, gesture based identification system is evolved.

Gesture is a representation of substantial activities or emotional appearance. It includes hand gesture, body gesture etc. It can be categorized into two: static and dynamic gesture where the sign in the first case and the movement of the body or the hand in the

Anand Kumar M et al. (Eds.): SPELLL 2022, CCIS 1802, pp. 279–292, 2023.
https://doi.org/10.1007/978-3-031-33231-9_20

second case. Sign language recognition involves hand gestures, facial expressions and body movements for communication. Hand gesture identification is possible through glove, vision and color dye based approaches. In glove based approach, glove tools are used to sense hand pose, finger pliant and movement of hand as shown in Fig. 1. However, the consumer should compulsorily put on an aid that is similar to glove in this approach. As a consequence, this cannot be easily affordable by all. In color dye based approach, colored markers or distinct gloves are used to convey the progression of locating palm, fingers and to track the hand which is depicted in Fig. 2. But the shortcoming is that they are aberrant and inappropriate for applications through numerous users owing to hygiene issues. In vision based approach, camera(s) are mainly used to capture hand gestures for easy interaction between humans and the computers. The main advantage in this segment is nothing to be worn by the consumer which it is portrayed in Fig. 3. The advantage of this approach is that it is fairly simple, usual and easily operated.

   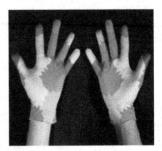

Fig. 1. Data Glove based identification   **Fig. 2.** Colour dye based re cognition

Fig. 3. Vision based identification

To conclude the hand gesture based identification system using camera is trustworthy, appropriate and cost effective solution for effectual communication between deaf and dumb and normal people. Hence, the literatures related to hand gesture recognition system is elaborated in the succeeding section.

2 Related Works

Spatio-temporal Hand gesture recognition based on fuzzy logic and neural network is presented [1]. Histogram thresholding algorithm considers gesture contour by a localized contour sequence [2]. Optimization based hand gesture recognition systems is discussed [3]. Spatiotemporal matching, classifier-based and sub-gesture reasoning algorithm for hand gesture recognition is proposed [4, 5]. Hand gesture based video game interaction using k-means clustering and support vector machine based classification is projected [6]. Hand gesture segmentation along with improved Kalman filter and TSL skin color model is proposed [7, 8]. Hand finger counting from skin color extraction using dominant points for hand gesture recognition is proposed [9]. Alphabets of Indian Sign Language recognition using real time hand tracking, hand segmentation, feature extraction and gesture recognition is projected [10]. Detection of meaningful gestures by fusing data from three-axis accelerometer (ACC) and multichannel electromyography (EMG) sensors is attempted [11]. Human-computer interaction with kinect sensor is projected [12]. Similarity matching algorithm and accelerometer based gesture recognition algorithm is presented [13]. Pyroelectric Infrared (PIR) sensors, kinect segment, accelerometer-based pen-type sensing device employed hand gesture recognition systems are presented [14–16].

Wireless, Electromyography (EMG) signals with artificial neural network based embedded system for hand gesture recognition is presented [17]. In addition, enhancing hand segmentation through wearing wristbands is attempted [18]. Deep neural networks-based recognition system is proposed for EgoGesture dataset [19]. Indian Sign Language (ISL) hand gestures into appropriate text message are attempted using segmentation and recognition system [20]. Sign Language Recognition system capable of recognizing 26 gestures from the Indian Sign Language by using MATLAB is discussed [21]. Hand contour model to reduce the computational complexity of gesture matching is presented [22]. Hand gesture based television control through automatic user state recognition scheme is proposed [23]. Vision-based system is employed to classify hand gestures with combined RGB and depth descriptor [24]. A complete gesture recognition framework based on maximum cosine similarity and fast nearest neighbor (NN) techniques for isolated recognition, gesture verification and gesture spotting on continuous data stream is attempted [27].

Automatic recognition of finger spelling using digital image processing techniques and artificial neural network in Indian sign language is recommended [26]. An algorithm that uses an articulated ICP minimization function that is initialized by the parameters obtained from a data set of hand gestures trained through a deep learning framework [27]. A deep convolutional neural network is proposed to directly classify hand gestures in images without any segmentation or detection stage that could discard the irrelevant not-hand areas [28]. A Recurrent Neural Network (RNN) trained by using the features i.e., the angles formed by the finger bones of the human hands acquired by a leap motion controller sensor is presented [29].

To conclude, hand gesture recognition system is a promising technique that can be adopted for hearing impaired to recognize their hand gestures through segmentation. Further, deep leaning based model is proposed to train large volume of images so that the model can be suitable for real time scenario.

3 Proposed System

The flow diagram of the proposed system is illustrated in Fig. 4. The input image is segmented using active contour segmentation. The segmented image is fed as input to the deep learning model. The trained data is stored in the data base. Whenever the input image is segmented, it is compared with the gestures stored in data base. If the gesture matches, the message will be generated as voice. On the other hand, if the gesture does not match, an error message will be displayed.

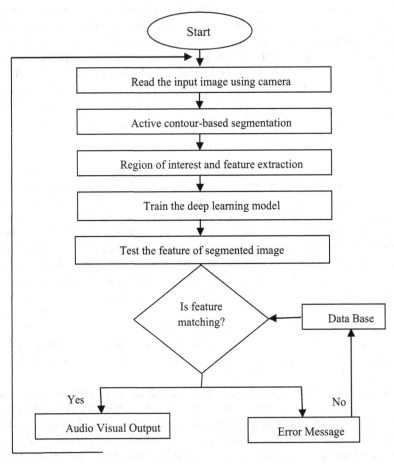

Fig. 4. Flow chart of the proposed system

The proposed system involves the following two phases and are elaborated in the subsequent sub-section:

(i)   Identification of appropriate segmentation method
(ii) Training and testing the deep learning based hand gesture recognition model

3.1 Image Segmentation

The accuracy of hand gesture recognition system relies on proper selection of segmentation method. To attain enhanced quality, image segmentation is carried out in input RGB image shown in Fig. 5 with the following four different techniques:

- Skin Segmentation
- k-Means Segmentation
- Edge-based Segmentation
- Active contour Segmentation

Further, their quality metrics such as mean square error, root mean square error, signal to noise ratio, peak signal to noise ratio and normalized cross correlation are analyzed. The process is elaborated in the following section.

3.1.1 Skin Segmentation

A pixel based skin color approach is used for detecting skin pixel and non skin pixel in color images. In this algorithm, RGB input image is chosen. The foremost step is to transform the skin- likelihood images with each pixel in RGB demonstration to CHROMA representation and critical likelihood value. Hence, all the skin regions are shown better than the non-skin region which is represented in Fig. 6. By using skin segmentation, code segmentation image is obtained. It neglects the backdrop of the original image.

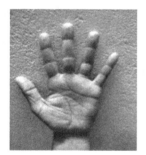  

| **Fig. 5.** Input Image | **Fig. 6.** Skin segmentation | **Fig. 7.** k-means segmentation |

3.1.2 K-Means Segmentation

k-Means clustering algorithm is a fragment of unsupervised algorithm and it is used to segment the RoI from the backdrop. To get better quality, the biased stretching enrichment is practical to the image prior to applying k-Means algorithm. This method follows least-square segmenting technique with the aim of dividing a collection of a group into k groups. This algorithm recapitulates over two steps namely,

- Calculate the mean of every cluster

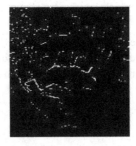

Fig. 8. Prewitt segmentation   **Fig. 9.** Robert segmentation   **Fig. 10.** Log segmentation

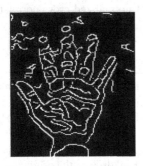

Fig. 11. Canny segmentation   **Fig. 12.** Active contour segmentation

- Allocate each point to its nearby cluster after computing the distance linking every point of all clusters with reference to the resulting cluster mean.
- Recapitulate the above two steps until the sum of squared error in the group cannot be lesser any longer.

Backdrop of the image is also measured and is not neglected in k-Means segmentation. The output image of k-Means segmentation is depicted in Fig. 7.

3.1.3 Edge Based Segmentation

Edge detection is a process of locating an edge of an image. Ever since edges repeatedly take place at image locations signifying objects boundaries, it is extensively used within image segmentation process as images are alienated into areas corresponding towards altered objects. This process is used to remove all needless false points on the boundaries in an image. This process will work only after filtering the noise from the image. The boundary operator is useful to detect the boundaries of the image after the boundaries are smoothed using a proper marginal value, which removes all the outmoded points. Edge based partitioning represents a collection of methods scheduled on information about boundaries in an image. Edge segmentation is accomplished through four different techniques listed below:

- Perwitt Segmentation
- Roberts's segmentation
- Laplacian of a Gaussian (LoG) based segmentation
- Canny segmentation

The output images of edge based segmentation are displayed from Fig. 8, 9, 10 and 11 respectively.

PERWITT SEGMENTATION.

Prewitt segmentation involves discrete differentiation operator that computes a rough calculation of the gradient image intensity function. In addition, it is used predominantly in edge detection algorithms.

ROBERT'S SEGMENTATION.

By computing sum of the squared difference among crosswise adjacent pixels and the gradient of an image, segmentation is obtained using cross operator during discrete differentiation.

LAPLACIAN OF A GAUSSIAN (LoG) BASED SEGMENTATION.

LoG operator computes the second derivative of an image. This means that in places anywhere the image has a non-changing intensity (i.e., where the gradient of intensity is 0), the LoG output will also be 0. However, while close to change of intensity, the LoG output response will be +ve on the darker side and lighter side will be −ve accordingly. This means that at a sharp edge among two regions of standardized but varying intensities, the LoG output will be:

- 0 at a far distance from the edge
- +ve just to one side of the edge
- −ve just to the other side of the edge
- 0 at a point in between, on the edge itself

CANNY SEGMENTATION

Canny edge detection algorithm involves the following five steps:

- Gaussian filter is applied for noise removal and to smooth the image
- The gradient image intensity is found out
- Spurious response to attain edge detection, minimum suppression speed is used
- Double threshold power is utilized by influencing its own potential edges,
- Suppressing weaker boundaries and connecting to stronger boundaries in the end, the edge detection is finalized

3.1.4 Active Contour Segmentation

Active contour model known as snake model involves the use of constraints and energy forces for segmentation of the significant pixels. Its boundaries are designed as active models and are based on the areas of interest necessary in an image. Contour is a compilation of points so as to experience interpolation progression. The interpolation progression should be splines, linear and polynomial which elaborates the curvature in an image. The contour model forms a parametric curve or object boundaries or any other which is different from the features of the image. Energy function is constantly linked through the curve defined in the image. External energy is defined as the mixture of forces owing to the image which is exclusively meant for controlling the contour location onto the images. Deformable changes are controlled using the internal energy. The essential color is attained by minimum of the energy function. Contour can be clearly derived from constraints as well as forces in the regions of the image. The Fig. 12 correspond to the output image of active contour segmentation is presented.

Further to choose the best method for segmentation, quality of the segmented image has to be analyzed. To facilitate this, the image quality metrics for the segmented methods are analyzed. Based on the quality metrics, the best segmented image is obtained. The image quality metrics [30] to analyse the segmentation methods are presented in Appendix 1.

3.2 Deep Learning Based Hand Gesture Recognition Model:

The best segmented image obtained through segmentation model is stored in data base. The segmented images are fed as input to deep learning model. The deep neural network is constructed using Convolutional Neural Network (CNN). The segmented images will train the network and stored in database. The input segmented hand gesture is compared with the data base and it is converted to text and voice message if it matches. Or else, error message will be displayed.

4 Implementation

Hand gestures are captured using camera and the data base is initially created. The raw data base is fed as input to the pool of image segmentation algorithms implemented in MATLAB. Segmentation of the hand gestures are accomplished using skin, k-Means, edge based segmentation, and active contour methods and the segmented images are presented from Figs. 6, 7, 8, 9, 10 and 11 respectively. Further, the quality of the segmented image is analyzed using image quality metrics such as mean square error, root mean square error, signal to noise ratio, peak signal to noise ratio and normalized cross correlation to identify high quality segmented image. From the quality metrics, it is observed that active contour based segmentation outperforms when compared with other methods. Further active contour based segmented image is fed as input to deep learning neural network for recognition. The result obtained through segmentation, their quality analysis and efficiency of the deep learning model are demonstrated in the succeeding section.

5 Result and Discussions

Segmentation algorithm such as skin, k-Means, Edge based and Active contour Segmentation are implemented in MATLAB. Thus, the original image and the segmented images are presented from Figs. 5, 6, 7, 8, 9, 10, 11 and 12 respectively. The comparison of all the segmentation algorithms is accomplished to identify high quality segmented image and the comparison of all the algorithms are tabulated in below Table 1.

Table 1. Comparison of Segmentation Methods along with the metrics

	MSE	RMSE	SNR	PSNR	NCC
Skin	9173	95.7424	8.51184	7.73349	–
K-Means	0.00064	0.02428	32.5824	28.4587	–
Perwitt	0.394	0.62684	4.06929	−11.27	− 0.1804
Roberts	0.39448	0.62725	4.063	−11.719	− 0.1871
Log	0.38919	0.62368	4.11498	−10.212	− 0.1204
Canny	0.39574	0.62818	4.05178	−9.0724	-0.249
Active Contour	0.4461625	0.6677875	3.5096625	−4.1675125	-0.9041875

From the table, it is evident that active contour proves to be better. With the basis of 10 different hand gestures are segmented and their segmented images are presented below in Fig. 13.

From Fig. 13, it is evident that active contour based segmentation performs better. However, when the number of images is higher, it is advisable to implement a hand gesture recognition system. Under such condition, Deep Neural Network based hand gesture recognition system is proposed and implemented. The hand gestures correspond to 20 positions in different angles are segmented and fed as input to the deep learning algorithm and the performance of the algorithm in terms of accuracy and loss is obtained. The input and output correspond to deep learning model is presented in Fig. 14 and 15 respectively.

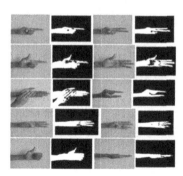

Fig. 13. Input and Segmented Images

From Fig. 13, it is evident that active contour based segmentation performs better. However, when the number of images is higher, it is advisable to implement a hand gesture recognition system. Under such condition, Deep Neural Network based hand gesture recognition system is proposed and implemented.

The hand gestures correspond to 20 positions in different angles are segmented and fed as input to the deep learning algorithm and the performance of the algorithm in terms of accuracy and loss is obtained. The input and output correspond to deep learning model is presented in Fig. 14 and 15 respectively.

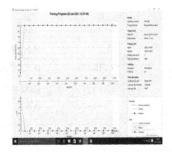

Fig. 14. Segmented Image   **Fig. 15.** Performance of DNN model

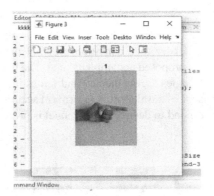

Fig. 16. Text and Speech display

From the above Fig. 15 and 16, it is clear that active contour segmented and DNN based Hand gesture recognition system yields better results in terms of accuracy. In addition, the algorithm converts speech into text which is clearly evident in Fig. 16.

6   Conclusion

Hand gesture recognition system is a prominent technique ought to be adopted to facilitate smooth communication of deaf and dumb people with others. Hence, active contour and deep neural network based hand gesture recognition system is proposed. The proposal is implemented in MATLAB. At first, image segmentation is carried out using skin, k-Means, edge and active contour methods. The quality of output image through these segmentation methods is analyzed based on the quality metrics. From results, it is evident that active contour segmentation suits better. Further, the segmented images are fed as input to Deep Neural Network to predict the hand gesture. The predicted gesture is converted to text and is further converted to voice through in-built system speaker in MATLAB. Implementation of hand gesture recognition system using real time videos is the future scope of the work.

Appendix 1

Image Quality Metrics

Mean Squared Error (MSE): Mean Squared Error method calculates the average of the squares of the errors (of a method intended for estimating an overlooked quantity). MSE is expected to be positive whose values closer to zero are expected.

$$\bar{x} = \frac{\sum x}{N} \tag{1}$$

where $\sum x$ - the sum of x
N - number of data
$\bar{x}$ - mean

$$\sigma^2 = \frac{\sum (x - \mu)^2}{N} \tag{2}$$

where
σ^2 - variance
N - Number of scores

Root Mean Square Error (RMSE): The Root Mean Square Error is a determination of the difference between the empirical and obtained values by a model predictor. RMSE correspond to square root of disparity among obtained values and empirical values. RMSE is expected to be always positive and a value of 0 (almost never achieved in practice) point out a perfect fit data. RMSE of a predictor with respect to an predicted parameter is defined as the square root of the mean square error and is given by

$$RMSE = \sqrt{MSE} \tag{3}$$

where RMSE- Root Mean Square Error
MSE - Mean Square Error

Signal to Noise Ratio (SNR): Signal-Noise Ratio (SNR or S/N) is a metric to compare level of a required signal near the backdrop noise and is denoted in dB. The ratio of 1:1, greater than 0 dB indicates less noise and more signals.

$$SNR = \frac{\sum_{x=0}^{M-1} \sum_{y=0}^{N-1} \hat{f}(x,y)^2}{\sum_{x=0}^{M-1} \sum_{y=0}^{N-1} \left[f(x,y) - \hat{f}(x,y) \right]^2} \tag{4}$$

The measurement of both noise and signal ought to be calculated at the similar and equal points in a system and it should be bounded within the same system. SNR for arbitrary noise ratio of 'N' with zero depends either on signal that should be constant or an arbitrary variable value should be one. It is characterized through Eq. (5).

$$SNR = \frac{S^2}{\sigma_N^2} \qquad (5)$$

Peak Signal to Noise Ratio (PSNR): The ratio among the greatest possible power of a signal and the power of humiliating noise

$$PSNR = \frac{Utmost\_Power}{Humiliating\_Noise} \qquad (6)$$

The quality of the compressed or reconstructed image is better when the PSNR value is higher.

Normalized Cross Correlation (NCC): Cross-correlation is the comparison of two different time series to detect if there is a correlation between metrics with the same maximum and minimum values. Normalized cross-correlation is also the comparison of two time series, but using a different scoring result.

References

1. Su, M.C.: A fuzzy rule-based approach to spatio-temporal hand gesture recognition. IEEE Trans. Syst. Man Cybern. Part C Appl. Rev. **30**(2), 276–281 (2000)
2. Gupta, L., Ma, S.: Gesture-based interaction and communication: automated classification of hand gesture contours. IEEE Trans. Syst. Man Cybern. Part C Appl. Rev. **31**(1) 114–120 (2001)
3. Wachs, J.P., Stern, H.I., Edan, Y.: Cluster labeling and parameter estimation for the automated setup of a hand-gesture recognition system. IEEE Trans. Syst. Man Cybern. Part A Syst. Hum. **35**(6), 932–944 (2005)
4. Alon, J., Athitsos, V., Yuan, Q., Sclaroff, S.: A unified framework for gesture recognition and spatiotemporal gesture segmentation. IEEE Trans. Pattern Anal. Mach. Intell. **31**(9), 1685–1699 (2009)
5. Yang, R., Sarkar, S., Loeding, B.: Handling movement epenthesis and hand segmentation ambiguities in continuous sign language recognition using nested dynamic programming. IEEE Trans. Pattern Anal. Mach. Intell. **32**(3), 462–477 (2010)
6. Dardas, N.H., Georganas, N.D.: Real-time hand gesture detection and recognition using bag-of-features and support vector machine techniques. IEEE Trans. Instrum. Measur. **60**(11), 3592–3607 (2011)
7. Mo, S., Cheng, S., Xing, X.: Hand gesture segmentation based on improved Kalman filter and TSL skin color model. In: 2011 IEEE Conference, pp. 3543–3546 (2011)
8. Tsai, T.-H., Huang, C.-C., Zhang, K.-L.: Design of hand gesture recognition system for human-computer interaction. Multimedia Tools Appl. **79**(9–10), 5989–6007 (2019). https://doi.org/10.1007/s11042-019-08274-w

9. Meng, Z., Pan, J.S., Tseng, K.K., Zheng, W.: Dominant points based hand finger counting for recognition under skin color extraction in hand gesture control system. In: 2012 Sixth International Conference on Genetic and Evolutionary Computing, pp. 364–367 (2012)
10. Ghotkar, A.S., Khatal, R., Khupase, S., Asati, S., Hadap, M.: Hand gesture recognition for Indian sign language. In: 2012 International Conference on Computer Communication and Informatics (ICCCI -2012), Jan. 10 – 12, Coimbatore, India (2012)
11. Zhang, X., Chen, X., Li, Y., Lantz, V., Wang, K., Yang, J.: A framework for hand gesture recognition based on accelerometer and EMG sensors. IEEE Trans. Syst. Man Cybern. Part A Syst. Hum. 41(6), 1064–1076 (2011)
12. Ren, Z., Yuan, J., Meng, J., Zhang, Z.: Robust part-based hand gesture recognition using kinect sensor. IEEE Trans. Multimedia 15(5), 1110–1120 (2013)
13. Xie, R., Sun, X., Xia, X., Cao, J.: Similarity matching-based extensible hand gesture recognition. IEEE Sens. J. 15(6), 3475–3483 (2015)
14. Erden, F., Cetin, A.E.: Hand gesture based remote control system using infrared sensors and a camera. IEEE Trans. Consum. Electr. 60(4), 675–680 (2014)
15. Ju, Z., Ji, X., Li, J., Liu, H.: An integrative framework of human hand gesture segmentation for human–robot interaction. IEEE Syst. J. 11(3), 1326–1336 (2017)
16. Xie, R., Cao, J.: Accelerometer-based hand gesture recognition by neural network and similarity matching. IEEE Sens. J. 16(11), 4537–4545 (2016)
17. Liu, X., Sacks, J., Zhang, M., Richardson, A.G., Lucas, T.H., Van der Spiegel, J.: The virtual trackpad: an electromyography-based, wireless, real-time, low-power, embedded hand-gesture-recognition system using an event-driven artificial neural network. IEEE Trans. Circ. Syst. II Express Briefs. 64(11), 1257–1261 (2017)
18. Lee, D.L., You, W.S.: Recognition of complex static hand gestures by using the wristband-based contour features. IET Image Process. 12(1), 80–87 (2017)
19. Zhang, Y., Cao, C., Cheng, J., Lu, H.: EgoGesture: a new dataset and benchmark for egocentric hand gesture recognition. IEEE Trans. Multimedia 20(5), 1038–1050 (2018)
20. Shangeetha, R.K., Valliammai, V., Padmavathi, S.: Computer vision based approach for Indian sign language character recognition. In: 2012 International conference on machine vision and image processing (MVIP), pp. 181–184. IEEE (2012)
21. Narayan, S., Sawant, S.N., Kumbhar, M.S.: Real time sign language recognition using PCA. In: 2014 IEEE International Conference on Advanced Communication Control and Computing Technologies, pp. 1412–1415 (2014)
22. Yao, Y., Fu, Y.: Contour model-based hand-gesture recognition using the kinect sensor. IEEE Trans. Circ. Syst. Video Technol. 24(11), 1935–1944 (2014)
23. Lian, S., Hu, W., Wang, K.: Automatic user state recognition for hand gesture based low-cost television control system. IEEE Trans. Consum. Electron. 60(1), 107–115 (2014)
24. Ohn-Bar, E., Trivedi, M.M.: Hand gesture recognition in real time for automotive interfaces: a multimodal vision-based approach and evaluations. IEEE Trans. Intell. Transp. Syst. 15(6), 2368–2377 (2014)
25. Poularakis, S., Katsavounidis, I.: Low-complexity hand gesture recognition system for continuous streams of digits and letters. IEEE Trans. Cybern. 46(9), 2094–2108 (2016)
26. Adithya, V., Vinod, P.R., Gopalakrishnan, U.: Artificial neural network based method for Indian sign language recognition. In: Proceedings of 2013 IEEE Conference on Information and Communication Technologies (ICT 2013), pp. 1080–1085 (2013)
27. Sanchez-Riera, J., Srinivasan, K., Hua, K.L., Cheng, W.H., Hossain, M.A., Alhamid, M.F.: Robust RGB-D hand tracking using deep learning priors. IEEE Trans. Circ. Syst. Video Technol. 28(9), 2289–2301 (2018)

28. Bao, P., Maqueda, A.I., del-Blanco, C.R., García, N.: Tiny hand gesture recognition without localization via a deep convolutional network. IEEE Trans. Consum. Electron. **63**(3), 251–257 (2017)

29. Avola, D., Bernardi, M., Cinque, L., Foresti, G.L., Massaroni, C.: Exploiting recurrent neural networks and leap motion controller for the recognition of sign language and semaphoric hand gestures. IEEE Trans. Multimedia **21**(1), 234–245 (2019)

30. https://www.mathworks.com/help/images/image-quality-metrics.html

Multimodal Hate Speech Detection from Bengali Memes and Texts

Md. Rezaul Karim[1,2(✉)], Sumon Kanti Dey[3], Tanhim Islam[2], Md Shajalal[1,4], and Bharathi Raja Chakravarthi[5]

[1] Fraunhofer Institute for Applied Information Technology FIT,
Sankt Augustin, Germany
rezaul.karim@rwth-aachen.de
[2] RWTH Aachen University, Aachen, Germany
[3] Noakhali Science and Technology University, Noakhali, Bangladesh
[4] University of Siegen, Siegen, Germany
[5] University of Galway, Galway, Ireland

Abstract. Numerous machine learning (ML) and deep learning (DL)-based approaches have been proposed to utilize textual data from social media for anti-social behavior analysis like cyberbullying, fake news detection, and identification of hate speech mainly for highly-resourced languages such as English. However, despite of having a lot of diversity and millions of native speakers, some languages like Bengali are under-resourced, which is due to lack of computational resources for natural language processing (NLP). Similar to other languages, Bengali social media contents also include images along with texts (e.g., multimodal memes are posted by embedding short texts into images on Facebook). Therefore, only the textual data is not enough to judge them since images might give extra context to make a proper judgement. This paper is about hate speech detection from multimodal Bengali memes and texts. We prepared the only multimodal hate speech dataset for-a-kind of problem for Bengali, which we use to train state-of-the-art neural architectures (e.g., Bi-LSTM/Conv-LSTM with word embeddings, ConvNets + pre-trained language models, e.g., monolingual Bangla BERT, multilingual BERT-cased/uncased, and XLM-RoBERTa) to jointly analyze textual and visual information for hate speech detection. Conv-LSTM and XLM-RoBERTa models performed best for texts, yielding F1 scores of 0.78 and 0.82, respectively. As of memes, ResNet-152 and DenseNet-161 models yield F1 scores of 0.78 and 0.79, respectively. As of multimodal fusion, XLM-RoBERTa + DenseNet-161 performed the best, yielding an F1 score of 0.83. Our study suggest that text modality is most useful for hate speech detection, while memes are moderately useful.

Keywords: Hate speech detection · Under-resourced language · Bengali · Multimodal memes · Word embeddings · Transformer language models

Anand Kumar M et al. (Eds.): SPELLL 2022, CCIS 1802, pp. 293–308, 2023.
https://doi.org/10.1007/978-3-031-33231-9_21

1   Introduction

The micro-blogging sites and social media not only empower freedom of expression and individual voices, but also tempts people to express anti-social behavior [13,14], like cyberbullying, online rumours, and spreading hatred statements [18]. Abusive speech expressing prejudice towards a certain group is also very common, and based on race, religion, and sexual orientation is getting pervasive. United Nations Strategy and Plan of Action on Hate Speech [10] defines hate speech as *any kind of communication in speech, writing or behaviour, that attacks or uses pejorative or discriminatory language regarding a person or a group based on their religion, ethnicity, colour, gender or other identity factors.*

Bengali is spoken by 230 million people in Bangladesh and India, making it one of the major languages in the world. Similar to other major languages such as English, anti-social behaviors like propagating hate speech is also getting rampant in Bengali. Karim et al. [13] have shown via some examples that hate speech in Bengali not only signify how severe Bengali hateful statements could be, but also show that hate speech is contextualized from the personal to religious, political, and geopolitical levels. Since such hate speech is getting more pervasive, there is a potential chance that these could lead to serious consequences such as hate crimes [13], regardless of languages, geographic locations, or ethnicity. Addressing and identifying hate speech does not mean limiting or prohibiting freedom of speech, rather keeping it from escalating to a more dangerous level [10].

Bengali: পাকিস্তানের প্রেতাত্মারা পাকিস্তানে ফেরত যা, মুক্তিযুদ্ধের বাংলায় রাজাকারের ঠাই নাই।

English: The ghosts of Pakistan should be deported to Pakistan, there's no place for Razakars in Bangladesh.

Bengali: বাংলাদেশ ব্যাংকের টাকা লোপাট হাসিনা চুন্নিকে আগেই জানানো হয়েছে বলে জানালেন গভর্নর আতিউর।

English: Governor Atiur Rahman on money laundering issue of Bangladesh Bank said that Hasina plunderer were already been informed about it.

Bengali: মুফতি ইলিয়াস আর জাকির নায়েক, এই দুই হিন্দু বিদ্বেষীকে জোটিয়ে ভারত ছাড়া করা হোক।

English: Mufti Ilyas and Zakir Naik, these two Hindu haters should be expelled from India.

Bengali: একজন মানবিক সিরিয়াল বলাৎকার কারীর ইতিহাস: ছাত্রদের কষ্ট আমি বুঝ, ওরা যাতে ব্যাথা না পায় তাই থুথু দিয়া করি।

English: The history of a humane serial rapist: I understand the suffering of the students, why I spit so that they do not get hurt.

Fig. 1. Some examples of multimodal hate speech memes in Bengali

Automatic identification of such hate speeches in social media and raising public awareness is of utmost importance for Bengali too [13]. Owing to unrestricted access, digitalization, and use of social media, we have access to a huge amount of online contents. Manual reviewing and verification of such large scale data is not only time-consuming and labor-intensive, but also prone to potential human errors [12]. Therefore, robust and scalable methods are required for accurate identification of hate speech in an automated way. Further, similar to other major language, recent Bengali social media content also include images along with texts (e.g., in Twitter, multimodal tweets are formed by images with short texts embedded into). As shown in Fig. 1[1], some of these multimodal contents are only hate speech because of the combination of the text with a certain image. The presence of only offensive terms does not signify the traces of hate speech, as the hate propagators tend to intentionally construct contents, where the text is not enough to determine they are really hate speech [12]. In such cases, images may provide extra context to make a proper judgement.

Numerous works that have been proposed to accurately identify hate speech in major languages like English that are based on machine learning (ML) and neural networks (DNNs) [12,23]. However, Bengali is severely low-resourced for natural language processing (NLP), albeit it is a rich language with a lot of diversity. One of the primary reasons is it lacks computational resources such as language models, properly annotated and labelled datasets, and efficient ML methods. Further, similar to other major languages, modern Bengali data consist of texts, images, and memes containing texts that could provide extra context and eventually improve the performance of identifying hate. State-of-the-art (SotA) transformer language models are becoming increasingly effective in various NLP tasks. Besides, multimodal ML is also being increasingly applied to handle multimodal contents. However, none of the existing works focus on jointly analyzing textual and visual information for hate speech detection in Bengali.

Inspired by the success of transformer-based language models and SotA multimodal ML learning, we propose a novel approach for accurate identification of hate speech from Bengali memes and texts. In our approach, Bengali memes and texts are first comprehensively preprocessed, before classifying them into either hate speech or neutral w.r.t political, personal, geopolitical, and religious contexts. We apply different multimodal learning techniques in combination with early- and late fusion techniques, including transformer-based neural architectures (i.e., Bangla BERT-base, multilingual BERT (mBERT), and XLM-RoBERTa) and CNN architectures (i.e., VGG, ResNet, DenseNet, and EfficientNet) for the text and imaging modality, respectively. We carried out a wide range of experiments by training several ML and DNN baseline models on which we provide comparative analysis. Overall contributions of our paper is 4-folds:

1. We prepared the largest and only multimodal hate speech detection dataset to date for the Bengali language.
2. We train state-of-the-art neural architectures to accurate identification of hateful statements from memes and texts.
3. We provide comprehensive evaluation and comparison with baselines.

---

[1] **Disclaimer**: memes and lexicons contain contents that are racist, sexist, homophobic, and offensive in different ways. Further, authors want to clarify that the dataset is collected and annotated from social media for research purposes only and not intended to hurt or offense any specific person, entity, or religious/political groups/parties.

4. To foster reproducible research, we make available computational resources such as annotated dataset, language models, and source codes that will further advance the NLP research for under-resourced Bengali language.

The rest of the paper is structured as follows: Sect. 2 critically reviews related works. Section 3 describes our proposed approach. Section 4 reports experiment results, including a comparative analysis with baseline models. Section 5 summarizes this research with potential limitations and points to some possible outlooks before concluding the paper.

2 Related Work

Numerous works have been proposed to accurately identify hate speech in major languages like English [12,23]. Many classic methods traditionally rely on manual feature engineering, e.g., support vector machines (SVM), Naïve Bayes (NB), logistic regression (LR), decision trees (DT), random forest (RF), and gradient boosted trees (GBT). Waseem et al. [24] use classical ML techniques to classify 16,000 tweets as racist and sexist. They used word n-grams and character n-grams in conjunction with other task-specific engineered features like gender information and location information. Davidson et al. [6] used LR along with L1 regularization to decrease the dimensionality of data. They have experimented with multiple traditional ML classifiers like RF, LR, NB, DT, and linear SVMs, where LR and linear SVMs perform significantly better than other models. Malmasi et al. [25] obtained 78% accuracy in identifying posts across three classes - hate, offensive, and neutral using an approach based on character n-grams, word n-grams, and word skip-grams along with SVM for multiclass classification.

DNN-based approaches that can learn multi-layers of abstract features from raw texts that are primarily based on convolutional neural networks (CNNs) or long short-term memory (LSTM) networks. In comparison with DNN-based methods, ML-based approaches are rather incomparable as the efficiency of linear models at dealing with billions of such texts has proven less accurate and unscalable, while DNNs architectures perform on average 10% better across classification tasks in NLP. CNN and LSTM networks are two popular DNN architectures. While CNN is an effective feature extractor, LSTM is suitable for modelling orderly sequence learning problems. CNN extracts word or character combinations and LSTM learns long-range word or character dependencies in texts. While each type of network has relative advantages, few works have explored combining both architectures into a single network [22]. Conv-LSTM is a robust architecture to capture long-term dependencies between features extracted by CNN and found more effective than structures solely based on CNN or LSTM (where the class of a sequence depends on its preceding sequence).

Further, various off-the-shelf word embeddings like Word2Vec, FastText, and GloVe, along with DNN classifiers i.e., CNNs, LSTMs, and GRUs, are employed in these approaches. Gomez et al. [7] experimented with three different models including feature concatenation model (FCM), spatial concatenation models (SCM), and textual kernel model (TKM). The basic FCM performed better than all, and they concluded that no additional improvement in performance could be obtained with the addition of images in hate speech detection. A multimodal approach by Blandfort et al. [2] provides a promising improvement over the best single modality approach, yielding an average precision of 18%. They use both early fusion and late fusion techniques in which a late fusion model with a stack of SVM classifiers showed a better performance.

Transformer-based language models are becoming increasingly effective at NLP tasks and have made a notable shift in the performance on all text classification tasks including hate speech detection [21]. In addition, research has exposed the ability of BERT variants such as mBERT and XLM-RoBERTa to capture hateful context within social media content by using new fine-tuning methods based on transfer learning [21]. Sai et al. [20] fine-tuned the XLM-RoBERTa and mBERT for offensive speech detection in Dravidian languages and experimented with inter-language, inter-task, and multi-task transfer learning strategies leveraging resources available for offensive speech detection in the English language. Ranasinghe et al. [17] also fine-tuned XLM-RoBERTa for offensive language identification in three languages Bengali, Hindi, and Spanish, improving other deep learning models by fine-tuning Transformers [21].

Further, autoencoder (AE)-based representation learning techniques have been employed to solve numerous supervised and unsupervised learning tasks. In AE architectures, weights of the encoder module are learned from both non-corrupted and unlabeled data. Subsequently, noisy supervised data with missing modalities is not suitable for learning latent features. Although, a simple AE can be used to reconstruct an output similar to the original input, it cannot handle multimodality. Therefore, AE-based multimodal representation learning techniques emerged, e.g., a new approach called deep orthogonal fusion (DOF) model is proposed by Braman et al. [3]. DOF first learns to combine information from multimodal inputs into a comprehensive multimodal risk score, by combining embeddings from each modality via attention-gated tensor fusion. To maximize the information gleaned from each modality, they introduce a new loss function called multimodal orthogonalization loss that increases model performance by incentivizing constituent embeddings to be more complementary.

Patrick et al. [16] proposed another multimodal concept of learning called shared latent representation (SLR) and latent representation concatenation (LRC) techniques. Based on several studies covering text classification, sequence data, and imaging, they identified several limitations of SLR. First, the reconstruction loss for LRC is significantly lower compared to SLR-based representation learning technique. Secondly, when a classifier is trained on features learned by LRC, accuracy improves significantly, which is largely backed by lower reconstruction loss. On the other hand, accurate identification of hate speech in Bengali is a challenging task. Only a few restrictive approaches [11,13,19] have been proposed so far. Romim et al. [19] prepared a dataset of 30K comments, making it one of the largest datasets for identifying offensive and hateful statements. However, this dataset has several issues. First, it is very imbalanced as the ratio of hate speech to non-hate speech is 10K:20K. Second, the majority of hate statements are very short in terms of length and word count compared to non-hate statements. Third, their approach exhibits a moderate level of effectiveness at identifying offensive or hateful statements, giving an accuracy of 82%.

Ismam et al. [11] collected hateful comments from Facebook and annotated 5,126 hateful statements. They classified them into six classes- hate speech, communal attack, insightful, religious hatred, political comments, and religious comments. Their approach, based on GRU-based DNN, achieved an accuracy of 70.10%. In a recent approach [13], Karim et al. provided classification benchmarks for document classification, sentiment analysis, and hate speech detection for Bengali. By combining fastText embedding with multichannel Conv-LSTM network, their approach is probably the first work among a few others on hate speech detection. Since fastText works well with rare words such that even if a word was not seen during the training, it could be broken down into n-grams to get its corresponding embedding. Therefore, using fastText-based embeddings were more beneficial than that of Word2Vec and GloVe models.

Nevertheless, there exists significant difference among texts and meme modalities. Therefore, instead of using manually engineered convolutional filters in CNN, convolutional and pooling layers can be stacked together to construct a stacked convolutional AE (SCAE), to leverage better feature extraction capability. CAE learns more optimal filters by minimizing the reconstruction loss, which results in more abstract features from the encoder. This helps stabilize the pre-training, and the network converges faster by avoiding corruption in the feature space [9], making it more effective for very high dimensional data compared to vanilla AE-based multimodal learning. Therefore, considering the limitations of vanilla AE and SLR and the effectiveness of multimodal ML architectures, we constructed both MCAE based on a CAE and DOF.

3   Methods

In this section, we discuss our proposed approach in detail, covering word embedding, multimodal learning, and training of different network architectures.

3.1   Data Preprocessing

We remove HTML markups, links, image titles, special characters, and excessive use of spaces/tabs, before initiating the annotation process. Further, following preprocessing steps are followed before training ML and DNN baseline models:

- **PoS tagging:** using BLSTM-CRF based approach [1].
- **Removal of proper nouns:** proper nouns and noun suffixes were replaced with tags to provide ambiguity.
- **Hashtags normalization**: Hastags were normalized, with the goal of supplying normalized hashtag content to be used for the classification tasks.
- **Stemming:** inflected words were reduced to their stem, base or root form.
- **Stop word removal:** commonly used Bengali stop words are removed.
- All emojis, emoticons, duplicates, and user mentions were removed.
- **Infrequent words**: tokens with low frequency (TF and IDF) were removed.

As BERT-based models perform better classification accuracy on uncleaned texts, we did not perform major preprocessing tasks, except for the lightweight preprocessing discussed above. On the other hand, for the imaging modality, we performed some preprocessing as the dataset has varying sizes. Therefore, images are converted into RGB format before extracting features, while the sizes are adjusted according to deep CNN model specification.

3.2 Neural Word Embeddings

We train the *fastText* [8] word embedding model on Bengali articles used for the classification benchmark study by Karim et al. [13]. The preprocess reduces vocabulary size due to the colloquial nature of the texts and some degree, addresses the sparsity in the word-based feature representations. We have also tested, by keeping word inflexions, lemmatization, and lower document frequencies[2]. The fastText model represents each word as an n-gram of characters, which helps capture the meaning of shorter words and allows the embeddings to understand suffixes and prefixes. Each token is embedded into a 300-dimensional vector space, where each element is the weight for the dimension for that token. Since the annotated hate statements are relatively short, we constrain each sequence to 100 words by truncating longer texts and pad shorter ones with zero values to avoid padding in convolutional layers with many blank vectors.

3.3 Training of DNN Baseline Models

We train three DNN baselines: CNN, Bi-LSTM, and Conv-LSTM. Weights of the embedding layer for each network are initialized with the embeddings based on the fastText embedding model. The embedding layer maps each hate statement into a *sequence* (for LSTM and CNN layers) and transforms it into feature representation, which is then flattened and fed into a fully connected softmax layer. Further, we add Gaussian noise and dropout layers to improve model generalization. AdaGrad optimizer is used to learn the model parameters by reducing the categorical-cross-entropy loss. We train each DNN architecture 5 separate times in a 5-fold CV setting, followed by measuring the average F1-score on the validation set to choose the best hyperparameters.

3.4 Training of Transformer-Based Models

As shown in Fig. 2, we train monolingual Bangla BERT-base, mBERT, and XLM-RoBERTa large models. Bangla-BERT-base[3] is a pretrained Bengali language model built with BERT-based mask language modelling. RoBERTa [15] is an improved variant of BERT, which is optimized by setting larger batch sizes, introducing dynamic masking, and training on larger datasets. XLM-RoBERTa [5] is a multilingual model trained on web-crawled data. XLM-RoBERTa not only outperformed other transformer models on cross-lingual benchmarks but also performed better on various NLP tasks in low-resourced language settings [20].

---

[2] We observe slightly better accuracy using lemmatization, hence we report the result based on it.
[3] https://huggingface.co/sagorsarker/bangla-bert-base.

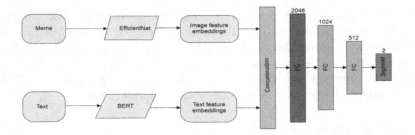

Fig. 2. Schematic representation of the approach for hate speech detection

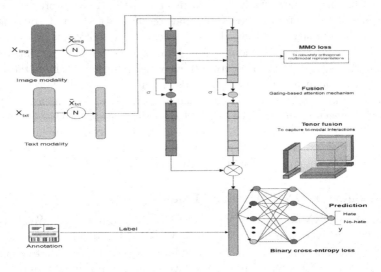

Fig. 3. DOF model for hate speech detection (recreated based on literature [3])

We shuffle training data for each epoch and apply gradient clipping to clip error derivative to a threshold during backward propagation of the network. We set the initial learning rate to $2e^{-5}$ and employ Adam optimizer with the scheduled learning rate. PLMs are fine-tuned by setting the maximum input length to 256. We experimented with 2, 3, and 4 layers of multi-head attention, followed by placing a fully connected softmax layer on top. Several experiments are carried out with different hyperparameters combinations, as shown in Table 1.

3.5 Multimodal Fusion and Classification

Let X be a training minibatch of data for N samples, each containing M modalities such that $X = [x_1, x_2, \ldots, x_M]$, where x_m represents the data for respective modality m. We employ two approaches to learn the joint embeddings (LRC and late fusion using DFO), followed by supervised-fine tuning for the classification. In LRC, first image, image-text, and textual embedding are first learned. Assuming input $x_m \in \mathbb{R}^D$ for each of $m \in \mathbb{R}^K$ modalities is consisting of N

Table 1. Hyperparam combinations for pre-trained language models (PLMs)

Hyper-parameters	Value
Learning-rate	{2e–5, 3e–5}
Epochs	{5, 6, 10, 20}
Max sequence length	{64, 128, 256}
Dropout	{0.1, 0.2, 0.3, 0.5}
Batch size	{16, 32, 64, 128}

samples. A convolutional layer of CAE calculates the convolutional feature map. Since the individual latent representation is required to have the same dimensionality [16], we generate a combined representation for all input modalities, instead of one latent representation for each input modality. Max-pooling operation is then performed, which downsamples the output of the convolutional layer by taking the maximum value in each non-overlapping sub-region. Thus, x_m is mapped and transformed into a lower-dimensional embedding space z_m. The latent-space representation $z_m = g_\phi(x_m)$ is learned in the bottleneck layer [16]:

$$z_m = h_m = g_\phi(x_m) = \sigma(W_m \oslash x_m + b_m), \tag{1}$$

where the encoder is a sigmoid function $g(.)$ parameterized by ϕ, while the decoder function $f(.)$ is parameterized by Θ. The final feature maps Z_m are latent variables, specific to modality m. In Eq. 1, where ϕ are trainable parameters (including a weight matrix $W_k \in \mathbb{R}^{p \times q}$ and a bias vector $b_m \in \mathbb{R}^q$ specific to respective modality m, where p and q are the numbers of input and hidden units), $\oslash$ is the convolutional operation, and σ is the exponential linear unit activation function. The decoder reconstructs the original input X_m from the latent representation Z_m using function $f(.)$. The hidden representation h_m is mapped back to reconstructed version x_m, similar to original input X_k [16]:

$$\hat{x}_m = f_\theta(z_m) = f_\theta(g_\phi(x_m)), \tag{2}$$

where parameters (θ, ϕ) are jointly learned to reconstruct the original input. As this is analogous to learn an identity function, such that $x_m \approx f_\theta(g_\phi(x_m))$, $f_\theta(g_\phi(x_m))$ is equivalent to $\Psi(\hat{W}_m * h_m + \hat{b}_m)$, which yields Eq. 2 into:

$$\hat{x}_m = \Psi(\hat{W}_m \odot h_m + \hat{b}_m), \tag{3}$$

where $\odot$ is the transposed convolution operation, θ are trainable parameters i.e., weight matrix $\hat{W}_m \in \mathbb{R}^{n \times p}$, bias vector $\hat{b}_m$) specific to modality m, and sigmoid activation function Ψ. Let x_t and x_i be the text and image modalities, then each x_m is transformed into following hidden representations [16].

$$\begin{aligned} h_t &= \sigma(W_t \oslash x_t + b_t) \\ h_i &= \sigma(W_i \oslash x_i + b_i), \end{aligned} \tag{4}$$

where $\{W_t, W_i\}$ are encoder's weight matrices, $\{b_t and b_i\}$ are bias vectors for the text and image modalities, respectively. Last element of the hidden dimension is the dimensionality of the modality-specific latent representation. The mean squared error is used as the reconstruction loss:

$$L_{\mathrm{m}}(\theta, \phi) = \frac{1}{n} \sum_{i=1}^{n} (x_m - f_\theta (g_\phi (x_m)))^2 + \lambda \|W_m\|_2^2. \qquad (5)$$

By replacing $f_\theta (g_\phi (x_m))$ with $\hat{x}_m$, above equation yields:

$$L_{\mathrm{m}}(\theta, \phi) = \frac{1}{n} \sum_{i=1}^{n} (x_m - \hat{x}_m)^2 + \lambda \|W_m\|_2^2, \qquad (6)$$

where λ is the activity regularizer and W_m is network weights specific to input modality m. In the cross-modality stage, a concatenation layer concatenates individual latent representations h_t and h_i into following single representation:

$$h_{mcae} = \sigma (W_{mcae} [h_t \oplus h_i] + b_{mcae}), \qquad (7)$$

where $\oplus$ signifies concatenation. As of DOF model, we customize it in a classification setting. First, a trainable unimodal network is trained that takes x_m as input and generates deep embeddings [3]:

$$h_m = \Phi_m (x_m) \in \mathbb{R}^{l_1 x N}, \qquad (8)$$

where Φ_m trainable unimodal network. When $M > 1$, embeddings from each modality are combined in a multimodal fusion network. For each h_m, an attention mechanism is applied to control its expressiveness based on information from other modalities. An additional fully connected layer results in h_m^S of length l_2. Attention weights of length l_2 are obtained through a bi-linear transformation of h_m with all other embeddings (denoted as H_{pr}), then applied to h_m^S to yield the following attention-gated embedding [3]:

$$h_m^* = a_m * h_m^S = \sigma \left(h_m^T * W_A * H_{pd} \right) * h_m^{S*} \qquad (9)$$

To capture all possible interactions between modalities, we combine attention-weighted embeddings through an outer product between modalities, known as tensor fusion. A value of 1 is also included in each vector, allowing for partial interactions between modalities and for the constituent unimodal embeddings to be retained. The output matrix is the following M-dimensional hypercube of all multimodal interactions with sides of length $l_2 + 1$ [3]:

$$F = \begin{bmatrix} 1 \\ h_1^* \end{bmatrix} \otimes \begin{bmatrix} 1 \\ h_2^* \end{bmatrix} \otimes \ldots \otimes \begin{bmatrix} 1 \\ h_M^* \end{bmatrix} \qquad (10)$$

Figure 3 depicts the schematic representation of multimodal fusion of memes and texts. It contains sub-regions corresponding to unaltered unimodal embeddings, pairwise fusions between 2 modalities. A final set of fully connected layers, denoted by Φ_F, is applied to tensor fusion features for a final fused embedding $h_F = \Phi_F(F)$ [3]. Unimodal embeddings before the fusion level should be orthogonal s.t. each modality contributes unique information to outcome prediction, rather than relying on signal redundancy between modalities [3]. Inspired by this, we updated each Φ_m through MMO loss to yield embeddings that better complement other modalities. For the set of embeddings from all modalities $H \in \mathbb{R}^{l_1 x M*N}$, the MMO loss is computed as follows [3]:

$$L_{MMO} = \frac{1}{M*N} \sum_{m=1}^{M} \max\left(1, \|h_m\|_*\right) - \|H\|_+ \tag{11}$$

where $\|\cdot\|$ denotes the matrix nuclear norm. As the loss is the difference between the sum of nuclear norms per embedding and the nuclear norm of all embeddings combined, it penalizes the scenario where the variance of two modalities separately is decreased when combined and minimized when all unimodal embeddings are fully orthogonal. Having the multimodal embeddings, we perform the supervised fine-tuning by optimizing the binary cross-entropy loss.

4 Experiment Results

We discuss experimental results both qualitatively and qualitatively. Besides, we provide a comparative analysis with baselines.

4.1 Datasets

We extend the *Bengali Hate Speech Dataset* [13] with 4,500 labelled memes, making it the largest and only multimodal hate speech dataset in Bengali to date. We follow a bootstrap approach for data collection, where specific types of texts containing common slurs and terms, either directed towards a specific person or entity or generalized towards a group, are only considered. Texts and memes were collected from Facebook, YouTube comments, and newspapers. While the "Bengali Hate Speech Dataset" categorized observations into political, personal, geopolitical, religious, and gender abusive hates, we categorized them into hateful and non-hateful, keeping their respective contexts intact.

Further, to reduce possible bias, unbiased contents are supplied to the annotators and each label was assigned based on a majority voting on the annotator's independent opinions[4]. To evaluate the quality of the annotations and to ensure the decision based on the criteria of the objective, we measure inter-annotator agreement w.r.t *Cohen's Kappa* statistic [4].

---

[4] A linguist, a native speaker & an NLP researcher participated in annotation process.

4.2   Experiment Setup

Methods[5] were implemented in *Keras* and *PyTorch*. Networks are trained on Nvidia GTX 1050 GPU. Each model is trained on 80% of data (of which 10% is used as validation), followed by evaluating the model on 20% held-out data. We report precision, recall, F1-score, and *Matthias correlation coefficient* (MCC).

4.3   Analysis of Hate Speech Detection

We report modality-specific results. The classification results based on text modality are shown in Table 2. We evaluated DNN or ML baseline and 4 variants of BERT on held-out test set and report the result, respectively. We observed that single text modality has comparable performance to DNN baseline models. Conv-LSTM outperformed other DNN baselines, giving an F1 score of 78%, which is 4% to 6% better other DNN models. In terms of MCC (i.e., 0.69), Conv-LSTM model is about 2% to 4% better than other DNN baselines.

Table 2. Hate speech detection based on texts

Method	Classifier	Precision	Recall	F1	MCC
DNN baselines	Vanilla CNN	0.74	0.73	0.73	0.651
	LSTM	0.74	0.73	0.73	0.651
	Bi-LSTM	0.75	0.75	0.75	0.672
	Conv-LSTM	**0.79**	**0.78**	**0.78**	**0.694**
BERT variants	Bangla BERT	0.80	0.79	0.79	0.592
	mBERT-cased	0.80	0.80	0.80	0.637
	XLM-RoBERTa	**0.82**	**0.82**	**0.82**	**0.808**
	mBERT-uncased	0.81	0.81	0.81	0.615

Table 3. Hate speech detection based on memes

Method	Classifier	Precision	Recall	F1	MCC
CNN baselines	Vanilla CNN	0.74	0.73	0.73	0.651
	ResNet-152	**0.79**	**0.78**	**0.78**	**0.694**
	VGG19	0.75	0.75	0.75	0.774
	DenseNet-161	**0.79**	**0.79**	**0.79**	**0.808**
	EfficientNet-B7	0.79	0.78	0.78	0.795

As shown in Table 2, XLM-RoBERTa outperformed all transformer models and turns out to be the best model, yielding an F1 score of 82%, which is 2% ≈ 3% better than other transformer models. mBERT model (cased and uncased) performed moderately well than Bangla BERT model. Results based on uni-modal visual only models are reported in Table 3. Among trained CNN architectures (i.e., ResNet-152, VGG19, DenseNet-161, EfficientNet-B7), DenseNet-161

---

[5] https://github.com/rezacsedu/Multimodal-Hate-Bengali.

Table 4. Hate speech detection for multimodality

Method	Classifier	Precision	Recall	F1	MCC
ConvNet + BERTs	Bangla BERT + EfficientNet-B7	0.79	0.79	0.79	0.57
	Bangla BERT + DenseNet-161	**0.80**	**0.80**	**0.80**	**0.60**
	Bangla BERT + ResNet-152	0.80	0.80	0.80	0.59
	Bangla BERT + VGG19	**0.80**	**0.80**	**0.80**	**0.60**
	XLM-RoBERTa + EfficientNet-B7	0.70	0.70	0.70	0.39
	XLM-RoBERTa + DenseNet-161	**0.84**	**0.83**	**0.83**	**0.67**
	XLM-RoBERTa + ResNet-152	0.73	0.72	0.72	0.44
	XLM-RoBERTa + VGG19	0.70	0.68	0.68	0.38
	mBERT-uncased + EfficientNet-B7	**0.82**	**0.82**	**0.82**	**0.64**
	mBERT-uncased + DenseNet-161	0.80	0.80	0.80	0.60
	mBERT-uncased + ResNet-152	0.80	0.80	0.80	0.60
	mBERT-uncased + VGG19	0.81	0.81	0.81	0.61

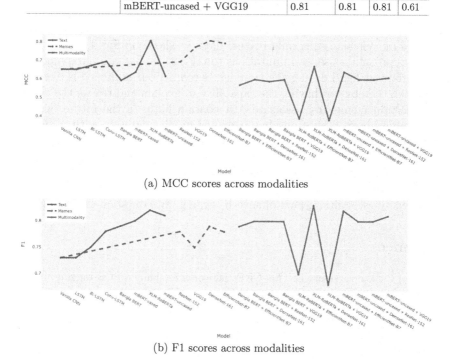

(a) MCC scores across modalities

(b) F1 scores across modalities

Fig. 4. Effects of individual modalities w.r.t MCC and F1 scores

achieved an F1-score of 79% and MCC score of 0.808, which is about 4% ≈ 6% (w.r.t F1) or 2% ≈ 15% (w.r.t MCC) better than that of other architectures.

We experimented with different combinations of multimodal models for textual feature extraction and vision modality. We report the results of top-4 models in Table 4. As shown, the multimodal fusion of mBERT-uncased + EfficientNet-B7 yielding F1-scores of 0.82 outperforms all mBERT + ConvNets fusion. At the same time, Bangla BERT + DenseNet-161 and Bangla BERT + VGG19 fusion combinations, which are the best performing models in Bangla BERT + ConvNets architectures by 2% w.r.t F1-score. On the other hand, the multimodal fusion of XLM-RoBERTa + DenseNet-161 turned out to be the best performing model w.r.t precision and F1-score, yielding the highest MCC score of 0.67, which is about 3 to 15% better than other multimodal fusions.

5 Conclusion

In this paper, we proposed hate speech detection for under-resourced Bengali language in multimodal setting that jointly analyze textual and visual information for hate speech detection. Our study suggests that: i) feature selection can have non-trivial impacts on learning capabilities of ML and DNN models, ii) texts are mot useful modality for the hate speech identification, while memes turns out to be moderately useful. However, none of multimodal models outperform unimodal models analyzing only textual data, as shown in Fig. 4.

Our approach has several limitations too. First, we had a limited amount of labelled data at hand during the training. Secondly, our approach is like blackbox model, thereby not having the capability to explain and reason the decision why a certain meme and associate text contain hate. In the future, we want to overcome above limitations by: i) extending the datasets with a substantial amount of samples, ii) improving explainability of the model by employing different interpretable ML techniques in order to provide global and local explanations of the predictions in a post-hoc fashion and measures of explanations w.r.t faithfulness. Besides, we want to focus on other interesting areas such as named entity recognition, part-of-speech tagging, and question answering.

References

1. Alam, C.: Bidirectional LSTMs-CRFs networks for bangla POS tagging. In: 19th IEEE International Conference on ICCIT, pp. 377–382 (2016)
2. Blandfort, P., et al.: Multimodal social media analysis for gang violence prevention. In: Proceedings of the International AAAI Conference on Web and Social Media, vol. 13, pp. 114–124 (2019)
3. Braman, N., Gordon, J.W.H., Goossens, E.T., Willis, C., Stumpe, M.C., Venkataraman, J.: Deep orthogonal fusion: multimodal prognostic biomarker discovery integrating radiology, pathology, genomic, and clinical data. In: de Bruijne, M., Cattin, P.C., Cotin, S., Padoy, N., Speidel, S., Zheng, Y., Essert, C. (eds.) MICCAI 2021. LNCS, vol. 12905, pp. 667–677. Springer, Cham (2021). https://doi.org/10.1007/978-3-030-87240-3_64
4. Chen, B., Zaebst, D., Seel, L.: A macro to calculate kappa statistics for categorizations by multiple raters. In: Proceeding of the 30th Annual SAS Users Group International Conference, pp. 155–230. Citeseer (2005)
5. Conneau, A., et al.: Unsupervised cross-lingual representation learning at scale. arXiv:1911.02116 (2019)

6. Davidson, T., Warmsley, D., Macy, M., Weber, I.: Automated hate speech detection and the problem of offensive language. In: Proceedings of the International AAAI Conference on Web and Social Media, vol. 11, pp. 512–515 (2017)
7. Gomez, R., Gibert, J., Gomez, L., Karatzas, D.: Exploring hate speech detection in multimodal publications. In: Proceedings of the IEEE/CVF Winter Conference on Applications of Computer Vision, pp. 1470–1478 (2020)
8. Grave, E., Bojanowski, P., Mikolov, T.: Learning word vectors for 157 languages. In: Proceedings of the International Conference on Language Resources and Evaluation (LREC) (2018)
9. Guo, X., Liu, X., Zhu, E.E.A.: Deep clustering with convolutional autoencoders. In: International Conference on Neural Information Processing, pp. 373–382. Springer, Guangzhou (2017). https://doi.org/10.1007/978-3-319-70096-0_39
10. Guterres, A.: United nations strategy and plan of action on hate speech. United Nations (20Strategy) (2019)
11. Ishmam, A.M., Sharmin, S.: Hateful speech detection in public facebook pages for the Bengali language. In: 2019 18th IEEE International Conference on Machine Learning And Applications (ICMLA), pp. 555–560. IEEE (2019)
12. Izsak, R.: Hate speech and incitement to hatred against minorities in the media. UN Humans Rights Council, A/HRC/28/64 (2015)
13. Karim, M.R., Chakravarthi, B.R., Cochez, M.: Classification benchmarks for under-resourced Bengali language based on multichannel convolutional-LSTM network. In: 2020 IEEE 7th International Conference on Data Science and Advanced Analytics (DSAA), pp. 390–399. IEEE (2020)
14. Karim, M.R., et al.: DeepHateExplainer: explainable hate speech detection in under-resourced Bengali language. In: 2021 IEEE 8th International Conference on Data Science and Advanced Analytics (DSAA), pp. 1–10. IEEE (2021)
15. Liu, Y., Ott, M., Goyal, N., Lewis, M., Zettlemoyer, L., Stoyanov, V.: RoBERTa: a robustly optimized BERT pretraining approach. arXiv:1907.11692 (2019)
16. Patrick, T., Hans, A.K., Friedhelm, S.: Multimodal deep denoising convolutional autoencoders for pain intensity classification based on physiological signals. In: The International Conference on Pattern Recognition Applications and Methods (2020)
17. Ranasinghe, T., Zampieri, M.: Multilingual offensive language identification with cross-lingual embeddings. arXiv preprint arXiv:2010.05324 (2020)
18. Ribeiro, M.H., Calais, P.H., Almeida, V.A., Meira Jr, W.: Characterizing and detecting hateful users on Twitter. In: AAAI Conference on Web & Social Media (2018)
19. Romim, N., Ahmed, M., Talukder, H., Islam, M.S.: Hate speech detection in the Bengali language: a dataset and its baseline evaluation. arXiv preprint arXiv:2012.09686 (2020)
20. Sai, S., Sharma, Y.: Towards offensive language identification for Dravidian languages. In: Proceedings of the First Workshop on Speech and Language Technologies for Dravidian Languages, pp. 18–27 (2021)
21. Sai, S., Srivastava, N.D., Sharma, Y.: Explorative application of fusion techniques for multimodal hate speech detection. SN Comput. Sci. **3**(2), 1–13 (2022)
22. Salminen, J., Almerekhi, H., Milenkovic, M., Jung, S.: Anatomy of online hate: developing a taxonomy and ml models for identifying and classifying hate in online news media. In: ICWSM, pp. 330–339 (2018)
23. Sherief, M., Kulkarni, V., Belding, E.: Hate lingo: a target-based linguistic analysis of hate speech in social media. In: AAAI Conference on Web & Social Media (2018)

308   Md. R. Karim et al.

24. Waseem, Z., Hovy, D.: Hateful symbols or hateful people? predictive features for hate speech detection on twitter. In: Proceedings of the NAACL Student Research Workshop, pp. 88–93 (2016)
25. Zampieri, M., Malmasi, S., Nakov, P., Rosenthal, S., Farra, N., Kumar, R.: Semeval-2019 task 6: identifying and categorizing offensive language in social media (offenseval). arXiv preprint arXiv:1903.08983 (2019)

Workshop 1: Fake News Detection in Low-Resource Languages (Regional-Fake)

A Novel Dataset for Fake News Detection in Tamil Regional Language

T. T. Mirnalinee, Bhuvana Jayaraman$^{(\boxtimes)}$, A. Anirudh, R. Jagadish, and A. Karthik Raja

Sri Sivasubramaniya Nadar College of Engineering, Chennai, India
{mirnalineett,bhuvanaj}@ssn.edu.in,
{anirudh19015,jagadish19039,karthik19048}@cse.ssn.edu.in

Abstract. Tamil is one of the very few ancient languages that have survived the passage of time. And yet even though a lot of pieces of literature are available for this language, not a lot of data is labeled. With the Internet boom and digitization in all mediums, it is important to build classifiers for data analysis and prediction. But the available labeled data is from little to none in each domain. With the internet being used in all walks of life, the news spread via this medium quickly. Misleading and distorted information will not only affect the individual but also impact on the public. This research work elaborates on the creation of one such corpus meant for fake new detection. News snippets were scrapped from the news media and are annotated into fake and real news. The news of two classes are further labelled manually as 5 classes namely Sports, Politics, Science, Entertainment and Miscellaneous. The corpus has a collection of 2949 fake news and 2324 samples of genuine news was also added to the corpus to provide for a balanced dataset. One of the main observations was that a major chunk of the fake news data was political. For bench-marking this dataset we have built 5 baseline models with our corpus, each model showed improvement in different areas. Four machine learning and one deep learning model were trained on this new corpus.

Keywords: Tamil corpus · Fake News · Real News · Classifiers · Exploratory Data Analysis

1 Introduction

In this digital era, almost all the day to day tasks are made possible via internet. The news media outlets use this medium to publish their news, where the credibility of the news remains an issue. Distorted and misleading news travel quickly and cause damage not only to any individual but most of the public as well. These news are often spread deliberately to cause confusion among the readers. Around 214% of increase in fake news was found in India [17], huge raise was observed during demonetisation, state, central elections and Covid.

Anand Kumar M et al. (Eds.): SPELLL 2022, CCIS 1802, pp. 311–323, 2023.
https://doi.org/10.1007/978-3-031-33231-9_22

India stands seventh in Digital Civility Index on online risks and fake news released by Microsoft [1] is a cause of concern.

Intelligence agencies under Government of India have taken severe actions on the entities that spread malignant news and its proliferation. IPC section 505 paves way for handling the fake news propagation, National Crime Records Bureau (NCRB) releases yearly statistics of the crimes involving the fake news/rumours. Spreading of fake news can only be handled, when the news is identified as fake, however fact checking is one potential solution. But the fact checking individually every news has its limitations on consistency and trustworthiness. With the insights from the recent pandemic, the world had realized the need to classify fake news. An automated system that checks the credibility of the news as real or fake is the dire need of the day. With a lot of machine learning work booming in for the English community, which has abundant labeled data it is the responsibility of the local communities to take care of labeling their regional language data to full fill the need for fake news classifiers.

It was found that no dedicated corpus was available in our regional language, Tamil that helps to build classifiers to detect the fake news. This deficit has prevented ML engineers from providing more classifiers for Fake News classification. The objective of this work is to give methods to extract news from new media and to annotate them as real and fake in the domains of Sports, Politics, Science, Entertainment and Miscellaneous. Here, a first ever news corpus in Tamil was created having a collection of fake and real news in our regional language with around 6 thousand news samples, which is well-balanced for fake and genuine news data with next level of labeling the data into 5 classes. The next section discusses about the similar and existing work, Sect. 3 elaborates on the methodology in developing the corpus, Sect. 4 deals with the base line classifiers constructed on this Tamil corpus and their performance and Sect. 5 concludes the paper.

2   Related Work

Prior to creating a Tamil fake news text corpus, a thorough literature was performed. It was found that, presently there is no Fake News Detection dataset in Tamil is available. There are Indian regional language text corpora [21], but they are very generic in nature. Our work was inspired by a shared task on fake news detection in the Urdu language hosted by HASOC in 2020 The dataset [9], called Bend-The-Truth, had 900 manually collected fake and real news headlines in Urdu, models from various research works were used for baselines. Some research works have used pre-processing on Indo-Aryan languages like Hindi and their comparison with English for offensive text classification. Models like SVM, Naive Bayes and LSTM was used to get a accuracy of over 80% [10]. Following are the different works that have been carried out on Tamil Corpus. [12] The research work classifies offensive text in south Indian regional languages like Malayalam, Tamil. The dataset used here uses transliterated words in English script. Deep Learning Models like BiLSTM proved to be better than ML models like Naive Bayes for the dataset provided.

Connectives also form an important part of any language. This research work identifies and labels connectives [14] from a Tamil data corpus of 511 words obtained from wikipedia.323 connectives were identified from the collected dataset. This was published as corpus resource.

Research works that label the intonation of words in a corpus have also been done [13]. This uses segmentation and clustering to identify the intonation for the stress labelling corpus. The features were identified to be pitch, energy and duration.

Some research works regarding Tamil corpus has quantitative analysis, frequency and position of appearances of different types [11] of words like verbs, their infinitives. This research work also supports tag based search for a given sub sentence.

Tamil being a rich language in grammar, various stemming algorithms were performed to identify various [19] types of words based on tenses ad other grammar rules. Various stemming algorithms were analysed and their stemmed data was tabulated and compared with the proposed light stemmer.

Parts of Speech based word embedding for Tamil was proposed that used POS annotated corpus. Feature vectors are created using bag of words, TF-IDF and Word2Vec methods [20]. Classifiers such as Linear SVM, Extreme Gradient Boosting, k- Nearest Neighbour are used to build POS taggers. SVM has given the better POS tagging in Tamil as per the authors observation.

Sentence similarity is Tamil was done by combining the corpus based approach and knowledge based approaches. Similarity of two sentences can be derived from similarity of words. The work has used Tamil wordNet as its lexical database [16]. Unique words from both sentences are taken as joint word set, followed by the creation of raw semantic vectors and similarity is determined as a cosine coefficient.

Named entity recognition for Tamil was proposed by extracting and classifying the NEs using word level Naïve Bayes classifier [18]. Initially the features are extracted using Regular Expression (REGEX) feature extraction, Morphological Feature Extraction and Context Feature Extraction.

A stemmer is a procedure that maps the root word with the derived word, often used in query based retrieval systems. Stemmer for Tamil language is proposed [15], where the authors removed n suffixes in different iterations. Authors decided to defer considering the irregular words and homographs. And have stemmed the proper nouns. The work has not handled the suffixes with usual suffix patterns.

3 Proposed Work

3.1 Data Scraping

To create a new corpus in Tamil for fake news, news headlines were scraped from various websites. For scraping news headlines from the internet, a Python library called *BeautifulSoup* was used. Prior to the scraping process, the following steps were done:

1. Identification of websites that could be scraped: as an example, certain websites had a very complex HTML structure which made scraping difficult like Reuters, CNN, etc.
2. Observation of the HTML structure of the candidate website: websites that could be scraped were inspected to identify the HTML elements holding the required information, and the class names of those HTML elements
3. Observation of the URL of the candidate: The URL changed slightly when moving from one page to another (in all cases, a page number was appended to the URL). This was taken into account during the scraping process to extract data from multiple pages in a single run.

Totally 5273 samples were collected by extracted data by running the scraping script, with minor modifications made to the URL, HTML Tags.

Beautiful Soup is a Python package for parsing HTML and XML documents. It creates a parse tree for parsed pages that can be used to extract data from HTML, which is useful for web scraping. Beautiful Soup has a class, BeautifulSoup which has a method to return the HTML structure of a given web page. Parameters passed to the BeautifulSoup class during instantiating are URL name, HTML version and the output will be the HTML structure of the web page. A BeautifulSoup object has the HTML contents of an entire web page, a particular element(or a set of elements) can be extracted from the HTML contents by using a method 'find_all'. In most of the online news web pages, the news articles are often enclosed in a HTML element such as $< div >$ and $< p >$ which have a common class attribute. Apart from the headline, these elements also contain various other metadata like the author name, date of publication, and sometimes the tag. The web pages were manually scanned using the browser's inspect tool to understand the structure. Then the find_all method of the BeautifulSoup object was used to extract the headline news, date, author and tag (if present). The format of the returned contents depend on the encoding format used in the web page. In our case, it was one of three types namely, UTF-8, UTF-16-le and ISO, where the encoding conflicts were resolved manually.

3.2 Real News Data Collection

Real news headlines were collected from reputed Indian regional and national newspapers. These websites had headlines written in Tamil, so no translation was necessary for such samples. Furthermore, these websites had separate sections for sports, politics, entertainment, and technology, that helped us to label the real news data samples. Two major news outlets were used for the real news data collection. The Hindu Tamil - e-version of a national-level newspaper [7], from where the sports, politics, technology, and miscellaneous news were collected. Daily Thanthi - e-version [2] of a regional newspaper is the second source of data collection in specific for entertainment news.

3.3   Fake News Data Collection

Certified fake news was collected from the fake news sections of reputed regional and national newspapers, as well as from certified online fact-checking websites namely politifact.com [4]. A mix of various types of news headlines were collected from these websites. for the regional and national News that are tagged as fake are from News18 [5], One-India [6], Tamil-Samayam [3], Zee-News [8] - news headlines in Tamil. News headlines scrapped were converted to Tamil using Google Translate API.

3.4   Challenges in Data Collection

The first and major issue faced during data collection was that certain websites have prevented the scrapping tool from scraping news headlines since we were using a web-scraping robot. In order to overcome this problem, we modified the header in the HTTP request sent to the website to fool the browser into thinking that it was interacting with a human. Certain websites had an un-scrapable structure, like CNN, it was evident that this was to prevent news scraping and other websites, it was due to poor programming practices. Certain websites had a huge difference in the URL between the first and second pages. It was done manually to scrape data from the first page and then automated for the rest of the pages. Certain websites did not display the author's details in the headline which was overcome by scrapping the associated meta information.

3.5   Data Cleansing

Final cleansed dataset is available at[1]. Dataset was saved in different encoding formats. So in order to overcome that problem, during dataset merging, appropriate encoding formats (utf-8, utf-16-le, ISO) were used. Final dataset saved in utf-16. As a part of data cleansing, we converted the manual labels into a homogeneous set viz. sports, politics, entertainment, tech (science & business), and miscellaneous; Fixed the spelling of the labels; Removed additional characters like square brackets; Removed the automatic column numbering for the merged real and fake news; Removed duplicate column headings (problem caused due to merging); Dropped extraneous columns; Removed the duplicated rows wherever required

3.6   Exploratory Data Analysis (EDA)

For both the real and fake news dataset, a common set of EDA operations were performed.

The shape of the real and fake news dataset was analyzed. The real news dataset has 2324 rows and the fake news dataset has 2949 rows. It is observed

---

[1] https://github.com/AAnirudh07/Fake-News-Headlines-In-Tamil.

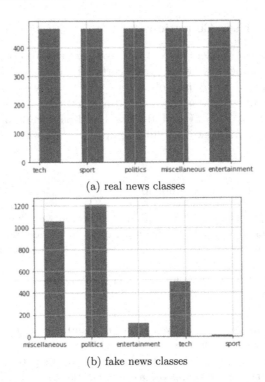

(a) real news classes

(b) fake news classes

Fig. 1. Histogram of the Corpus

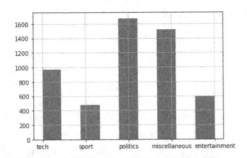

Fig. 2. Histogram of the 5 classes in the Tamil Corpus

that there are 5178 unique words in the entire Tamil corpus and the word *politics* appearing for 1674 number of times. For each news headline in the corpus, has both English and Tamil versions labeled as one of the five categories namely Politics, Sport, Tech, Entertainment and Miscellaneous. Google Translate API was used to translate Tamil versions to English and vice versa. Histogram representation of the multi-class samples across sports, Tech, politics, entertainment, miscellaneous for the entire corpus shown in Fig. 2.

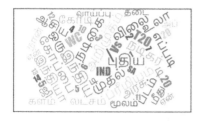

(a) Real dataset

(b) Fake dataset

Fig. 3. Word cloud for the corpus

Class	Real News Sample	Fake News Sample
Tech	இந்தியாவின் முதல் மின்சார டபுள்-டெக்கர் பஸ்: அறிந்ததும் அறியாததும்	க.பேஸ்புக்கில் இப்போது "சூனியக்காரி" உள்ளது என்று கூறுகிறது.
Sport	பும்ராவுக்கு மாற்று வீரரை இன்னும் அடையாளம் காணவில்லை' - ரோகித் சர்மா தகவல்	க.பாக்ஸ் ஸ்போர்ட்ஸ் அனைத்து என்எப்எல் ஒளிபரப்புகளையும் ரத்து செய்கிறது, 'வீரர்கள் கொடியை மதிக்கும் வரை.
Politics	பள்ளி பேருந்துகளில் கேமரா கட்டாயம்: தமிழக அரசு உத்தரவு	பிரேக்கிங்: டிரம்ப் துணை அட்டர்னி ஜெனரல் ராட் ரோசன்ஸ்டைனை நீக்குகிறார். முல்லரின் தலைவிதி மீது கேள்விகளை எழுப்பினார்
Miscellaneous	சென்னை தினம்: இணையத்தில் சென்னை புராணம்!	ஒபாமா டெக்சாஸில் உணவு பரிமாறுகிறார்!
Entertainment	தீபாவளிக்கு வெளியாகிறது 'வாரிசு' படத்தின் முதல் பாடல் - ரசிகர்கள் உற்சாகம்	டேனியல் ராட்கிளிஃப் கொரோனா வைரஸால் பாதிக்கப்பட்டுள்ளார்.

Fig. 4. Sample instances from real and fake news datasets of the corpus

The dataset was analyzed for the number of null values and duplicates, which were not found in the real-news dataset but has 78 null values (for the authors field) and 47 duplicated rows in the fake news dataset. Used standard python methods to get the overview statistics of the real and fake news datasets These overview statistics depicted various parameters viz. Unique count in each column, data type, examples.

When we plotted the number of samples/rows per label (entertainment, sport, politics, tech, miscellaneous), it is observed that Real news dataset had an equal representation of each class with approximately 450 news instances per class as shown in Fig. 1a. While the fake news dataset had an unequal distribution having more than 70% of the dataset belonging to politics and miscellaneous

Table 1. Overlapping words

Label	Overlap between real and fake news
Entertainment	147
Miscellaneous	195
Politics	548
Sport	22
Tech	403

fake news as shown in Fig. 1b. With respect to the actual news headlines, we collected nearly equal samples from all classes (around 450) due to the availability of verified, actual news headlines in these labels However, when it came to fake news headlines, most of the headlines were political since, logically, most controversial or fake news are tied to politics. We were only able to find verified fake news headlines with these sources.

The sample instances of fake and real news instances from the corpus for each class is shown in Fig. 4.

As a part of EDA, to get the insight of the news instances the headlines are grouped by 'author' and visualized the top-5 author contributions. In both the real and fake news datasets, the author contribution was skewed, where around 3 authors contributed to more than 50% of the news headlines. 'Authors' are a confounding factor and by using the author information in the classification would thus lead to very poor generalization.

The number of unique words for both the real and fake news datasets were calculated and found that the real news dataset has 8518 unique words and the fake news dataset has 15897 unique words. The word cloud for real and fake news datasets were also generated that help to visualize the data (in Figs. 3a, 3b, where the words that are appearing large in word cloud are the words that have occurred more number of times than others.

Certain number of overlapping words were observed in each class between the real and fake datasets and reported in Table 1. The number of overlapping words between the real and fake news dataset will confuse the classifiers from making discrimination properly. Proper features should be identified to improve the classification performance better.

3.7   Corpus Statistics

The total number of rows in the Dataset for Fake News Detection is 5273, with 2324 instances of real headlines and 2949 instances of fake headlines, details are listed in Table 2.

Any classifier require to learn the important information from the corpus to discriminate them. The presence of stop words may not help the classifiers to focus more important discriminating information. Hence removal of stop words is essential as a pre-processing activity. Few of the usual stop words in tamil script

Table 2. Overall statistics of the dataset

Label	Count	Real	Fake
Entertainment	589	468	121
Miscellaneous (mostly political news, but that of an individual's opinion)	1521	464	1057
Politics	1674	464	1210
Sport	476	464	12
Tech	966	464	502

ஒரு	ஆகும்	என்ன	அவன்
என்று	அல்லது	இருந்து	தான்
மற்றும்	அவர்	சில	பலரும்
இந்த	நான்	என்	என்னும்
இது	உள்ள	போன்ற	மேலும்
என்ற	அந்த	வேண்டும்	பின்னர்
கொண்டு	இவர்	வந்து	கொண்ட
என்பது	என	இதன்	இருக்கும்
பல	முதல்	அது	தனது
என்றும்	ஆகிய	மிகவும்	உள்ளது
அதன்	இருந்தது	இங்கு	போது
தன்	உள்ளன	மீது	இந்தக்
பிறகு	வந்த	ஓர்	பற்றி
அவர்கள்	இருந்த	இவை	நீ
வரை	அவள்	வரும்	வேறு

Fig. 5. Sample set of stop words in the Corpus

have been identified and have been shown in Fig. 5 and the rest is available in Github[2].

Some of the Tamil words are most often prone to be mis-spelt, such words are shown in Fig. 6. The team has taken enough efforts to avoid the occurrences of mis-spelt words in the corpus.

4 Benchmark Models

4.1 Data Representation

Two methods were used to represent the Tamil news headlines namely Bag-Of-Words and TF-IDF. The scatter plots for the same are shown in Fig. 7a and 7b. It is observed from the bag of words plot that there are more number of clusters

---

[2] https://github.com/AAnirudh07/Fake-News-Headlines-In-Tamil/Tamil-News-Headlines.csv.

S. No	English Meaning	Tamil word	Misspelt as	English Meaning
1	head	தலை	தழை	leaf
2	sound	ஒலி	ஒளி	light
3	mountain	மலை	மழை	rain
4	brain	மூளை	மூலை	corner
5	half	அரை	அறை	room
6	Tear apart	கிழி	கிளி	parrot
7	morning	காலை	காளை	bull
8	tail	வால்	வாள்	sword
9	school	பள்ளி	பல்லி	lizard
10	strength	பலம்	பழம்	fruit
11	shore	கரை	கறை	dirt
12	tiger	புலி	புளி	tamarind
13	wave	அலை	அழை	call
14	pain	வலி	வழி	path
15	plough	உழவு	உலவு	tillage
16	mind	மனம்	மணம்	smell
17	mine	என்	எண்	number
18	snow	பனி	பணி	work
19	lake	ஏரி	ஏறி	Climb up
20	hole	குழி	குளி	bath

Fig. 6. Some of the words that are often mis-spelt

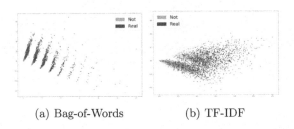

(a) Bag-of-Words   (b) TF-IDF

Fig. 7. Representation of data

with similar words in real and fake domains. However, the outliers of real domain shown in blue coloured dots help the classifiers to discriminate the fake and real news instances. Similarly, in case of TF-IDF plot, that appears to have cone like structure, the real instances (blue dots) scattered on the right side of the plot play significant role in classifying the instances into real news and fake news.

4.2   Classifiers

Four machine learning models and one deep learning model were trained on the dataset as baseline classifiers, namely SVM, Logistic Regression, Naive Bayes, XG-Boost as the machine learning classifiers and a deep learning classifier, RNN with 2 LSTM layers. No preprocessing steps were applied to the dataset before training the models. The TF-IDF representation was used the features for classification. While using the logistic regression model the regularization lambda was made smaller so that the model does not get over fit and is added with perturbations. Here, we have used regularization parameter lambda to be 1, by giving C = (1/lamdba) = 1, thereby giving no place for overfitting. Reducing C i.e. increasing lambda reduces the overall accuracy in both cases of TF-IDF and bag of words. This gives a general idea that all news don't follow the same pattern.

The MultinomialBayes model was trained with smoothening and prior probabilities are learned based on input, and no additional changes were made. The next model was trained on a support vector machine specifically that gives probabilities. As discussed before the regularization parameter C was set to 1. XGB Classifier used has a maximum depth of 7, and sub-sample ratio was set to 0.8, with 10 threads the learning rate was set to 0.1. Lastly a LSTM based deep Learning model was trained with inputs converted to one-shot format, and then passed to a simple embedding layer followed by 2 LSTM layers, whose output is passed on to 2 dense layers for classification. The embedding layer has a max capacity of 1000 words. The LSTM had 128, 64 units respectively, and was reduced by dense layers of size 32 and 1.

4.3   Results

Table 3. Performance of four Baseline classifiers

Model	Accuracy	Precision	Recall	F1-Score
Support Vector Machine	87.85	88	87.5	88
Logistic Regression	86.80	86.5	87	86.5
Naive Bayes	85.46	85	84.5	85
XG-Boost	85.08	84.5	84.5	84.5
RNN (2 LSTM Layers)	75.04			

From the TF-IDF and the bag-of-words representation, it was evident that there are certain words that are unique to the real class, near the bottom-right corner of the TF-IDF and bag of words in Figs. 7a and 7b. These words helped the machine-learning models understand whether sentences were real or fake and help them to discriminate between real and fake news. The Support Vector Machine had the highest accuracy 87.85% as it was able to separate the real and fake news datasets on some higher dimensional plane than the other classifiers. The intention here is not to study the performance of the classifiers, but to establish a baseline of classifiers, so that the people interested can build better classifiers than this (Table 3).

5   Conclusion

A novel text corpus consisting of real and fake news headlines in the Tamil regional language was created. The inspiration has stemmed from the fact that there were no fake news text corpora in Tamil and hence through the literature survey, the authors have identified and implemented the following:

1. Credible online sources for real and fake news
2. Extracting headlines and meta-data from these websites
3. Cleansing the dataset
4. Performing exploratory data analysis on the cleansed data
5. Training baseline models on the dataset

This research work has also provided a rigorous description of the dataset, in particular, the summary statistics for the dataset was provided with the number of unique words and the overlap of words between real and fake news headlines. Visualizations such as word clouds, Bag-of-Words, and TF-IDF representations have also been provided. Five baseline models were also developed for the dataset. Out of these, four were based on Machine Learning and one was based on Deep Learning. The model that performed the best in terms of accuracy is the Support Vector Machine, with an accuracy of 87.85%.

In the future, state-of-the-art machine learning models can be built for this dataset by fine tuning them further. A pre-processing package for the Tamil language in Python can be developed. Finally, the authors also plan to host a shared NLP task to help domain experts and researchers contribute to the developing robust algorithms to detect fake news in the Tamil language.

References

1. Business insider. https://www.businessinsider.in/india-has-more-fake-news-than-any-other-country-in-the-world-survey/articleshow/67868418.cms
2. Daily Thanthi. https://www.dailythanthi.com/
3. Samayam Tamil: Tamil News — News in Tamil — Online. https://tamil.samayam.com/
4. Stand up for the facts!-Politifact, Poynter Institute. https://www.politifact.com/
5. Tamil News - Get Latest and breaking News in Tamil. https://tamil.news18.com/
6. Tamil News — One India Tamil. https://tamil.oneindia.com/
7. The Hindu News in Tamil, Latest Tamil News India. https://www.hindutamil.in/
8. Zee News: Latest News, Live Breaking News. https://zeenews.india.com/
9. Amjad, M., Sidorov, G., Zhila, A., Gómez-Adorno, H., Voronkov, I., Gelbukh, A.: "bend the truth": benchmark dataset for fake news detection in Urdu language and its evaluation. J. Intell. Fuzzy Syst. **39**(2), 2457–2469 (2020)
10. Anand, A., Golecha, J., Bharathi, B., Jayaraman, B., MirnalineeT., T.: Machine learning based hate speech identification for English and Indo-Aryan languages. In: FIRE (2021)
11. Ganesan, M.: Tamil corpus generation and text analysis. In: Conference papers, p. 193

12. Jayaraman, B., MirnalineeT., T., Anandan, K.R., Kumar, A.S., Anand, A.: Offensive text prediction using machine learning and deep learning approaches. In: FIRE (2021)
13. Narayana, L., Ramakrishnan, A.: Defining syllables and their stress labels in mile Tamil TTS corpus. In: Workshop in Image and Signal Processing (WISP-2007) (2007)
14. Rachakonda, R.T., Sharma, D.M.: Creating an annotated Tamil corpus as a discourse resource. In: Proceedings of the 5th Linguistic Annotation Workshop, pp. 119–123 (2011)
15. Ramachandran, V.A., Krishnamurthi, I.: An iterative stemmer for Tamil language. In: Pan, J.-S., Chen, S.-M., Nguyen, N.T. (eds.) ACIIDS 2012. LNCS (LNAI), vol. 7198, pp. 197–205. Springer, Heidelberg (2012). https://doi.org/10.1007/978-3-642-28493-9_22
16. Selvarasa, A., Thirunavukkarasu, N., Rajendran, N., Yogalingam, C., Ranathunga, S., Dias, G.: Short Tamil sentence similarity calculation using knowledge-based and corpus-based similarity measures. In: 2017 Moratuwa Engineering Research Conference (MERCon), pp. 443–448. IEEE (2017)
17. Singhal, S., Kaushal, R., Shah, R.R., Kumaraguru, P.: Fake news in India: scale, diversity, solution, and opportunities. Commun. ACM 65(11), 80–81 (2022)
18. Srinivasan, R., Subalalitha, C.: Automated named entity recognition from Tamil documents. In: 2019 IEEE 1st International Conference on Energy, Systems and Information Processing (ICESIP), pp. 1–5. IEEE (2019)
19. Thangarasu, M., Manavalan, R.: Stemmers for Tamil language: performance analysis. arXiv preprint arXiv:1310.0754 (2013)
20. Thavareesan, S., Mahesan, S.: Word embedding-based part of speech tagging in tamil texts. In: 2020 IEEE 15th International Conference on Industrial and Information Systems (ICIIS), pp. 478–482. IEEE (2020)
21. Venugopal-Wairagade, G., Saini, J.R., Pramod, D.: Novel language resources for Hindi: an aesthetics text corpus and a comprehensive stop lemma list. arXiv preprint arXiv:2002.00171 (2020)

Fake News Detection in Low-Resource Languages

Rajalakshmi Sivanaiah[(✉)], Nishaanth Ramanathan, Shajith Hameed,
Rahul Rajagopalan, Angel Deborah Suseelan,
and Mirnalinee Thanka Nadar Thanagathai

Department of Computer Science and Engineering, Sri Sivasubramaniya Nadar
College of Engineering, Chennai, Tamil Nadu, India
{rajalakshmis,nishaanth2010302,shajith2010537,
rahul2010222,angeldeborahs,mirnalineett}@ssn.edu.in

Abstract. Fake news spreads much faster than real news. False information and misleading texts are the most important elements that lead to
disasters and even life threats. One such strategy is fake news, which has
become a never-ending phenomenon with the rise of the internet. There
can be several devastating consequences due to fake news spreading. It is
therefore important to prevent the spread of fake news. This paper shows
how we prepared fake news data sets for a few low-resource languages and
how we used Logistic Regression and BERT models to perform fake news
classification in low-resource languages. Through rigorous experiments,
we show that BERT-based-multilingual-cased and Logistic Regression
models reach maximum F1 scores of around 98% and 95% respectively.
We have done fake news classification with the models for low-resource
Indian languages like Tamil, Kannada, Gujarati, and Malayalam.

Keywords: Fake news · low resource Indic languages · Logistic
Regression · Sigmoid Function · Bert-base · F1 score

1 Introduction

Humanity is evolving rapidly. New inventions and technologies are becoming
more common. This is also accompanied by ever-improving communication standards. We are currently living in the information age. This brings with it a lot of
advantages, such as near instantaneous communication and social media, which
is proving to be a robust platform for nearly everyone to voice their opinions. But
there are some glaring disadvantages as well. Information is extremely sensitive
and something that can be easily tampered with. In 2018, there was chaos due
to the rise of fake news in Brazil, where almost 44% of voters were influenced by
it [11]. This is slowly turning out to be a major concern.

Anand Kumar M et al. (Eds.): SPELLL 2022, CCIS 1802, pp. 324–331, 2023.
https://doi.org/10.1007/978-3-031-33231-9_23

There are different types of fake news, such as propaganda that is adopted by governments and religious groups that try to appeal to emotions, etc. Clickbait, which is an eye-catching detail that is used to sway off the main topic at hand, and finally, errors made by even the biggest of news organizations, which are not intentional but can mislead people nonetheless,

People tend to visualize media as the greatest and purest form of information, so they fail to understand the very fact that not everything a person sees or hears might be true.

This tactic can be devastating if the right audience is targeted [1]. Rural people who are denied education turn out to be gullible and tend to believe everything they see or hear [2]. This situation is prevalent in India, where the literacy rate is relatively low compared to other countries. It is therefore very important to get over this obstacle of fake news spreading in order to develop as human beings and thrive.

Machine learning plays a critical role in achieving this. Several machine learning algorithms are applied to large datasets to perform desired tasks [3]. These algorithms include supervised, unsupervised, and reinforcement learning algorithms, to name a few [4].

2 Related Work

There are limited number of literature work available for the low resource languages in the research area of fake news detection. The existing work and future challenges lying in the low resource languages are discussed in [7]. The usage of logistic regression in detecting the fake news content is explained in detail in [15] with the F1 score of 0.72. BERT multilingual based model is used to identify the fake news in COVID dataset for Indic languages with an F1 score of 0.89 in [5]. The different types of machine learning techniques used for detecting fake news in English language are discussed in [1,3,4]. Pretrained embeddings for multilingual data are described in [9,10]. Deep learning techniques are used to detect the fake content by [11].

Our objective is to detect fake news. We propose a fake news detection model that focuses on Indic languages and an approach where besides network and user-related features, the text content of messages is given high importance. To deal with text processing we used Natural language processing tools and techniques [7]. We train the model based on data that is originally in English. This is then translated into several Indic languages [9]. The model is then trained with new datasets (translated Indic languages) and fed to the machine learning models which then predict a piece of news based on its credibility. Any form of data needs to be converted to numbers before further processing. This is accomplished by using the BERT framework for natural language processing. The introduction of pretrained BERT text attachment model [16] in the year 2019 enables unprecedented results in many automated word processing tasks in natural language processing field. This model is considered as a good replacement for the popular word2vec model and becomes an industry standard.

3   Fake News Dataset

The fake news detection task aims to discover and differentiate fake news from real news with high accuracy. In general, the input data is divided into two halves: training and testing data, and the former is fed to the machine learning model for learning purposes; the model then makes predictions on the testing data. The data set for fake news in low-resource languages like Tamil, Telugu, Malayalam, and other low-resource languages is not available in the research domain, as this research is a budding area, so we have used the Kaggle English fake news data set to produce data sets in low-resource languages. Our intention was to produce fake news data sets in four Indian languages: Tamil, Malayalam, Kannada, and Gujarati. First, an English training data set was translated into these low-resource languages using the Google translation API [5]. In the resultant translated data file, we detected the presence of other languages and incorrect translations. We cleaned the data file by removing all the rows that contained characters from other languages with the help of the pycld2 library [14]. Figure 1 shows some example sentences in each language.

index	Language	Title	Author	Label
0	Tamil	அமெரிக்க வான்வழித் தாக்குதலில் கொல்லப்பட்ட 15 பொதுமக்கள் அடையாளம் காணப்பட்டுள்ளனர்	ஜெசிகா பர்கிஸ்	1
1	Malayalam	ഫ്ലിൻ: ഹിലാരി ക്ലിന്റനെ, കാമ്പസിലെ വലിയ സ്ത്രീ - ബ്രീഡ്ബാർട്ട് ഡാനിയൽ	ജെ. ഫ്ലിൻ	0
2	Kannada	ವ್ಯಭಿಚಾರಕ್ಕಾಗಿ ಕಲ್ಲೆಸೆದು ಕೊಲ್ಲಲ್ಪಟ್ಟ ಮಹಿಳೆಯ ಬಗೆ, ಕಾಲ್ಪನಿಕ ಅಪ್ರಕಟಿತ ಕಥೆಗಾಗಿ ಇರಾನ್ ಮಹಿಳೆಗೆ ಜೈಲು ಶಿಕ್ಷೆ ಹೊವಾರ್ಡ್	ಪ್ಲೊಟಾನ್ಸ್ಕಾಯ್	1
3	Gujarati	એક યુએસ એરસ્ટ્રાઇકમાં માર્યા ગયેલા 15 નાગરિકોની ઓળખ કરવામાં આવી છે જેસિકા	પુર્કિસ	1

Fig. 1. Sample sentences for each language

Table 1. Data distribution for real and fake labels

Language	#Real News	#Fake News
Tamil	9782	7124
Kannada	8876	5745
Gujarati	8435	5672
Malayalam	9495	6134

Table 1 shows the number of real and fake entry labels in the training dataset for each language.

4   Methodologies Used

4.1   Logistic Regression

Logistic Regression is a popular model that is used for binary classification [15]. It predicts an outcome to be 1 or 0 after considering all the available features and assigning weights to them. The sigmoid activation function is a mathematical function that is used to map the predicted values from the Logistic Regression model to probabilities. In Logistic Regression, the concept of threshold value is used, and if the values are above the threshold value, then they are classified as 1, and if they are below the threshold value, then they are classified as 0. Techniques like Term Frequency -Inverse Document Frequency (TF-IDF), Bag of Words, etc. may be used to convert data into features [17]. In this work, feature vectors are formed from texts and fed to Logistic Regression model. The model assigns weights to all features to produce predicted values (linear), which are mapped to probabilities by sigmoid function (non-linear). Each probability is then compared with the threshold value to be classified as either of the two labels.

4.2   BERT-Base Model

BERT is a type of transformer model that was developed by Google. The model is pre-trained and built with the help of a large corpus of multilingual data [6]. A transformer is an encoder-decoder network that applies mathematical technique called self-attention on the encoder side and attention on the decoder side to detect relationship between distant data [10].

Pre-training and fine-tuning are the two important steps in building the BERT model. The model is pre-trained with large corpus of data over different tasks in pre-training phase and during fine-tuning, most of the hidden layers are initialized with parameters of pre-trained model, while output layer (few more layers before output layer) are trained with new labeled data. For each task there is a separate fine-tuned model available, even though the pre-trained parameters in hidden layers are same. The architecture of BERT model uses a multi-layer bidirectional transformer encoder and the generation of embeddings are shown in Fig. 2. .

For this work, we have used BERT-based-multilingual-cased model [3,13] which has 768 hidden layers, 110M parameters and 12 attention heads. The model is pre-trained with the help of the content from top 104 languages using a masked language modeling (MLM). Figure 3 depicts the input and different embeddings of BERT model. MLM is pre-trained with two objectives:

– Masked Language Modeling (MLM): It involves masking certain percentage of the sentence and giving the masked sentence to the learned model. The model predicts the masked part of the sentence. Undergoing this process would allow the model to gain bidirectional knowledge.

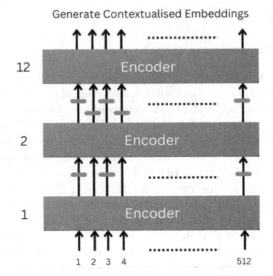

Fig. 2. Generation of Contextualised Embeddings

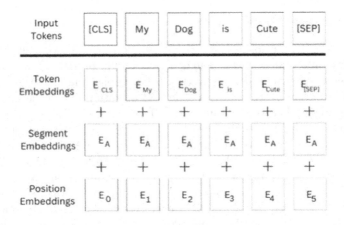

Fig. 3. Input for the BERT Model

- Next sentence prediction (NSP): It involves passing concatenated sentences as inputs to model during pre-training. The job of the model is to predict whether any two sentences follow one another or not.

We have used a library called Simpletransformers to create the above-mentioned model. Simpletransformers is a library that lets us create models that are present in Hugging Face - an AI community that contains SOTA models.

5   Implementation

Our first step was the classification of fake news and non-fake news in the English data set. The data set was divided as follows: 80% for training and 20% for testing. Training data was then vectorized using the TfidfVectorizer [12], which assigns scores to each word based on its repetition. TfidfVectorizer gives more weight to the words that seem to be important (term frequency) as well as less weight to the words that seem to be less important and repetitive (inverse document frequency). These scores were then transformed into feature vectors and fed to the Logistic Regression model for training purposes; the model was evaluated with both training and testing data. To obtain better accuracy, we used the simpletransformers library to create the bert-base-multilingual-case (BERT model type) model, which is a Transformers-compatible pre-trained model [6,8]. For each language, the model was trained with training data and evaluated with both training and testing data. The learning rate and regularisation values were adjusted to avoid overfitting. After training and evaluating the model with different combinations of learning rate and regularisation values, we found that the learning rate value of 7E-5 and regularisation values with a square gradient of 1E-4 and a parameter scale of 1E-3 provided good results.

6   Result and Analysis

We found that the F1 scores for the English training data set (97%) and testing data set (95.03%) data under Logistic Regression approach were really good, and hence, we decided to implement the model in the same way for Indian languages. Table 2 shows the performance metrics for Logistic Regression model used for Tamil, Malayalam, Kannada, and Gujarati languages. As Table 2 shows, the F1 scores for Tamil and Kannada are very low, whereas the F1 scores for other languages are good. So, we decided to do the classification with the help of a deep neural network model, and hence, we used a BERT-based model. Table 3 shows the performance metrics for the BERT model. As Table 3 shows, the F1 scores for Tamil and Kannada are higher in the latter approach. We also observe that our Logistic Regression approach performs nearly as well as the BERT type model approach for the other three languages.

Table 2. Performance scores for Logistic Regression

Languages	Training data			Testing data		
	Precision (%)	Recall (%)	F1 score (%)	Precision (%)	Recall (%)	F1 score (%)
Kannada	77.93	61.46	68.72	71.52	55.96	62.79
Gujarati	89.82	94.18	91.95	87.43	93.21	90.23
Malayalam	91.69	90.64	91.16	88.69	87.61	88.15
Tamil	77.12	58.61	66.60	71.90	50.04	59.01

Table 3. Performance scores for BERT-base-Multilingual-cased

Languages	Training data			Testing data		
	Precision (%)	Recall (%)	F1 score (%)	Precision (%)	Recall (%)	F1 score (%)
Kannada	87.63	88.96	88.29	88.71	89.64	89.17
Gujarati	80.90	99.73	89.33	89.53	99.31	89.82
Malayalam	86.24	98.22	91.84	86.10	98.45	91.86
Tamil	87.03	99.50	92.85	87.01	99.19	92.70

7 Conclusion

The data set under consideration is the Kaggle fake news data set. This data set was converted from English to various Indian languages. It was then fed to Logistic Regression model for training. We observed that the model performed well for Malayalam and Gujarati, with F1 scores of 88.15% and 90.23% respectively, and poorly for Tamil and Kannada, with F1 scores of 59.01% and 62.79%. From the variation in accuracy, we infer that the vectorizations (using TfidfVectorizer) of Tamil and Kannada texts were not as efficient as they were for Malayalam and Gujarati. In order to improve the scores, the data was fed to BERT-based-multilingual-cased model for training; the newly evaluated scores were significantly higher. The BERT model is pre-trained in English, whereas the BERT-based-multilingual-cased model is pre-trained on the top 104 languages, so usage of this model for Indian languages provided good results. It provided exceptionally good results for Malayalam and Tamil, as contextualised embeddings for the words in Tamil and Malayalam were appropriate for training. We observed that the model performed well for all four languages: Malayalam with an F1 score of 91.86%, Gujarati with an F1 score of 89.82%, Kannada with an F1 score of 89.17% and Tamil with an F1 score of 92.70%. As a future work we would like to investigate on other low resource languages and concentrate on extracting the important features for differentiating the various language contents.

References

1. Batailler, C., Brannon, S.M., Teas, P.E., Gawronski, B.: A signal detection approach to understanding the identification of fake news. Perspect. Psychol. Sci. **17**(1), 78–98 (2022)
2. Wickens, T.D.: Elementary Signal Detection Theory. Oxford University Press, Oxford (2001)
3. Pandey, S., Prabhakaran, S., Reddy, N.V.S., Acharya, D.: Fake news detection from online media using machine learning classifiers. In: Journal of Physics: Conference Series, vol. 2161, no. 1, p. 012027. IOP Publishing (2022)
4. Kareem, I., Awan, S.M.: Pakistani media fake news classification using machine learning classifiers. In: 2019 International Conference on Innovative Computing (ICIC), pp. 1–6. IEEE (2019)

5. Kar, D., Bhardwaj, M., Samanta, S., Azad, A.P.: No rumours please! a multi-indic-lingual approach for COVID fake-tweet detection. In: 2021 Grace Hopper Celebration India (GHCI), pp. 1–5. IEEE (2021)

6. Lee, J., Devlin, M., Chang, K., Toutanova, K.: Pre-training of deep bidirectional transformers for language understanding. arXiv preprint arXiv:1810.04805 (2018)

7. Magueresse, A., Carles, V., Heetderks, E.: Low-resource languages: a review of past work and future challenges. arXiv preprint arXiv:2006.07264 (2020)

8. Slovikovskaya, V.: Transfer learning from transformers to fake news challenge stance detection (FNC-1) task. arXiv preprint arXiv:1910.14353 (2019)

9. Kakwani, D., et al.: IndicNLPSuite: monolingual corpora, evaluation benchmarks and pre-trained multilingual language models for Indian languages. In: Findings of the Association for Computational Linguistics: EMNLP 2020, pp. 4948–4961 (2020)

10. Saurav, K., Saunack, K., Kanojia, D., Bhattacharyya, P.: A Passage to India: Pre-trained Word Embeddings for Indian Languages. arXiv preprint arXiv:2112.13800 (2021)

11. Kong, S.H., Tan, L.M., Gan, K.H., Samsudin, N.H.: Fake news detection using deep learning. In: 2020 IEEE 10th Symposium on Computer Applications & Industrial Electronics (ISCAIE), pp. 102–107. IEEE (2020)

12. Guo, A., Yang, T.: Research and improvement of feature words weight based on TFIDF algorithm. In: 2016 IEEE Information Technology, Networking, Electronic and Automation Control Conference, pp. 415–419. IEEE, 2016

13. Kula, S., Choraś, M., Kozik, R.: Application of the BERT-based architecture in fake news detection. In: Herrero, Á., Cambra, C., Urda, D., Sedano, J., Quintián, H., Corchado, E. (eds.) CISIS 2019. AISC, vol. 1267, pp. 239–249. Springer, Cham (2021). https://doi.org/10.1007/978-3-030-57805-3_23

14. Sommers, J.: On the characteristics of language tags on the web. In: Beverly, R., Smaragdakis, G., Feldmann, A. (eds.) PAM 2018. LNCS, vol. 10771, pp. 18–30. Springer, Cham (2018). https://doi.org/10.1007/978-3-319-76481-8_2

15. Nada, F., Khan, B. F., Maryam, A., Zuha, N., Ahmed, Z.: Fake news detection using logistic regression. Int. Res. J. Eng. Technol. (IRJET) 6 (2019). https://www.irjet.net/archives/V6/i5/IRJET-V6I5733.pdf

16. Koroteev, M.V.: BERT: A review of applications in natural language processing and understanding. arXiv preprint arXiv:2103.11943, 2021

17. Hirlekar, V.V., Kumar, A.: Natural language processing based online fake news detection challenges-a detailed review. In: 2020 5th International Conference on Communication and Electronics Systems (ICCES), pp. 748–754. IEEE (2020)

Workshop 2: Low Resource Cross-Domain, Cross-Lingual and Cross-Modal Offensive Content Analysis (LC4)

MMOD-MEME: A Dataset for Multimodal Face Emotion Recognition on Code-Mixed Tamil Memes

R. Ramesh Kannan[1]🆔, Manikandan Ravikiran[2]🆔,
and Ratnavel Rajalakshmi[1(✉)]🆔

[1] Vellore Institute of Technology, Chennai, India
rajalakshmi.r@vit.ac.in
[2] Georgia Institute of Technology, Atlanta, Georgia

Abstract. Multimodal Facial Emotion Recognition (MFER) for Low resourced Language like Tamil is handled with code-mixed text of Tamil and English. The newly created dataset addresses the multimodal approach on facial emotion recognition with the help of code-mixed memes. The dataset provides facial emotions for the memes and the code-mixed comments for the memes. The memes posted in websites and social media are collected to prepare the dataset. Overall dataset contains 4962 memes with annotated facial emotions and the code-mixed memes in it. Each are annotated by the 3 different annotators with single face emotion and double face emotions with code-mixed Tamil memes. Convolutional Neural Network (CNN) has been applied for detecting the emotions on this dataset containing single faces alone. The preliminary results on the single face emotion dataset has resulted in an accuracy of 0.3028.

Keywords: Code-mixed Tamil Meme · Facial Emotion · Social Media and Multimodal

1 Introduction

In this digital world, users share their opinion/emotions on the social medium platforms like Whatsapp, Twitter, Facebook, Instagram, YouTube etc. In their day-to-day life people express their beliefs and viewpoints on the current event or an activity through the social media networks. This viewpoints of expression shows the drastic increase of the social media users in recent years. The recent statistics [1] shows that, around 59% of the world population use social media. Around the world, 4.70 billion people are using social media and 227 million new users have started using social media in the past one year. The survey findings revealed that, the average time spent on social media is 2 h and 29 min.

Emotion is a mental reaction directed towards the opponent in the form of physiological and behavioural changes in the activity. For expressing the emotions, language is a powerful and important medium. The social interaction is essential for day-to-day life on the internet era, which helps in communicating

Anand Kumar M et al. (Eds.): SPELLL 2022, CCIS 1802, pp. 335–345, 2023.
https://doi.org/10.1007/978-3-031-33231-9_24

and expressing our thoughts [5] in the form of blogs, micro-blogs, wikis, video-sharing sites and through other social mediums.

There are different categories of people who use internet to share their opinion on the activity or an event. It includes educated/un-educated people and of different age groups. As the people have different opinions, it becomes a challenge in analysing their opinions/views in terms of emotions. This shows the interest on analysing the opinions on the social media by the users. For this purpose, we have created a face emotion dataset from social media contents. Various works have been carried out in the multimodal emotion recognition [2,7,25]. In this article, we have contributed: Facial Emotion Recognition dataset that contains real face emotions with the code-mixed Tamil memes contents. To the best of our knowledge, this is the first attempt in the combination of multimodal face emotion with code-mixed tamil meme contents. In this we have used memes to analyse the emotions of the people on the social media. We have collected and used internet trending memes, troll memes and actor/actress memes for the face emotion recognition. Facial emotion recognition are used to analyse diagnosing mental diseases, human social interaction and human physiological interactions. The emotion from the memes are taken as Single face emotion and Double face emotion. Single face emotion contain only one subject in the meme and Double face emotion means there are two subjects with same or different emotions on their faces on memes.

The paper is organized as follows: Sect. 2 deals with related works and Sect. 3 describes about the dataset collection. Section 4 discusses about the dataset construction. Section 5 shows the detailed analysis of dataset followed by conclusion in Sect. 6.

2   Related Works

Multimodal face emotion recognition deals with various inputs such as audio, image and video. In [8] the authors have introduced, CNN-LSTM (Long Short Term Memory) for voice feature extraction and for facial expression from videos the pretrained architecture model Inception-ResNetV2 is used as feature extractor. The extracted features are selected using chi-square test and the selected features are fused to form a new feature vector. The selected features are given to LIBSVM on multimodal opinion level sentiment intensity corpus (MOSI) and Multimodal Emotion Lines Dataset (MELD) dataset and obtained 87.56% and 90.06% in terms of accuracy. Improved models of Deep Convolutional Neural Network (DCNN) and Deep Separation CNN (DSCNN) are involved in the process of multimodal emotion recognition model on Speech and Video images respectively. After classification, decision level features are fused to form a new feature space. Multiobjective optimization algorithm [7] proposed and shown better performance on Interactive Emotional Dyadic Motion Capture (IEMO-CAP) dataset. In [2] authors collected subject images and the emotions were trained on Bayesian classifier with different modalities like facial expressions, body movement, gestures and speech. The each modality were fused at feature level and decision level separately. Multimodal approach on fusion level shown better results than decision levels and unimodal approaches with 240 sample collected data.

In real world, head pose, illumination variation and subject dependency can be handled by analysing sensor information rather than videos or images. The authors [25] of the system proposed to analyse three sensors to capture the information. First sensor to detect dynamic changing face component with the help of eye trackers. Second sensor to capture audio, depth and EEG signals which provides non-visual information. Third sensor to filter out visual information. All three sensors helped in capturing visual, non visual and filter visual information for analysing emotion system. Text classification have been studied with various Machine Learning [9,10,13,15,23], SVM [14], XGB [26] and Deep Learning approaches were applied for short text classification [11,19,28], CNN [18], RCNN [12] as well. Short text sentiment analysis [3,16,20,24] have been studied with attention [27,29] based approaches.

In [21], author proposed Bidirectional Encoder Representations from Transformers (BERT) for offensive text classification on code-mixed Tamil-English tweet contents. Author [17] proposed Bidirectional Long Short-Term Memory (BiLSTM) for offensive span identification on code-mixed Tamil contents. To detect Hate or Offensive comments from YouTube comments, authors [22] proposed Multilingual Representations for Indian Languages(MuRIL) a multilingual model with a input of Stemmed YouTube comments. Majority Voting classifier is for the final classification. IndicBERT [6] based approach is a variant of BERT, which is proposed for sentiment analysis of Code-mixed Tamil tweets. A translation based offensive content identification MTDOT [4] proposed on various south Indian languages like Tamil, Malayalam and Kannada on YouTube comments. Feature selection based on Deep learning methods were explored by many authors on various datasets were discussed for image based and video based classification. Short text classification handled with various approaches like feature weighting, transformer approach and deep learning approaches. We will try to apply these various approaches for our Multimodal face emotion recognition dataset.

3   Dataset Collection

In this work, we have reused the part of the dataset from Troll Multimodal Meme classification [30] consisting of 2967 memes in code-mixed language. Existing dataset usage is beneficial in terms of time consumption for dataset creation. This encourages the dataset collection process easy and by annotating the previously available dataset. From the existing dataset [30], we have analysed the images manually and collected additional images for constructing this dataset based on our objective. In this work, we have collected new data from the search engines like Google, Bing and from few of the websites like oneindia, Dailyhunt. We have collected images using some of the keywords for the dataset creation, which include Tamil actors names, actress names, political party names and comedy actor names. Search queries include Vadivelu meme, Vijaykanth meme, Jayam Ravi meme, Yogibabu meme, Senthil Goundamani meme etc., and the results were collected using Google search. In google search, we have mentioned the image size as Large, type of image as face and the usage rights was set to all. We have not set the number of images to be collected. We have collected all the images which were fetched from google search.

Table 1. Overall Data Distribution

S.No	Emotions	Double face		Single face
1	Angry	491	431	646
2	Contempt	30	27	72
3	Disgust	73	88	127
4	Fear	139	148	225
5	Joy	406	423	729
6	Neutral	337	242	565
7	Sad	370	460	556
8	Surprise	65	92	131
Total		1911	1911	3051
		4962		

For annotation of the face emotion on memes three annotators were assigned and the label for the face emotion guidelines were prepared and followed for annotation. The data are collected using public domain, and hence the annotators were instructed not to influence their personal opinions on the images annotated. Dimensionality is one of the biggest problem in image classification task. Various pre-trained image architectures and deep learning architectures requirements differ in the input size of images. This poses difficulty in processing collected images on the architectures with different input sizes. Most of the pre-trained architectures were analysed to fix the dimension of the image for classification. The minimum size of the images were set to at least 150*150 for all the images. We have considered only "jpg" images for creating the dataset.

4   Details of Dataset Construction

The dataset was collected in two different ways viz., 1) extracting/filtering existing dataset, 2) web resources. The details of the summary are shown in the Table 1. Initial retrieval was conducted in google search, then the search was conducted using Bing search.

Initial collection were done from the available Troll meme classification, which contains 2300 odd number of training sets and 667 number of test values with categorised as troll and not-troll. The data set contains text extracted from the images and also the images of memes. The text in memes is represented not only in English, but also in Tamil and Code-Mixed Tamil. Out of 2967 samples, only 579 images with the Single face emotions and 380 images with Double face emotions were selected. From the troll meme dataset around 30% of the samples were reused in dataset creation process.

The second part of dataset was collected from the news related websites. One of the online news website is used to collect the data. A program using Javascript, was used to extract the memes which are posted on the websites. Totally 135 web pages of one india website contain 1064 memes. The collected images from oneindia website were processed and we annotated the images with the help of annotators. Later it was segregated into 2 groups viz., Single face emotion images (153) and Double face images (263). Same process was followed in extracting images from dailyhunt website. Daily hunt website contains 9 different categories of memes. They include cric memes, latest tamil memes, central memes, Memes trend, Inraiya Memes, Memes boys, Foryou Memes, Kollywood Memes and Memes ulagam. From this collection, 1425 memes were collected, processed and annotated. After annotation 268 Single face memes, 376 Double face memes and a total of 644 memes were annotated for dataset creation.

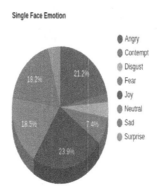

Fig. 1. Distribution on Single face emotions.

The third part of dataset collection was done by web scraping. The keywords from the web pages and general keywords were used to extract images. Using the different keywords we have collected memes from the different websites using web scraping. Different parameters were set to scrap the images from google search.

5   Dataset Analysis

From Table 1, the meme annotated into emotions with different categories. The categories are mentioned in the table with the individual count of the category images of Double face and Single face. Total of 4962 images were annotated with 3051 with Single face emotions and 1911 images with Double face emotions.

From Fig. 1, the percentage of Single face emotions with the annotations are plotted in bar graph with how much percentage category in the particular class. Angry with 646 images are with 21.2% in overall Single face emotions. Contempt with 2.4%, Disgust with 4.16%, Fear with 7.4%, Joy with 23.9%, Neutral with 18.5%, Sad withe 18.2% and Surprise with 4.3%.

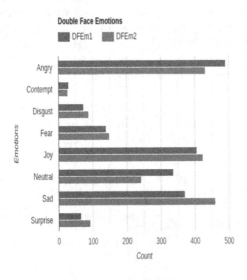

Fig. 2. Distribution on Double face emotions.

From Fig. 2, the emotions from the faces are taken with multi label category. Each and individual image may contain both the categories. For example, from Fig. 3, the emotion from the first male face is angry and the second face from image is lady face, which shows the contempt state. The emotion of a first person, here the male object is mentioned as Double Face Emotion1(DFEm1) and female object emotion is mentioned as Double Face Emotion2(DFEm2). The distribution of DFEm1 and DFEm2 are shown in Fig. 2.

From Fig. 4, the comparison of all the categories of Single face emotions, Double face emotions were plotted. The count of angry in Single face images is 646 and DFEm1 is 491 and DFEm2 is 431. The percentage of distribution of all

Fig. 3. Double face emotion - A sample image.

the angry category is around 21–25% with in their category, but when compared to the count of images, Single face emotion images contains high numbers compared to Double face emotions. Like wise the other category distributions also with in the difference of 1–5% in the same category labels. Fear category almost same distribution around the category with 7.3–7.5%. Figure 5, the Single face emotion is shown with single subject face in the meme. Here the emotion is expressed as sad from the sample image.

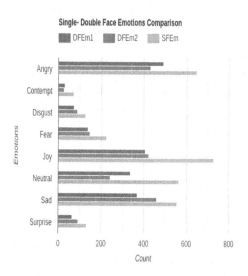

Fig. 4. Comparison of Single and Double face emotions.

Fig. 5. Single face emotion - A Sample image

As a baseline experiment, Convolutional Neural Network is implemented with Single face emotion alone on 3051 dataset. Dataset is splitted into 80% for training and 20% for testing. Images of RGB are resized to 150*150. First layer as input layer, Conv2d, Maxpooling, Dropout and Dense layer are used. Dropout of 0.2 is used in all the operations. Convolution 2D operation with 128 hidden units, kernel size of 2 and activation function as relu is used for further operation. In the fully connected layer softmax activation function is used and optimizer as adam is used. Obtained a training accuracy score of 0.4857 and training loss of 1.3654. The parameter values are Epochs = 28, batch size = 128. Since maximum accuracy is achieved on 28 epoch without fine tuning the parameters. Early stopping applied on test set with maximum accuracy score. All the metrics are macro average score. Since it is a imbalanced dataset, macro weighted metrics is observed for all the metrics. Precision score of 0.1825, recall score of 0.1836 and F1score of 0.1665 is obtained as macro weighted score on the test set.

6   Conclusion

Identifying the emotion is the toughest problem. For identifying the emotion of social media contents, we have webscraped the images and annotated the images into 8 categories. The categories of the Face emotions are Angry, Contempt, Disgust, Fear, Joy, Neutral, Sad and Surprise. The social media content meme contains so many objects, from that object, we have categorised the human face based emotion identification. The meme contains Single face Emotion and Double face Emotions. The distribution and Comparison of the Face Emotions were plotted as graph and Tables. We have collected very few amount of data for this face emotion detection. Deep learning implementation using CNN was implemented and obtained a accuracy score of 0.3028. In future, we will try to implement recent transformer based approach on the Face emotion recognition.

References

1. https://www.smartinsights.com/social-media-marketing/social-media-strategy/ new-global-social-media-research/#::text=more%20than%20half%20of%20the, social%20media%20is%202h%2029m
2. Caridakis, G., et al.: Multimodal emotion recognition from expressive faces, body gestures and speech. In: Boukis, C., Pnevmatikakis, A., Polymenakos, L. (eds.) AIAI 2007. ITIFIP, vol. 247, pp. 375–388. Springer, Boston, MA (2007). https:// doi.org/10.1007/978-0-387-74161-1_41
3. Ganganwar, V., Rajalakshmi, R.: Implicit aspect extraction for sentiment analysis: a survey of recent approaches. Procedia Comput. Sci. **165**, 485–491 (2019)
4. Ganganwar, V., Rajalakshmi, R.: MTDOT: a multilingual translation-based data augmentation technique for offensive content identification in Tamil text data. Electronics **11**(21) (2022). https://doi.org/10.3390/electronics11213574. https:// www.mdpi.com/2079-9292/11/21/3574
5. Hirat, R., Mittal, N.: A survey on emotion detection techniques using text in blogposts (2015)
6. Kannan, R.R., Rajalakshmi, R., Kumar, L.: IndicBERT based approach for sentiment analysis on code-mixed tamil tweets **3159**, 8 (2021)
7. Li, M., et al.: Multimodal emotion recognition model based on a deep neural network with multiobjective optimization. Wirel. Commun. Mob. Comput. **2021**, 6971100:1–6971100:10 (2021)
8. Liu, D., Wang, Z., Wang, L., Chen, L.: Multi-modal fusion emotion recognition method of speech expression based on deep learning. Front. Neurorobotics **15** (2021). https://doi.org/10.3389/fnbot.2021.697634. https://www.frontiersin.org/ articles/10.3389/fnbot.2021.697634
9. R., R.: Supervised term weighting methods for url classification. J. Comput. Sci. **10** (06 2014). https://doi.org/10.3844/jcssp.2014.1969.1976
10. R., R., Aravindan, C.: An effective and discriminative feature learning for url based web page classification. In: 2018 IEEE International Conference on Systems, Man, and Cybernetics (SMC), pp. 1374–1379 (2018). https://doi.org/10. 1109/SMC.2018.00240
11. Rajalakshmi, R., Tiwari, H., Patel, J., Kumar, A., Karthik., R.: Design of kids-specific url classifier using recurrent convolutional neural network. Procedia Comput. Sci. **167**, 2124–2131 (2020). https://doi.org/10.1016/j.procs.2020. 03.260. https://www.sciencedirect.com/science/article/pii/S1877050920307262, international Conference on Computational Intelligence and Data Science
12. Rajalakshmi, R., Tiwari, H., Patel, J., Kumar, A., Karthik, R.: Design of kids-specific URL classifier using recurrent convolutional neural network. Procedia Comput. Sci. **167**, 2124–2131 (2020)
13. Rajalakshmi, R., Xaviar, S.: Experimental study of feature weighting techniques for url based webpage classification. Procedia Comput. Sci. **115**, 218–225 (2017). https://doi.org/10.1016/j.procs.2017.09.128. https://www.sciencedirect. com/science/article/pii/S1877050917319567. 7th International Conference on Advances in Computing & Communications, ICACC-2017, 22-24 August 2017, Cochin, India
14. Rajalakshmi, R.: Identifying health domain URLs using SVM. In: Proceedings of the Third International Symposium on Women in Computing and Informatics, pp. 203–208 (2015)

15. Rajalakshmi, R., Agrawal, R.: Borrowing likeliness ranking based on relevance factor. In: Proceedings of the Fourth ACM IKDD Conferences on Data Sciences (2017)
16. Rajalakshmi, R., Duraphe, A., Shibani, A.: DLRG@ DravidianLangTech-ACL2022: Abusive comment detection in tamil using multilingual transformer models. In: Proceedings of the Second Workshop on Speech and Language Technologies for Dravidian Languages, pp. 207–213 (2022)
17. Rajalakshmi, R., More, M., Shrikriti, B., Saharan, G., Samyuktha, H., Nandy, S.: DLRG@TamilNLP-ACL2022: offensive span identification in Tamil using BiLSTM-CRF approach. In: Proceedings of the Second Workshop on Speech and Language Technologies for Dravidian Languages, pp. 248–253. Association for Computational Linguistics, Dublin, Ireland (May 2022). https://doi.org/10.18653/v1/2022. dravidianlangtech-1.38. https://aclanthology.org/2022.dravidianlangtech-1.38
18. Rajalakshmi, R., Ramraj, S., Ramesh Kannan, R.: Transfer learning approach for identification of malicious domain names. In: International Symposium on Security in Computing and Communication, pp. 656–666. Springer (2018)
19. Rajalakshmi, R., Reddy, B.Y.: Dlrg@hasoc 2019: an enhanced ensemble classifier for hate and offensive content identification. In: FIRE (2019)
20. Rajalakshmi, R., Reddy, P., Khare, S., Ganganwar, V.: Sentimental analysis of code-mixed Hindi language. In: Congress on Intelligent Systems, pp. 739–751. Springer (2022). https://doi.org/10.1007/978-981-16-9113-3_54
21. Rajalakshmi, R., Reddy, Y., Kumar, L.: DLRG@DravidianLangTech-EACL2021: transformer based approach for offensive language identification on code-mixed Tamil. In: Proceedings of the First Workshop on Speech and Language Technologies for Dravidian Languages, pp. 357–362. Association for Computational Linguistics, Kyiv (Apr 2021), https://aclanthology.org/2021.dravidianlangtech-1.53
22. Rajalakshmi, R., Selvaraj, S., Mattins R., F., Vasudevan, P., Kumar M., A.: Hottest: hate and offensive content identification in Tamil using transformers and enhanced stemming. Comput. Speech Lang. **78**, 101464 (2023). https://doi. org/10.1016/j.csl.2022.101464. https://www.sciencedirect.com/science/article/ pii/S0885230822000870
23. Rameshkannan, R., Rajalakshmi, R.: Dlrg@aila 2019: context - aware legal assistance system (2019)
24. Ravikiran, M., et al.: Findings of the shared task on offensive span identification from Code-mixed Tamil-English comments. In: Proceedings of the Second Workshop on Speech and Language Technologies for Dravidian Languages, pp. 261–270. Association for Computational Linguistics, Dublin, Ireland (May 2022). https:// doi.org/10.18653/v1/2022.dravidianlangtech-1.40. https://aclanthology.org/2022. dravidianlangtech-1.40
25. Samadiani, N., et al.: A review on automatic facial expression recognition systems assisted by multimodal sensor data. Sensors **19**(8) (2019). https://doi.org/10.3390/ s19081863. https://www.mdpi.com/1424-8220/19/8/1863
26. Sharen, H., Rajalakshmi, R.: DLRG@ LT-EDI-ACL2022: detecting signs of depression from social media using XGBoost method. In: Proceedings of the Second Workshop on Language Technology for Equality, Diversity and Inclusion, pp. 346–349 (2022)
27. Soubraylu, S., Rajalakshmi, R.: Analysis of sentiment on movie reviews using word embedding self-attentive lstm. Int. J. Ambient Comput. Intell. **12**, 33–52 (2021). https://doi.org/10.4018/IJACI.2021040103

28. Soubraylu, S., Rajalakshmi, R.: Hybrid convolutional bidirectional recurrent neural network based sentiment analysis on movie reviews. Comput. Intell. **37**(2), 735–757 (2021). https://doi.org/10.1111/coin.12400. https://onlinelibrary.wiley.com/doi/abs/10.1111/coin.12400

29. Soubraylu, S., Rajalakshmi, R.: Context-aware sentiment analysis with attention-enhanced features from bidirectional transformers. Soc. Netw. Anal. Min. **12**(1), 1–23 (2022). https://doi.org/10.1007/s13278-022-00910-y

30. Suryawanshi, S., Chakravarthi, B.R., Verma, P., Arcan, M., McCrae, J.P., Buitelaar, P.: A dataset for troll classification of TamilMemes. In: Proceedings of the WILDRE5- 5th Workshop on Indian Language Data: Resources and Evaluation, pp. 7–13. European Language Resources Association (ELRA), Marseille, France (May 2020). https://aclanthology.org/2020.wildre-1.2

End-to-End Unified Accented Acoustic Model for Malayalam-A Low Resourced Language

Rizwana Kallooravi Thandil$^{(\boxtimes)}$ ⓘ, K. P. Mohamed Basheerⓘ, and V. K. Muneerⓘ

Sullamussalam Science College, Areekode, Kerala, India
ktrizwana@gmail.com

Abstract. Accented Automatic Speech Recognition(AASR) takes into account the accent information that poses a great challenge to the construction of ASR. The authors in this work have constructed multiple unified acoustic models for the Malayalam language that captured the accented and accent unspecific knowledge which also worked fine with unknown accents. Malayalam is a Dravidian language rich in accents that are spoken in the Indian state of Kerala. Accented speech dataset was constructed initially comprising five different accents. The paper discusses various experiments in the feature engineering of accented speech data. The accented features were extracted using Mel Frequency Cepstral Coefficients(MFCC), Short Term Fourier Transform (STFT), Mel Spectrogram, and Tempogram approaches individually and combined approaches to find the better feature set. Different experiments were conducted to construct different Unified accented models using machine learning, deep learning, and LSTM-RNN for all individual feature set extracted. The experiment resulted in finding a novel approach to constructing accented ASR for the Malayalam language with a reduced WER than many other baseline models. The model worked fine with known accents, unknown accents, and accent unspecific standard accents.

Keywords: Accented Malayalam Speech · Accented Automatic Speech Recognition · Unified acoustic model

1 Introduction

The majority of the accented ASR systems work fine for known accents and on the other hand, fail for unknown accents. Here in this experiment, we propose a novel approach for handling unknown accents for the model. The experiments were conducted in different phases both for feature engineering and also for acoustic modeling. The paper discusses the novel approach to feature extraction for the audio data that better represents the audio waves which make the AASR model a unified one.

There are no publicly available benchmark datasets for accented Malayalam speech and hence the authors constructed the accented speech corpus to conduct this study. The corpus contains audio data from five different districts of Kerala(Malappuram, Wayanad, Kannur, Kozhikode, and Kasaragod) where five different accented Malayalam are spoken.

Anand Kumar M et al. (Eds.): SPELLL 2022, CCIS 1802, pp. 346–354, 2023.
https://doi.org/10.1007/978-3-031-33231-9_25

The proposed system pipeline includes:

- Data collection
- Feature Engineering
- Unified Model Construction

The feature engineering experiment is conducted in several phases to find the best approach for the accented Malayalam speech. Multiple unified models are constructed using different machine learning methods, deep learning, and also LSTM-RNN approaches. Unified models were constructed using Multi-Layer Perceptron (MLP), Decision Tree Classifier (DTC), Support Vector Machine (SVM), K-Nearest Neighbour (KNN), Stochastic Gradient Descent (SGD), Random Forest Classification (RFC), and ensembled methods. Multiple unified models are constructed using deep learning and LSTM-RNN approaches. Models are constructed for each feature set and finally, the performance of each model is evaluated.

2 Related Work

The success of AASR systems is in the ability to identify the utterances regardless of the accent and style of the pronunciation. The research should focus on building benchmark datasets, appropriate feature engineering methods, and ideal model construction methods.Some of the relevant study in the area is discussed below.

Alëna Aksënova et.al. [1] proposed methodologies for constructing benchmark datasets and constructing pre-trained models for accented speech using wav2vec methods. Nilaksh Das et.al. [2] proposed a semi-supervised method for accent identification combining transfer and adversarial training methods.

Muhammad Ahmed Hassan et. al. [3] proposed a two-level pipeline in constructing the accented model both for accented and non-accented data. The model constructed had a reduced WER as compared to the baseline models.A Jain et. al. [5] proposed architecture called the mixture of experts for modeling multiple accented data. They proposed a methodology to better classify the speech regardless of phonetics and accents.Y.Qian et. al. [6] proposed a layer-wise embedding for a faster adaptation for accent classification in their work. Ryo Imaizumi et.al. [7] proposed a multi-dialect model for Japanese accent identification using multi-task learning.

3 Proposed Methodology and Design

The primary objective of this study is to propose a better approach for modeling accented Malayalam speech that works fine with known and unknown accents. The dataset of 7070 accented multi-syllabic speech data has been constructed for the study. The speech was donated by 30 male and female speech donors of different age groups. The dataset was constructed on 40 classes of speech data. The entire corpus was constructed using a crowdsourcing method that recorded the speech samples under a natural recording environment. A portion of the data in the set was collected through different community

348   R. K. Thandil et al.

platforms over the internet while the other portion is recorded directly under a natural recording environment.

The data is initially cleaned to remove any noise in the signal. The data is then preprocessed before performing the feature engineering task. Once the data is preprocessed it undergoes a series of experiments in the feature engineering phase. Feature extraction is done in eight phases and eight different feature sets are constructed. All eight sets are used in the model constructions in the following experiments. Different accented acoustic models are constructed using machine learning, deep learning, and LSTM-RNN approaches. The architecture of the proposed methodology is shown below (Fig. 1).

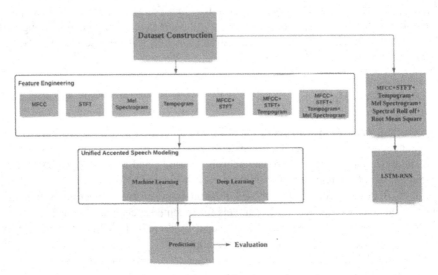

Fig. 1. Architecture of the proposed system

3.1 Dataset Construction

A speech corpus of 7070 samples has been constructed using crowdsourcing methods for experimenting. Accented speeches have been collected from 30 different speakers(both male and female). The corpus includes data from 5 different districts to represent 5 accents in the Malayalam language. The corpus contains 5.8 h of speech data collected from donors of different age groups. The data that has been collected is sampled to 16 kHz and converted to.wav format for further processing.

We have collected speech data from donors of all age groups for constructing the corpus.1160, 1160, 2370, 1190, 1190 samples have been constructed from children below 13, from an age group of 14 to 20, 21 to 45,46 to 65, and 66 to 85 respectively.

3.2 Feature Engineering

Feature engineering involves extracting prominent features from the accented speech signal. In this work, feature engineering is performed in eight different phases. The different phases include MFCC, STFT, Mel Spectrogram, Tempogram, and a combined approach of all these features (Fig. 2).

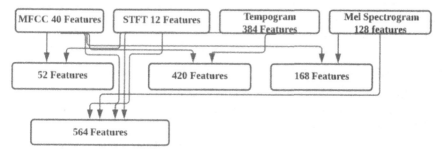

Fig. 2. Feature Engineering Approaches

The different phases are

1. Phase I Using MFCC
   MFCC is used to extract 13 frequency coefficients from the speech signal. Here we extract the 13 coefficients plus the second and third derivatives to get the 39 coefficients. And at last, we find the mean value of these coefficients as the 40th value and hence we get the 40 values in this phase to represent the audio data.
2. Phase II Using STSFT
   STFT is used to extract the prominent 12 amplitude values from the audio signals for time-frequency decompositions. It provides a time-localized frequency situation where the frequency components of a signal vary over time[8].
3. Phase III Using Tempogram Features
   Tempogram features are used to extract the rhythmic components of the speech data. Here in this experiment, we use 384 tempogram features to experiment. The rhythmic features are closely related to the accented features of the speech signal.
4. Phase IV Using Mel Spectrogram Features
   Here we extract 128 features from the audio signals using Mel Spectrogram that extracts the hidden features of the speech data.
5. Phase V MFCC and STSFT
6. Phase VI MFCC and Tempogram
7. Phase VII MFCC and Mel Spectrogram
8. Phase VIII MFCC, STFT, Tempogram and MelSpectrogram

3.3 Building the Accented ASR System

Multiple accented ASR system is constructed in this study in different feature engineering phases. The unified accented models are constructed in eight different phases using three different approaches. The different approaches involved in the AASR model construction are:

1. Machine learning methods
2. Deep learning methods and
3. LSTM-RNN

3.3.1 AASR Model Construction Using Machine Learning Methods

MLP, Decision Tree, SVM, SGD, KNN, RFC, and ensembled methods are used for constructing the multiple AASR models in this study. Eight models are constructed for each phase of feature engineering.

3.3.2 AASR Model Construction Using Deep Learning Methods

Deep Learning AASR models are constructed using the different features extracted at different phases. The different phases in this experiment include model construction using different feature sets.

Eight models are constructed here in this phase of the study using this approach. Each model is trained for 6000 epochs and the neural network architecture is composed of the input layer and three hidden layers with a dense layer of 32 neurons, then a dropout layer, and then a dense layer of 16 neurons. The model is adapted to learn slowly at a learning rate of 0.0001.

3.3.3 AASR Model Construction Using LSTM-RNN

The combined set of features is used for the accented model construction using the LSTM-RNN approach. Single AASR is constructed using the combined feature sets obtained by applying MFCC, STFT, Mel Spectrogram, Root Mean Square and Tempogram. The model is trained for 2000 epochs in each experiment. The model performed well both in terms of accuracy and match error rate.

4 Experimental Results

Eight models are constructed in the machine learning approach and eight models are constructed in the deep learning approach. One model is constructed using the LSTM-RNN approach. Performance evaluation metrics are Word Error Rate (WER), Match Error Rate (MER), and Word Information Loss (WIL) in accent ASR [3].WER is the most commonly used evaluation metric for the ASR models.WER is the calculation of the measure of disparity in the prediction of the model to the original transcript.WER can be calculated as:

$$W.E.R = \frac{St + I + D}{T} \tag{1}$$

where T is the total number of words in the set.

$$T = St + D + H_t \tag{2}$$

where S_t is the total number of substitutions, I is the number of insertions and H_t is the total number of correct predicted words.

M.E.R is the mismatch in the given input-output predictions and can be calculated

$$\text{as } \frac{St + I + D}{Ht + St + I + D} \tag{3}$$

$$\text{and } T = St + I + D + HT \tag{4}$$

$$\text{W.I.L} = \frac{Ht^2}{(H + S + I)(H + S + D)} \tag{5}$$

All the evaluation metrics discussed above are used for measuring the performance of the model. The lesser the measurement the more accurate the model will be. WER can be used for comparison with the other models since it has no upper bounds due to the insertion parameter. M.E.R and W.I.L can be used for the evaluation of the models.

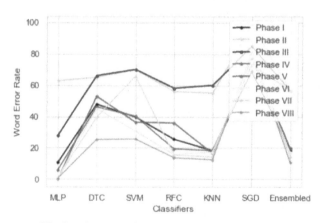

Fig. 3. The WER of Machine Learning Approaches

Figure 3 illustrates the WER rate observed in the experiment in different phases. Although the WER is found to be lowest for phase VIII and hence the experiment proves that the combined approach in feature extraction generates least WER for the accented data we used here in this experiment.

Table 2 shows the MER of deep learning experiments on speech data. The performance evaluation is calculated for each phase and compared against each other (Fig. 4) (Table 1).

Table 1. Districtwise Distribution of Samples in the Dataset

District	Size of Audio Samples
Kasaragod	1360
Kannur	1360
Kozhikode	1690
Malappuram	1360
Wayanad	1330
Total	7070

Table 2. M.E.R of Deep Learning Approaches

Phase I	Phase II	Phase III	Phase IV	Phase V	Phase VI	Phase VII	Phase VIII
49%	80%	71%	69%	61%	27%	39%	18%

Figure 5 and Fig. 6 show the performance evaluation of the AASR model constructed using LSTM-RNN methods at multiple runtimes. The model was constructed at 6,72,000 steps and obtained a training accuracy of 94%. The model obtained a validation accuracy of 64% . The training loss was 2.5 in the beginning and later it got reduced to 3%. The model obtained an M.E.R of 9%.

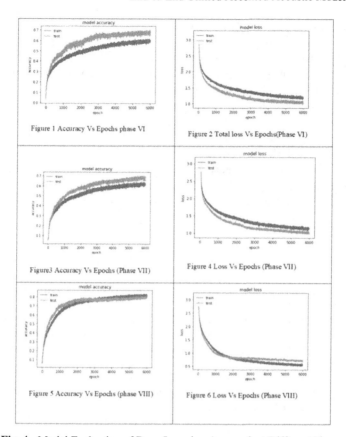

Fig. 4. Model Evaluation of Deep Learning Approach at Different Phases

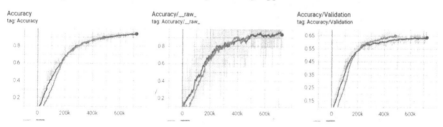

Fig. 5. Train and Test the Accuracy of the LSTM-RNN at different phases

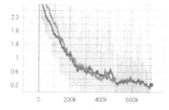

Fig. 6. Train and Validation loss at LSTM-RNN model at different phases

5 Conclusion and Future Scope

The authors propose a novel approach to model accented Malayalam speech. An accented speech corpus has been constructed for the study. The utterances have been annotated using IPA format. The authors experimented with the feature engineering approach to find the best feature set for working with the accented speech data for the Malayalam language. Multiple accented models were constructed using each feature set using three different approaches. The performance of all the AASR models is compared against each other with W.E.R and M.E.R metrics and hence concludes that the ensembled feature set obtained by combining all feature sets had the best performance than the ones with single feature sets.MLP in machine learning LSTM-RNN generated the least errors in prediction. The deep learning model with a combined feature set performed well than the other models with reduced feature sets.

References

1. Aksënova, A., et al.: Accented Speech Recognition: Benchmarking, Pre-training, and Diverse Data, arXiv:2205.08014,https://doi.org/10.48550/arXiv.2205.08014 (2022)
2. Das N, Bodapati S, Sunkara M, Srinivasan S, Chau DH.: Best of both worlds: Robust accented speech recognition with adversarial transfer learning,2021,https://www.amazon.science/pub lications/best-of-both-worlds-robust-accented-speech-recognition-with-adversarial-transfer-learning,Interspeech 2021
3. Hassan, M.A., Rehmat, A., Ghani Khan, M.U., Yousaf, M.H.: Improvement in automatic speech recognition of south asian accent using transfer learning of deepspeech2. Math. Prob. Eng. 6825555, 12 (2022). https://doi.org/10.1155/2022/6825555
4. Ni, J., Wang, L., Gao, H., et al.: Unsupervised text-to-speech synthesis by unsupervised automatic speech recognition (2022). https://arxiv.org/abs/2203.15796
5. A. Jain, V. P. Singh and S. P. Rath, "A multi-accent acoustic model using mixture of experts for speech recognition", Proc. Interspeech, pp. 779–783, 2019
6. Qian, Y., Gong, X., Huang, H.: Layer-wise fast adaptation for end-to-end multi-accent speech recognition. IEEE/ACM Trans. Audio Speech Lang. Process. 30, 2842-2853 (2022)
7. Imaizumi, R., Masumura, R., Shiota, S., Kiya, H.: End-to-end Japanese Multi-dialect Speech Recognition and Dialect Identification with Multi-task Learning, Tokyo Metropolitan University, 6–6 Asahigaoka, Hino-shi, Tokyo, 191–0065, Japan 2NTT Media Intelligence Laboratories, NTT Corporation, Japan
8. https://www.sciencedirect.com/topics/engineering/short-time-fourier-transform

Author Index

© The Editor(s) (if applicable) and The Author(s), under exclusive license
to Springer Nature Switzerland AG 2023
Anand Kumar M et al. (Eds.): SPELLL 2022, CCIS 1802, pp. 355–356, 2023.
https://doi.org/10.1007/978-3-031-33231-9

Printed in the United States
by Baker & Taylor Publisher Services